VIRUSES, PLAGUES, AND HISTORY

VIRUSES, PLAGUES, AND HISTORY

Past, Present, and Future

MICHAEL B. A. OLDSTONE

Revised and Updated Edition

UNIVERSITY PRESS

2010

OXFORD

UNIVERSITY PRESS

Oxford University Press, Inc., publishes works that further
Oxford University's objective of excellence
in research, scholarship, and education.

Oxford   New York
Auckland   Cape Town   Dar es Salaam   Hong Kong   Karachi
Kuala Lumpur   Madrid   Melbourne   Mexico City   Nairobi
New Delhi   Shanghai   Taipei   Toronto

With offices in
Argentina   Austria   Brazil   Chile   Czech Republic   France   Greece
Guatemala   Hungary   Italy   Japan   Poland   Portugal   Singapore
South Korea   Switzerland   Thailand   Turkey   Ukraine   Vietnam

Published by Oxford University Press, Inc.
198 Madison Avenue, New York, New York 10016

www.oup.com

Oxford is a registered trademark of Oxford University Press

Library of Congress Cataloging-in-Publication Data
Oldstone, Michael B. A.
Viruses, plagues, and history : past, present, and future / by Michael
B. A. Oldstone. — Rev. and updated ed.
p. cm.
Includes bibliographical references and index.
ISBN 978-0-19-532731-1
1. Virus diseases—History. I. Title.
RC114.5.O37 2010
616.9—dc22
2009003550

5   7   9   8   6   4

Printed in the United States of America
on acid-free paper

For Betsy,
Jenny, Beau, and Chris
and six sweethearts,
  Caroline Anne
  Aileen Elizabeth
  Madeleine Rose
  Faye Annastasia
  Raina Elizabeth
  Marilee Kate

You need not fear the terror by night,
nor the arrow that flies by day,
nor the plague that stalks in the darkness.

—91st Psalm

PREFACE

My book, *Viruses, Plagues, and History*, is now modified to include three new plagues that play important roles in this twenty-first century. The first two are Sudden Acute Respiratory Syndrome (SARS), the first new plague of this century, and West Nile virus, a virus similar to yellow fever virus in being transmitted by mosquito but appearing for the first time in North America, in New York City during the late 1990s. West Nile virus is currently the most common cause of encephalitis (brain infection) in the Americas where it has now spread. Third, bird flu, or influenza virus, in which a bird hemagglutinin gene (H5) has replaced the known hemagglutinin genes of human influenza virus (H1, H2, or H3), is lethal for nearly two-thirds of humans hospitalized or seriously ill with this infection. Bird flu has now migrated on the wings of its avian hosts and/or by shipment of poultry initially from China, throughout Asia to Europe and while not yet in the Americas, its arrival is imminent.

Considerable insight concerning understanding those plagues previously discussed and containment of several such viruses has been made over the last decade. These advances are presented here. Also discussed is the dampening of prior euphoria that poliomyelitis virus and measles virus would be eliminated as targeted by the World Health Organization (WHO) in the early twenty-first century. Although containment of such infections has been remarkable, elimination has not occurred. Similarly, cows with bovine spongiform disease (mad cow disease) have now been found in North America and raise alarms about the safety of the beef supply. Lastly, while the complete genomic structure of influenza 1918/1919 fossil virus has now been reconstructed and the virus manipulated to cause infection, conclusions of how and why the 1918/1919 flu was so lethal is still a puzzle to solve.

Conflicts between culture, politics, and government versus science have continued. Unfortunately, science is most often poorer and a loser for it being often overruled by faith, myths, and ignorance. This results in the continuation and increased incidence of disease and greater susceptibility of populations rather than disease control. Nevertheless, the incredible advancements in detective virology, therapeutics, and understanding basic functions of the immune system, the genetics of viruses and their hosts, coupled with the continued dedication of newly entered investigators and scientists to join ranks of those already present gives optimism that public apathy and misguided governmental decisions (like denial by some in South African government in leadership roles that AIDS is caused by a virus or that antiviral therapy is of value) will fall in time.

This book was conceived in the spirit of Paul deKruif's book *Microbe Hunters*, which I first read in junior high school. His heroes were the great adventurers of medical science who engaged in a struggle to understand the unknown and relieve human suffering. In retrospect, those stories initiated the spark that led me to medical school and a career in biomedical research. From those opportunities, I came to know Frank Dixon, Bernie Fields, Hilary Koprowski, Jonas Salk, Albert Sabin, John Enders, Tom Weller, Frank Fenner, Joe Smadel, Bernie Moss, Joe Esposito, Bob Shope, Fred Murphy, Bob Gallo, Luc Montagnier, D. A. Henderson, Jordie Casals, Rob Webster, D. Carlton Gajdusek, Joe Gibbs, Stanley Prusiner, Bruce Chesebro, Jeffery Taubenberger, Peter Palese, Ed Kilbourne, Yoshi Kawaoka, Gary Nabel, Ian Wilson, and James Paulson, all of whom figure in the stories told here about viral diseases.

In tracing the history of struggles to find each agent of these diseases, I have asked what was known from its initial description, what unique problems existed, what actions were the most critical in solving the problems, why these decisions were made, and at what point community and governmental support provided the essential resources or stood in the way of progress. To accomplish this task, I selected as examples four viral diseases—smallpox, yellow fever, measles, and poliomyelitis—that science has controlled despite the unrestrained devastation and misery they once caused. These success stories are contrasted with those of seven viral infections that currently remain out of control—Lassa fever virus, Ebola virus, Hantavirus, SARS, West Nile virus, and human immunodeficiency virus—and with the continuing threat from influenza, now reasonably contained but with the potential to revert to a worldwide pandemic disaster. I also tell the story of an unusual group of progressive neurologic disorders, the spongiform encephalopathies (scrapie, mad cow disease, variant Creutzfeldt–Jakob disease, chronic wasting disease of deer and elk), and the debate as to whether they are caused by a virus or a prion (protein). A common thread of fear, superstition, and irrational behavior runs through all twelve stories, testifying to our human fallibility. Unsubstantiated rumors or beliefs that the poliovirus vaccine was the cause of HIV, that autism results from vaccination with measles virus, and so forth, have led to refusal to take vaccines with resultant outbreaks of virus infections that should not have occurred. However, the motivation and skill of scientists along with the right community and governmental leaders and support have led to important victories over some viral plagues, and there will be more.

This book commemorates the enormous magnitude of these achievements too often forgotten. Recall that smallpox killed over 300 million people in the twentieth century alone and now has been totally eradicated from our planet. Measles, which once killed millions each year globally and still kills roughly 400,000 in Third World countries, today harms few in the industrial countries of the world. Yellow fever virus devastated populations along the Mississippi River and several port cities in the United States and was responsible for closing operations of the American government in 1793. Now this infectious disease has been largely eradicated from the United States with only a handful of cases imported into the country, although it still exists in rain forests of South America and Africa. Poliomyelitis virus, the cause of infantile paralysis, was at one time the fifth leading killer of children in Scandinavia and pervasive in North America. I remember my parents' fear of poliomyelitis each summer, a fear that is still vivid in the minds of many of us over fifty years of age who saw siblings, schoolmates, or friends stricken, then either die or become crippled. Yet once the American people and a private foundation as well as governments invested in scientific research, poliomyelitis was brought under control, so that in neither Scandinavia nor North America is there a case of wild-type poliomyelitis today.

The most important benefit of controlling infectious diseases is alleviation of pain and suffering. There is also substantial benefit, the monetary savings. Thus, funds are no longer required for hospitalization and treatment. Individuals who would otherwise have been incapacitated are now healthy and are able to work, buy goods, and pay taxes. A safe estimate is that for each dollar invested by the government in basic research to study these diseases, a return of at least 1,000- to 10,000-fold has been realized in terms of those who are financially productive, instead of requiring long-term care. Yet with success comes complacency, and a lessening of general awareness that viral diseases will always remain a threat. Only with continuing research, investigation, surveillance, and education can humankind hope to control those diseases that remain or are newly discovered and prevent the reemergence of viruses that were once tamed.

This book is based largely on the personal reports, letters, and messages of the principal persons involved. I have tried as far as possible to write from the original sources and from contemporary accounts by participants who saw the events firsthand as they unfolded. I have been fortunate to have the opportunity to become friends with many of those who played commanding roles in the fight to control and eradicate the viruses and to discuss with them many episodes described in this book. At medical school, I came under the influence of Theodore Woodward, a superb teacher and clinician who, as Chairman of Medicine at the University of Maryland, educated me in clinical aspects of infectious diseases. Through his urging and that of Charles Wisseman, Chair of the Microbiology Department, I spent one summer working at Walter Reed Hospital and Institute of Research. There I came in direct contact with Joseph Smadel, a dean of the scientific discipline of virology. Soon afterward through Dr. Smadel I met John Enders, who recommended that, upon completion of my medical program, I apply my training in infectious diseases and graduate work in viruses and rickettsia into the interphase of virology and immunology. Both Enders and Smadel play prominent roles in this book. Following Enders's advice and suggestion, I moved to La Jolla to train under Frank Dixon, one of the major figures of modern immunology, at the Scripps Clinic and Research Foundation in La Jolla, California (now The Scripps Research Institute). The late 1960s and early '70s brought the opportunity to complement my immunologic training under Dixon and receive virologic training by working directly with a major figure in virology, Karl Habel.

I am especially grateful to Hilary Koprowski, Jonas Salk, Albert Sabin, Tom Weller, Samuel Katz, D. A. Henderson, Frank Fenner, John Skehel, Brian Mahy, Jordie Casals, Luc Montagnier, Robert Gallo, W. Ian Lipkin, Jeffery Taubenberger, Peter Palese, Rob Webster, and Ken Tyler as contributors to this history. Of course, I have consulted the voluminous literature on the subject, and I am indebted to Paula King and Marisela Perez-Meza of The Scripps Research Institute Medical Library for their assistance, the Medical Library at the Medical Research Council at Mill Hill, and the Burroughs-Wellcome Medical Library, both in London. I am also indebted to Brian Mahy and C. J. Peters, both personal friends and senior virologists at the Centers for Disease Control, Atlanta, Georgia, for their discussions on Lassa fever, Ebola virus, and Hantavirus infections. I am grateful for the insight and education I received on China, Chinese culture, and policy from Jennifer Oldstone-Moore, Professor and Chair of Far Asian Studies at Wittenberg University.

I am particularly indebted to both the Burroughs-Wellcome Trust that provided a Visiting Professorship to allow me to work at Mill Hill in London, and the Rockefeller Foundation, which provided me with a scholarship to live at the Villa Serbelloni, Bellagio, Italy, a sanctuary where I put many of my thoughts into words and constructed the outline for this book. Throughout the project I was fortunate to have the assistance of Gay Wilkins-Blade, who provided expert secretarial services, Phyllis Minick, who gave editorial advice, and Madeleine Rose Oldstone for indexing. I also thank my scientific colleagues: the late Frank J. Dixon, J. Lindsay Whitton, and Curtis Wilson (The Scripps Research Institute, La Jolla), Thomas Merigan (Stanford Medical School, Palo Alto), John Skehel (Medical Research Council, Mill Hill, London), Rob Webster (St. Jude Children's Research Hospital, Memphis), Bruce Chesebro (Rocky Mountain Laboratory, National Institutes of Health, Hamilton, Montana), Joe Esposito (Centers for Disease Control and Prevention, Atlanta, Georgia), Ken Tyler (University of Colorado Medical School), and Sven Gard and Erling Norrby (Karolinska Institute, Stockholm), who offered valuable suggestions and comments on several of the chapters.

La Jolla, California
M.B.A.O.
Spring 2009

CONTENTS

Part One
Viruses, Plagues, and History

1

A General
Introduction

Individual viruses have evolved intriguing and unique lifestyles. Many have altered the world we live in and continue to do so. The ravages of smallpox and measles viruses, long ago brought inadvertently to the New World by Europeans, decimated the native populations, allowing the newcomers to invade and colonize without restraint. Since antiquity, smallpox and measles viruses had infected populations in Asia, the Middle East, and Europe. Selective pressures then weeded out the most susceptible victims and provided immunity (protection) for the survivors of infection. For example, New World natives who had never been exposed to these infectious agents were highly susceptible, readily infected, and died in huge numbers. Simultaneously, Europeans, including members of the military in the New World, died from yellow fever, especially the French forces in Haiti. As his soldiers fell victim to this virus, Napoleon decided to sell a large component of France's New World holdings to the newly formed U.S. government headed by Thomas Jefferson. Acquisition of this huge area, termed the Louisiana Purchase, allowed the United States to extend from the Caribbean shores to Canada and then expand westward to the Pacific Ocean. Additionally, the millions paid for this purchase enabled the new Americans to avoid war with their stronger European adversaries. Thus, viruses played a commanding role in the defeat of America's native warriors, the conquest by Europeans throughout much of this continent, the dramatic increase of the slave trade, and the manifest destiny of Western expansion across the United States.

Currently, we continue to witness virally caused changes in our landscape. The plague of human immunodeficiency virus (HIV)-associated immunodeficiency disease (AIDS) has infected, according to some sources, over 34 million persons but more likely closer to 39 million, of which over one-half have died. This epidemic's devastation in the African continent has resulted in severe economic and cultural changes, untold misery, loss of family structure, and enormous increases in the number of orphans. Further, the first pandemic of the twenty-first century, sudden acute respiratory syndrome (SARS), has already struck. Governments and international organizations like the Pan American Union, the European Union, and the World Health Organization have now set up surveillance systems to monitor such diseases. They have planned countermeasures to prevent a future plague from influenza viruses, such as those that killed 40–60 million people from 1918 to 1919. Perhaps more humans could succumb to mad cow-like diseases, the spongiform encephalopathies caused by a still incompletely understood agent, prions.

Then, what are these infectious agents called viruses, what do they do, and how do they do their work? Some of these infectious agents have decided the winners of battles, for example, when a particular virus infected one army but not its adversaries. Viruses have depleted the native populations of several continents and countries. They have caused geographic, economic, and religious changes.

Smallpox alone, in the twentieth century, has killed an estimated 300 million individuals, about threefold as many persons as all the wars of that century (1).[1] In the sixteenth and seventeenth centuries, smallpox killed emperors of Japan and Burma, as well as kings and queens of Europe, thereby unseating dynasties, altering control of countries, and disrupting alliances (2). Smallpox decimated the combined French/Spanish-led naval invasion of England and played a key role in preventing the continental army in the American Revolution from conquering Canada. The successful conquest of Mexican Aztec and Peruvian Inca empires by a handful of Spanish conquistadors led by Hernando Cortés and Francisco Pizarro, respectively, resulted in large

---

[1] Numbers in parentheses refer to References listed at the end of the book.

part from epidemics of smallpox and measles virus infection that deci-mated the native defenders. Most of the conquistadors had been exposed to these viruses in Europe, so were immune to their effects, but those of the New World were completely vulnerable. In fact, neither the obvious technical superiority of the Spaniards, the superstitions that Aztec god Quetzalcoatl or other gods would destroy the natives, nor the Spaniards' alliances with tribes subjugated by the Aztecs or Incas account for the Spanish victory. History asserts that the Aztecs, once incited to fight, sav-agely attacked and defeated the Spanish. However, on the very evening that the Aztecs drove the conquistadors out of what is now Mexico City, killing many while routing the rest, a smallpox epidemic began. As it ravaged in the city (3), not only did the susceptible Aztec forces die in droves, but the psychological aspect of seeing Spaniards, who fought under a Christian god, resist this new malady while warriors of the Aztec gods were dying of infection demoralized the natives even further. The Aztecs could not have known that smallpox was endemic in Europe at this time and that many in Spain exposed to smallpox earlier were resistant or immune to subsequent infection by this virus. The stricken Aztecs interpreted the death of their people while the Spaniards went untouched as a clear indication that the Christian god held dominance over native gods. Therefore, one direct consequence of mass smallpox infection was the subjugation and subsequent exploita-tion of Native Americans and Mexicans by the Spaniards. A second and more lasting effect was destruction of the native culture; as the Spaniard culture assumed sovereignty, millions of Native Americans were converted to the Christian faith. During the time of the Spanish con-quest in the New World, an estimated one-third to one-half or more of the total native population had been killed by smallpox and measles viruses.

In addition to propelling the establishment of Christianity in Mexico and Latin America, viruses played a role in enlarging the African slave trade throughout the Americas. African blacks are relatively resistant to yellow fever virus, whereas Caucasians and Native Americans are much more susceptible. Because so many Native Americans had died from yellow fever, too few workers remained to do chores in the fields and mines. The Spaniards then imported black slaves as labor replace-ments (3). The net result was expansion of black slave importation to the Americas (4); ironically, the yellow fever virus initially came from Africa aboard trading and slave ships.

In addition to Spain, other European countries staked out colonies in the Americas. The French colonized Haiti and, in keeping with their observation that the Africans resisted infection by yellow fever and therefore were stronger workers, used primarily black labor for their plantations. But viruses altered human history again when black slaves revolted in the early years of the nineteenth century. To put down that uprising, Napoleon sent over 27,000 crack troops to Haiti. Before long, the vast majority of these Frenchmen came in contact with the yellow fever virus transmitted by mosquitoes and died from the infection. This huge loss influenced the decision not to risk the even larger numbers of troops necessary to protect other French territories in the New World and was one of the major considerations leading Napoleon to negotiate the sale of the Louisiana Territory to the United States (5).

England also colonized large parts of North America, including what was to become the early United States and Canada. During the Revolutionary War, the American colonial government sent an army to wrest Canada away from the English. Having captured Montreal, the colonial army, superior in numbers, marched on to engage in the conquest of Quebec City. But smallpox entered their ranks. The decimated American army (6), soon after burying their dead in mass graves, retreated in disorder from Quebec.

The bigger picture lies in the aftereffects of smallpox, measles, and yellow fever viruses. Some historians link the Spaniards' New World riches with the initial dominance of Spain in Europe. Nevertheless, the later demise of Spain in European politics is attributed by some primarily to wealth acquired from the Americas, which fostered a leisure population that was slow to enter the industrial revolution. The situation may have been very different had the natives not been susceptible to the diseases carried by the Spanish. Viruses interfered so that Canada and the United States never united into a single country. Further, the virus-promoted Louisiana Purchase provided an opportunity for the United States to enhance its size by unprecedented western expansion, without precipitating a potential geopolitical conflict with France. The aftermath of virus infection uprooted native cultures and peoples of South, Central, and Latin America and replaced them with a European culture, where Christianity flourished. Enhanced transport and introduction of ever more valuable black African slaves into the New World filled a niche created by smallpox, measles, and yellow fever viruses.

But at that time, who would have imagined that the ancient diseases of humankind, smallpox and measles, would eventually be controlled? Smallpox, after decimating the ancient Mexican population, still continued to kill, for example, until the early 1940s, when this virus was responsible for the deaths of over 10,000 Mexicans a year. Yet, smallpox has now been eradicated not only from Mexico but also from the entire world as a result of vaccination programs. Eradication of measles virus may or may not be a reasonable goal in view of its strong infectivity, but control is achievable. Measles is no longer a problem in most industrialized countries where the vaccine is given routinely. In 1970, measles viruses infected an estimated 130 million individuals and killed nearly 8 million. Today most cases occur in the underdeveloped countries of the Third World, where measles virus still infects about 40 million individuals per year with a death rate approaching one-half million.

Poliomyelitis virus is a relatively new virus. Polio epidemics were not recorded until the nineteenth century, followed by an increasing incidence in the twentieth century (7). At one time, poliomyelitis virus infection was responsible for one-fifth of the deaths from acute disease in Sweden (8). No one would have guessed then that poliomyelitis would now be under control or that its eradication from this planet would be a goal of the World Health Organization. Similarly, because of vaccination, yellow fever virus no longer spreads the havoc and fear it once did. These triumphs of medicine reflect the achievements that are possible when medical scientists and government agencies work together and devote their resources to solving health problems.

In contrast to these viruses now harnessed by the innovations of health care, new viral plagues of fearful proportions have appeared. Although HIV has reportedly infected up to 39 million persons, no vaccine exists to prevent it. The drugs currently used for its treatment successfully lower the amount of viruses but do not completely rid them from the infected individual. Thus, those infected can still transmit HIV and AIDS. There are no known spontaneous cures.

Among other plagues now emerging, SARS has already killed thousands in this new century. Spreading from China to Toronto, Canada, it closed down that city and overtaxed its medical/health services. Hemorrhagic fevers made their formidable appearance in the second half of the twentieth century. Evident on all continents, exhibiting frightening death rates, the hemorrhagic fever viruses Ebola, Hanta, and Lassa have claimed numerous victims. Just the names of these viruses provoke the fear today that yellow fever, poliomyelitis, and smallpox did in previous times. Another virus never before seen in North America made its appearance in 1998 by first killing birds in Queens and New York City before affecting humans. This virus, West Nile, has subsequently spread across North America, Canada, Mexico, Central and South America, and the Caribbean, killing thousands along the way. Still another former plague caused by a type of human influenza virus that killed over 40 million persons between 1918 and 1919—more victims than died in World War I—may make a comeback in its previous form or in a new variation, the so-called bird flu. In bird flu, a major protein of human influenza virus, the hemagglutinin is replaced by hemagglutinin 5 of birds, which represents a new threat to humans. Last in this list is the current scare that beef from cattle with mad cow disease is causing human dementia. However, the probability that this disease can reach epidemic proportions as well as identification of the causative agent as a virus remains debatable. Another mad cow–like sickness is called chronic wasting disease of deer and elk. Although we have no evidence, as yet, that this disease agent can infect humans, surveillance units are now in place to investigate and evaluate that possibility.

To assist the reader in understanding how plagues of the past were first discovered and then controlled, despite numerous difficulties, the next two chapters briefly review the principles of virus infection and its course. Chapter 2 defines what a virus is, how it replicates, and how it causes disease. The third chapter explores how the human immune system combats viruses, either by spontaneously eliminating infections or by becoming stimulated via vaccination to prevent viral diseases. For those interested in virology and immunology, Chapters 2 and 3 are recommended. Otherwise, the reader may wish to skip directly to Chapter 4. Knowing how vaccines were envisioned and developed helps to explain why devising a vaccine for HIV is so difficult, and what steps are required for successfully attacking and combating a virus infection. The balance of power between any virus and the host it infects reflects the strength, or virulence, of the virus and the resistance or susceptibility of the host.

Readers of this book will encounter the major personalities who became microbe hunters in the fight against smallpox, measles, yellow fever, poliomyelitis, Lassa fever, Ebola, Hantaviruses, SARS, West Nile virus, HIV, influenza, and spongiform encephalopathies. The history of viruses and virology is also the history of men and women who have worked to combat these diseases. The conquest or control of any disease requires the efforts of many. However, several who became prominent by identifying, isolating, or curing viral infections have been singled out by history as heroes. This book also examines the research of medical investigators who eventually linked certain diseases with specific viruses, leading to their ultimate control. Because these scientists—virologists— are human, inevitable conflicts arose among them, and some of these stories are also told.

The history of virology would be incomplete without describing the politics and the superstitions evoked by viruses and the diseases they cause. For example, armed private citizens and militias attempted to prevent frightened crowds from fleeing Memphis in 1878–79 during an epidemic of yellow fever, tried to blockade those leaving New York City in 1916 because of poliomyelitis, and endeavored to halt the abandonment of Zwitheba, Zaire (renamed Congo Republic in 1997), in 1995 to escape Ebola. Thus, woven into the fabric of the history of viral plagues are the fear, superstition, and ignorance of humankind.

Even as measles and poliomyelitis disappeared from countries like the United States and the United Kingdom, apathy toward vaccination arose among those who had never observed the devastation caused by these viruses. In fact, organizations evolved for the express purpose of preventing vaccination. Encouraged by this misinformed culture, parents who participated in the antivaccination movement not only put their own children in harm's way but also the children of others, because unprotected children frequently become sick and circulate infection to playmates, schoolmates, and their communities. In turn, the likelihood increases that these infectious agents will return with their enormous potential for causing devastation. It is unfortunate but true that when culture or politics confronts science, culture and politics most often trumps until a disaster occurs.

Lastly, it is worth considering how the people of a country like the United States could unite in a crusade to prevent a disease like poliomyelitis, yet succumb to controversy in alleviating the spread of and suffering from HIV. Believe it or not, a similar lack of support by industrialized countries of the world, including the United States, once halted the plans to eradicate smallpox (1).

2

Introduction to the Principles of Virology

Peter Medawar, a biologist awarded the Nobel Prize for Medicine and Physiology in 1960, defined a virus as a piece of nucleic acid surrounded by bad news (1). True, viruses are nothing more than a tiny bit of genetic material—a single kind of nucleic acid (segmented or nonsegmented, DNA or RNA) and a coat made of protein molecules. Viruses multiply according to the information contained in this nucleic acid. Everything other than the DNA or RNA is dispensable and serves primarily to ensure that the viral nucleic acid gets to the right place in the right sort of cell in the organism hosting the virus. Viruses cannot multiply until they invade a living cell. However, viruses can enter all cellular forms of life from plants and animals to bacteria, fungi, and protozoa. Together, viruses, plants, and animals form the three main groups that encompass all living things. As opposed to plants and animals, which are made up of cells, viruses lack cell walls and are, therefore, obligatory parasites that depend for replication on the cells they infect.

Viruses have relatively few genes compared with other organisms. Measles virus, yellow fever virus, poliomyelitis virus, Lassa fever virus, Ebola virus, Hantavirus, as well as the human immunodeficiency virus (HIV), have fewer than ten genes each, whereas a smallpox virus and

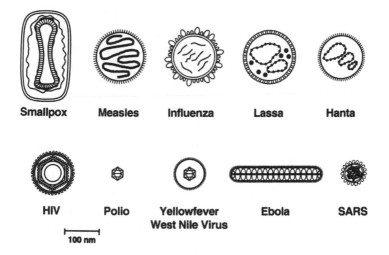

FIGURE 2.1 *Viruses have differing lifestyles and have evolved a variety of shapes and sizes in which to place their genetic material. A scaled comparison of the various viruses discussed in this book is shown. Viruses vary from the smallest, poliovirus, to the largest, smallpox virus.*

herpes virus may contain between 200 and 400 genes. These numbers compare with 5,000 to 10,000 genes for the smallest bacteria and approximately 30,000 genes for a human.

Some have argued that the nucleic acid of viruses evolved from the genes of normal cells. Through the alterations of mutation, reassortment, and recombination, viruses could then have evolved their own genetic structures. Perhaps some viruses stayed within the parental host from which they evolved and displayed symbiotic or near-symbiotic relationships. But as viruses moved from one host species to another or mutated to form new genetic mixtures, some of these formerly symbiotic viruses achieved a high level of virulence. Researchers suspect that the canine distemper virus of dogs or rindepest virus of sheep may have crossed species to enter humans in whom they mutated sufficiently to become the measles virus. This concept is postulated because the genomic sequences of canine distemper virus, rindepest virus, and measles virus have more in common than do sequences from other types of viruses. Such interrelationships between these three viruses likely occurred at the time when large human populations first lived in close proximity to domestic animals. A similar event enabled simian (monkey) viruses to infect humans, become HIV, and cause AIDS. The virus carried in monkeys does not cause disease in that host. Thus, whenever a virus encounters an unfamiliar organism, the virus may undergo multiple mutations and emerge as a variant that produces a severe and novel disease. For example, human influenza virus contains one of three viral hemagglutinins, which are outer glycoproteins of the virus whose purpose is to bind to molecule(s) on a host's cell. Termed H1, H2, or H3, the hemagglutinin of human influenza virus has been replaced by a bird hemagglutinin termed H5 in what we call bird flu. Infectious for certain birds, H5 bird flu has now infected humans for the first time, and the resultant mortality is high in humans hospitalized with bird flu. However, the H5 bird virus that infected humans has not yet undergone significant transmission from one human to others. When or if that happens, then another serious pandemic of influenza is likely to occur.

To maintain itself in nature and to replicate, a virus must undergo a series of steps. First, the virus must find a way of entering a susceptible host. The virus contacts the cell to be infected and then attaches to its surface. A major function of the plasma membrane or outer "skin" of nucleated cells is to act as a barrier against infecting viruses. Yet viruses often cross through this membrane to carry their genetic material and accessory proteins into the cell's cytosol (inner compartment). Next, the virus penetrates into the cell's interior, leading to the uncoating or removal of the virus's outer husk. Thereafter, the virus uses its evolved strategies to express its genes, replicate its genome (genes placed in the correct order and orientation), and assemble its component parts (nucleic acids and proteins) in multiple copies or progeny (offspring). Upon completion of this sequence, mature viruses formed during the replication process exit from the infected cell by a process called budding. In some cases the virus, once it has made multiple progeny, will kill the cell as a mechanism for releasing new viruses.

Generally, the attachment and entry of viruses into cells are dependent both on the activities of the host cell and on the properties of selected viral genes. The cell has on its surface receptors to which viruses attach and bind with proteins evolved specifically for that purpose. The cell must also provide the mechanism for viral penetration after binding has occurred and for the internal highway that viruses travel to reach sites in the cell's cytoplasm or nucleus where replication processes can proceed.

As described above, the attachment or binding of a viral protein (specifically, an amino acid sequence within that protein) to a cell receptor is the first step that initiates infection of a cell. The unique distribution of certain receptors and either their limitation to a few cell types or, instead, their broad range on many different cell types dictates how many portals of entry exist for a virus. Further, the type of cells with such receptors and/or with the ability to replicate a given virus often determines the severity of illness that a virus can cause, the distribution of areas (organs, tissues, cells) in the body that can be affected, and the host's potential for recovery. For example, infection/killing of the irreplaceable neuronal cells in the central nervous system or of cells in the heart whose function is essential to life is extremely ominous. Less so is infection of skin cells, which are not as critical for survival and are readily replaced.

An example of a cellular receptor is a molecule called CD4, which is abundant on the surfaces of some lymphocytes (white blood cells) derived from the thymus (CD4$^+$ T cells). The CD4 molecule is also present, but less plentiful, on monocyte/macrophages (macrophages are infection fighting cells, an activated form of monocytes) in the blood and in certain tissues of the body. The CD4 molecule along with certain chemokine (cell-attracting) molecules is the receptor for HIV. Because the CD4 receptor appears on relatively few cell types that HIV can infect, these viruses attack only limited sites in the body (2,3). In contrast, a molecule called CD46, one of the cell receptors for measles virus (the other is SLAM), appears on many types of cells (4–7). CD46 is found on epithelial cells, which line most cavities including the nose, pharynx, respiratory tree, and gut; on endothelial cells lining blood vessels; on lymphocytes/macrophages; and on neuronal cells in the brain. The common presence of the CD46 receptors accounts for the widespread replication of measles virus during infection.

In addition to access through specific cell receptors, viruses can enter cells by other means. When an unfamiliar agent composed of foreign proteins (antigens), such as a virus, enters the body, a defensive response by the host produces antibodies that bind to the antigen in an attempt to remove it. Because antibodies are shaped roughly like the letter "Y," they can bind to cells in two ways. First, via their arms (the two upper parts of the "Y"), antibodies use a combining site (the so-called FAb'2 site) to interact specifically with antigens on cells. Second, with a part of their stalk (the bottom part of the "Y") called the Fc region, antibody molecules can bind to receptors (Fc receptors) on certain cells.

After antibodies made by the host's immune system in response to viral antigens bind to those antigens, an infectious virus–antibody complex forms (8). By binding to the cell via the Fc receptor, the virus as part of the virus–antibody complex can enter that cell even though its surface may not contain a specific receptor for the virus.

Not all cells that bind and take in a virus have the appropriate machinery to replicate that virus. Therefore, binding of a virus to a receptor and entry into a cell may not result in the production of progeny. To summarize, the susceptibility of a specific cell for a virus is dependent on at least three factors. First, a functional receptor must be present on the cell. Second, a specific viral protein, or sequence within the protein, must be available to bind to the cell receptor. Third, the cell must possess the correct machinery to assist in replication of the virus.

The postbinding step in which viruses can penetrate a cell is an active process and depends on energy. Occurring within seconds of binding/attachment, penetration follows either by movement of the entire virus across the cell's plasma membrane, a process called phagocytosis (more specifically, endocytosis), so that the virus particle is pinched off inside a vacuole or compartment of the cell, or by fusion of the cell's membrane with the virus's outer envelope. After penetration, the virus sheds its protective protein coat and then releases its viral nucleic acids. This procedure is followed by replication of the viral genome, during which the host cell's protein-manufacturing equipment actually synthesizes new viruses—their progeny. To produce abundant amounts of their own proteins, viruses must evolve strategies that provide advantages for synthesizing viral materials instead of host cells' materials. Viruses accomplish this feat either by abolishing the cell's ability to make its own products or by conferring a selective advantage for the making of viral products.

Whatever the route, once the viral genome and proteins form, they assemble as multiple progeny viruses, they mature, and they leave the infected cell. Individual viruses have evolved unique processes and "patented" them for success in this process. Once formed as a mature particle, viruses assume distinctive sizes and shapes.

How do viruses cause disease? Three distinct pathways are available (9,10). By the first, the virus or its proteins are directly toxic to a cell. In this instance, the virus kills its host cell. With some viruses this process serves to release viral particles from the inside of a cell to the outside environment. Alternatively, a second mechanism enables a virus to avoid killing the cell but instead to alter its function. By this means, the synthesis of an important product made by a cell is turned down or turned up. For example, a nonlethal virus infection of cells that make growth hormone can diminish the amount of this hormone made by the infected host cell. As a result the host fails to grow and develop normally. The third way in which injury and disease can follow a viral infection is through the participation of the host's immune response. As stated in Chapter 3, the immune response to viruses is generated to rid infected cells of viral progeny and to remove an infectious virus from the host's blood and other body fluids. By destroying virally infected cells, the immune system can damage tissues that are critical to healthy function of the organism. The idea is to destroy the factories that make new viruses, with luck, before complete infectious virus particles form. As discussed in Chapter 3, a specialized arm of the immune response, so-called cytotoxic CD8 T cells, can recognize parts of viral proteins (peptides) presented on the cells' surface along with the host's "self" units (major histocompatibility complex molecule I) and kill the infected cell at an early stage during infection but before assembly of infectious viral particles. Additionally, virus–antibody immune complexes can form and subsequently deposit or become trapped in kidneys and blood vessels, which are then injured. Thus, another side of the usually protective immune response is its destructive potential. The study of such processes is called immunopathology. The balance between the protective and destructive processes of the immune system is in large part responsible for the clinical symptoms (what the patient feels or sees) and signs (what the doctor finds) that accompany a virus infection.

How were viruses recognized as dangers to health? Although the diseases caused by viruses were known in antiquity, viruses were not acknowledged as separate infectious agents until the late 1890s, after bacteria and other parasites had been recognized.

The mid-1800s was the time when bacteria were discovered, and Louis Pasteur, Robert Koch, and their associates accomplished pioneering work. During that period, the laboratory culturing process was developed so that bacteria could be grown in enriched agar preparations or broths, then fixed on glass slides, stained, and observed under the microscope. Bacteria were retained on filters with specific pore sizes, which allowed calculation of each bacterium's size. After their identification, specific bacteria could be linked with particular disease states. This was the framework in which the first viruses were uncovered. In 1898, Dmitri Losifovich Ivanovski (11) in Russia and Martinus Beijerinck (12) in

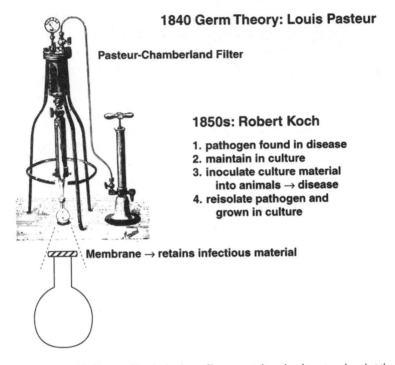

1840 Germ Theory: Louis Pasteur

Pasteur-Chamberland Filter

1850s: Robert Koch

1. pathogen found in disease
2. maintain in culture
3. inoculate culture material
   into animals → disease
4. reisolate pathogen and
   grown in culture

Membrane → retains infectious material

FIGURE 2.2 *The Pasteur-Chamberland-type filter connected to a hand pump and used at the Pasteur Institute toward the end of the nineteenth century.*

the Netherlands demonstrated that the material responsible for a disease of tobacco plants, instead of being retained, passed through the pores of a Pasteur-Chamberland filter without losing infectivity (i.e., the material was smaller than bacteria). The investigators found that this soluble residue of filtration could somehow grow on healthy tobacco leaves, but not on media used to grow bacteria. Their result was the first report of a plant virus, the tobacco mosaic virus. Similarly, Friedrich Loeffler and Paul Frosch (13) in Germany concluded that the agent causing foot-and-mouth disease of cows also passed through porcelain filters and induced symptoms of disease when inoculated into previously healthy cattle. These observations, highly controversial at the time, provided the basis for defining viruses as subcellular entities that could cause distinct forms of tissue destruction, which became marks of specific diseases. The uniqueness of this detective work is even more dramatic when one

FIGURE 2.3 *Louis Pasteur, one of the founders of microbiology. Pasteur also attenuated (reduced virulence in) several infectious agents, including rabies virus, to make vaccines.*

considers that the infectious virus particles were too small to see and could not grow on the culture media available. Visualization of viruses awaited the use of electron microscopy in the mid-1930s, and the culturing of living cells necessary for viral replication was not possible until the late 1940s to early 1950s.

Most viral infections are recognized as acute illnesses. That is, the causative virus enters the body, multiplies in one or more tissues, and spreads locally through the blood or along nerves. The incubation period of two days to two or three weeks is followed by signs and symptoms of disease and local or widespread tissue damage. Viruses can be isolated from the patient's blood (serum or blood cells) or secretions for a short time just before and after the appearance of symptoms from these

FIGURE 2.4 *Friedrich Loeffler (right) and his teacher and mentor Robert Koch (left), who with Louis Pasteur cofounded the field of microbiology. Loeffler and Paul Frosch isolated the first animal virus, foot-and-mouth virus, in 1898. The virus was separated from bacteria by its ability to pass through a Pasteur-Chamberland filter. Photos courtesy of the National Library of Medicine.*

sources and from infected tissues. Afterward, the infected host either recovers from the infection, and is often blessed with lifelong immunity to that virus, or dies during the acute phase of illness.

Distinct from acute infections are persistent infections in which the immune response fails to completely remove viruses from the body, and those remaining viruses then persist for months or years. As in the case of HIV infection, viruses can be recovered for years throughout the long course of infection. Although all components (antibodies and T cells) of the immune response are generated during HIV infection, and for a considerable period of time the amount of virus load decreases markedly, the response is not capable of terminating the infection. Then, during the terminal stage of the illness, T cell immunity declines or vanishes; that is, T cells become exhausted and function poorly, and a high viral load recurs. Figure 2.5 shows the differences between acute and persistent infection. How the immune response is constituted and how it attacks viruses are described in the next chapter. A list of important virologic observations recently compiled by Fred Murphy, a longtime worker in the field, is provided at the end of this chapter (Table 2.1, courtesy of Fred Murphy).

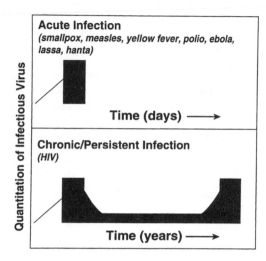

FIGURE 2.5 *Infections caused by viruses differ. Some are acute, and the outcome—survival or death—is decided within a week or two. Others, like HIV, routinely run a years-long or lifetime infectious course in the human host. The darkened area indicates the presence of virus.*

TABLE 2.1 The Foundations of Medical and Veterinary Virology—Discoverers and Discoveries, Inventors and Inventions, Developers and Technologies

Date	Discoverer(s) Inventor(s) Developer(s)	Discovery(ies) Invention(s) Technology(ies)
400 BCE	Hippocrates	Greek physician, father of medicine, important epidemiologic observations on many infectious diseases
1546	G. Fracastoro	Theory that epidemic diseases are disseminated by minute particles carried over long distances
1660	R. Hooke	Invention of the compound microscope and illumination system

TABLE 2.1 *(continued)*

Date	Discoverer(s) Inventor(s) Developer(s)	Discovery(ies) Invention(s) Technology(ies)
1668	A. Van Leeuwenhoek	Invention of a simple microscope, observation of bacteria
1775	L. Spallanzani	First growth of bacteria in culture
1796	E. Jenner	Application of cowpox virus for vaccination against smallpox
1835	M. Schleiden, T. Schwann, others	Development of the concept that all organisms are composed of cells
1838	J. Graunt, W. Farr, J. Snow, L. Villerme, P. Panum, M. Pruden, H. Biggs, others	Founding of epidemiology
1840s	I. Semmelweis, O. Holmes	Development of practical methods of hygiene and antimicrobial disinfection
1850	C. Davaine	First association of a specific infectious organism with a specific disease (*bacillus anthracis*-anthrax)
1857	L. Pasteur, R. Koch	Founding of microbiology
1858	C. Darwin, A. Wallace	Development of the concepts of evolutionary progression, common descent, natural selection
1860s	W. Henderson, R. Paterson	Discovery of the inclusion body of molluscum contagiosum virus
1865	G. Mendel	Founding of genetics
1868	F. Meischer	Discovery and characterization of nucleic acids
1880s	J. Buist	Discovery of the elementary bodies of vaccinia and variola viruses
1880s	C. Chamberland	Development of the Chamberland-Pasteur unglazed porcelain ultra-filter and the autoclave
1882	A. Mayer	Development of the concept of transmissibility of tobacco mosaic disease and the earliest concept of filterable virus

1883	E. Metchnikoff, J. Bordet, P. Ehrlich	Founding of immunology
1884	J. Henle, R. Koch, F. Loeffler	Henle-Koch postulates, criteria for proof of causation
1885	L. Pasteur, E. Roux	Development of rabies vaccine
1888	Institut Pasteur	Opening of the Institut Pasteur at 15 Rue du Docteur-Roux, Paris
1888	F. Loeffler, P. Rous, A. Yersin, E. Von Behring	Discovery of microbial toxins and antitoxins
1892	D. Ivanovski	Discovery of tobacco mosaic virus (the first virus)
1898	M. Beijerinck	Discovery of tobacco mosaic virus (the first virus)
1898	F. Loeffler, P. Frosch	Discovery of foot-and-mouth disease virus (the first vertebrate virus, the first picornavirus)
1898	G. Sanarelli	Discovery of myxoma virus (the first poxvirus)
1900	J. M'Fadyean, T. Edgington, A. Theiler	Discovery of African horse sickness virus (the first orbivirus)
1900–1901	W. Reed, J. Carroll, A. Agramonte, J. Lazear, C. Finlay	Discovery of yellow fever virus (the first human virus, the first flavivirus) and its transmission cycle
1901	E. Centanni, E. Savonuzzi, A. Lode, J. Gruber	Discovery of fowl plague virus (avian influenza virus, the first orthomyxovirus)
1902	M. Nicolle, M. Adil-Bey	Discovery of rinderpest virus (the first morbillivirus)
1902	A. Aujeszky	Discovery of pseudorabies virus (the first herpesvirus)
1902–1906	J. Spruell, A. Theiler	Discovery of bluetongue viruses
1903	A. Negri	Discovery of the rabies inclusion body—negri body
1903	M. Remlinger, Riffat-Bay	Discovery of rabies virus (the first rhabdovirus)
1903	E. De Schweinitz, M. Dorset	Discovery of classical swine fever virus (hog cholera virus, the first pestivirus)
1904	H. Vallée, H. Carré	Discovery of equine infectious anemia virus (the first retrovirus)

TABLE 2.1 *(continued)*

Date	Discoverer(s) Inventor(s) Developer(s)	Discovery(ies) Invention(s) Technology(ies)
1905	H. Carré, P. Laidlaw, G. Dunkin	Discovery of canine distemper virus
1907	P. Ashburn, C. Craig	Discovery of dengue viruses
1908	V. Ellermann, O. Bang	Discovery of avian leukemia virus (the first leukemia virus)
1909	K. Landsteiner, E. Popper	Discovery of poliovirus (the first enterovirus)
1909	R. Doerr, K. Franz, S. Taussig	Discovery of sandfly (phlebotomus) fever viruses (the first phleboviruses)
1910	A. Carrel, H. and M. Maitland, E. Steinhardt, H. Eagle, G. Gey, T. Puck, R. Hamm, J. Enders, T. Weller, F. Robbins, others	Development of cell culture methods
1910	T. Morgan	Nature and role of the chromosome and the use of *Drosophila* in genetics research
1911	J. Goldberger, J. Anderson	Discovery of measles virus
1911	P. Rous, J. Beard	Discovery of rous sarcoma virus (first solid tumor virus)
1911–1934	G. Von Hevesey, R. Schoenheimer, D. Rittenberg	Development of radioisotopic labeling
1914–1938	A. Hess, Y. Hiro, S. Tasaka	Discovery of rubella virus (the only rubivirus)
1915–2004	American Public Health Association	Publication of the book, *Control of Communicable Diseases Manual*, 18 editions
1917–1919	F. Twort, F. D'herelle	Discovery of bacteriophages
1918–1919		Influenza pandemic, 40–100 million deaths worldwide
1918–1952	A. Breinl, J. Cleland, E. French	Discovery of Murray Valley encephalitis virus
1919	A. Löwenstein	Discovery of herpes simplex virus

1920s	J. Barnard	Visualization of several poxviruses by darkfield and UV microscopy
1921	R. Montgomery	Discovery of African swine fever virus (the only asfarvirus)
1923	T. Svedberg	Development of the ultracentrifuge
1925–1952	K. Kundratitz, H. Ruska, T. Weller, M. Stoddard	Discovery of varicella-zoster virus—chickenpox and zoster
1926	W. Cotton, P. Olitsky, J. Traum, H. Schoening	Discovery of vesicular stomatitis virus(es)
1927	T. Doyle	Discovery of Newcastle disease virus
1928	F. Griffith	Discovery of transformation in bacteria, a foundation of molecular genetics
1928	T. Rivers, others	Beginning of clinical virology
1928	T. Rivers (Ed)	Publication of the first major virology book, *Filterable Viruses*
1928	J. Verge, N. Christoforoni	Discovery of feline panleukopenia virus (the first parvovirus)
1928	R. Lancefield, E. Lennette, P. Halonen, others	Beginnings of viral disease diagnostics
1929	S. Nicolau, I. Galloway	Discovery of borna virus (the only bornavirus)
1930	R. Green, N. Ziegler, others	Discovery of canine hepatitis virus (the first adenovirus)
1931	A. Woodruff, E. Goodpasture, M. Burnet	Development of embryonated hen's eggs as host for viruses
1931	R. Shope	Discovery of swine influenza virus (the first influenzavirus)
1931	K. Meyer	Discovery of western equine encephalitis virus (the first alphavirus)
1931	R. Daubney, J. Hudson, P. Garnham	Discovery of Rift Valley fever virus
1931	J. Furth	Development of mice as host for viruses
1931	W. Elford	Use of graded collodion membranes to determine virion size
1933	R. Shope, P. Rous, J. Beard	Discovery of rabbit papillomavirus (the first papillomavirus)

TABLE 2.1 *(continued)*

Date	Discoverer(s) Inventor(s) Developer(s)	Discovery(ies) Invention(s) Technology(ies)
1933	A. Tiselius	Development of electrophoresis
1933	W. Smith, C. Andrewes, P. Laidlaw	Discovery of human influenza virus
1933	E. Ruska, M. Knoll	Development of the electron microscope
1933	Staff of Jackson Memorial Laboratory	Discovery of mouse mammary tumor virus
1933	J. Leake, E. Musson, H. Chope	Discovery of St. Louis encephalitis virus
1933–1954	W. Dimmock, P. Edwards, E. Doll, J. Kintner	Discovery of equid herpesvirus 1 (equine rhinopneumonitis virus) and equid herpesvirus 4 (equine abortion virus)
1934	C. Johnson, E. Goodpasture	Discovery of mumps virus
1934	M. Merrill, C. Lacaillade, C. Ten Broeck	Discovery of eastern equine encephalitis virus
1934	M. Hayashi, S. Kasahara, R. Kawamura, T. Taniguchi	Discovery of Japanese encephalitis virus
1935	M. Theiler	Development of yellow fever vaccine
1935	W. Stanley	Purification, "crystallization" of tobacco mosaic virus
1935	J. Bittner	Discovery of mouse mammary tumor virus
1936	F. Bawden, N. Pirie	Discovered that tobacco mosaic virus is comprised of nucleoprotein and that the nucleic acid is RNA
1936	J. Cuillé, P. Chelle	Transmission of scrapie to normal sheep by cell-free material from diseased sheep
1936	C. Armstrong, T. Rivers, E. Traub	Discovery of lymphocytic choriomeningitis virus (the first arenavirus)

1936	P. Rous, J. Beard	Induction of carcinomas in other species by rabbit papillomavirus
1936	J. Traub	Discovery of vesicular exanthema virus of swine (the first calicivirus)
1937	F. Beaudette, C. Hudson	Discovery of infectious bronchitis virus of chickens (the first coronavirus)
1937	M. Theiler	Demonstration of persistent CNS infection (theiler's virus)
1937	T. Rivers	Criteria for proof of viral disease causation: the Henle-Koch postulates revisited
1937	L. Zilber, M. Chumakov, N. Seitlenok	Discovery of tick-borne encephalitis virus (Russian spring summer encephalitis virus)
1938	C. Beck, P. Wyckoff, V. Kubes, F. Rios	Discovery of Venezuelan equine encephalitis virus
1938	R. Doerr, C. Hallauer (Eds.)	Publication of the major virology book, *Handbuch der Virusforschung-Erste Halfte*
1938	B. Von Borries, E. Ruska, H. Ruska	First electron micrograph of a virus (ectromelia virus)
1939	E. Ellis, M. Delbrück	Development of the one-step virus growth curve
1939	R. Doerr, C. Hallauer	First international virology journal, *Archiv für die Gesamte Virusforschung* (now *Archives of Virology*)
1940	K. Smithburn, T. Hughes, A. Burke, J. Paul	Discovery of West Nile virus
1940s	M. Burnet, D. Talmadge	Discovery of clonal selection as the central mechanism in the immune response
1941	G. Hirst	Discovery of virus hemagglutination, hemagglutination-inhibition, receptor destroying enzyme (neuraminidase) (influenza virus)
1941	N. Gregg	Discovery of rubella virus congenital abnormalities
1944	O. Avery, C. Macleod, M. Mccarty	Identification of DNA as the material of inheritance

TABLE 2.1 *(continued)*

Date	Discoverer(s) Inventor(s) Developer(s)	Discovery(ies) Invention(s) Technology(ies)
1945	T. Francis, J. Salk, G. Hirst, F. Davenport, T. Eickhoff, G. Meiklejohn, E. Kilbourne	Development of inactivated influenza vaccines
1945–1956	M. Chumakov, G. Courtois, colleagues	Discovery of Crimean-Congo hemorrhagic fever virus (the first nairovirus)
1946	M. Delbrück	Discovery of genetic recombination (bacteriophage)
1946	K. Smithburn, A. Haddow, A. Mahaffy	Discovery of Bunyamwera virus (the first bunyavirus)
1946–1953	M. Delbrück, S. Luria, S. Benzer, G. Stent, A. Hershey	Founding of the "phage school" at the California Institute of Technology, with "branches" at the Cold Spring Harbor Laboratory and the University of California Berkeley
1947	F. Fenner	Experimentation with ectromelia virus in mice and the beginning of viral pathogenesis research
1947–1955	M. Burnet, A. Gottschalk, E. Klenk	Discovery of virus receptors
1947–2007	C. Clifton, S. Raffel	Publication of *Annual Review of Microbiology*, 60 volumes
1948	G. Dalldorf, G. Sickles	Discovery of coxsackieviruses
1948	K. Sanford	Culture of single animal cells
1948–1965	T. Rivers, F. Horsfall, I. Tamm	Initial publication of book, *Viral and Rickettsial Infections of Man* (eventually four editions)
1948–1995	American Public Health Association, E. Lennette, N. Schmidt	Publication of book, *Diagnostic Procedures for Virus and Rickettsial Diseases*, seven editions
1949	J. Enders, T. Weller, F. Robbins	Development of cell culture methodology for polio, measles, and other vaccines

1949	A. Lwoff, L. Siminovitch, N. Kjeldgaard	Discovery of lysogeny and induction (bacteriophage)
1950	L. Florio, M. Miller, E. Mugrage	Discovery of Colorado tick fever virus (the first coltivirus)
1950–1960s	C. Mims	Development of immunofluorescence in viral pathogenesis research
1950–1960s	M. Delbrück, A. Hershey, S. Luria	Discovery of mechanisms in virus replication and genetics
1951	J. Lederberg	Discovery of bacteriophage λ
1951	L. Gross	Discovery that murine leukemias and lymphomas caused by viruses are transmitted through the embryo
1951	Univac 1 and Ferranti Mark I	Development of the first commercial electronic digital computers
1952	A. Hershey, M. Chase	Biological proof of DNA as the material of inheritance
1952	R. Dulbecco	Development of virus quantification by plaque assay
1952	J. Lederberg, N. Zinder	Discovery of transduction: transfer of genetic information between bacteria by viruses
1952	W. Stanley	Establishment of the Virus Laboratory at the University of California Berkeley
1953	W. Rowe	Discovery of human adenoviruses
1953	J. Watson, F. Crick, M. Wilkins, R. Franklin	Discovery of the structure of DNA
1953	J. Murphy, F. Bang	Discovery of virus release by budding at the cell surface
1953	N. Ishida, N. Kuroya	Discovery of Sendai virus (parainfluenza virus 1)
1953	S. Stewart, L. Gross, B. Eddy	Discovery of polyoma virus (the first polyomavirus)
1953	A. Coons, colleagues	Development of immunofluorescence
1953	W. Plowright	Discovery of bovine malignant catarrhal fever virus
1953	S. Luria	Publication of the major book, *General Virology*

TABLE 2.1 *(continued)*

Date	Discoverer(s) Inventor(s) Developer(s)	Discovery(ies) Invention(s) Technology(ies)
1953	R. Billingham, P. Medawar, L. Brent, F. Fenner, M. Burnet, R. Owens	Discovery of immunologic tolerance in virus infections
1953	K. Smith	Publication of the first major virology review series, *Advances in Virus Research*
1953–1959	A. Sabin	Discovery of orthoreoviruses (the first reoviruses)
1954	J. Salk, J. Youngner, T. Francis	Development of inactivated polio vaccine
1954	M. Smith	Discovery of murine cytomegalovirus
1954	B. Sigurdsson	Development of the concept of slow viruses (maedi-visna virus, scrapie prion)
1954	G. Takatsy	Development of microtiter plate technology
1955	S. Benzer	Definition of a gene (cis-trans test)
1955	W. Schäfer	Discovery that fowl plague virus is an influenza virus, and likely zoonotic
1955	R. Taylor, T. Hurlbut, T. Work, J. Kingston, T. Frothingham	Discovery of Sindbis virus
1955	M. Minsky	Development of confocal microscopy
1955	G. Hirst, L. Black, S. Luria	Publication of the journal, *Virology*
1956	J. Morris, R. Chanock, colleagues	Discovery of respiratory syncytial virus (the first pneumovirus)
1956	W. Pelon, W. Mogabgab, W. Price	Discovery of human rhinoviruses
1956	A. Gierer, G. Schramm, H. Fraenkel-Conrat, B. Singer	Discovery of the infectivity of viral RNA (tobacco mosaic virus)

1956	S. Madin, C. York, D. Mckercher	Discovery of infectious bovine rhinotracheitis virus
1956	R. Ross	Discovery of Chikungunya virus
1956	R. Chanock	Discovery of human parainfluenza viruses
1956	M. Smith, W. Rowe, T. Weller	Discovery of human cytomegalovirus
1957	A. Isaacs, J. Lindenmann	Discovery of interferons
1957	T. Work, F. Rodriguez, P. Bhatt	Discovery of Kyasanur Forest disease virus
1957	H. Fraenkel-Conrat, R. Williams	First in vitro assembly of a virus (tobacco mosaic virus)
1957	E. Doll	Discovery of equine arteritis virus (the first arterivirus)
1957	J. Enders, M. Hilleman, A. Gershon, S. Katz, S. Plotkin, M. Takahashi, others	Development of vaccines against measles, mumps, rubella, Marek's disease, hepatitis A, hepatitis B, varicella-zoster, adenoviruses
1958	M. Meselson, F. Stahl	Discovery of the semiconservative mode of replication of DNA
1958	E. Berger, J. Melnick	Publication of virology review series, *Progress in Medical Virology*
1958	R. Kissling, R. Goldwasser	Development of rabies immunofluorescence diagnostics
1958	A. Parodi, D. Greenway, others	Discovery of Junin virus
1958	D. Burkitt	Description of Burkitt's lymphoma in African children
1958	K. Åström, E. Richardson, J. Cavanaugh, G. Zu Rhein, B. Padgett, D. Walker, M. Bouteille, L. Horta-Barbosa	Discovery of progressive multifocal leukoencephalopathy (JC, SV40 viruses—polyomaviruses)
1959	A. Sabin, H. Cox, H. Koprowski	Development of attenuated live-virus polio vaccine
1959	L. Kilham	Discovery of murine parvoviruses
1959	S. Brenner, R. Horne	Invention of negative stain electron microscopy
1959	K. Porter, R. Edelman, A. Nisonoff	Discovery of the structure and molecular function of antibodies

TABLE 2.1 *(continued)*

Date	Discoverer(s) Inventor(s) Developer(s)	Discovery(ies) Invention(s) Technology(ies)
1959	R. Yalow and S. Berson	Development of radioimmunoassays (RIAs)
1959–1962	A. Shubladze, K. Chzhu-Shan, K. Schneweis	Differentiation of herpes simplex viruses 1 and 2
1960	Digital Equipment Corporation	Development of the first minicomputer
1960	B. Sweet, M. Hilleman	Discovery of simian virus 40 (SV40)
1960	V. Riley, colleagues	Discovery of lactate-dehydrogenase elevating virus
1960	W. Thompson, B. Kalfayan, R. Anslow	Discovery of La Crosse virus
1960–1970s	G. Palade, A. Claude, K. Porter, C. De Duve	Description of the fine structure and biochemistry of cellular organelles
1960s	J. Casals, R. Shope, R. Tesh, J. Digoutte, O. and C. Causey, R. Taylor, C. Calisher, F. Murphy, others	Discovery and characterization of many arthropod-borne alphaviruses, flaviviruses, bunyaviruses, rhabdoviruses and orbiviruses
1960s	R. Johnson, N. Nathanson, R. Blanden, B. Fields, M. Oldstone, A. Haase, D. Griffin, others	Founding of the modern era of viral pathogenesis research
1961	F. Jacob, J. Monod, A. Lwoff, S. Brenner, F. Gros, M. Meselson	Discovery of messenger RNA and how ribosomal genes control the expression of other genes
1961	F. Crick, J. Griffith, L. Orgel, S. Brenner, L. Barnett, R. Watts-Tobin	Discovery of the triplet coding of DNA (bacteriophage)
1961–1966	M. Nierenberg, S. Ochoa, J. Matthaei, H. Khorana	Cracking of the genetic code

1962	A. Chovnick, R. Dulbecco, J. Cairns, G. Hirst, A. Lwoff, H. Rubin, M. Stoker	Cold Spring Harbor symposium on quantitative biology: *Basic Mechanisms in Animal Virus Biology*
1962	L. Kraft	Discovery of mouse hepatitis virus (lethal intestinal virus of infant mice)
1962	D. Caspar, A. Klug	Discovery of the principles of icosahedral virus structure
1962	P. Gomatos, I. Tamm	Discovery of double-stranded RNA in a virus (reovirus)
1962	A. Cosgrove	Discovery of infectious bursal disease virus (the first birnavirus)
1962	F. Rauscher	Discovery of the first virus-induced lymphoid leukemia in mice
1962	J. Trentin, Y. Yabe, G. Taylor	Discovery of induction of tumors in hamsters by human adenoviruses
1963	W. Downs, C. Anderson, C. Spence, others	Discovery of Tacaribe virus
1964	M. Epstein, B. Achong, Y. Barr	Discovery of Epstein-Barr virus and its association with Burkitt's lymphoma
1964	O. Jarrett	Discovery of feline leukemia virus
1965	K. Johnson, N. Wiebenga, P. Webb, others	Discovery of machupo virus
1965	D. Tyrrell, M. Bynoe, J. Almeida, D. Hamre, J. Procknow	Discovery of human coronaviruses (B814 and 229E)
1965	F. Jacob, A. Lwoff, J. Monod	Discovery of messenger RNA, ribosomes, and genes controlling the expression of other genes
1965	M. Bouteille, T. Chen, L. Horta-Barbosa, J. Sever, others	Discovery of subacute sclerosing panencephalitis (measles virus)
1965	R. Atchison, J. Melnick, colleagues	Discovery of adeno-associated viruses
1966	C. Gajdusek, C. Gibbs, W. Hadlow	Discovery of transmissible spongiform encephalopathies (Kuru, scrapie)

TABLE 2.1 *(continued)*

Date	Discoverer(s) Inventor(s) Developer(s)	Discovery(ies) Invention(s) Technology(ies)
1966	P. Wildy, F. Fenner, R. Matthews, others	Founding of the International Committee on Nomenclature of Viruses (now the International Committee on Taxonomy of Viruses)
1966	P. Bhatt, R. Jacoby, H. Morse, A. New, others	Development of diagnostic virology of laboratory rodents
1967	B. Blumberg, H. Alter, A. Prince, others	Discovery of Australia antigen, hepatitis B virus (the first hepadnavirus)
1967	J. Kates, B. Mcauslan	Discovery of DNA-dependent RNA polymerase in a virion (vaccinia virus)
1967	W. Siegert, R. Slenczka, G. Martini, R. Kissling, R. Robinson, F. Murphy, others	Discovery of Marburg virus (the first filovirus)
1967	B. Van Der Westhuizen, Y. Inaba, Y. Tanaka, colleagues	Discovery of bovine ephemeral fever virus
1967	R. Wagner, L. Kozloff, N. Salzman	Publication of the journal, *Journal of Virology*
1967	C. Kaplan, P. Wildy	Publication of the journal, *Journal of General Virology*
1967	J. Maizel, U. Laemmli	Development of SDS polyacrylamide gel electrophoresis of proteins
1968	J. Kates, B. Mcauslan, A. Shatkin, J. Sipe	Discovery of RNA-dependent RNA polymerase in a virion (reovirus)
1968	U.S. Advanced Research Projects Agency	Development of the Internet
1968	W. And G. Henle	Association of Epstein-Barr virus with mononucleosis
1968	H. Doerr	Publication of virology review series, *Monographs in Virology*
1968	S. Gard, C. Hallauer, K. Meyer	Publication of virology review series, *Virology Monographs*

1968	P. Wildy, J. Melnick, N. Oker-Blom, V. Zhdanov	The First International Congress for Virology
1968	P. Vogt, H. Hanafusa, C. Moscovici, W. Okazaki, B. Burmester, others	Discoveries elaborating the molecular biology of avian retroviruses
1969	R. Huebner, G. Todaro	Development of the viral oncogene hypothesis
1969	S. Buckley, J. Casals	Discovery of Lassa virus
1969	C. Mebus, N. Underdahl, M. Rhodes, M. Twiehaus	Discovery of bovine rotavirus (the first rotavirus)
1970	D. Baltimore, A. Huang	Discovery of RNA-dependent RNA polymerase in an enveloped RNA virion (vesicular stomatitis virus)
1970	H. Temin, D. Baltimore	Discovery of the reverse transcriptase of retroviruses
1970	T. Kelly, H. Smith, D. Nathans, K. Danna	Discovery and characterization of first restriction endonucleases, cleaving DNA only at specific sites
1970s	S. Kalter, R. Heberling	Development of nonhuman primate virology
1970s	G. Elion, R. Whitley, L. Corey, others	Development of the antiviral chemotherapeutic, acyclovir, for treatment of herpesvirus infections
1971	P. Doherty, R. Zinkernagel	Discovery of how the cellular immune system recognizes virus-infected cells
1971	P. Perlmann, E. Engvall, A. Schuurs, B. Van Weemen	Development of enzyme immunoassays—EIAs and ELISAs
1972	R. Tomlinson	Development of e-mail
1972	A. Kapikian, colleagues	Discovery of Norwalk virus
1972–1973	P. Berg, H. Cohen, C. Boyer	Development of recombinant-DNA technology-genetic engineering
1973	R. Bishop, G. Davidson, I. Holmes, T. Flewett, others	Discovery of human rotaviruses
1973	A. Hellman, M. Oxman, R. Pollack	Asilomar Conference: *Biohazards in Biological Research*

TABLE 2.1 *(continued)*

Date	Discoverer(s) Inventor(s) Developer(s)	Discovery(ies) Invention(s) Technology(ies)
1973	S. Feinstone, A. Kapikian, R. Purcell	Discovery of hepatitis A virus
1973	D. Nathans	Completion of the restriction enzyme map of a viral genome (SV40 virus)
1974	G. Kohler, C. Milstein	Development of monoclonal antibodies
1974	F. Blattner, P. Leder, L. Enquist, K. Murray, T. Maniatis, others	Development of phage λ as a viral vector for recombinant DNA technology
1974–1982	I. Tischer, H. Gelderblom	Discovery of porcine circovirus (the first circovirus)
1975	P. Sharp, L. Chow, R. Roberts, T. Broker	Discovery of RNA splicing and split genes (adenovirus)
1975	Y. Cossart, A. Field, A. Cant, D. Widdows	Discovery of parvovirus B-19 and its association with aplastic crisis in hemolytic anemia
1975	C. Madeley, B. Cosgrove, T. Lee, J. Kurtz	Discovery of human astrovirus 1 (the first astrovirus)
1975	B. Blumberg, B. Larouze, W. London, B. Werner, J. Hesser, I. Millman, G. Saimot, M. Payet	Discovery of the relationship of hepatitis B virus with hepatocellular carcinoma
1975	B. Moss, A. Shatkin	Discovery that messenger RNA contains a specific nucleotide 5' cap for correct processing during translation (vaccinia, reovirus)
1976	T. Diener	Discovery of viroids (infectious naked RNA molecules)
1976	K. Johnson, P. Webb, J. Lange, F. Murphy, S. Pattyn, W. Jacob, G. Van Der Groen, P. Piot, E. Bowen, G. Platt, G. Lloyd, A. Baskerville, colleagues	Discovery of Ebola virus

1976	H. Lee, colleagues	Discovery of Hantaan virus—hemorrhagic fever with renal syndrome, Korean hemorrhagic fever
1976	J. Bishop, H. Varmus	Discovery of the cellular origin of retroviral oncogenes
1976	A. Evans	Special criteria for proof of viral disease causation: the Henle-Koch postulates revisited again
1976	C. Weisman, colleagues	Development of the first infectious recombinant clone of a virus (phage qβ in *E. coli*)
1976–1977	W. Fiers, F. Sanger colleagues	First complete sequencing of viral genomes (bacteriophage MS2 and φχ174)
1977	D. Henderson, F. Fenner, I. Arita, others	Global eradication of smallpox
1977	A. Maxam, W. Gilbert, F. Sanger, colleagues	Development of the technology for rapid sequencing of DNA
1978	L. Carmichael, M. Appel, M. Parrish, others	Discovery of canine parvovirus (CPV-2)
1978	D. Botstein	Discovery of restriction-fragment-length polymorphisms (RFLPs)
1978	A. Waterson, L. Wilkinson	Publication of the book, *An Introduction to the History of Virology*
1978	Genentech Inc.	The first biotech company on the NY stock exchange
1978–1985	S. Harrison, A. Olson, J. Hogle, M. Rossman, R. Rueckert	Determination of the atomic structure of a plant virus (tomato bushy stunt virus) and vertebrate viruses (poliovirus, rhinovirus)
1979	L. Enquist, M. Madden, P. Schiop-Stanley, G. Vande Woude	Development of the technology for cloning viral DNA fragments into phage λ vector (herpes simplex virus)
1980	R. Gallo, Y. Hinuma, J. Yoshida, B. Poiesz, I. Miyoshi, colleagues	Discovery of human T lymphotropic viruses 1 and 2

TABLE 2.1 *(continued)*

Date	Discoverer(s) Inventor(s) Developer(s)	Discovery(ies) Invention(s) Technology(ies)
1980	E. Williams, S. Young	Discovery that chronic wasting disease of deer and elk is a spongiform encephalopathy and caused by a prion
1981	Centers for Disease Control and Prevention *Morbidity and Mortality Weekly Report (MMWR)*	Publication of reports of *pneumocystis carinii* pneumonia in five previously healthy young men in Los Angeles, and an unusual number of cases of Kaposi sarcoma in gay men—AIDS
1981	V. Racaniello, D. Baltimore	Development of the first infectious recombinant clone of an animal virus (poliovirus)
1981	G. Binnig, H. Rohrer	Development of the scanning tunneling microscope
1981	D. Wiley, J. Skehel, I. Wilson, others	Discovery of the structure of the influenza virus hemagglutinin
1981	W. Burnette, R. Reiser, H. Towbin	Invention of western blotting—electrophoretic transfer of proteins from polyacrylamide gels to nitrocellulose sheets and detection with antibody
1981	W. Joklik, H. Ginsberg, others	Founding of the American Society for Virology
1982	S. Prusiner	Development of the concept of the prion and the etiologic role of prions in spongiform encephalopathies
1982	M. Oldstone, Y. Sinha, P. Lampert, colleagues	Development of the concept of virus-induced alterations in cellular homeostasis and luxury functions of infected cells
1982–1997	G. Woode, D. Reed, M. Weiss, F. Steck, M. Horzinek, M. Koopmans, R. Glass, R. Guerrant, colleagues	Discovery of bovine, equine, and human toroviruses

1983	F. Barré-Sinoussi, J. Chermann, L. Montagnier, R. Gallo, others	Discovery of human immunodeficiency virus 1 (HIV1)
1983	M. Balayan, colleagues	Discovery of hepatitis E virus (the only hepevirus)
1983	A. Murray, J. Szostack	Development of the yeast artificial chromosome—vector to clone large DNA fragments
1984	B. Mahy, R. Compans	Publication of the journal, *Virus Research*
1984	M. Hilleman, others, Merck Sharp & Dohme Inc.	Development of the first recombinant vaccine for humans (hepatitis B vaccine made in yeast)
1985	K. Mullis, colleagues, Cetus, Perkin-Elmer	Invention of the polymerase chain reaction (PCR)
1985	Biomérieux, Bio-Rad Genetic Systems, Abbott	Development of the first FDA approved HIV antibody tests (EIAs)
1985	N. Letvin, R. Desrosiers	Discovery of simian immunodeficiency virus
1985	F. Barin, F. Clavel, M. Essex, P. Kanki, F. Brun-Vézinet, others	Discovery of human immunodeficiency virus 2 (HIV2)
1985–1995	R. Rott, H. Ludwig, I. Lipkin, others	Discovery of Bornavirus as a human pathogen and possible cause of psychiatric disease
1986	R. Gallo	Discovery of human herpesvirus 6A
1986	S. Kit	Development of the first recombinant DNA vaccine for animals (pseudorabies virus, TK-deletion mutant)
1986	N. Pedersen, E. Ho, M. Brown, J. Yamamoto	Discovery of feline immunodeficiency virus
1987	M. Houghton, colleagues	Discovery of hepatitis delta virus (the only deltavirus)
1987	S. Broder, H. Mitsuya, M. Fischl, D. Richman, Burroughs Wellcome Co, others	Development of the first anti-HIV drug approved by the FDA (AZT-zidovudine)

TABLE 2.1 *(continued)*

Date	Discoverer(s) Inventor(s) Developer(s)	Discovery(ies) Invention(s) Technology(ies)
1987	L. Hood, Applied Biosystems	Development of commercial DNA sequencing technology
1987	M. Capecchi, M. Evans, O. Smithies	Development of knockout and other genetically manipulated mice
1988	C. Lopez, P. Pellett, K. Yamanishi, T. Kurata, colleagues	Discovery of human herpesvirus 6B and its association with exanthem subitum
1988	National Center For Biotechnology Information (NCBI)	Development of GenBank
1988	M. Eigen, C. Biebricher, J. Holland, E. Domingo, E. Koonin, A. Gibbs, L. Villarreal, D. De La Torre, R. Adino, S. Weaver, others	Development of modern concepts of virus evolution and quasispecies
1989	M. Houghton, H. Alter, D. Bradley, colleagues	Discovery of hepatitis C virus
1989	D. Gelfand, S. Stoffel, T. Brock	Discovery of taq polymerase
1989	S. Fodor, I. Herskowitz, M. Schena, R. Davies, P. Brown	Development of microarray technology
1990	U.S. Department of Energy	Launching of the human genome project
1990	N. Frenkel	Discovery of human herpesvirus 7
1991	G. Reyes, J. Kim	Development of SISPA (sequence-independent single primer amplification)
1991	R. Salas, N. De Manzione, R. Tesh, R. Rico-Hesse, R. Shope, colleagues	Discovery of Guanarito virus and its association with Venezuelan hemorrhagic fever
1991	C. Venter, H. Smith, colleagues (TIGR)	Invention of shotgun cloning methods

1993	S. Nichol, C. Peters, T. Ksiazek, colleagues	Discovery of sin nombre virus and its association with Hantavirus pulmonary syndrome
1993	S. Falkow	Molecular criteria for proof of viral disease causation: the Henle-Koch postulates revisited again
1994	Y. Chang, P. Moore	Discovery of human herpesvirus 8—Kaposi sarcoma herpesvirus
1994	M. Schnell, T. Mebatsion, K. Conzelmann	Development of reverse genetics for negative-strand RNA viruses, infectious virus derived from cloned cDNA (rabies virus)
1994	T. Lisieux, M. Coimbra, E. Nassar, F. Pinheiro, colleagues	Discovery of sabiá virus and its association with Brazilian hemorrhagic fever
1995	A. Philbey, K. Murray, P. Hooper, colleagues	Discovery of Hendra virus
1996	R. Will, J. Ironside, J. Collinge, colleagues	Discovery that bovine spongiform encephalopathy prion is the cause of variant Creutzfeldt-Jakob disease
1996	D. Fredricks, D. Relman	Development of sequence-based identification of microbial pathogens: the Henle-Koch postulates revisited again
1996	M. Hirsch, D. Ho, T. Merigan, S. Hammer, others	Development of HAART treatment for aids
1997	T. Nishizawa, H. Okamoto, colleagues	Discovery of torque teno virus (TTV) (anellovirus) and its association with acute hepatitis
1998	T. Folks, W. Heneine	Discovery of simian foamy virus infection in humans
1998	L. Page, S. Brin	Development of Google
1999	K. Chua, S. Lam, W. Bellini, T. Ksiazek, B. Eaton, colleagues	Discovery of Nipah virus
2001	B. Van Den Hoogen, A. Osterhaus, colleagues	Discovery of human metapneumovirus
2001	TIGR, others	Completion of draft version of the nucleotide sequence of the human genome

TABLE 2.1 *(continued)*

Date	Discoverer(s) Inventor(s) Developer(s)	Discovery(ies) Invention(s) Technology(ies)
2002–2006	I. Frazer, J. Zhou, S-J. Ghim, A. Jenson, R. Schlegel, R. Kirnbauer, D. Lowy, J. Schiller, R. Reichman, W. Bonnez, R. Rose, Sanofi Pasteur, Merck Sharp & Dohme, Glaxosmithkline	Development of papillomavirus vaccine (cervical cancer)
2003	C. Urbani, J. Peiris, S. Lai, L. Poon, G. Drosten, K. Stöhr, A. Osterhaus, T. Ksiazek, D. Erdman, C. Goldsmith, S. Zaki, J. Derisi, many others	Discovery of SARS coronavirus
2003	D. Raoult, J-M. Claverie	Discovery of mimivirus, from amoebae, the largest virus known
2005	P. Palese, T. Tumpey, A. Garcia-Sastre, J. Taubenberger	1918 influenza virus genome reconstructed and sequenced
2005	N. Wolfe, T. Folks, W. Heneine, D. Burke, W. Switzer	Discovery of human T lymphotropic viruses 3 and 4
2005	C. Rice, F. Chisari, T. Wakita	Manipulation of virus and cells for the first in vitro hepatitis C virus culture system
2006	T. Allander	Discovery of human bocavirus (parvovirus)
2008–2015	Who Global Polio Eradication Initiative	Planned global eradication of poliomyelitis

3

Introduction to the Principles of Immunology

A misunderstanding of the term "immune" has arisen because the general public usually interprets immunity to mean that no disease occurs. However, the medical scientist knows that a pathogen can infect its host but in such a mild form that no serious or life-threatening consequences follow. In fact, such an infection often has no visible sign at all. Therefore, immunity refers to a bodily system (immune response) that, instead of precluding infection, enables the infected host to respond to infection by resisting disease.

The proteins in viruses and bacteria that trigger an immune response are called antigens, and the result of a satisfactory immune response to these antigens is immunity—long-term protection from repeated disease caused by a specific type of virus or bacteria (1). Similarly, a vaccine primes the immune response by programming it to anticipate and resist future pathogens like those in that particular vaccine.

The immune system has evolved to deal with enormous numbers and varieties of every conceivable foreign antigen. A consequence of viruses' entry and replication in an organism—the host—is the manufacture of viral antigens that, in most cases, elicit an immune response by that host. The success of this system defines an organism's capacity for survival.

In addition, the immune system must discriminate between foreign antigens, such as viral proteins, that are nonself and those antigens that are self, one's own proteins (i.e., hormones such as insulin and cell proteins that make up muscle).

After an initial exposure to viral infection, the acute phase, a race is on between the virus, which is replicating rapidly, and the host's immune system, which functions first to limit the amount of virus made and second to clear the virus from the host. At stake is whether the virus can successfully replicate itself. To combat the virus, the host mobilizes and uses many weapons, that is, both the immunologically specific and nonspecific responses. The nonspecific factors are all early combatants against the virus and the cells it infects. Included in this group are natural killer lymphoid cells, phagocytic macrophages—large cells that ingest or eat viruses—and proteins in the blood called complement factors that are capable of interacting with viruses and also destroying cells. Most important is the innate immune system that provides the initial defense against pathogens and primes the subsequent adoptive immune response (see below). The major players in the innate immune response are toll-like receptors (TLRs) that recognize different microbial patterns and type 1 interferons (IFNs) made primarily by plasmacytoid dendritic cells (DCs) (1,2). These innate systems are mutually complementary and are involved in developing the ensuing adoptive immune response. For example, the engagement of a pathogen with a TLR can result in release of type 1 IFNs. Type 1 IFNs are the key molecules that augment and sustain the T cell response (defined below). They upregulate costimulatory molecules and major histocompatibility complex (MHC) molecules on DCs, a requirement for the optimal interaction of DCs with $CD4^+$ and $CD8^+$ T cells. Thus, in summary, after a virus infection or vaccination, so-called "professional" antigen-presenting cells, primarily DCs but also B cells and macrophages, present endogenously (from inside the cell) and exogenously (from outside the cell) processed antigens. Viruses' obligatory intracellular pathogens primarily present by the MHC class I pathways to T cells, an action termed "priming" that literally prepares an infected host to resist disease. The external or MHC class II pathway is primarily used for processing bacteria and toxins. When stimulated correctly, these antigen-presenting cells (primarily DC) display costimulatory molecules like B7.1 and B7.2 on their surfaces and manufacture substances (cytokines) that activate T cells to provide an immune response that eliminates invading viruses.

The effectiveness of the antiviral immune response correlates directly with the size and power of this adoptive immune response and the resulting memory that prevents further ill effects from that particular virus. The total strength of the immune response that follows infection or vaccination reflects the balance between those factors (cytokines) that enhance or drive the immune response and those host molecules that function to modulate or downgrade the immune response. Factors that downgrade or suppress immunity (molecules like IL-10, PD-1, CTLA4, T regulatory cells) represent a defensive mechanism by the host to prevent an excessive immune response that may lead to injury. Yet, several viruses have turned the tables; these viruses have actually found a way to induce the formation of suppressive molecules, thereby stifling the vigorous host immune response required to purge the infection. As a result, the host's ordinarily effective antiviral T cells no longer function adequately, become exhausted, and cannot terminate the virus infection. The viruses can then persist in the host in the form of a chronic infection. As discussed in the chapter on human immunodeficiency virus (HIV), these immunosuppressive molecules are found in patients with this and other persisting viral infections. One current strategy under exploration is the blockade or neutralization of such suppressive molecules in the expectation of restoring function to the exhausted T cells as a means of combating and removing the persisting viruses.

The major combatants against viruses are antibodies and T lymphocytes (defined further below). For smallpox, measles, yellow fever, poliomyelitis, hemorrhagic fever, and influenza viruses, the generation of antigen-specific immune responses by antibodies, CD4 T cells, and cytotoxic CD8 T lymphocytes (CTLs) purges the infecting virus and terminates the infection in those that survive. Thus, the host immune response to specific viruses is mounted by both antibodies and T cells.

A clearly defined winner in the race between a virus and its host is often decided in less than ten to fourteen days. If the immune response wins, the viruses are vanquished, and the host survives with enduring immunity to that virus. However, if the immune response is overcome, an acute viral infection ends in either death of the host or a chronic-persistent infection. During chronic-persistent infection, the time scale of disease is lengthened, and ongoing viral replication can continue despite an immune response that, by definition in this situation, has not terminated the infection or eliminated the virus. In contrast to the short duration of acute infection, this longer term scenario plays out during HIV infection, for example.

The course of HIV infection is as follows. Soon after HIV enters a host's cells and replicates there, a vigorous immune response generates CTLs, and this response correlates directly with a decrease in the host's viral load. An antibody response is also generated, although it appears for the most part after reduction of the viral load. Reduced but not eliminated are the key words because even the combined vigorous CTL and antibody responses fail to terminate HIV infection. Instead, anti-HIV CTLs as well as anti-HIV antibodies now coexist with the virus. Later in the course of HIV infection, the anti-HIV CTLs lose effectiveness; the viral load increases, and the patient approaches death. The loss of CTL activity late in HIV infection likely results from the increasing loss of CD4 helper/inducer cells, cells that are necessary to help maintain CTL activity over prolonged periods of time, and from newly generated virus variants that escape CTL recognition. In contrast, acute infection evokes a vigorous CTL and antibody response that removes all the viruses.

Vaccination is the medical strategy for stimulating the immune system to protect against a specific disease agent preceding real-life exposure. In fact, vaccination preconditions components of the immune response to have a ready and rapid start when the host is first exposed to virus infection (1). Provoking an immune response in this way before a natural viral infection occurs acts to "blueprint" immunologic memory so that cells involved in making the potential antiviral immune response are primed and held alert. When confronted with the full-strength infectious virus, these primed cells react quickly and with greater intensity than unprimed cells, thus enhancing the host's ability to successfully combat and control the infection.

Historically, three different routes have been taken in developing antiviral vaccines. The first employs "live viruses." These are usually prepared by passing viruses (injection into and then withdrawal) through a laboratory animal and tissue culture or in tissue culture alone, which decreases the disease-causing ability of virus. This process, called attenuation, yields a form of the virus with just enough potency to cause an immune response but not enough to cause disease. The attenuated, live virus is then tested initially in animal models and later in human volunteers to assess its safety and immunizing capacity. This was the method followed to formulate the successful smallpox, measles, yellow fever, and Sabin poliomyelitis vaccines. By the second route, the virulent virus is inactivated, essentially killed, by use of a chemical such as formalin. The killed virus is then tested for its capacity to cause an immune response as above. The Salk poliomyelitis virus vaccine is a successful example of this approach. The third option is preparation of a viral subunit, recombinant, or DNA vaccine. The successful hepatitis B virus vaccine is an example of a recombinant vaccine; other subunit and DNA vaccines are currently under experimental analysis but have not had sufficient testing in clinical trials for general use.

Cells process live viruses differently from killed viruses. Processing of viral antigens by cells follows two distinct pathways called the MHC class I and MHC class II (1). For the class I pathway, antigens inside cells from living, replicating viruses (virulent or attenuated) are broken into smaller components called peptides. According to several physical–chemical parameters, some of these antigenic peptides bind to grooves within host proteins (called MHC class I proteins), then travel to and wait on cells' surfaces to be recognized by CTLs that react with a CD8 receptor (CD8$^+$). The class II pathway primarily handles antigens that are initially outside the cell. These antigens (usually killed viruses or toxins) enter the cell (endocytosis) via phagocytosis, and the protein is broken down into peptides inside vesicles where it then binds to the host's proteins (called MHC class II proteins). The complex is then presented on the surface of a cell to await recognition by CD4$^+$ T cells (as described in Chapter 2). To summarize, the key is the location where the antigen finally stops. Viral antigens synthesized inside cells join to MHC class I proteins, whereas those captured outside cells attach to MHC class II proteins. Although this division is not absolute due to a process called cross-priming, it is an accurate generalization. Vaccines made from killed viruses do not necessarily induce a good CD8$^+$ T cell (defined below) response, and the immunity so-induced is not as long lasting as that from attenuated live viruses.

What are these CD8$^+$ and CD4$^+$ T cells? The T stands for thymus-derived and CD8$^+$ or CD4$^+$ indicates specific molecules on the cells' surfaces. The thymus is a two-lobed gland of the lymphoid system located over the heart and under the breastbone. Lymphocytes formed in the bone marrow (hemopoietic stem cells) travel to and enter the thymus where they are educated (mature) and are then selected to become either CD8$^+$ or CD4$^+$ T cells. (The terms "T lymphocytes" and "T cells" are used interchangeably.) CD8$^+$ T cells function as surveillance and killer cells, which accounts for their name "cytotoxic T lymphocytes"

(CTLs). They travel along the highways of blood vessels and wander among tissues throughout the body seeking cells that are foreign (not like self) because they express viral proteins or are transformed by cancers. $CD8^+$ CTLs then recognize, attack, and kill such cells. $CD8^+$ T cells also release cytokines like interferon (INF)-gamma (γ) and tumor necrosis factor (TNF)-alpha (α) that have antiviral effects without killing the virus-infected cell (1). $CD4^+$ T cells usually serve a different role. They release soluble materials (proteins) that help or induce bone marrow–derived (non-thymic-educated) B lymphocytes to differentiate and make antibodies. $CD4^+$ T lymphocytes also assist $CD8^+$ T lymphocytes and macrophages, prompting their designation as helper/inducer T cells (1, 3–8). Additionally, $CD4^+$ T cells release soluble factors (cytokines) that also participate in clearing a virus infection. In some instances $CD4^+$ T cells may also have killing activity against virally infected cells.

T lymphocytes use their cell surface receptors to interact with protein fragments or peptides of the viral antigen attached to MHC molecules on the surfaces of infected cells. These MHC proteins actually carry the viral peptides to cells' surfaces. Thus, T lymphocytes seek foreign antigens (in this case, viral antigens—peptides derived from the viral protein) on the surfaces of infected cells being parasitized by the virus. T cells that recognize an infected cell as "foreign" (contains virus) become activated and either directly kill the infected cell and/or release soluble factors (lymphokines, cytokines) that alert and arm other cells of the host to join the battle. In addition, some of these cytokines can directly interfere with viral replication. By such means, the spread of viruses is inhibited, and the nidus of infection removed.

Antibody and CTL responses rely on lymphocytes, which originate from hemopoietic stem cells during the blood-forming process (1,9). Antibodies and CTLs represent the two arms of antigen-specific immune responses, and both play important roles in combating infection. In fact, overall immunity has a built-in plasticity such that the relative contribution of each arm of the immune response varies according to the identity of an infecting virus. Antibodies primarily react with viruses in the body fluids and are, therefore, most effective in limiting the spread of virus through the blood or in cerebrospinal fluids that bathe the brain and spinal cord. By this means, antibodies decrease a host's content of virus and diminish infectivity, thereby lowering the numbers of infected cells. However, the eradication of virus-infected cells and their removal is the primary job of CTLs. By removing infected cells, CTLs eliminate the factories that manufacture viral progeny. As the number of virus particles released is reduced, the work of antibodies becomes easier.

Before continuing the story of T lymphocytes (below), I'll diverge here to describe antibodies, which are large protein molecules. Antibodies are made by B lymphocytes, named for their source, the bone marrow (1,2). B cells are small resting lymphocytes with nuclei that virtually fill these cells; little cytoplasm is present. When a virus or viral protein is encountered by a specific lymphocyte with a preconceived receptor for the antibody that matches the virus's protein structure, the lymphocyte becomes stimulated to divide and the amount of cytoplasm composing the cell's volume increases. The expanded cytoplasm factory then manufactures antibodies designed to interact with the virus that stimulated their production and exports these antibody molecules into the immediate milieu. One such activated B lymphocyte can pump out 100 million antiviral antibody molecules per hour.

Antibodies latch onto and neutralize viruses by one of several mechanisms: (1) Antibodies can coat or block the outer spike protein of the virus that attaches to receptors on a cell and initiates viral entry into the cell. By this means antibodies can prevent infection. (2) Antibodies can aggregate or clump viruses so that the net number of infectious particles is reduced. (3) With the assistance of complement, a group of proteins in the blood, antibodies can lyse (disintegrate) viruses (10), and (4) antibodies can react with virus antigens on the outer membrane of the infected cells to limit the manufacturing or transcription of virus molecules inside the cells thereby restricting the amount of virus made (11). Each antibody molecule generated acts on a specific antigen or target molecule of the virus. The host has the capacity to synthesize billions of different antibodies via genes that dictate their manufacture.

Now, returning to T cells, the CD4$^+$ T lymphocytes can in some specialized instances also function as cytotoxic cells. Conversely, the CD8$^+$ cells can release soluble molecules so they also have a helper/inducer activity, although their primary function is to recognize and destroy virus-infected cells. In tissue culture, one CD8$^+$ CTL can kill up to ten or more virally infected cells by engaging an infected cell, lysing it, moving to the next infected cell, and so on. Further, in living animals, one CD8$^+$ CTL has been observed to bind and lyse up to three target cells at one time (12). An important matter here is that these CTLs can recognize viral peptides on infected cells before virus particles are assembled and thus effectively and efficiently kill these cells before viral progeny form.

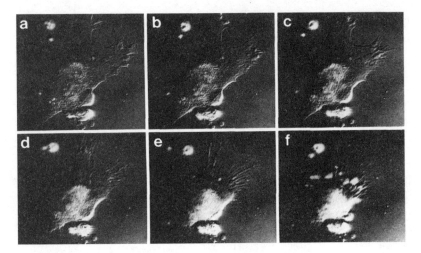

FIGURE 3.1 *Steps in the killing of a virus-infected cell by cytotoxic T lymphocytes (CTLs) (a–f). This sequence of images shows a virus-specific CTL clone killing a fibroblast target cell presenting the LCMV NP peptide. Images were taken at 4-sec intervals and show the final period of CTL-target interaction when the target cell undergoes strong morphological changes. Contraction of the target cell is accompanied by retraction of cell fibers, thickening of the cytoplasm in the center of the cell, and finally by massive blebbing. Similar scenario for LCMV infected target cells. Photomicrographs by Klaus Hahn and Michael B. A. Oldstone.*

When a host is initially exposed to an infecting virus or to a vaccine containing viral antigens, antibodies specific for that virus as well as CTLs are generated. The CTL response is initiated on the first day of infection, expands over 10^5 to 10^6 times by doubling roughly every twelve hours with peak expansion seven to eight days after exposure. Thereafter, the quantity of these cells contracts and is maintained at 1 to 2 percent of the total generated; these become immune memory cells (1,3–6). Antibody responses peak after the CTL response, and unattached or free antibodies are often weakly detectable during the acute phase of infection. The number of antibodies then rises over a period of two to four weeks after infection, and they linger for years. B cells as well as T cells can be memory cells, that is, cells that were previously in contact with a particular virus. Such CD8[+] CTL and B memory cells (or antibodies) frequently last for the host's entire lifetime and function to protect the host from reinfection with the same virus (1,13–15). CD4[+] memory T cells decline over time (16,17). This is the likely scenario played out in those who survive infection from smallpox, measles, yellow fever, poliomyelitis, or hemorrhagic fever viruses.

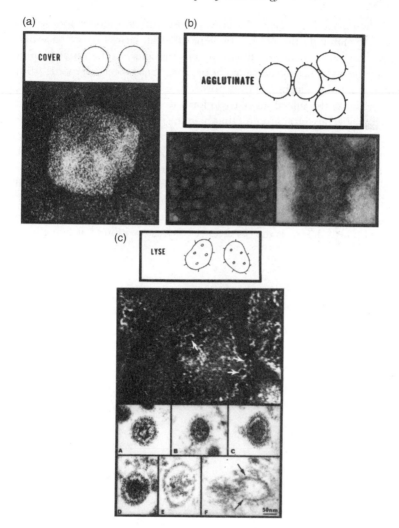

FIGURE 3.2 *Antibodies can, with or without the complement proteins in the blood, blanket virus particles (A, antibody acts on coronavirus to cover viral particles); (B, antibody acts on polyomavirus with the participation of antibody to directly clump the virus); (C, top, retrovirus; C, bottom, arenavirus). Lysis of the retrovirus produces holes (arrows), but lysis of the arenavirus begins a progression of events that climaxes in the release of virus nucleic acids to the outside environment away from the protective virus coat. Photomicrographs from the laboratory of Michael B. A. Oldstone.*

When a viral infection like HIV persists, the immune response has failed to eliminate the virus. The genes that all viruses carry have one of two primary functions. One group of genes ensures the replication of viral progeny. These genes encode proteins that protect the virus from harsh conditions during its transport from one host to the next; that is, they stabilize the infectious particle for travel through the environment. Also encoded are viral proteins that bind the virus to its receptors on cells, assist in internalization of the virus into cells, and provide the appropriate signaling for replication, assembly, and exit of the viral progeny from the parasitized cell. The second group of genes has among its main purposes the subjugation and/or modification of a host's immune system. By such strategies the virus can manipulate the normal function of the immune system to escape surveillance and destruction for itself and the cells it infects. The outcome is the persistence of viruses within their living host.

Part Two
Success Stories

4

Smallpox

THE GEOPOLITICAL IMPACT OF SMALLPOX

Smallpox, which killed nearly 300 million people in the twentieth century alone—three times more than all the wars in that century—has been eradicated (1,2). The story of this most universally feared disease, its elimination, and whether it could return again to cause havoc is the topic of this chapter. Two of the more interesting commentaries about this major accomplishment of mankind in eradicating smallpox from our planet is, first, that considerable opposition stood in the way of its conquest 200 years ago, as well as in the recent past, and second, that significant controversy remains about the possible return of smallpox and what to do about it.

September 11, 2001, changed America and the world. The plot to deliberately crash commercial airplanes into the twin towers of Manhattan's World Trade Center announced to every country on the globe its vulnerability to fanatics who value death over life and have no regard for innocent civilians. This scenario of suicide bombings had played out earlier in the Middle East, Africa, Asia, and Europe.

With the understanding that suicide attacks can kill large populations, the fear of deliberate biological attacks surfaced. Of the several devastating biological agents available, smallpox virus is at or near the top of the list. The virus had been field tested and shown effective as early as the mid- to late 1700s in battles between the French and

English, termed in North America the French and Indian War, then during the American Revolution and later during World War II (1–7). In World War II, smallpox attack was studied and quantified at the notorious Japanese experimental biowarfare center in Ping Fan at Unit 731 against Manchurian and Chinese civilians and captured soldiers (8). There, aerosol delivery systems were used to infect their human captives. The seeds of those macabre investigations germinated in the hands of victorious Russian and American forces, as each developed their own biological warfare programs. Research into the offensive use of biological weapons as agents of war was terminated unilaterally by the United States during the Nixon administration in the 1960s. Nevertheless, tests using indicator but relatively harmless bacteria continued to gauge dispersals of microorganisms over selected cities and in the New York City subway system. Thus, the technology was in place for dispersal but not for the intent to follow through. Yet, the Russian biowarfare program continued secretly during the Cold War and into the late 1980s based in part on the potential usefulness of biological reagents for terrorism or war and Soviet suspicions that the United States was secretly continuing their biological warfare programs. However, with the September 11 attacks the sub-rosa testing programs changed into a very real possibility that smallpox could become a weapon in the hands of terrorist groups or rogue nations.

When a biological agent becomes a candidate for weaponry, among the first considerations is its virulence. Virulence refers to the ability of an organism, in this case the smallpox virus, to cause disease. Virulence factors are encoded within the genes of a virus and can be manipulated by present day technology to increase in potency beyond anything nature has yet provided. Before September 11, smallpox virus was known to come in two flavors: smallpox major that was lethal to about one in three people so infected, and smallpox minor, a naturally occurring variant that killed as few as one of one hundred people infected. Smallpox is one of the largest viruses known, and the vast majority of its genes are similar between these major and minor forms. Thus, just a small number of genes that differ determines whether the number of deaths it causes is high rather than low. There is no doubt that smallpox virus major in its natural form or one altered to increase virulence would be the bioterror weapon of choice.

Susceptibility refers to the predisposal of the host, in this case humans, to become infected. The smallpox virus in nature infects only humans. Before vaccination became accepted, two of every three people infected with smallpox lived. Yet, because the human genome consists of approximately 30,000 genes, we have only fragmentary knowledge of which genes or factors decide who would survive or who would die.

The first vaccine ever developed was formulated to protect humans from smallpox infection. The long fight to implement vaccinations, led by the World Health Organization (WHO), eventually overcame objections from many sources, with the result that this virus no longer afflicted mankind, the only vaccine ever to accomplish this feat. Ultimately, because smallpox was eradicated from the world, the vaccination program ended, yielding enormous savings in governmental budgets for public health and medical services. Also avoided were the few but ever-present adverse effects that accompanied vaccination. With the exceptions of some government officials and military personnel, no smallpox vaccinations have been given worldwide since 1980, and in some countries like the USA, since the 1960s. Consequently, most of the world's current population has not been vaccinated and is, therefore, susceptible to smallpox if the virus were to reappear.

To prevent viruses from circulating, a population at risk needs protection, that is, immunity. This so-called herd immunity is achieved via vaccination. Viruses differ in the immunity coverage required to prevent their spread. One of the most contagious is measles virus (discussed later in Chapter 6), which likely requires a herd immunity of over 90 to 95 percent. Smallpox, although also contagious, is less so than measles, and is estimated to require an immunity level of about 80 percent to prevent its spread. The herd immunity in the United States and in the world, that is, the percentage of persons immune to smallpox, is well below that level.

Then how would or could enemies spread smallpox? A likely scenario is inoculation of smallpox into multiple suicide volunteers outside the USA, Europe, etc., who would then travel by airplane to the target areas while incubating the virus yet appearing to be healthy. Perhaps such "death volunteers" would arrive in many large cities before their disease activates into clinically infectious smallpox. Another scenario would be aerosol spread of the virus, perhaps as delivery into the air over metropolitan areas or tourist sites like Las Vegas, New York, London, or Paris, which are visited by more than 35 million travelers per year.

Once exposed, these visitors return to their homes throughout the world and carry the infectious agent within.

The first part of this chapter records selected events throughout the course of history in which smallpox has played a decisive role. Instances of populations and individuals exposed to smallpox before the development of the vaccine are compared to those after vaccination became widespread. That history is presented as context for the chapter's second part, which discusses whether or not to revaccinate today: the issues, risks, and benefits involved. That perspective comes through the author's eyes, a medically and scientifically trained research physician working at the interface of virology and immunology for over four decades. His work's focus is how viruses cause disease, that is, who wins the battle between virulence—potential death-dealing infection—and host resistance (immunity) or susceptibility to that infection and the inherent disease.

The story of smallpox is interwoven with the history of human migrations and wars, dramatically favoring one population or army over another. Smallpox actually changed the course of history by killing generals and kings or decimating their enemies.

The smallpox virus has no animal reservoir; its infection is limited to humans (3). Subclinical, or medically undetectable, infections are rare, if they occur at all. The typical course of smallpox is an acute disease that produces obvious and distinct skin lesions and, after recovery, leaves its well-defined fingerprints as clearly visible, distinctive pock marks, usually numerous, on the faces of survivors. After an incubation period of ten to fourteen days during which the infected subject is well and mobile, fever, weakness, and headache suddenly begin, followed in two to three days by the distinctive rash. When the rash appears, the patient can infect others, as lesions on the mucosal membranes allow viruses to spread through the air. Skin-to-skin contact is less important as a route of spreading the infection. Therefore, people in small, isolated communities can avoid contact with the smallpox virus, but once it is introduced, the effects are devastatingly pervasive.

How smallpox evolved as an infectious agent and when it first infected man are unclear (1,3–7). The virus probably made its appearance as the first agricultural settlements were being established in 10,000 B.C. along the great river basins. The earliest hint of smallpox infection is the extensive lesions found on three Egyptian mummies, the most renowned being Ramses V. We know that Ramses died of an acute illness in 1157 B.C.,

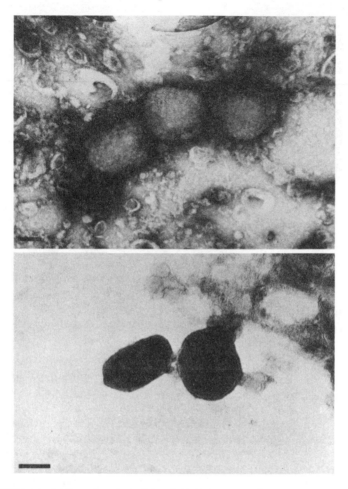

FIGURE 4.1 *Smallpox virus obtained from fluid of a human smallpox vesicle. Bar, 100 μm. Photomicrograph from E. L. Palmer and M. L. Martin,* An Atlas of Mammalian Viruses *(1982), courtesy of CRC Press, Inc., Boca Raton, FL.*

his fortieth year of life. When his mummified remains were discovered in 1898, his face and neck displayed a striking rash of pustules strongly resembling smallpox. Other ancient plagues considered to result from smallpox (1,3–7,9) were recorded in 1346 B.C. by the Hittites, in 595 B.C. at Syracuse, in 490 B.C. at Athens, in A.D. 48 throughout China, in

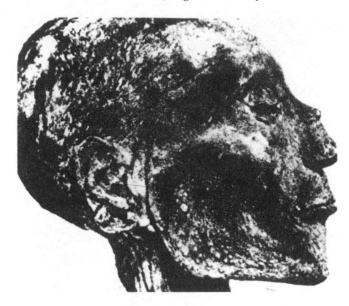

FIGURE 4.2 *Mummy of Ramses V, who died in his early thirties probably from smallpox in 1158* B.C. *Smallpox lesions are visible on his lower face and neck.*

A.D. 583 on the Korean Peninsula, and in A.D. 585 within Japan. Ho Kung, a Chinese medical writer (A.D. 281–361) wrote this:

> Recently there have been persons suffering from epidemic sores which attack the head, face, and trunk. In a short time, these sores spread all over the body. They have the appearance of hard boils containing white matter. While some of the pustules are drying up, a fresh crop appears. If not treated early the patients usually die. Those who recover are disfigured by purplish scars (on the face) which do not fade until after a year.

The lack of any written description of the rash and the inability of physicians of antiquity to distinguish the rash of smallpox from other skin rashes like measles, however, makes these diagnoses suggestive rather than definitive.

In A.D. 570, an army from Abyssinia (now Ethiopia) attacked the Arabic capital of Mecca for the purpose of destroying the Kaaba and subjugating the native population. The Kaaba was a shrine sacred to the Arabs, who at this time were not yet Moslems. According to the

Koran, God sent flocks of birds that showered the attacking armies with stones, producing sores and pustules that spread like a pestilence. The Abyssinian troops soon became decimated and Abraha, their leader, died from the disease. This war was recorded in the Koran:

> *In the name of Allah, the Beneficent, the Merciful,*
> *Hast thou not seen how the Lord dealt with the possessors of the elephant.*
> *[Ahraha arrived mounted on a white elephant.]*
> *Did He not cause their wars to end in confusion?*
> *And send against them birds in flocks?*
> *Casting at them decreed stones—*
> *So He rendered them like straw eaten up?*

Coincidentally, the year A.D. 570 was also the birth year of Mohammed, the prophet of Islam. By 622, Ad Ahrun, a Christian priest living in Alexandria, described the pox lesion, and in 910 the Arab physician Al-Razi descriptively separated the skin rash of smallpox from that caused by measles in his patients (10).

The great Islamic expansion across North Africa and into the Iberian Peninsula in the sixth through eighth centuries spread smallpox across Africa and into Europe. This migration was defined by the Saracens' (now known as Moors) capture of Tripoli in 647, the invasion of Spain in 710, and crossing of the Pyrenees to invade France in 731.

By 1000, smallpox epidemics had been recorded in populated areas from Japan to Spain and throughout African countries on the southern rim of the Mediterranean Sea. The eleventh to thirteenth centuries abounded with the movement of people to and from Asia Minor during the Crusades (1096–1291) and of African caravans crossing the Sahara to West Africa and the port cities of East Africa, carrying smallpox as well as goods.

By the sixteenth century, multiple smallpox outbreaks in European countries were reflected by statistics then being collected in several large cities including London, Geneva, and Stockholm. Because the sixteenth century was a time of exploration, often on ocean-going ships, smallpox was spread across oceans by mariners as well as over land routes by armies and caravans (3). These European explorers, and the colonists who soon followed to the newly discovered continents of America, Australia, and South Africa, brought smallpox as part of their baggage. Indeed, the inadvertent arrival of smallpox played a crucial role in the

Spanish conquest of Mexico and Peru, the Portuguese colonization of Brazil, the settlement of North America by the English and French, as well as the settlements of Australia.

In the Americas, the decimation of native Indian populations made both conquest and colonization easier (11). The native population, initially considered by the conquistadors and church as not having souls, therefore not human but similar to lower animals, was worked in mines and plantations as beasts of burden. Such inhuman working conditions, coupled with diseases brought from Europe, reduced the labor pool available. With so much of the native Indian labor force lost, the impetus grew to bring slaves from West African ports as replacements. This was especially so in Hispaniola (now the Dominican Republic) and Cuba, greatly stimulating the establishment of slave trade to the New World. There, the epidemic of smallpox began with an outbreak in Hispaniola, and by 1518 it had killed much of the native population. By 1519, the plague had spread to Cuba. Within the next year, smallpox occupied the Yucatan and other parts of Mexico (11).

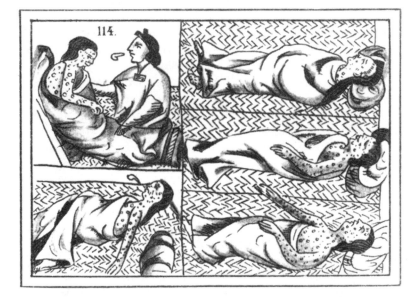

FIGURE 4.3 *Smallpox victims in this sixteenth-century Aztec drawing from the Códue Florentino.*

Hernando Cortés, initially with fewer than 500 conquistadors and followers, set out to explore and claim the territory of the Yucatan and other parts of Mexico for the King of Spain. At that time, in the early 1500s, the Aztecs ruled over Mexico, forcing many tribes into submission and obtaining tribute from them. With an elaborate system of messengers and roads, their emperor, Montezuma, was kept up to date on the landings and movements of Cortés from the isle of Cozumel in the Yucatan to the east and north until he reached what is now Veracruz. Cortés shrewdly convinced a number of native tribes to become his allies by promising to remove the yoke of Aztec domination. He was favored in this endeavor by the legend of Quetzalcoatl, a god predicted to arrive from the east on the wind and destroy the Aztec empire. Cortés must have seemed like the living manifestation of this legend, arriving from the east in boats with sails. Cortés and his men, because their landing was on Good Friday, were dressed in black, one of Quetzalcoatl's fabled colors. The Spaniards were themselves of a different (lighter) complexion than the natives, and wore beards, so might even resemble the god. Finally, the Spaniards rode horses and brought attack dogs as well as cannons and rifles, materials of war never seen before by natives. With the abundance of such unfavorable signs, Montezuma decided to appease Cortés and his followers when they reached Tenochtitlan (now Mexico City), capital of the Aztec empire. Yet in reality, the Spanish were greatly outnumbered. The Aztecs later united under Montezuma's brother Cuitlahuac, his cousin Cuauhtémoc, and other nobles to fight the Spaniards who suffered heavy casualties, forcing their retreat to a coastal settlement. The Spaniards had lost nearly one-third of their men, and their defeat on the bridges of Tenochtitlan was the biggest loss suffered until then by Europeans. If the Aztecs had continued their pursuit, the Europeans would have been expelled from Mexico. But, instead, the Aztecs stopped. Why did they not follow up their initial victory and annihilate the remaining Spaniards?

The answer, by a devious route, lies in the appearance of smallpox. Diego Velázquez, the governor of Cuba and rival of Cortés, had initially but hesitantly sent Cortés on his mission to Mexico. Not only had Velázquez been suspicious of Cortés's ambition, but he also wanted the power and the riches of the new land for himself, of course after providing the appropriate one-fifth taxation to the King of Spain. To achieve his goal, Velázquez had sent a second expedition commanded by Panfilo de Narváez, a conquistador more loyal to Velázquez than to Cortés, and including an "old crowd" of Caribbean conquistadors. Presumably, they were to aid and strengthen Cortés, but in reality their purpose was to take control from him. Unknown to the Narváez expedition, a slave among the crew carried smallpox. From this expedition, the Spaniards spread smallpox throughout the Yucatan, where they stopped before joining Cortés at Veracruz. Hunyg, the Indian king of the Yucatan, and his eldest son died, as did other native royalty. When Narváez's conquistadors arrived at Veracruz, Cortés won them over, which strengthened his army to slightly under 900 men. It was this small force that occupied Tenochtitlan, the capital of the Aztecs, and imprisoned Montezuma.

On Montezuma's death, his successor as Emperor of Mexico gathered the Aztec forces and led a night attack to drive the conquistadors out of the city. But on that night, smallpox also reached Tenochtitlan. One after another, the Emperor of Mexico, many of his family and subjects, and the Aztec troops died of smallpox. As area after area succumbed to infection, many streets filled with people dead or dying from smallpox, left there without the manpower or method of removing bodies. In some places half the population died. Kings and noblemen died as swiftly as farmers and serfs (11):

> Great was the stench of the dead. After our fathers and grandfathers succumbed, half the people fled to the fields. The dogs and vultures devoured the bodies. The mortality was terrible. Your grandfathers died and with them the sons of kings and their brothers and kings men. So it was that we became orphans, oh my sons. So we became when we were young. All of us were thus. We were born to die.

The disease spread from family to family and from town to town, and famine followed, because too few people were alive to farm the land.

The havoc wrought by smallpox also brought a morbid state of mind to the Aztecs. They thought the disease supernatural because it preferentially killed them but spared the conquistadors. The Aztecs could not have known that most of the Spaniards, having survived to adulthood despite epidemics at home, were immune to smallpox. However, for the Aztecs this exposure was a first-time event. The only interpretation obvious to them was that they were being punished by angry gods. It seemed that the Spanish god was supreme over the Aztec gods, just as the Spanish conquerors came to dominate and obliterate their Aztec foes. Three million Indians, an estimated one-third of the total population in Mexico, were killed at this time by smallpox. The aftermath is not surprising. As the natives docilely accepted commands from the priests and the Spanish authorities, mass conversions to Christianity and to a Spain-like country followed.

This story is by no means the only example of smallpox spreading throughout an isolated, indigenous population with horrendous consequences. By the seventeenth and eighteenth centuries, smallpox was the most devastating disease in the world, in Europe alone killing an estimated 400,000 people each year. One-third of all cases of blindness resulted from smallpox. In 1853, some 80 percent of the native population of Oahu, Hawaii, died when first exposed to smallpox. Even as late as 1903, the South American Cayapo tribe was decimated by smallpox. A single missionary priest, inadvertently carrying the virus, arrived to work among the 6,000 to 8,000 Indians. After fifteen years only 500 natives survived.

Rich and poor alike were victims. In Europe, the use of makeup began among the wealthy who were infected but survived smallpox then attempted to hide their pitted faces. Even the European monarchs were not sequestered from the disease. During this time, Queen Mary of England died of smallpox in 1694 at the age of thirty-two. The ruling monarchs Joseph I of Germany, Peter II of Russia, Louis XV of France, and William II of Orange met the same fate.

Puritan settlers of the fledgling New England colonies in North America faced an unkind land and high death rate. However, they were mentally prepared for their travails owing to their belief that having voluntarily withdrawn from England, they were serving God's will as a chosen people. When, in 1634, John Winthrop, the Massachusetts Bay Company Governor, heard of an epidemic among local Indian tribes, he wrote in his diary, "They are all dead of the smallpox so the Lord clearath our title to what we possess" (12,13). In addition to this belief in divine intervention, subjugation of the native American Indians was reinforced by purposeful infection with smallpox under the orders of Sir Geoffrey Amherst, the British Commander-in-Chief in North America (12,14,15). By Amherst's direction, hostile Indian tribes were provided with blankets contaminated with smallpox: "Could it not be contrived to send the smallpox among those disaffected tribes of Indians? We must, on this occasion, use every stratagem in our power to reduce them" (14). Amherst considers the Indians as savages beneath regard by civilized men.

In response to this request by Amherst, Colonel Henry Bouquet, the ranking British officer for the Pennsylvania frontier replied: "I will try to inoculate the Indians with some blankets that may fall in their hands and take care not to get the disease myself" (15). Captain Ecuyer recorded in his journal that he had given two blankets and a handkerchief from the garrison smallpox hospital to hostile chiefs (Indian) with the hope "it will have the desired effects." Aided by the smallpox epidemic, Bouquet destroyed an Indian army at Bushy Run near Fort Pitt and rolled back Indian advances, after many of them had perished from disease.

British troops were variolated (inoculated with smallpox), but in the early years of the war the rebelling American colonists were not. In 1776, Benedict Arnold led an army of American colonial troops to attack Quebec with the hope of freeing that Canadian city from British rule and adding it to the territory of the thirteen colonies (5,16,17). Of the 10,000 American troops in the attack, 5,500 developed smallpox. One of Arnold's officers wrote, "Those regiments, which had not the smallpox, expected every day to come down with it."

There were not enough tents to shelter even the desperately sick men. The moans of the sick and dying could be heard everywhere. Pits were opened as common graves and filled day after day with corpses, as the men died like flies. Governor Jonathan Trumble of Connecticut, who visited the retreating American troops ill with smallpox, wrote, "I did not look into a tent or hut in which I did not find a dead or dying man."

In the same war, the fear of smallpox limited and delayed George Washington's attack on Boston to free it from British control. Washington was concerned about the British use of smallpox as a weapon in the war (1,18):

> The information I received that the enemy intended spreading smallpox among us I could not suppose them capable of. I now must give some credit to it as it made its appearance on several of those who last came out of Boston. Every necessary precaution has been taken to prevent its being communicated to the Army, and the General Court will take care that it does not spread throughout the country.

As a consequence of smallpox outbreaks among American colonial troops, in 1777 Washington ordered the entire Continental Army variolated.

Andrew Jackson, a seminal figure in American history and the first "common man" to become President was a teenager in the Revolutionary War serving as an irregular and messenger. Taken prisoner by the British, along with his older brother Robert, he was sent to a prison in Camden, South Carolina. Smallpox ravaged the prison camp leading to the death of Robert, then the illness and recovery of Jackson with permanent smallpox scars.

George Washington's own pockmarked face attested that he also knew smallpox first hand, having survived an attack in Barbados. In the Fall of 1751, nineteen-year-old George Washington set sail from Virginia to the island of Barbados with his older brother Lawrence. Lawrence had a persistent cough and congested lungs, the signs and symptoms of tuberculosis that killed him within a year. Travel abroad was a favored treatment for tuberculosis. Because physicians believed that the disease could be alleviated by salt air, mountain breezes, or fair weather conditions, Washington hoped that this trip to Barbados would serve as a healing tonic to Lawrence.

Smallpox was almost uncontrolled in the Caribbean Islands as infected Africans imported to become slaves continued to be a dangerous source of the disease. Yet, the populations of most islands were tiny enough that epidemics frequently died out until another ship arrived to reintroduce smallpox. Unfortunately, at the time of Washington's visit in the mid-1700s, an epidemic of smallpox had resurfaced.

After a rough voyage, George and Lawrence Washington disembarked at Bridgetown and dined at the home of Gedney Clarke, a prominent merchant, planter, and slave trader. Washington noted in his diary, ". . . we (Lawrence and I) went, myself with some reluctance, as the smallpox was in his family" (18). Washington's misgivings were justified for, shortly afterwards, he was infected with smallpox. He was so severely ill that he could not write in his diary for nearly a month. Later he did write about the episode, saying that fourteen days after dining in the Clarke home, he came down with symptoms and not until the end of December, almost two months later, was it clear that he had survived the infection. His face bore the telltale pockmarks, which remained a recognizable characteristic for the rest of his life. Even then, anyone having a pockmarked face from a previous attack of smallpox was considered immune (resistant) against a second attack. But those not previously exposed to smallpox remained at great risk of death.

In 1775 at Philadelphia, the Continental Congress convened to discuss the options of separation from Britain or reconciliation. After much debate, the majority but not unanimous decision was to devise a "Declaration of Independence." Smallpox, an uninvited visitor, also came to these proceedings. The disease killed one of New England's most prominent delegates to the Congress, Samuel Ward of Rhode Island. As smallpox penetrated throughout the colonies, hundreds then thousands of people traveled from the countryside to be variolated (inoculated with living smallpox viruses).

John Adams, a prominent voice at the Congress, later to succeed Washington as the country's president, knew from first-hand experience of variolation. After he recommended the procedure to his wife, Abigail, she wrote him from Boston (19,20):

"Such a spirit of inoculation had never been known. The town and every house in it are as filled as can hold." Abigail Adams and her children were part of a family group numbering seventeen that included Abigail's sister Elizabeth, Louisa, a three-year-old daughter of her brother William Smith, three servants, two cousins, and the former law clerk of Adams who was currently a tutor of the Adams' children; all gathered to be variolated. Abigail Adams continued:

"We have our bedding, etc., to bring. A cow we have driven down from Braintree (Adams' farm) and some hay. I have put into the stable wood, etc., and we have really commenced housekeeping here . . . our little one (three-year-old Thomas) stood the operation manfully. I wish it was so you could have been with us."

"The little folks are very sick then and puke every morning, but after that they are comfortable."

Although Abigail Adams was well enough to turn out on July 18, 1776, for Boston's celebration for the Declaration of Independence, the children's difficulties from variolation continued. They stayed in her uncle's house for nearly two months. "Nabby (Adams' daughter) has enough of the smallpox for all the family beside." "She is pretty well covered, not a spot of what is so sore that she can neither walk, sit, stand, or lay with any comfort." She wrote of six-year-old Charles burning with fever and going into delirium that lasted forty-eight hours. "The pustules were the size of a large pea."

John Adams wrote (21) to his uncle, Isaac Smith, expressing his gratitude for all Smith was doing for his family. Adams said he would leave Philadelphia for Boston immediately if he could, but could not ". . . in honor and duty to the public stir from this place...We are in hourly expectation of some important event." Writing to Abigail, he told her how proud he was of her for what she had done. He wished the whole population could be so inoculated. Once, while walking through Potter's Field in Philadelphia, Adams was overcome by the thought that more than 2,000 Americans lay buried there, most of them victims of smallpox. But it was mostly the well-to-do who were flocking to be variolated. The prevalence of smallpox also rendered George Washington's mind uneasy for his wife. However, she agreed to submit to variolation during a trip to Philadelphia, which greatly relieved his anxiety.

King Louis XVI, who decided to assist the Americans in their War of Independence, did so in an effort to limit English power and protect France's interests in the New World. Louis himself was variolated in June 1774. The inoculation was mandated because his predecessor, Louis XV, who had initially engaged the British in the French and Indian war, died earlier of smallpox.

In June 1779, France formally declared war on England. France had, for almost two years prior, been assisting the colonists in their fight against Britain. France was joined in the war by her ally Spain, and by August, 40,000 troops had been assembled to invade England, at a time when much of Britain's military might was on the other side of the Atlantic ocean, fighting the Americans. As described in *History of the French Navy* (22):

"The plan for the invasion of England was comparatively simple. Two armies, each of 20,000, were to be assembled with their transports, one at St. Malo, the other at Le Havre. D'Orvilliers was to take the main French fleet from Brest, join the Spanish fleet, and the combined force of over sixty of the line (ships), which would give them odds of three to two over any force the English could put to sea, was to take command of the Channel. The troop transports were then to unite north of Cherbourg and be escorted to land the soldiers on the Isle of Wight and round Portsmouth, destroying the English naval base in the Channel preparatory to a march on London."

The French and Spanish fleets united, and the combined armada of sixty-six ships and fourteen frigates appeared off the coast of Plymouth, "with the wind in their favor." British Admiral Hardy and his thirty-eight British ships were nowhere in sight. To the English on shore, "nothing was certain except that the most powerful armada that ever walked the waters had inserted itself between the British fleet and the British arsenals and dockyards." "Never perhaps has England been in more serious danger of invasion than in July 1779."

"Yet the French did not attack. It was for them the golden opportunity, but they lay there for three days and made no effort. The reason was that they had smallpox on board, and far from being in a condition to fight, they were so weakened that it would have been impossible to maneuver their ships. On August 16, their sick were at least equal to the number of sound men. Many of their line-of-battle ships had from 50 to 60 percent of their crews [out of combat] and the dead were flung overboard. On August 18, a wind increasing to a gale blew from the East and the weakened French and Spanish fleets were blown a hundred miles into the Atlantic."

Thus, smallpox saved Britain but did not spare it from infection (23). Nearly 2,500 deaths from the disease were recorded in London during 1779, and another 3,500 two years later. During the last two decades of the eighteenth century, smallpox killed over 36,000 persons in London and an equal number in Glasgow, Scotland. This constituted almost one of every ten deaths in London, and nearly a fifth of all the deaths in Glasgow. The overwhelming majority of the victims were young children, since nearly all surviving adults were immune. In English towns, nine of every ten persons who died of smallpox were under the age of five years.

Smallpox continued to play a role in American history. Abraham Lincoln was elected the twelfth President of the United States, and this event precipitated the secession of the Southern states; South Carolina, Mississippi, Florida, Alabama, Georgia, Louisiana, and Texas. The causes of conflicting pressures, prejudices, and principles, all fueled by North/South differences, had already festered for many years. The root of these problems was slavery, which had been introduced into North America by colonial planters (24–26). Mostly gone from the Northern states by the time of the Revolutionary War, slavery continued to expand in the Southern states, especially to supply labor for the cultivation and harvesting of cotton on large plantations. This huge, low-cost labor force enabled planters to take advantage of the cotton gin, a new invention that made cotton production a very profitable enterprise. Thus, the debate over slavery involved not only moral principles but also the acquisition of wealth and personal power (24–27). Further, governmental power was declining in the South from the early- to mid-nineteenth century. In 1800, half the population of the United States was in the mainly agricultural South. However, with industrial expansion in the North and immigration from Europe, by 1850 less than one-third of the country's occupants lived in the South. Since the number of members eligible for election to the House of Representatives of the U.S. Congress depends on state population, the North's explosive growth brought a majority of Northerners to the House. Consequently, Southern political strategists strove to maintain parity in the Senate, where regardless of population's size, only two representatives were allowed for each state. Thus, the Southerners fought to have "slave, not slave-free new states" enter the Union. As Jefferson Davis, then a senator from Mississippi, said to the Northerners about the slavery issue:

"It is not humanity that influences you . . . it is that you may have a majority in the Congress of the United States and convert the Government into an engine of Northern aggrandizement . . . you want by an unjust system of legislation to promote the industry of the United States at the expense of people in the South."

As the South veered toward withdrawal from the Union, Davis was to become president of the Confederacy.

In that background of paranoia, the presidential election of 1860 established the battle lines (27). Stephen Douglas of Illinois became the nominee of the Northern wing of the Democratic party with the Southern wing breaking away to nominate John Breckinridge of Kentucky. The newly formed Republican party nominated Abraham Lincoln. South Carolina announced that it would secede from the Union if Lincoln were elected.

Despite gathering less than 45 percent of the popular vote, Lincoln was elected. South Carolina first, then followed by other Southern states, seceded. Beginning the day after Christmas in 1860, and four months between Lincoln's election and inauguration as President of the United States, federal fortifications and arsenals in Southern states were seized by local authorities without a shot being fired. Following Lincoln's inauguration as president on April 12, 1861, a federal ship carrying supplies was sent to Fort Sumter in Charleston Harbor, South Carolina. Cannons of the Southern forces fired on the fort, and the shooting war between the states began.

However, smallpox took no sides in this war. The disease was widely present throughout both the North and South in farms, villages, and towns (28). Earlier, in 1812, the U.S. Army command had ordered mandatory vaccination for all troops, yet another proof of

Jenner's success in preventing smallpox. But, in spite of the army's regulations requiring vaccination at the beginning of hostilities and throughout the war, new recruits continuously arrived, mostly from rural farms and cities where vaccination was not regularly given. Neither the Northern nor Southern states had any central authority to make, test, or certify the effectiveness of smallpox vaccines being used. Often the vaccine was inactive or weakened to a degree that it did not give protection. More often, it was contaminated with other microbes. So smallpox outbreaks continued throughout the war. An example was at the battle of Chancellorsville in May 1863, where as many as 5,000 Confederate troops became infected and unfit for duty (29). Similar examples abounded in the Northern army (30,31). In addition, Union and Confederate soldiers who were captured often carried smallpox deep into the South and North, respectively. Alternatively, prisoners developed smallpox afresh in the prison camps. For example, over 2,000 cases of smallpox, with 618 deaths, were recorded among Confederate prisoners of war in the Union prison at Camp Douglas, Illinois, between February 1862 and June 1865. The outbreak at Camp Douglas was a major source of an epidemic in nearby Chicago that lasted for over five years. Of over 600,000 Union and Confederate soldiers, estimates were that 29,000 developed smallpox and over 10,000 died of the disease.

During the first days of July, 1863, an epic battle that was to decide the war was fought at Gettysburg. Gettysburg is a small town near the Pennsylvania and Maryland boundary line. Meade's Union army of the Potomac withstood the charge and challenge of Lee's army of northern Virginia, causing Lee to withdraw his troops from the field. This defeat terminated the Confederacy's attempt to invade the North. It also ended the willingness of European countries to recognize the Confederacy.

Abraham Lincoln journeyed to Gettysburg in November of that year to commemorate the battle and honor the fallen soldiers (27). Lincoln was invited to attend the dedication of the cemetery at Gettysburg where thousands had died. Many who were not identified but quietly buried throughout the area were now to be reinterred within the cemetery grounds. The president was not the major speaker for the occasion, that honor belonging to Edward Everett, former President of Harvard College, former U.S. senator and former secretary of state. Lincoln was asked as "Chief Executive" of the nation to formally set apart the burial grounds as a sacred field of honor. Despite Lincoln's careful preparations for his address, he almost did not go to Gettysburg.

His son Todd was ill, and Mary Lincoln, his wife, hysterically recalling the deaths of her other sons, pleaded with her husband not to leave. But the occasion was too important, and Lincoln brushed off his wife's pleas. Soon afterward, he gave his famous *Gettysburg Address*. However, in those moments, he was already incubating the smallpox virus.

Smallpox was alive and well in Washington, DC in the 1860s, and by 1863, the spread of disease intensified (30). It was said ". . . scarcely a neighborhood in Washington was free of smallpox." Lincoln wrote to his older son, Robert, who was in Cambridge, Massachusetts, ". . . there is a good deal of smallpox here." The *Chicago Tribune* reported ". . . great terror . . ." in Washington because of smallpox (31). Even before then, smallpox had spread to the White House.

Returning to Washington by train the afternoon after giving the *Gettysburg Address*, Lincoln developed a severe headache and fever (31–34). When he arrived back in Washington, the President was placed at bed rest, while complaining of increasing headache, backache, fever and generalized fatigue. Two days later the rash appeared. The diagnosis of smallpox was made, and for the next three weeks Lincoln remained under quarantine at the White House. The case was mild, but upon recovery, Lincoln's face became pockmarked. His illness lasted slightly less than one month although, like George Washington, he did not recover his full strength until nearly two months later. The White House was placed on "penetrable quarantine," meaning limited access to allow the daily business of government. Lincoln joked that his illness gave him an answer to the continuous requests for appointments and demands of office seekers: ". . . now I have something I can give to everybody." Visitors, including his wife, were prohibited, and cabinet meetings canceled. Eight days after giving the *Gettysburg Address*, Lincoln sent a shakily handwritten note to Secretary of State Stanton, "I am improving but I cannot meet with the Cabinet." Once the diagnosis was made, Lincoln's staff attempted to prevent the news from becoming public fare that might influence the ongoing war.

How and where Lincoln became infected are not clear (28,31,34). The most common belief is that Lincoln was infected by his young son, Todd, who had an illness and rash diagnosed, likely mistakenly, as "scarlatina" when Lincoln left Washington for Gettysburg. No evidence has ever surfaced that Lincoln was vaccinated. Although Lincoln survived his smallpox infection, during its course death remained a strong possibility. So, when the news of his illness eventually did leak out, the prospect caused major concern, not only in North America, but also in Europe. China and Japan both lost emperors to smallpox, and centuries earlier rulers of European countries had died of smallpox. In Washington, Congress sent prayers for the president's recovery, and those visiting the president were vaccinated. Even so, Lincoln's valet, William Johnson, suffered a severe smallpox infection. United States Senator Lemuel Bowden, Republican for Virginia, became infected and died of smallpox.

On the European continent during the Franco-Prussian War of 1870–1871, the Prussian army of over 800,000 soldiers was vaccinated every seven years; these Germans lost fewer than 300 out of 8,360 infected. In contrast, the French army commanders who did not believe in repeated vaccination lost over 23,000 soldiers to smallpox and more than 280,000 became infected.

CHARACTERISTICS OF THE SMALLPOX VIRUS, DISEASE, AND VACCINATION

Smallpox is a severe, contagious, febrile disease characterized by a skin rash with fluid-containing vesicles that enlarge to hold pus (3). What is known about its course and pathogenesis stems from clinical and pathological studies in patients and from detailed laboratory investigations of mice infected with mousepox virus (ectromelia) and rabbits infected with vaccinia virus (35). The smallpox virus gains access to the body by the respiratory route (mouth and nose), where it multiplies first in the mucous membranes and then in nearby lymph nodes. The virus enters the bloodstream and travels to internal organs such as the spleen, lymph nodes, liver, and lungs. The virus then goes through cycles of replication that result in the manufacture of a large viral population. The incubation period from the time of the initial exposure to the onset of disease is approximately twelve days, with a range of seven to seventeen days. Thereafter, the virus invades the blood a second time, and this incursion terminates the incubation period, as the infected individual now feels ill. At this acute stage, patients have temperatures of 102°F to 106°F, headache, muscle pain, abdominal pain, vomiting, and prostration. The viruses then spread to the skin, where they multiply in epidermal cells. The characteristic skin eruptions follow in three to four days. Initially the rash is a spot on the skin (macule) then progresses to a raised skin lesion (papule) that fills with fluids (vesicular stage). Finally, the fluids become infected and form pustules in the second week of infection.

The individual with smallpox can transmit the infection at any time from a day before the rash appears until all the lesions have healed and the scabs have fallen off. During the early phase of illness, the virus is transmitted from nasal secretions and cough.

Although the route of spread through air had been suspected (36), a description of the first details appeared in a classic paper recording the observations of John Thresh (37), a Medical Officer of Health in the County of Essex, England, in 1902. Thresh was evaluating the excessive prevalence of smallpox in the Orsett Union district—with an exceedingly high incidence occurring in the town of Purfleet. Reflecting on his investigations during the years beginning in 1892, he concluded that the sole source was ships belonging to the London Metropolitan Asylum Board and anchored just offshore on the river Thames to isolate patients with active cases of smallpox. Thresh and his assistant, Mr. Sowden, noted that by 1902 one-tenth of the population in Purfleet had smallpox. Thereafter, the disease spread to the town of West Thurrock, and less expansively to adjacent parishes like Stafford, Aveley, Wennington, and Erith. A map from Thresh's report in *Lancet* (37) published in February 1902 displayed the position of the hospital ships in relationship to Purfleet and surrounding towns. Vaccinations were uniformly lax throughout the entire area, yet significantly more citizens of Purfleet contracted smallpox than in the other towns. "Why?" asked Thresh. After showing that the numbers of unvaccinated susceptible individuals were equivalent in all parishes of Orsett Union in the county of Essex, he calculated the distances to these hamlets of hospital boats carrying smallpox patients and the pattern of wind flow along the Thames. The proximity of the hospital ships to Purfleet and the mapping of wind currents solved the riddle of why, in proportion to the total population in Essex, Purfleet had fourfold more smallpox cases than in West Thurrock and thirtyfold more cases than in the remaining hamlets. As recorded by Thresh, "... Still more cogent proof, however, is obtained when the relation between the prevalent wind and the distribution of the disease is considered ... by far the most prevalent wind has been from south-west and west-south-west and would therefore blow over that portion of Purfleet to the south of the railway. Between the cottages here and those to the west of the railway there is a considerable area upon which there are very few houses. To the west of the railway there is a group of 32 houses lying almost due north of the ships. On very few occasions has the wind blown in this direction; hence, if the infection is airborne the inhabitants of this portion of Purfleet should have almost escaped. This is exactly what is found. In West Purfleet, with a population of 137, there has been only one case, whilst in South Purfleet, with a population of 342, there have been 41 cases." In other words, in the cottages nearest and exposed to the prevailing wind out of every eight persons one has been attacked. If such an epidemic prevalence had occurred in London there would have been over half a million cases during the past seven months."

Clearly, the wind carried smallpox from the hospital ships anchored on the Thames causing a 43-fold enhancement of cases occurring in those hamlets in its path compared to the other surrounding hamlets not visited by the wind. The distance traveled by the smallpox virus in the wind was approximately three-fourths of a mile. The alternative hypothesis, that smallpox was spread by infected sewage poured into the river, was deemed less likely, although several persons from the hamlets who bathed in the Thames did contract smallpox. Nevertheless, there was no correlation between the high incidence of cases in Purfleet and the few incidences of this infection among river bathers elsewhere.

Further, when the patient's skin eruptions are fully formed, these lesions themselves also become a source of infectious material. Smallpox virus may contaminate clothing, bedding, dust, or other inanimate objects (fomites) and remain infectious for months. It was blankets such as this that General Jeffrey Amherst requested to be given to the Indians of Massachusetts, an early example of premeditated germ warfare.

The terror of smallpox has been constant throughout recorded history. By the turn of the eighteenth century, the disease had become endemic in the major cities of Europe and the British Isles. Nearly one-tenth of all mankind had been killed, crippled, or disfigured by smallpox: "No man dared to count his children as his own until after they had had the disease." The nursery rhyme that symbolized both smallpox and the bubonic plague and their usual outcome was: "Ring around the rosie, pocket full of posies, a-tishoo, a-tishoo, all fall down."

It was in this milieu of terror with the deaths of peasants, bourgeoisie, and kings alike that a way of preventing smallpox was sought. Variolation, the transfer of smallpox as an inoculum into susceptible individuals, is believed to have occurred in China as early as the first century. Documents record its practice in the Sung Dynasty from 960 to 1280. Variolation consisted of obtaining dried smallpox scabs, converting them into a powder, and inhaling the substance through the nose. From China to India the technique of variolation spread, reaching Persia and Turkey.

The most common alternative to this technique of variolation was to remove the thick liquid from the smallpox pustule and rub it into a needle scratch made on the arm.

The Royal Society of London was first informed of the practice of variolation around 1700 and began collecting data on the procedure during the first decade of the eighteenth century, primarily from one of its members, the physician Emanuel Timoni (38). Dr. Timoni had received his medical degree from the University of Padua and from Oxford. He later served as the physician to the British Ambassador's family in Constantinople. There he observed variolation and documented the procedure for the Royal Society. His reports detailed withdrawal of the fluid from a pustule of a patient with uncomplicated smallpox on day twelve or thirteen of illness, then pressing the fluid into a clean glass container and transferring this material onto fresh cuts made by a needle through the fleshy part of a recipients' arm. Lady Mary Montagu, wife of the British Ambassador to Turkey, observed this procedure done in 1718.

As a great beauty, Lady Montagu had a horrifying experience with smallpox when, at the age of twenty-six, she became infected. Although she recovered, her face was permanently disfigured. Her brother was not as lucky; he died of the disease. Fearing a smallpox attack on her six-year-old son, she had him variolated during her husband's absence from Constantinople, presumably because he objected to the procedure. But Lord Montagu was not alone in his reluctance toward variolation. The British Embassy chaplain raged that variolation was un-Christian and could succeed only in infidels. However, the variolation done in spite of his fierce and sustained opposition was supervised by Dr. Timoni and performed by Dr. Maitland, the Scottish Embassy surgeon. The procedure was a success and Lady Montagu's son resisted smallpox infection.

Lady Montagu later informed her friend, Carolene of Anspach, the Princess of Wales and later the Queen of England during George II's reign, of the variolation procedure. Lady Montagu described vividly its effectiveness in the many cases that she had seen, particularly her son. In 1721, during an outbreak of smallpox in London, the Princess of Wales asked Dr. Maitland to variolate her three-year-old daughter. Shortly thereafter, the Prince and Princess of Wales, along with members of the Royal Society, had Dr. Maitland variolate six condemned prisoners at Newgate. The prisoners' reward for undergoing variolation was freedom if they survived the procedure and resisted an active exposure to smallpox. Witnessed by over twenty-five members of the Royal

Society and reported publicly by newspapers, variolation showed a dramatic protective effect. One of the three women variolated, Elizabeth Harrison, later went to Hertford during a smallpox epidemic. There she failed to develop the disease despite nursing a hospitalized patient with active smallpox and lying in bed with a child of six, who had smallpox for six weeks. This and other accounts of successful variolation were published by Maitland in a book dedicated to the Prince and Princess of Wales. Maitland later traveled to the European continent to variolate Prince Frederick of Hanover. Thereafter physicians came from all parts of Europe to learn the procedure, which was supervised by the Royal Society and sponsored by the Prince and Princess of Wales. The end result was that variolation protected many recipients exposed to smallpox later in life, although its use was associated with a 2 percent death rate.

Variolation in the United States began along an independent path. In 1706, the Reverend Cotton Mather of Boston heard about variolation as practiced in Africa from his African slave. After acquiring additional information from slave traders, Mather obtained and read Dr. Timoni's article (38) describing variolation as published in *Philosophical Transactions*. Mather then began actively seeking physicians in Boston to perform variolation as a defense against the attacks of smallpox that frequently cycled through the community. One physician, Zabdiel Boylston, of Brookline, Massachusetts, successfully variolated his six-year-old son, his thirty-year-old slave, and the slave's two-year-old son. Boylston reported these results in the *Boston Gazette* on the July 17, 1721, along with those from the successful variolation of seven other persons. By 1722, he had variolated 242 patients, 6 of whom died. His data indicated a mortality rate of 2.5 percent in those variolated as compared with the ordinarily 15 to 20 percent dead during most smallpox epidemics. It was this report detailing the experience of Boylston, coupled with deaths of soldiers in his army from smallpox, that led George Washington to variolate troops of the Continental Army and to the variolations of John and Abigail Adams and many others. The popularity of variolation continued until Edward Jenner provided the safer alternative of vaccination in 1798. Louis Pasteur, the great microbiologist who in 1879 attenuated fowl cholera bacteria by lengthening its passage in culture and who experimentally worked out the conditions for attenuation of bacteria and viruses, adopted the word "vaccine" to describe the generalized group of immunizing products. He chose the word in recognition of Jenner's work on the cowpox (*vacca*, Latin for cow) vaccine and vaccination procedure.

With use of the most attenuated cowpox virus vaccines instead of variolation with smallpox virus, the incidence of death from immunization was reduced from two to three per hundred to one per hundred thousand to one per million.

Edward Jenner, an eighteenth-century country physician in the market town of Berkeley in Gloucestershire, England, had observed that cowmaids in his area had fair and almost perfect complexions when compared with the disfiguring pockmarks of villagers infected with smallpox:

> *Where are you going, my pretty maid*
> *I'm going a-milking, sir, she said*
> *May I go with you, my pretty maid*
> *You're kindly welcome, sir, she said*
> *What is your father, my pretty maid*
> *My father's a farmer, sir, she said*
> *What is your fortune, my pretty maid*
> *My face is my fortune, sir, she said.*

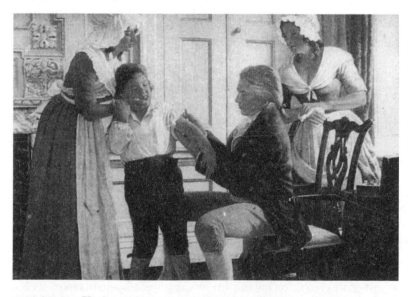

FIGURE 4.4 *The first vaccination is depicted in this painting. Edward Jenner is seen vaccinating eight-year-old James Phipps with vesicle fluid taken from the cowpox lesion on the hand of milkmaid Sarah Nilmes. Courtesy of the Wellcome Trust.*

He was aware that cowmaids who had been exposed to the pox infection of cows (cowpox) did not develop smallpox. In 1796, he obtained a vesicle induced by cowpox from the hand of his patient Sarah Nilmes and transferred it to the skin of a young lad, James Phipps. Later, when Phipps was exposed to and even inoculated with smallpox, he resisted smallpox infection. These and similar observations convinced Jenner of the feasibility and the benefits of vaccinating susceptible individuals with cowpox (current vaccine is called vaccinia) as a preventive therapy against the development of smallpox. Jenner eventually provided a detailed protocol for vaccination accompanied by illustrations of the procedure and the expected findings (39). Yet, Jenner was not the first to vaccinate against smallpox. Benjamin Jesty, a farmer and cattle breeder in Dorchester, vaccinated his wife and two sons with materials taken directly from cowpox lesions on the udder of a cow from the herd of his neighbor, Mr. Elford. Jesty had been aware of the beneficial effect of using cowpox to protect against smallpox. Previously he had noticed that two of his servant girls who had cowpox showed solid resistance to smallpox upon repeated exposure to the disease. He had known of other similar instances from reports of his neighbors. No doubt other laymen also performed similar prophylactic measures using materials obtained directly from infected cows. In 1764, thirty-two years before Jenner inoculated James Phipps with cowpox, Angelo Gatti published *Reflexions on Variolation*, which described its benefits and the nature of smallpox infection. He even discussed the need to find a means of attenuating the smallpox virus so as to diminish the morbidity and mortality it caused.

In addition to his medical practice, Jenner was a keen naturalist. He collected fossils and biological specimens for study and investigated the breeding of toads and eels. Then, when Joseph Banks returned from Captain Cook's circumnavigation of the Pacific in 1771, he approached Jenner for assistance in the classification of botanical materials he had collected. Jenner was the first to describe cuckoo hatchlings ejecting the other eggs from the nest and their adoption by nestling of foster parents. On the basis of these studies and publication of *The Natural History of the Cuckoo* he became a Fellow of the British Royal Society. Although Jenner had published in the *Royal Society Journal*, he was refused the opportunity either to present or publish his observations about smallpox. This rejection by the Royal Society was accompanied by the message that "he was in variance with established knowledge" and that "he had better not promulgate such a wild idea if he valued his reputation."

The Cow-Pock __ or __ the Wonderful Effects of the New Inoculation! __ vide. the Publications of ŷ Anti Vaccine Society

FIGURE 4.5 *Not all persons thought the procedure of vaccination was wonderful. Painting by the antivaccinationist James Gillnay in 1802 shows vaccinated persons with parts of cows growing out of their arms and bodies. Courtesy of the Wellcome Trust.*

Luckily for mankind, Jenner disregarded the rebuff from this learned and prominent society and published his results at his own expense two years later. Jenner's pamphlet, *An Inquiry into the Causes and Effects of the Variolae Vaccinae, a Disease Discovered in Some of the Western Counties of England, Particularly Gloucestershire and Known by the Name of Cowpox,* contained careful descriptions of twenty patients whose lasting immunity to smallpox followed vaccination with cowpox. The importance of this singular contribution was recognized by many, but not all, of his contemporaries. Opponents argued that vaccination was a revolting practice, that to infect a healthy person with repugnant material from an animal was an outrage, that vaccinated victims sprouted horns and looked like cows, and that one was interfering with God's way, since vaccination was not mentioned in the Bible. This opposition was mounted by those in the medical and business professions as well as by religious leaders. Even the poet Lord Byron classified cowpox as a passing fancy.

Now look around, and turn each trifling page,
survey the precious works that please the age;
what varied wonders tempt us as they pass!
The cowpox, tractors, galvanism, and gas in turn appears

But Jenner weathered these blows; his pamphlet was read and his technique rapidly applied in areas of Britain, the European continent, as well as North and South America. Jenner himself received letters of gratitude from admirers worldwide. For example, in 1806, President Thomas Jefferson wrote to congratulate Jenner on his great achievement: "Yours is the comfortable reflection that mankind can never forget that you have lived. Future nations will know by history only that the loathsome smallpox had existed and by you has been extirpated." Napoleon, who was at the time at war with Britain, released English prisoners of war and permitted English citizens to return home upon the request of Jenner. Napoleon remarked that he could not "refuse anything to such a great benefactor of mankind." The Chiefs of the Five Nations of the North American Indians sent a wampum belt with a letter of thanks to Jenner in 1807. Their people had suffered grievously from smallpox, both inadvertently as passed by infected Europeans and directly by deliberate introduction of blankets contaminated with smallpox. The results were the killings of hundreds of thousands of their tribe members. Their letter said, "Brother: Our Father has delivered to us the book you sent to instruct us how to use the discovery which the Great Spirit made to you whereby the smallpox, that fatal enemy of our tribe, may be driven from the earth.... We sent with this a belt and a string of wampum in token of our appreciation of your precious gift." Of his many awards, Jenner especially valued the belt. He wore it with pride on ceremonial occasions. In Britain he received financial rewards of £10,000 and £20,000 in 1802 and 1807, respectively. Jenner was appointed Physician Extraordinary to his majesty, King George IV.

Yet there was overt and noisy controversy over vaccination. One example is the case of Benjamin Waterhouse and James Smith in the United States (40,41). Benjamin Waterhouse was appointed Professor of Theory and Practice of Physics at the newly established Harvard Medical School in 1783 after returning to Boston from several years of study abroad. For eight years he had studied at the best medical schools of that time, the University of Edinburgh, Scotland, and the University of

Leiden, Holland. After receiving his medical degree from the University of Leiden, he stayed at the university for an additional session and boarded with John Adams, the American minister. Adams would later become the second president of the United States. Waterhouse arrived at Harvard in 1783. From friends in England he received a copy of Jenner's publication in 1799. Thereafter, Waterhouse devoted his energies to advocating the use of cowpox to vaccinate against smallpox, rather than using variolation. Waterhouse received a glass vial containing cowpox directly from Jenner. He used it to vaccinate his son and others. Those vaccinated resisted infection when exposed to natural smallpox or when variolated with smallpox. However, many other physicians in the Boston area were opposed to vaccination. A coalition of physicians from Harvard and the Boston community petitioned the Boston Board of Health in 1802 to set up and conduct a public test of the new vaccine. Although it may not have been their intent, this investigation clearly proved the superiority of vaccination over variolation. The board then urged doctors to accept the principle of vaccination. Subsequently Waterhouse wrote to Thomas Jefferson and sent him his pamphlet on "A Prospect of Eliminating Smallpox." Jefferson wrote back, "Every friend of humanity must look with pleasure at this discovery, by which one more evil is withdrawn from the condition of man; and most contemplate the possibility that future improvements and discoveries may still more and more lessen the catalogue of the evils."

Jefferson himself became actively involved in the fight to vaccinate (42,43). Through his efforts, vaccine material received from Waterhouse was distributed to Jefferson's native Virginia, then to Pennsylvania and numerous areas within the South. Jefferson also sent Jenner's vaccine with Meriwether Lewis and William Clark on their journey to explore the Louisiana Purchase and find passage to the Pacific Ocean. He instructed Lewis on its use and requested it be brought to the frontier and Indians (44). Finally, James Madison, the fourth president of the United States, who was familiar with both Jefferson's and Waterhouse's activities, signed legislation, the first of its kind, to encourage vaccination.

To put this critical medical therapy into practice, Dr. James Smith of Maryland was appointed as the federal agent for the distribution of the vaccine. However, the winds still blew strongly against the use of vaccination. Politically, Waterhouse was a religious Quaker and, as such, a pacifist. Despite its popularity, he had objected to the Revolutionary War. To avoid entanglement in the war he traveled to and lived in

Britain in the early part of 1775. Further, he was born in Rhode Island and was considered an outsider by many in the Boston community. Finally, his political sympathies were with Thomas Jefferson and his style of government, a Populist democracy. By contrast to Waterhouse, the Boston elite supported Federalism and considered Jefferson immoral. As so often repeated in history, political power overcame good sense. A coalition of physicians at Harvard and throughout Boston, in concert with church leaders, arranged the dismissal of Waterhouse from his chair at the Harvard Medical School in 1812. Accordingly, the changing political climate in Washington in the 1820s led to repeal of the vaccine law followed by the dismissal of James Smith from his office in 1822. The result was that by 1840, epidemics of smallpox and deaths that followed once again increased in the United States.

Jenner and Jefferson expressed the hope in the early nineteenth century that smallpox might someday be eliminated. However, it was over 150 years after Jenner proved the effectiveness of vaccination that the first serious proposal to undertake smallpox eradication appeared. In 1950, the Pan-American Sanitary Organization made the commitment to conquer smallpox throughout the Americas. A program of mass vaccinations eliminated smallpox by the 1970s from all countries in the Americas except for Argentina, Brazil, Colombia, and Ecuador; in the countries with vaccination programs, the number of cases decreased markedly.

With governments around the world promoting vaccination, outbreaks of smallpox came under control in many but not all countries. In 1953, Dr. Brock Chisholm, the first Director General of the World Health Organization (WHO), proposed that smallpox eradication be undertaken as a global effort, and he challenged member states of WHO to join this crusade (2,45–47). However, the initial response of the World Health Assembly was not encouraging. Representatives of virtually every industrialized country, including the United States, argued that such a program was too complicated, too vast. So Chisholm's proposal was dropped (2). In fairness, at this time, WHO was preoccupied with a costly program to eradicate malaria, which occupied the majority of its efforts and budget. Unfortunately, this program turned out to be disappointing, even as smallpox was successfully eliminated from several more countries, including China. Five years later the Vice Minister of Health of the Soviet Union, Victor Zhadnov, proposed a ten-year program for the eradication of smallpox. Reasoning that the USSR had eradicated smallpox throughout its vast and ethnically heterogeneous country, he argued that there was no reason why other countries around the world could not do likewise. With the prodding of Zhadnov and others, the WHO Assembly finally did vote to accept the program, in principle, but unrealistically delegated only $100,000 of its budget. This lack of funding effectively defeated the proposal. At this time even the influential and prominent microbiologist Rene Dubos, like Lord Byron 150 years earlier, referred to smallpox eradication as a passing fancy: "Make it probably useless to discuss the theoretical flaws and technical difficulties of eradication programs, because more earthly factors will certainly bring them soon to a gentle and silent death.... Eradication programs will eventually become a curiosity item on library shelves, just as have all social utopias."

Nevertheless, the fight for eradication did not stop. In 1966, the WHO Director General, Marcelino Candau, proposed a budget of $2.4 million for smallpox eradication. Incredibly, almost every industrialized country again protested the size of the budget, and most expressed doubts about the wisdom of the program. Thus, the pivotal discovery by Jenner that would lead to one of the major accomplishments of mankind became implemented by a margin of only two votes. Under the direction of D. A. Henderson and his colleagues, WHO directed considerable effort toward the eradication of smallpox.

Donald Ainslie Henderson was born in Lakewood, Ohio, in 1928. He received his medical training at the University of Rochester and public health training at Johns Hopkins. He worked in the area of disease surveillance at the Centers for Disease Control (CDC) until assuming the position of Chief Medical Officer for the Smallpox Eradication Program of the WHO in 1966. He directed that program until its work eradicated smallpox. Henderson used two principal strategies. First, international vaccine testing centers were developed to ensure that all vaccines met the standards of safety and effectiveness. This guaranteed that only active vaccines would be used. Second, reducing the number of smallpox cases to zero became the established goal rather than documenting the number of vaccine doses given. With this goal, effective surveillance teams were set up to both report and contain outbreaks of smallpox. In the early years of the program, it became clear that the number of smallpox cases was underreported and that only 10 percent of vaccines being produced or provided met the accepted international standards. Subsequently, with more accurate surveillance and reporting, with the use of only those vaccines approved by the international vaccine testing centers, and with a program for vigorous vaccination of peoples in Africa and Asia, by 1970 smallpox was eliminated from twenty countries of western and central Africa. In 1971, smallpox was eliminated from Brazil, in 1972 from Indonesia, in 1975 from the entire Asian continent, in 1976 from Ethiopia, and in 1977 the last case was reported in Somalia. Thus by 1980, 184 years after Edward Jenner inoculated James Phipps and 182 years after he published *An Inquiry into the Causes and Effects of the Variolae Vaccinae*, the World Health Assembly announced worldwide eradication of smallpox. This singular event is one of the greatest accomplishments undertaken and performed for the benefit of mankind anywhere or at any time.

COULD SMALLPOX RECUR?

The microbe hunters who accomplished this deed are many but can be placed into two groups. First and unquestionably the most innovative was Edward Jenner for his work, perseverance, and influence. Second is the large group of dedicated health-care workers who traveled to the distant corners of the earth to track cases of smallpox and to vaccinate all peoples on the globe. This group was led by D. A. Henderson. Henderson reflects the best qualities of many in the long line of public health officers in the United States and throughout the world who have devoted their energies both scientifically and politically toward the control and elimination of infectious diseases.

The success of the Smallpox Eradication Program indicates clearly that other viruses with characteristics similar to smallpox—that is, whose natural host is man, that have no animal intermediate, and that do not cause persistent infection—such as measles and poliomyelitis, can and should be controlled. Scientific research has provided the tools; all that remains is the political and economic willpower and desire to apply them effectively. Thus smallpox, one of the viruses most intently studied by newly emerging practitioners of medicine, and a killer of millions of people, was to become no more than a curiosity, likely to be removed from the teaching curriculum of medical schools. Prior to September 11, plans were made to eliminate all stocks of smallpox within the next several years, thus making the virus the first species purposely eliminated from this planet.

Despite the eradication of smallpox as a disease, could the virus return? The virus's only natural host is man; no lower animals are susceptible. Since the virus does not linger in the form of a persistent infection, it is amenable to permanent eradication—that is to say, removal from the world. But because the virus no longer circulates in any community, the numbers of never-vaccinated or never-infected susceptible individuals increases continually. Further, complete or efficient immunity of those previously vaccinated is believed to wane in ten to twenty years. Consequently, the pool of highly susceptible individuals is expanding enormously.

In the last few years, some countries and individuals with hidden stores of smallpox viruses have actually chosen to develop more dangerous varieties by inserting materials alongside its genes. For example, the Soviet Biologic-Weapons Program near Novosibirsk in western Siberia continued such work engineering a component of Ebola virus into the smallpox virus, despite attempts from Gorbachev to curtail it. With the breakup of the Soviet Union, government-funded research decreased dramatically, and scientists working in biowarfare programs often found themselves without jobs. Some went abroad looking for employment by the highest bidder. Several emigrated to the United States or Great Britain as consultants in the defense against such biological weapons, even as the Offensive Biological Weapons Program was discontinued in the United States during the Nixon presidency. Others, perhaps mercenary biologists, have simply disappeared from Russia. One can only guess that they ended up in Iraq, Syria, Libya, Iran, or perhaps other areas with their stocks of smallpox and their technical knowledge to initiate and expand a bioweapons program. However, no one really knows where they are. But because of that threat, several specialists who earlier led the fight to remove smallpox from our planet and destroy the virus as a species have recently advised that funds be earmarked to stockpile vaccines against smallpox and other pathogens and to store the deadly virus in American and Russian designated laboratories. The Clinton administration agreed in late 1998 to request $300 million for this purpose. Implicit in the goal of eradication and elimination of smallpox or other plague-inducing agents is the need not to vaccinate the population. The billions of dollars saved by not having to make or use vaccines would then be available to control other health problems. Also advised is the retraining of physicians and public health officials in diagnosis of smallpox.

The last natural case of smallpox occurred in 1977 in Somalia at a time when many countries had already discontinued routine vaccination. However, in 1978, a photographer working at the University of Birmingham, England, became infected and died. Supposedly, the source of infection was a secure laboratory for smallpox research located a considerable distance from the room in which the photographer worked. This lethal episode emphasizes the danger of any viable smallpox virus during the posteradication era. As a result of that accident, all strains of smallpox stored in laboratories were supposedly destroyed or transferred to depositories at the CDC in Atlanta or the Research Institute for Viral Preparations in Moscow. The World Health Organization Ad Hoc Committee established to deal with this issue recommended in 1986 and 1994 that all remaining smallpox stocks in Atlanta and Moscow be destroyed if no serious objections were received from the international health community and that vaccination to protect military personnel be terminated. Despite the passage of years, neither recommendation has been implemented. The possibility was raised that smallpox in the hands of evildoers will resurface to be seen once again by practitioners of medicine. If smallpox should ever reappear, then potentially everyone on earth may be in danger. Since the time that vaccination was stopped, over 50 percent of the current population in the USA, Europe, and the world have never received the smallpox vaccine. Every year that number grows. Further, immunity to smallpox lessens generally seven to ten years after vaccination, and the precise time of protection following vaccination or revaccination is unknown. Owing to the Geneva Accord and other such agreements, rechallenge with live smallpox is, and rightfully so, unacceptable and not allowed. Hence, the time that vaccines completely protect is estimated from epidemiologic observations and outbreaks occurring in vaccinated populations. To better evaluate the risk/benefit ratio for reinstitution or not of vaccination, three observations are worth recalling. The first occurred during the Franco-Prussian War of 1870–1871 and represents Europe's last serious large outbreak of smallpox. The Prussian army of over 800,000 soldiers was vaccinated every seven years. These Germans lost fewer than 300 out of 8,360 infected. In contrast, the French army commanders who did not believe in repeated vaccination lost over 23,000 soldiers to smallpox and more than 280,000 became infected. The second incident occurred in Montreal and surrounding villages in Canada in the mid-1880s and represented the last great plague in

North America. French-Canadians living in and around Montreal had low vaccine coverage. Vaccination against smallpox for them was sporadic, largely not encouraged and in many cases actively resisted. In contrast, British, Scottish, and Northern Irish immigrants to the area were more actively supportive of vaccination. In addition to this cultural divide, there was an economic division of substandard housing, schools, and jobs in the French-Canadian community. Smallpox broke out in this area on February 28, 1885 and continued until mid-1886. Over this 15 month period there were over 9,600 cases reported in Montreal and an additional 10,305 in the surrounding province or a total of 19,905 (47a,b). The true number was likely threefold or around 60,000 or more infected with smallpox because of incomplete recording. Nevertheless, from the documented cases, over 3,000 died in Montreal and almost 3,000 more in French-Canadian villages. Of those dying over 95 percent were French-Canadian. Overall, Montreal lost 2 percent of its population to smallpox, primarily of unvaccinated individuals. The third lesson is from the outbreak that occurred in Meschede, Germany, in 1969 and is more accurately choreographed.

In 1969 newspapers and broadcasts described the murder trial of Robert Kennedy's killer in the United States and the seizing of the American ship *Pueblo* by the North Koreans. The good news broadcast at that time noted amazing achievements in space, the docking of spacecrafts and walking in space. But even as the Concord supersonic jet took flight, Palestinian terrorists detonated bombs and a TWA jet was hijacked. Also in that year, a twenty-year-old traveler (name withheld for confidentiality) from Meschede, Westphalia, Germany, was returning from adventures in the Orient and Pakistan. Eleven days after his return, he fell ill, and two days later developed a fever that rapidly rose to 102° and then 103° along with a severe headache and delirium. The next day (day sixteen after returning to Germany), he was taken to a local hospital, St. Walburga Krankenhaus, because of high temperature, sickness, and mental confusion (48,49). The initial diagnosis was typhoid fever, so the patient was placed in an isolation ward and was visited by Father Kunibert, a Benedictine monk who offered communion. Two days later the patient's fever rose, and a rash developed that later formed massive blisters over his body. When a clinical diagnosis of possible smallpox followed, one of the blisters was biopsied and the fluid removed was sent to the State Health Laboratory in Düsseldorf. The next day, the report came back stating that smallpox viruses were seen by electron microscopy (48,49). The morphologic picture of smallpox was easily recognizable, and The World Health Organization in Geneva, Switzerland, was notified.

Aware of the danger to hospital personnel, since smallpox roughly kills one of three people it infects, the hospital administration mobilized the local police. A few hospital personnel, as well as Father Kunibert, had been exposed to the patient, and several other patients and visitors in the hospital might be at risk. The police closed the hospital to prevent people from entering or leaving. The patient was placed in a biocontainment bag and transported by motor escort thirty miles away to Mary's Heart Hospital in the town of Winbern because this hospital had a newly built isolation unit specifically designed to handle highly contagious patients. A chain-link fence was installed to surround the hospital, and sentinels were posted to keep people out or in.

Although the patient survived his infection, the story did not end there. What of Father Kunibert and the other patients and staff who were at St. Walburga's hospital at the time of this episode? Potentially, all of them were exposed directly or indirectly to the smallpox virus. The same risk of exposure was true for visitors to other patients on the same and different floors for five to six days after the patient was first admitted to St. Walburga. To be sure and for public health safety, all these potential carriers of smallpox were placed in quarantine. Subsequently, German health authorities ordered a massive vaccination for smallpox in and around the hospital as well as throughout the Meschede area. This ring-type vaccine containment approach was modeled after the successful plan used by the World Health Organization that efficiently eliminated outbreaks of smallpox in Africa and Asia. As for St. Walburga's Hospital, it was boarded up, surrounded by a fence and sequestered by police barricades. Then, eleven days after this smallpox-infected traveler entered isolation at Mary's Heart Hospital, the Benedictine priest came down with smallpox, albeit a mild form. Next, a five-year-old girl in an isolation room diagonally across a hall from the patient's quarters developed a severe case of smallpox but survived. Thereafter one nursing student who worked on the second floor above the patient developed smallpox, soon followed by yet another nursing student who came down with smallpox and subsequently died. Overall, nineteen people in the area fell prey to smallpox infections, seventeen associated with the initial patient exposure (48). Most of these individuals had never entered the patient's room, and several were not on the same floor of the hospital. The smallpox evidently spread via air ducts or air currents. Another two persons caught smallpox secondarily while visiting other patients in the hospital. Of the nineteen infected persons, there were four deaths. The reason why four infected persons died while the remaining fifteen lived is not known. Their genes, the amount of exposure, a competent immune system, and a vigorous anti-smallpox immune response are all likely possibilities. Interestingly, except for Father Kunibert, the majority of those developing smallpox never came into direct contact with the patient. Of particular concern is that seventeen persons who contracted and became ill from smallpox had been vaccinated previously. That some who are vaccinated later become susceptible to smallpox infection is a fact, but why these unfortunates are different from those protected by vaccination is unclear.

In 2001, the Bush administration expanded manufacture of the vaccine and, following the recommendation of the Institute of Medicine of the National Academy of Sciences (50), began the program of revaccinating health-care and emergency workers, government officials, and the military (51). However, some of these designees resisted the revaccination plan, especially health-care providers, and far fewer received vaccinations than planned. The arguments against vaccination were vigorous and focused on five central issues. First, about 20 percent of the population cannot be vaccinated because their immune systems are compromised by disease or medications, by eczema and other skin lesions, or by pregnancy. This group also includes young children and a large segment of the population who take medication that suppresses the immune system. Second, general apathy has accompanied the decreased urgency to vaccinate, that is, the philosophy of "it is not likely to happen to me." Third, conservative or libertarian opposition insists that vaccination should be a self-choice and not one of a general public health concern, in line with suspicion of governments' dictums. Fourth, the unlikely possibility remains that vaccines may be contaminated or may expose recipients to secondary bacterial infections. Fifth, economics do not favor vaccine production. According to Glaxo-Smith-Kline, the world's largest vaccine maker, worldwide sales of vaccines in the year 1999 were slightly over $4 billion, but sales of just one drug like the cholesterol-lowering drug, Lipitor, yield $6 billion per year. Tamas Bartfai, currently a professor at The Scripps Research Institute and Chair of the Molecular and Integrative Neurosciences Department and previously the Director of Research for Hoffman-LaRoche Pharmaceuticals, told me that because of the economic reality for pharmaceutical houses, coupled with the public health and natural interest, the United States and most western European countries guarantee a profit for the manufacture of vaccines. In addition, these countries limit medical malpractice lawsuits for the manufacturers, an event that does not occur with any other of their produced drugs. These five arguments all have their champions. Economics and political philosophy about individual rights oppose group or public safety rights.

Other serious concerns hinder smallpox vaccination. One is an issue of the vaccine's side effects. Past experience in the United States and elsewhere when smallpox vaccine was routinely administered yielded records that one individual in every thousand vaccinated persons required related medical attention, and one death from complications occurred for every one million persons vaccinated. However, the most perplexing dilemma is that, from the time of the vaccine's discontinuation in the United States in the 1960s and in the world in the 1980s to the present, a large segment of the population has engaged in medical therapies that suppress the immune system to control such ailments as arthritis, diabetes, multiple sclerosis, and skin conditions. These medications did not exist in the 1960s. Further, immunosuppressive diseases like human immunodeficiency virus infection and AIDS, which were not present until the 1980s, now afflict millions. Currently, physicians and public health officials are being retrained in the diagnosis and management of smallpox.

As stated previously, an immune system that is suppressed for any reason is sufficient cause for exclusion from smallpox vaccination. This includes persons with genetic immune deficiencies and pregnant women because pregnancy suppresses the immune system and fetuses (whose immune systems have not yet matured) are highly susceptible to infection. Also at high risk for complications from smallpox vaccination are those with chronic skin conditions like eczema or psoriasis and individuals undergoing or recently given medical treatments to weaken their immune system. The latter group consists of patients receiving steroid or other immunosuppressive therapy for autoimmune diseases like diabetes, multiple sclerosis, rheumatoid arthritis, lupus erythematosus, and collagen-vascular disease like scleroderma or dermamyositosis. Further, individuals who would be in close physical contact with someone who falls into these categories should not get the smallpox vaccine because of the risk to those contacts. Examples of close contacts would be persons in potential vaccinees' household, school, or place of employment.

Also to be excluded from smallpox vaccination are those individuals having illnesses that can weaken the immune system. Included in this group are persons with HIV/AIDS, cancer, leukemia, or lymphoma; recipients of bone marrow, kidney, or other transplants; patients given radiation therapy within three months before proposed vaccination; or those taking steroid or immunosuppressive medication. If the dose of steroids received has been given long enough to significantly suppress the immune response, then a waiting period of one to three months after treatment ends would be recommended before vaccination. However, the waiting time required after discontinuing steroid therapy is still controversial.

If approximately 15 to 20 percent of the population of the United States cannot be vaccinated for protection from smallpox infection because of diseases they have or medication they take, the unresolved issue is, what about the remaining 80 to 85 percent of the population? Consider this: if smallpox is reintroduced as a bioterror weapon, then everyone on earth who was not vaccinated within the seven preceding years is likely in danger of infection. One plan for a protective program is to vaccinate everyone never exposed (naïve) and revaccinate all previously vaccinated persons. Despite the risks, the benefit-to-risk ratio dramatically favors vaccination. The second strategy is to vaccinate or revaccinate only health-care workers, military, and selected government personnel, then stockpile vaccine in multiple storage areas in case of a smallpox attack. In the event of an attack, begin vaccinating the population in a wide ring surrounding the outbreak site. Implicit in this approach is acceptance of loss of life from smallpox outbreaks, surveillance and isolation of all contacts, the enforcement of quarantine regulations, and travel restrictions. Implicit in this argument are the low probability of a terrorist attack using smallpox and the development of antiviral drugs to treat smallpox infection.

The first strategy, or universal vaccination, would eliminate most episodes of disarray, confusion, and panic that could occur and would alleviate the need for massive quarantine. This was the initial strategy used to eradicate smallpox. It was successful in industrialized countries where good public health/medical services are present. It was not as successful in Third World countries where, in addition to poorer health care, the lack of refrigeration (for vaccine storage) and difficulties in travel were problems. In those instances, ring vaccination around outbreaks was successfully utilized.

The second strategy weighs the possibility that a smallpox attack is unlikely and accepts that with a smallpox outbreak in a densely populated city perhaps as many as 5,000 to 50,000 may die from the primary exposure before the remaining population is protected with active vaccination after the infection has been verified.

What is the sequence of recent events to frame the decision of whether to be vaccinated?

Before knowledge of the ongoing Russian smallpox biowarfare program (52) and the defection and disappearance of several Soviet scientists working on that program, the Secretary of Health in President Clinton's administration, Dr. Louis Sullivan, advocated the government's position: destroy the world's stock of smallpox kept in only two known repositories, the Communicable Disease Center in Atlanta, Georgia, and the Research Institute for Virus Preparation in Moscow. He argued that, with the sequencing of the smallpox genome, ". . . There is no scientific reason not to destroy the remaining stocks of wild virus. So I am pleased to announce today that after we complete our sequencing of the smallpox genome, the United States will destroy all remaining virus stocks. I invite our colleagues in the Soviet Union to consider the same course of action. Perhaps we can jointly announce the final elimination of the last traces of this lethal virus."

This effort would effectively eliminate smallpox as a potential weapon, consistent with the aims of the International Biological and Toxic Weapons Convention of 1972, and eliminate the military's need for smallpox vaccination.

But nine years later, on April 22, 1999, President Clinton, acting on the advice of independent scientific investigators (53–55) and a report by the Institute of Medicine of the National Academy of Sciences (56) decided to delay the planned destruction of smallpox stocks in the United States. The decision was based on the importance of obtaining additional scientific knowledge about how smallpox works, how to chemically attack it with antiviral medical therapy, and concern over the possible use of smallpox as a terrorist weapon. The president wished to review the issue of eliminating smallpox with a re-evaluation and a decision to be made in June 1999 and to explore the possibility of joint research on smallpox with the Russians.

D. A. Henderson, who was largely responsible for leading the successful campaign to eradicate smallpox retorted,

"I'll wager over the next five years you'll see no work whatsoever... except in the Russian laboratory where smallpox was weaponized. You can draw your own conclusion about that."

At this same time, intelligence reports suggested that clandestine supplies of smallpox were elsewhere, most likely in North Korea, Iraq, and perhaps in other areas.

Henderson continued,

"I find it very regrettable that within the World Health Organization, 74 of 79 countries want to destroy the virus but four, including the United States and Russia, favor its preservation."

The new American position, to keep smallpox viruses rather than eliminate them, reversed the 1996 U.S. policy to destroy the virus. Arguments then, as now, for keeping smallpox rested on four points. By maintaining stocks of smallpox, first, the opportunity to develop antiviral antidotes remained. Second, a new and safer vaccine could be devised using modern technology. Third, even with the best intentions of all, smallpox could not be eliminated from the world because dead smallpox victims buried and preserved in permafrost were akin to having smallpox in a freezer. Fourth, we live in a wicked world, so who is to guarantee that smallpox would be eliminated from all laboratories, freezers, and countries?

So, the momentum began to swing the pendulum toward keeping smallpox. An editorial appeared in the journal *Nature* on April 29, 1999, advocating the preservation of smallpox in the two restricted areas. Then, in Geneva, after the World Trade Center attack on September 11, 2001, the WHO Governing Board agreed in January 2002 to delay the destruction of known samples of smallpox and revisit the issue again in 2005–2006.

However, at the time of the Geneva meeting, Soviet defectors now living in the United States and Great Britain who previously worked in the Russian smallpox bioweapons program told of an ongoing program in Russia (52). Iraqi and Iranian scientists were heavily engaged in research on camelpox, a close cousin of smallpox. Although camelpox has not been shown to infect humans, research to change its tropism to man may be a scientific possibility and therefore of great concern.

With that background came the legacy of the September 11, 2001, tragedy at the World Trade Center. The stakes now rose dramatically.

Plans were implemented to seek sufficient vaccinia vaccine for all or a large segment of the American population. However, production of the vaccine had been discontinued by the large pharmaceutical companies and federal contracts to smaller companies so often led to disappointing results in production. By April 17, 2002, only 15 million doses of aging smallpox vaccine were found. However, when tested in human volunteers at a dilution of one to five, that vaccine successfully immunized 99 percent of tested subjects, thus increasing the supply of smallpox vaccine from 15 million to 57 million doses. Further, even when the vaccine was diluted tenfold, the results proved efficient in 97 percent of those inoculated and now yielded 150 million doses of vaccine. The pharmaceutical firm Aventis Pasteur found and donated an additional 85 million doses. Finally, the government ordered from a private company, Acambis, an additional 155 million vaccine doses. Hence, the drive was accelerated to obtain, store, and use smallpox vaccine. With the will and production to increase vaccinia vaccine stocks came a chance to reflect on the path that the world's experience with smallpox has traveled.

The timetable of smallpox virus control

1796   Jenner successfully vaccinates against smallpox and shows complete protection against reinfection.

1967   Global eradication of smallpox undertaken by the World Health Organization.

1969   Outbreak of smallpox in Meschede, Germany, with transmission by the index case, a man returning from Pakistan.

1971   Controversial report of smallpox outbreak in the Soviet Union suggesting Russian experiments with aerosol delivery of smallpox as a weapon of war.

1972   Vaccination discontinued in the United States.

1977   Last natural case of smallpox in Somalia.

1978   Last transmitted case due to laboratory accident.

1979   Global commission for certification of smallpox eradication recommends destruction of all remaining stocks of smallpox or transfer to one of four countries: USA, Russia, United Kingdom, Netherlands.

1980   The WHO Assembly announces the worldwide eradication of smallpox. This singular event is one of the greatest accomplishments undertaken and performed for the benefit of mankind anywhere at any time.

1983 South Africa destroys its smallpox stocks. Smallpox stocks collected in the United Kingdom or The Netherlands are transferred to the Centers for Disease Control (CDC) in Atlanta, Georgia. Only secured facilities at the CDC and Research Institute for Virus Preparation in Moscow are designated as world centers for storage of smallpox.

1985 Routine smallpox vaccination ceases throughout the world.

1986 The WHO Ad Hoc Committee recommends that smallpox stocks in the USA and Moscow be eliminated and that vaccination of military personnel be discontinued.

1992 Ken Alibek, a head of secret smallpox and other biohazardous microbial research in the Soviet Biologic Weapons Program near Novosibirsk in Siberia, defects to the United States and briefs U.S. intelligence about the Russian Biological Warfare Program.

1994 The WHO Ad Hoc Committee issues a warning to any terrorist group or country planning to use smallpox as a biological weapon. The Committee states that possessing the virus is illegal and a crime against humanity.

1998 A U.S. intelligence report concludes that Iraq, North Korea, and Russia are concealing smallpox virus for possible military use.

D. A. Henderson, the leader of the eradication of smallpox effort by the WHO and a long-time advocate for the destruction of smallpox stocks, now calls for new smallpox vaccine production to deal with the potential of a deliberate terrorist release.

"It's (smallpox) potential for devastation today is far greater than at any previous time."

"In a now highly susceptible, mobile population, smallpox would be able to spread widely and rapidly throughout this country (U.S.A.) and the world."

President Clinton asks Congress to add $300 million to the next year's federal budget to protect Americans from biological and biochemical war.

1999 The WHO adopts a resolution calling for a delay in the destruction of smallpox in the two known storage sites in the USA and Russia. An editorial by Donna Shalala, Secretary of the U.S. Department of Health and Human Services in the Clinton administration, justifies the preservation of smallpox stocks, as does the Institute of Medicine of the National Academy of Sciences (USA) with a report that states, "The most compelling need for long-term retention of live variola virus would be for the development of antiviral agents or novel vaccines to protect against a re-emergence of smallpox due to accidental or intentional release of variola virus."

2000   Clinical research begins at St. Louis University with three groups of twenty volunteers each receiving vaccines either full-strength or diluted five- or tenfold.

2001   Clinical research to establish the efficacy of diluted smallpox vaccine expands to over 650 volunteers in clinical trials at St. Louis University, the University of Rochester, the University of Maryland, and Baylor College of Medicine.

2002   Calculation of results from this multicenter program indicates that a tenfold dilution of vaccine stock is efficient in causing the characteristic skin lesion and scab and proves generation of an immune response to smallpox. By this means, the available vaccine in the United States is now 150 million doses.

Other countries begin to stock smallpox vaccine: Israel and Great Britain each with 30 million doses, Germany 6 million doses, etc.

U.S. public health officials instruct state public health laboratories to prepare to vaccinate up to one million people in ten days in the event of a smallpox attack.

The CDC releases guidelines for states to run clinics and recruit 4,680 public health workers and volunteers. Dr. Judith Gerberding, Head of the CDC, advocates precautionary vaccines for health workers: "Those people need to be protected...if we do not do that then these workers will be standing in line to get their vaccines rather than helping."

Dr. Mohammed Akhter, Executive Secretary of the American Public Health Association: "This (smallpox vaccination) is a high undertaking, the likes of which we've never seen."

Israel announces successful vaccination of 15,000 soldiers and public health workers without serious side effects. Israel screens out from vaccination women who are pregnant and immune-suppressed individuals.

President Bush lays out plans for smallpox vaccination in the United States; 500,000 frontline military are to be vaccinated, along with one million health-care workers. The President himself is vaccinated and calls for voluntary vaccination of over 400,000 doctors, nurses, and emergency workers to begin in January 2003. The general public is to begin vaccination in 2004 or later. President Bush announces,

"Since our country was attacked fifteen months ago, Americans have been forced to prepare for a variety of threats we hope will never come."

"One potential danger to America is the use of the small-pox virus as a weapon of terror. Smallpox is a deadly but preventable disease. Most Americans who are thirty-four or older had a smallpox vaccination when they were children. By 1972, the risk of smallpox was so remote that routine vaccinations were discontinued in the United States."

"We know, however, that the smallpox virus still exists in laboratories. And we believe that regimes hostile to the United States may possess this dangerous virus."

"To protect our citizens in the aftermath of September 11, we are evaluating old threats in a new light. Our government has no information that a smallpox attack is imminent. Yet it is prudent to prepare for the possibility that terrorists would kill indiscriminately; those who do kill indiscriminately, would use diseases as a weapon."

"Today, I am directing additional steps to protect the health of our nation. I'm ordering that the military and other personnel who serve America in high-risk parts of the world receive the smallpox vaccine. Men and women who could be on the front lines of a biological attack must be protected."

"This particular vaccine does involve a small risk of seri-ous health considerations. As Commander-in-Chief, I do not believe I can ask others to accept this risk unless I am willing to do the same. Therefore, I will receive the vaccine along with our military."

"These vaccinations are a precaution only, and not a response to any information concerning imminent danger. Given the current level of threat and the inherent health risks of the vaccine, we have decided not to initiate a broader vaccination program for all Americans at this time. Neither my family nor my staff will be receiving the vaccine, because our health and national security experts do not believe vaccination is necessary for the general public."

Israel expands vaccination to 40,000 individuals. Of the first 17,000 persons vaccinated, two had ill effects but recovered.

2003 Several health-care workers resist vaccination and other scientists favor a cautious approach to the government's plan.

At a U.S. Senate hearing, Louis Bell, Chief of Pediatrics at Children's Hospital, Philadelphia, the country's largest children's hospital, states that his institution will not immunize the medical/hospital staff. Concerned about side effects of vaccination and spread of smallpox to immunosuppressed children (3, 49, 56) and other complications, James August, the health and safety director representing 350,000 health-care workers, asks for a delay in smallpox vaccinations. He warns that, "The worries of this group are: 1) health-care workers could suffer side effects; 2) could infect their own families or patients with vaccinia virus; 3) lack of workman's compensation, hospitalization or insurance coverage; 4) higher rates today of side effects anticipated because of the considerable number of people in the population today on medication that suppresses the immune system or having immunosuppressive diseases."

Andrew Stern, President of the Service Employees International Union says, "President Bush and Congress have not done enough to protect and care for health-care workers, their families and patients who could be harmed by the vaccine." He argues that workers who refuse vaccination should not be subject to repercussions at their job, and workers taking the vaccine should not lose income if they have to stay at home because of reactions to the vaccine.

The numbers of hospitals not cooperating are believed to be 100 or so. Vaccination of health-care workers, doctors, and nurses is voluntary and therefore spotty instead of uniform.

2007   American soldier vaccinated for smallpox three weeks before shipping out to Iraq returns home to visit his family. His two-year-old son, two weeks later, develops a severe and dangerous skin infection caused by vaccinia virus. Critically ill, the child spends seven weeks in the hospital and is successfully treated with new anti-smallpox viral therapy. Soldier's wife also ill from smallpox, has a mild case, and recovers.

What are the data for large populations on the risk of introducing infection from health-care workers? The best statistics indicate that from the years 1907 up to 1970, a total of eighty-five children and adults were infected by viruses originating from health-care workers due to shedding virus. Nine died, with the highest risk being to hospitalized children. In recent analysis of over 11 million Americans vaccinated for the first time in 1963 and 1968, John Neff (*Journal of the American Medical Association*, 2002) found that for every hundred thousand individuals vaccinated for the first time, smallpox spread by contact from two to six others who were not vaccinated. Of these, one or two became ill with fever and rash but recovered.

The current dilemma about smallpox vaccination is profound, and knowledgeable decisions about compliance are urgently required. Head of the Institute of Allergy and Infectious Disease at the National Institutes of Health, Dr. Anthony Fauci, has written an important and provocative paper titled "*Smallpox Vaccination Policy: Need for Dialogue*" (*New England Journal of Medicine*, Vol. 346, pp. 1319–1320, 2002). D. A. Henderson, the leader of the WHO's successful and spectacular campaign that led to the worldwide eradication of smallpox, initially fought for the removal of all smallpox virus stocks and total elimination of the virus. However, with the knowledge of a secret Russian smallpox bioterror program, the failure to account for the missing Russian scientists who worked on the smallpox research program, and coupled with the terrorist attacks of September 11, 2001, Henderson has now spoken out in favor of universal vaccination, a 180 degree turnaround for him. Henderson, as a scientific advisor to President Bush, and his colleagues have also written recent position papers that support smallpox vaccination, "*Smallpox Vaccination: A Review, Part I. Background, Vaccination Technique,*

Normal Vaccination and Revaccination, and Expected Results" and *"Smallpox Vaccination: A Review, Part II. Adverse Effects on Clinical Infectious Diseases"* in *Clinical Infectious Diseases,* Vol. 37, pp. 241–271, 2003, that, along with Fauci's article, should be required reading for everyone. Similarly, on the web anyone can access information to more intelligently reach a decision about vaccination. Specifically:

http://www.bt.cdc.gov/agent/agentlist.asp (bioterrorism agents/ diseases);

http://www.cdc.gov/mmwr/preview/mmwrhtml/rr5207a1.htm (recommendations for using smallpox vaccine: pre-event vaccination program).

The chance that a smallpox carrier will come into contact with and infect others depends on the geographic compactness and susceptibility of the population at risk. The same factors impact the magnitude and quickness of the infection's spread. Because each city, country, and village varies in size and the population's resistance to infection, estimating the likely spread of infection and the degree of vaccine coverage required for vaccination also varies. Initially the WHO sought 100 percent smallpox immunization but then settled for 80 percent coverage. Although 80 percent coverage allowed some smallpox infections to slip through, that lower percentage of vaccination combined with containment and surveillance procedures stopped the spread of smallpox.

To better evaluate the effectiveness of vaccination in preventing the spread of smallpox, epidemiologists have studied secondary infection rates; that is, in a single household with an index case (initial carrier) infected with the disease, the rate of spread to other members of that household is compared for differences among those who are or are not vaccinated. Despite some fluctuation based on the variable susceptibilities of family members and the amount of smallpox shed by the infected index case, on average 58 percent of unvaccinated subjects develop the disease compared to only 4 percent of those vaccinated (57). Further, examples of a worse-case scenario are the last known victim of natural smallpox infection (not in a laboratory), the unvaccinated cook, Ali Maow Maalin, who was exposed to the disease for only a few minutes while directing a vehicle transporting two patients with active smallpox from the hospital in Merea, Somalia, to the home of the local smallpox surveillance team leader (49). Similarly, in Meschede, Germany, a person who had never come in direct contact with a smallpox-infected patient contracted the disease after briefly visiting elsewhere in the hospital, probably from transient exposure to the airborne virus (48,49). Both episodes exemplify how extremely infectious smallpox can be.

Weighing all the options, as for my own opinion, I would prefer that my children and grandchildren receive primary smallpox vaccination now.

5

Yellow Fever

Yellow fever, after a seventy-two-year absence from North America, returned to the United States at Knoxville, Tennessee, in 1996 (1). Also called yellow jack or the yellow plague, yellow fever has the distinction of being one of the most devastating and feared diseases throughout the Americas in the eighteenth and nineteenth centuries. The 17D yellow fever vaccine developed in the mid-1930s miraculously controlled but did not eliminate this menace, so the potential for its return still exists as long as the disease-bearing mosquito remains alive to transmit the infection from humans or primates to susceptible victims.

In July 1996, a forty-five-year-old Tennessean vacationed in Brazil but had neglected to receive the mandatory vaccination for yellow fever required for traveling to an area where the infection abounds. During a nine-day fishing trip on the Amazon and Rio Negro rivers, he was bitten by a mosquito carrying the yellow fever virus. He incubated the infection and, upon returning to Knoxville, developed fever and chills. His health deteriorated; he vomited blood and soon died. Ninety-eight years earlier, the city of Memphis was devastated as a direct result of the yellow fever virus in Kate Bionda's blood that set off an epidemic in 1878, as described below. The *Aedes aegypti* mosquito was loose in Knoxville after traveling there from Brazil aboard a fisherman in 1996 as it had been in Memphis in 1878. But unlike that earlier plague when thousands died, no other yellow fever infections developed in Knoxville. However, during

1996, 254 cases of yellow fever resulted in 103 deaths in South America, including Brazil, where the virus is endemic, where the mosquito vector dwells, and where the Tennessee traveler was infected. The World Health Organization estimates (2) that 200,000 humans host this infection each year, primarily in Africa, and 30,000 of them die. Yellow fever continues to cause infections and deaths, and with increased airplane travel to exotic places, remains a threat to reappear anywhere in the world. Indeed, in 1999 and 2002, two other fatal cases of yellow fever occurred in California (3,4). Two travelers, one returning from a holiday in Venezuela and the other from a fishing trip on the Rio Negro in Brazil, both neglected to obtain the required yellow fever vaccine. This chapter tells their stories, the history of yellow fever, the role it played in shaping slavery in the United States, and its part in the country's westward expansion.

Yellow fever was an endemic disease of West Africa that traveled to the New World (5) and elsewhere aboard trading ships with their cargoes of slaves. Recent genetic analysis of nucleic acids from 133 samples of yellow fever virus taken from twenty-two countries over the last seventy-six years indicates that the virus reached South America 300 to 400 years ago, likely via ships carrying slaves. Yellow fever is an RNA virus, and analysis of RNA sequences revealed that the original (5) South American virus isolates were most closely related to Western African strains, West Africa being the location of ports for shipping slaves, and later to Eastern African viral strains. Further, these viruses could be traced back to an ancestral strain that existed in Africa for the past 1500 years (5). The black African peoples, although easily infected, nevertheless withstood the effects in that fewer died from the infection than did Caucasians, Native Americans, or Asians. Ironically, as smallpox and measles devastated natives along the Caribbean coast and islands, growing numbers of African slaves were brought to replace those plantation laborers. When the value of Africans over natives became apparent, by virtue of the blacks' resistance to yellow fever, the importation of these Africans increased still further (6,7). Thus, the yellow fever virus ventured into the Americas as human cargo along with the *Aedes aegypti* mosquito carried in the bilges and buckets of vessels sailing from Africa to the New World as slave transports.

Because it was so lethal to susceptible humans, yellow fever actually disrupted exploration into the Caribbean. In fact, American expansion became possible only after a team led by Walter Reed arrived in Cuba to combat the disease and prove it was transmitted by the *Aedes aegypti* mosquito. In 1901, a campaign was launched to eliminate yellow fever from Havana by attacking mosquito breeding places, a plan that proved effective. Finally, in 1937, a successful vaccine was developed.

From the sixteenth to the early twentieth century, yellow fever remained a dread and mysterious disease of unknown cause. Not even imagined hundreds of years ago was the possibility that the *Aedes aegypti* mosquito dwelling in the jungles of West Africa carried the yellow fever virus as part of a monkey-to-mosquito cycle. When humans penetrated into areas traveled by infected monkeys, the disease was then transmitted via infected female mosquitoes. The insects live only about 70 to 160 days, although maximal survival of 225 days has been reported, and the flight range of the insect is less than 300 meters. The mosquito lays its eggs in still water, a breeding habitat that includes water-filled cans, bottles, urns, and crevices (8,9). Consequently, the mosquito is an excellent traveler on boats and migrated successfully from West Africa to the Caribbean by that means. Because yellow fever was unknown in pre-Columbian America, and Native Americans showed the same susceptibility as the colonists, along with the epidemiologic evidence from molecular analysis (5) stated above, it is safe to assume that the disease arrived here along with transoceanic shipping (10,11). The disease was first recorded in 1648 in the Yucatan and Havana as an abrupt and short-lived fever lasting three to four days followed by a brief remission stage and then a second feverish stage when jaundice or yellowing appeared. Because liver injury associated with infection disrupted normal clotting of blood, many patients bled from nose and gums and frequently vomited blood (black vomit). Most of these victims died within eight days of the fever's reappearance.

As trade by ocean-going vessels continued, yellow fever struck Brazil in 1686, Martinique in 1690, Cadiz, Spain, in 1730, and later Marseilles, France, and the port of Swansea (1878) in Wales. Knowing that victims of yellow fever must be isolated from other patients and the general population, the staff of Greenwich Hospital in England dressed the segregated patients in jackets with yellow patches to forewarn others about the contagion. They were nicknamed "Yellow Jackets," and a yellow-colored flag that flew over the quarantined area was referred to as the "Yellow Jack."

Outbreaks in North American port cities included those in New York and Philadelphia. In the Philadelphia epidemic of 1793, some

4,044 individuals (over 10 percent) among the city's population of less than 40,000 perished in four months (12–15). Most likely the source was mosquitoes in water barrels aboard ships that transported French refugees fleeing the yellow fever scourge of 1792–99 in Santo Domingo, Haiti, and the West Indies (12,13,15).

In 1793 Philadelphia was America's capital. George Washington, John Adams, Thomas Jefferson, Alexander Hamilton, and John Knox witnessed the yellow fever plague and watched as it shut down the U.S. government. In July, one ship, then another, then fleets flocked in from Santo Domingo and the West Indies discharging hordes of refugees, white and black. Hungry and sickly, they poured into Philadelphia bringing news of the ongoing revolution in the islands. They told of the carnage, slaughter, destruction of plantations, and pestilent fever raging throughout the islands, and the agony of fevers on board the ships.

During that summer heavy rains descended on Philadelphia and produced a great increase of mosquitoes, a nuisance to those living in the city. Denny's Lodging House on North Water Street was a favorite place of residence for sailors and new arrivals; several from Santo Domingo and the other Caribbean islands found their way there upon arriving in Philadelphia (15). Two French sailors had taken a room at Denny's, and one was soon stricken with fever and died. Several days later the second sailor died. Two other boarders at Denny's died shortly thereafter, and many others in the city became feverish then perished. The fever had begun to spread. Stories told of a victim's "wretched state without a pulse, with cold clammy hands and his face a yellow color," of his "great distress, feverish, with yellow color on his skin, nauseated, throwing-up black vomit and given to nose-bleeds."

When a quarantine was ordered but failed to stop the yellow fever, the authorities decided that the disease was not imported. Instead, they asserted that local conditions of rotting coffee by the wharf and garbage in the streets caused putrid air that transmitted the disease (15,16). Dr. Benjamin Rush, one of the leading physicians of the time advised everyone who could to leave the city, to travel into the countryside where the air was clear (16): "There is only one way to prevent the disease—fly from it."

Philadelphia had suffered a previous yellow fever plague in 1762, when a hundred had died, but now thousands were dying. Thomas Jefferson wrote from Philadelphia to James Madison in Virginia, telling about the fever, how everyone who could was fleeing, and how one of every three stricken had died. Alexander Hamilton, the Secretary of the Treasury, came down with the fever. He left town, but when he was refused entry to New York City, he turned to upstate New York, to the home of his wife's father in Green Bush near Albany. There he and his wife were obliged to stay under armed guard until their clothing and baggage had been burned, their servants and carriage disinfected.

Clerks in departments of the federal government could not be kept at their desks. In the Treasury Department, six clerks got yellow fever and five others fled to New York; three sickened in the post office and seven officers in the customs service. Government papers were locked up in closed houses when the clerks left. By September, the American government came to a standstill. George Washington left for Mount Vernon:

> It was my wish to continue there longer—but as Mrs. Washington was unwilling to leave me surrounded by the malignant fever—I could not think of hazarding her and the children any longer by my continuance in the city—the house in which we lived being, in a manner, blockaded by the disorder and was becoming every day more and more fatal.

Washington recommended removing the clerks and the entire War Office out of Philadelphia. Washington, Jefferson, Hamilton, and Secretary of War Knox all left.

Philip Freneau wrote in 1793 in Philadelphia:

PESTILENCE
Written During the Prevalence of a Yellow Fever

Hot, dry winds forever blowing,
Dead men to the grave-yards going:
> *Constant hearses,*
> *Funeral verses;*
Oh! what plagues—there is no knowing!
Priests retreating from their pulpits!—
Some in hot, and some in cold fits
> *In bad temper,*
> *Off they scamper,*
Leaving us—unhappy culprits!
Doctors raving and disputing,
Death's pale army still recruiting—
> *What a pother*
> *One with t'other!*

Some a-writing, some a-shooting.
Nature's poisons here collected,
Water, earth, and air infected—
O, what pity,
Such a city,
Was in such a place erected!

The cause of yellow fever, a virus, would not be discovered until 100 years later in Cuba, and the route of transmission (mosquito as the vector) would not be implicated until eight years after that discovery. These plagues in New York and Philadelphia were limited primarily to the summer because *Aedes aegypti* mosquitoes prefer warm, tropical climates and do not survive in the frost. So it was throughout the tropics in and around the Caribbean, Central and Latin America, and the southern United States that the mosquito flourished and caused repeated epidemics. These outbreaks could be dramatic, as on the island of Santo Domingo, where in three months of 1793 over 44 percent of British soldiers forming the forty-first Foot Regiment and twenty-third Guard died. Refugees from such attacks who incubated the virus as they fled to cities of North America and Europe continued to spread the disease when they came in contact with the carrier mosquitoes.

Most black Africans and their descendants respond to yellow fever infection with mild to moderate symptoms such as headache, fever, nausea, and vomiting, and then recover in a few days. This outcome reflects the long relationship between the virus and its indigenous hosts, who through generations of exposure to the virus have evolved resistance. In some victims, the fever is more pronounced, rising to 104°F, along with generalized joint pains and bleeding. Still, even these patients recover within a few days. In contrast, among Caucasians and Native Americans, the disease assumes epidemic proportions and unfolds in a severe, three-stage course. During the first stage, an infection with fever of 102°F to 105°F lasts three to four days, during which the patient is infectious. Headache, back and muscle pain, nausea, and vomiting are severe. Thereafter, a remission stage without fever, or a period of calm ensues, sometimes lasting for just a few hours as the temperature falls to 99°F–100°F; the headache disappears, and the patient feels better. Then the third stage occurs. The temperature rapidly rises again, and symptoms present in the first stage recur but in more severe form, as the patient becomes increasingly agitated and anxious. Liver, heart, and/or

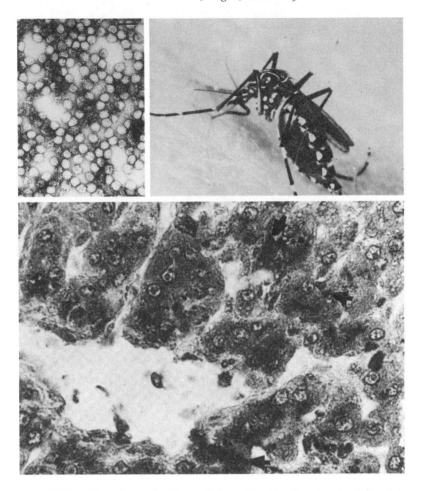

FIGURE 5.1 *Photomicrograph of the morphology of the yellow fever virus (top left) and the vector, the* Aedes aegypti *mosquito (top right). The virion particles are morphologically indistinct except that they are compact and relatively homogeneous in size. Bar, 100 μm. Electron micrograph from E. L. Palmer and M. L. Martin,* An Atlas of Mammalian Viruses *(1982), courtesy of CRC Press, Inc., Boca Raton, FL. (bottom). Liver destruction of a patient who died from yellow fever virus infection. The arrows point to deposits of yellow fever virus antigen. This picture courtesy of* Fields' Virology *(Philadelphia: Lippincott-Raven, 1996).*

renal failure follow, which leads to delirium. Jaundice, or yellowing of the skin, develops at about the fourth or fifth day during this third stage of disease. Within six to seven days, death frequently follows. Those who survive remain ill, usually for another seventeen to thirty days. Thereafter, recovery is slow and marked by intense fatigue.

Imagine this setting at a time when Napoleon had plans for an American empire. His base was French-controlled areas in the Caribbean, parts of Central America, Mexico, New Orleans, and the North American Midwest extending to Canada. Haiti, colonized by the French, was run by African labor. In 1801, a rebellion of this work force headed by the black leader Toussaint Louverture caused Napoleon to counter with a military expedition under his brother-in-law, General LeClerc (17). But within a few months after this force arrived in Santo Domingo, yellow fever destroyed over 27,000 of the veteran French troops, including LeClerc, leaving but few survivors. The disease had little effect on the black troops under Louverture. The results of this French defeat were twofold. First, Haiti gained its freedom from France. Second, Napoleon's ambitions in the New World dissolved. Disenchanted with his American venture, he decided to sell the Louisiana Territory to the United States (17). This act changed the destiny of the New World, since removal of the French influence allowed American growth westward and eliminated potential agitation between the two countries over land that America would have fought to acquire. Napoleon then redirected his empire building toward new efforts on Malta and in Egypt.

Unlike the sporadic record keeping for early smallpox and measles epidemics, the events of yellow fever epidemics in the nineteenth century are relatively clear because of the careful documentation and the rapid communication available. The spread of yellow fever and the devastation and fear it brought were portrayed by word of mouth and newspapers as this disease rampaged along the Mississippi and into Memphis, Tennessee, in the dark year of 1878. Just before the American Civil War in 1861, Memphis had a population of 22,000, which rose to 48,000 by 1878. In a few months, this vibrant and expanding town found its population reduced by over one-half from the devastation and deaths caused by yellow fever (18,19).

According to eyewitnesses of that time, Memphis was the hub of one of the world's major cotton-producing regions. It was located on America's major trade routes—the Mississippi River and three railroad lines. Its citizens were old-stock Southern whites, newly freed African

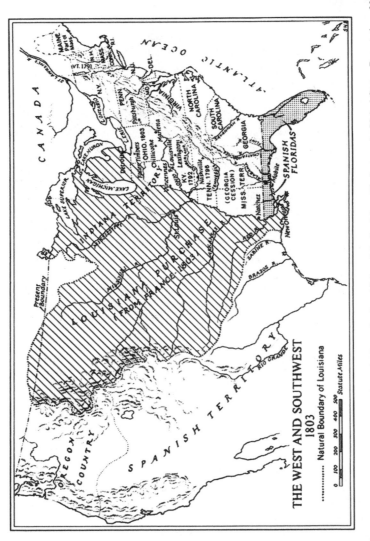

THE WEST AND SOUTHWEST
1803
·········· Natural Boundary of Louisiana

0 100 200 300 400 500
Statute Miles

FIGURE 5.2 *The effect of yellow fever on history is shown by the addition of the Louisiana Territory to the United States. Devastation of Napoleon's troops in Haiti from yellow fever and the need to focus his resources on the Egyptian campaign and wars against England led to the sale of this territory to the U.S. government in 1803 under the direction of Thomas Jefferson.*

Americans, and immigrants mainly from Ireland but also from Germany, France, Italy, and China. None living in Memphis at that time or elsewhere in the world knew that insects could transmit disease. But the *Aedes aegypti* mosquito lurked everywhere up and down the Mississippi River. All that was missing was a person whose blood contained the yellow fever virus. Once the mosquitoes bit an infected human and ingested that infected blood, the insects became carriers, or vectors, of the disease whose subsequent bites infected every susceptible individual contacted. Thus, the spread of disease began. The event and its progress were recorded in the Memphis *Daily Appeal* by J. M. Keating, its editor, who stayed in Memphis throughout the ordeal and published his recollections (20).

Mrs. Kate Bionda of Memphis and her husband ran a small restaurant/snack house located in Front Row along the great Mississippi River, where their main trade was catering food and drink to riverboat men. Mosquitoes were nuisances, especially during this summer of 1878. In late July, cases of yellow fever were noted in New Orleans. The *Daily Appeal* reported on July 24th:

> We learn from New Orleans that 24 people have died of yellow fever there in the past few days. We need not fear in Memphis. We were never in as good a condition from the sanitary point of view. Our streets and alleys were never as clean, and strict attention is now being paid to the enforcement of sanitary regulations on private premises. Nothing in our atmosphere invites that dread disease. There are no grounds for alarm on the part of our people. The yellow fever is not indigenous to our latitude and unless imported there is no reason to fear it. It cannot be imported as long as our sanitary laws are enforced.

Nevertheless, public apprehension increased on August 6 when the press carried news of a New Orleans steamboat hand's death from yellow fever at the quarantine hospital on President's Island. The victim, William Warren, had slipped into Memphis, stopped at the Bionda's restaurant on the night of August 1, and had become sick on August 2. He was admitted to the city hospital, where his illness was diagnosed as yellow fever, and then moved to the quarantine hospital where he died on August 5. A few days later, Mrs. Bionda, age thirty-four, became ill, and she died on August 13. On the basis of her clinical course including jaundice, her physician diagnosed her condition as the first case of yellow fever in Memphis in 1878.

Yellow fever was no stranger to people living along the Mississippi River or in the Mississippi Valley. But, as yet, Memphis had not suffered anything like the great New Orleans epidemic of 1853 that killed 9,000 persons. However, yellow fever had visited Memphis before—killing 75 people in 1855, 250 in 1867, and 2,000 in 1873—so the citizenry knew that the attacks were growing worse as the city grew. Even so, the greatest fear of yellow fever came from the unknown—how it came about, how it spread. Yellow fever was as mysterious to nineteenth century people everywhere, including Memphis, as were the great plagues of the Middle Ages to its populations. What was known about yellow fever was that it could spread relatively easily from city to city and that quarantine of incoming goods or people from yellow fever-infected areas limited or prevented the spread of disease.

The practice of quarantine presumably began in 1374, first in the Venetian Republic, later in the Republic of Dubrovnik, and then in Milan. Quarantine was derived from the Italian word *quaranta*, or forty, and indicated the number of days allotted for isolation. Its purpose then, as now, was to isolate people from infected places and sufferers, especially during the bubonic plague. The penalty for breaking of quarantine was frequently death. In 1383, Marseilles practiced quarantines regularly, setting a limit of forty days, and by the fifteenth century most European countries had detention stations to confine the infected.

But yellow fever, unlike the plagues of smallpox or measles, did not spread from person to person by contact. Yet the authorities understood that people fleeing from a community where yellow fever struck could in some unexplained way spread the disease to the place where they sought asylum. Thus, cities attempted to prevent entry by escapees from disease centers and prohibited their inhabitants from entering affected areas.

The tracking of yellow fever in the American South of 1878 began in late spring and early summer when the disease was reported in the West Indies, an area involved in trade with cities along the Mississippi River. The possibility of another epidemic like the one of 1873 grew in the minds of some Memphis citizenry, especially physicians and health board members, who argued vigorously for quarantine measures before the city council. But business interests on the council rejected quarantine for fear of disrupting their lucrative trade. As a result, the president of the Board of Health, Dr. R. W. Mitchell, resigned in protest. The quarantine debate continued as yellow fever spread closer, first reported in cities along the West Indies and then by July 26 in New Orleans roughly 500 miles away from Memphis. With outbreaks in New Orleans on July 26, and in Vicksburg, only 240 miles away, on July 27, Memphis finally established quarantine stations for goods and travelers from those cities. But would quarantine or any man-made edicts work? Fear and rumor spread through Memphis and multiplied when, on August 5, a man taken from a riverboat and hospitalized in Memphis was diagnosed as having yellow fever. By August 9, yellow fever was on the march as reports from the city of Grenada, just ninety miles South of Memphis, announced attacks. The news spread quickly by word of mouth. Memphis newspapers tried to calm an increasingly agitated public:

> The public may rely upon it that whenever yellow fever shows itself, as is not likely, the Board of Health through the press of the city will promptly report it. Keep cool! Avoid patent medicines and bad whiskey! Go about your business as usual; be cheerful and laugh as much as possible (20–22).

The advice was not easy to take. Although some calm returned to the city, residents began to leave Memphis, and others considered the possibility of doing so or began making preparations, just in case. By this time Mrs. Bionda was dying from yellow fever. On August 14, the day after she died, fifty-five additional cases were announced; by August 15 and 16, a full panic was under way. By foot, by railroad, by horse, by wagon, thousands of people began to leave: "On any road leading out of Memphis was a procession of wagons piled high with beds, trunks, small furniture, carrying also women and children. Beside walked men, some riotous, with the wild excitement, others moody and silent from anxiety and dread" (23).

Railroad companies attached extra cars, but these were not enough for all the people trying to push inside. Civic institutions collapsed. As city councilmen and aldermen fled, the city council was unable to assemble a quorum. One-third of the police force deserted. The fear of refugees evacuating Memphis mimicked the emotions of refugees fleeing advancing German armies during the Second World War in Europe. They ran from the unknown, from death. By four days after Mrs. Bionda's death, over half the population of Memphis, more than 25,000 locals, had fled to small towns along the Mississippi River, to Virginia, East Tennessee, St. Louis, Cincinnati, Louisville, and elsewhere.

Bitter experiences met some of these refugees. Towns along their route established quarantines against those coming from Memphis. Citizens enforced barricades with rifles and shotguns. Officials in Little Rock,

Arkansas, refused to let railroad trains from Memphis near their city. Others fleeing on riverboats, like the steamship *John D. Porter*, traveled up the Mississippi but were forced to stay on board for two months as port after port refused them permission to land, akin to the cursed *Flying Dutchman*, which was condemned to roam the seas eternally.

Many of the refugees did carry yellow fever and entered areas where the *Aedes aegypti* mosquito lived, thereby continuing the spread of disease along the Mississippi. Over 100 of those fleeing from Memphis died outside the city. But what about the 20,000 who remained in Memphis? Of these citizens, roughly 14,000 were African Americans and 6,000 were whites (23). Terror-stricken, they awaited their unknown fate, aware that the mysterious disease would rage until the frost came in late October. The question was: could they stay alive for the remaining forty-five or so days?

The epidemic struck with frightening swiftness and severity. Within a week of Kate Bionda's death, thousands were sick. As recorded by a minister in attendance, "weeks of suffering before us . . . numbers dying for want of attention which we are powerless to give . . . . God help us." At least 200 people died per day through the first half of September. Eleven weeks after the initial case, there were 17,000 cases, 5,000 of which were fatal (23).

During these harrowing weeks, the city was tomblike. Few ventured into the street; all commercial activity stopped. Robert Blakeslee, a New Yorker who came to Memphis by train to help fight the disease, described for the *New York Herald* the following interview on walking from the railroad depot:

> The city was almost deserted. . . . We had not gone far, however, before the evidence of the terrible condition of things became apparent. The first thing in the shape of a vehicle that I saw was a truck, loaded with coffins, going around to collect the dead. As this was within four blocks of the depot you may imagine how soon I came to a realizing sense of the desolation. Two blocks further on, coffins were piled in tiers on the sidewalk in front of the undertaker's shop, and we were compelled to walk between them. . . . Everyone was thoroughly frightened, a young doctor said to me. "It takes a man of great moral courage to stay in this place. You talk with a man tonight and tomorrow hear that he is in the grave."

The summer of 1878 was hot and wet. Accordingly, the 1878 attack of yellow fever was so virulent that those physicians who had witnessed the epidemic five years earlier thought they were confronted by a new, deadlier strain of yellow fever. In this assessment they were likely correct. Even the African Americans, usually resistant to yellow fever, also succumbed as never before, with over 11,000 infected, or 77 percent of their population in Memphis. Their illness was generally more severe than in previous epidemics, and their mortality was considerably higher at 10 percent, although much lower than the 70 percent death rate among Caucasians (of the 6,000 who remained, more than 4,000 died).

Many victims of this plague died alone covered with the black vomit characteristic of the disease. Whole families were wiped out. For example, Mrs. Barbara Flack, a widow, and all her seven children, from twenty-eight to three years of age, were killed. A nun helping in the care of the sick noted:

> Carts with 8 to 9 corpses in rough boxes are ordinary sights. I saw a nurse stop one day and ask for a certain man's residence. . . . The Negro driver just pointed over his shoulder with his whip at the heap of coffins behind him and answered, "I've got him here in this coffin" (22).

The Surgeon General, Dr. John M. Woodworth of the U.S. Marine Hospital, reported, "Scenes enacted here during the height of the epidemic would seem more appropriate to the domain of sensational fiction than to the serious pages of a medical journal; but the facts come under my own observation."

Doctors had enormous loads of patients and were mentally and physically exhausted. One wrote, "I wish I could go to some secret spot where there would be no burning heads and hands to feel, nor pulses to count, for the next six weeks. It is fever, fever all day long and I am weary. . . . I do not know what to think or do . . . . Nothing but distress and death on all sides" (24).

In an attempt to understand the cause of this disease and how to treat it, physicians performed about 300 autopsies. But afterward, they knew little more than they had before: "We can write and talk learnedly of epidemics and other forms of disease but when in the midst of a visitation . . . we are so overwhelmed with our impotence, and the unsatisfactory result of treatment" (25).

Yellow fever did not seem to be directly transmitted by person-to-person contact or by food or drinking water. Although germs were the suspected cause, attempts to demonstrate the agent had failed. Was yellow fever spread by inhalation of infected air? What were the conditions, so far unidentified, that allowed the disease to spread? What were the local sites where this disease occurred, and why was there an association with a warm climate? These questions had no answers in 1878.

The Memphis telegraph office kept lines open to other parts of the nation. Informed of the plight, states in the North, South, East, and West quickly sent supplies and funds. Then yellow fever struck those in the telegraph office as well. Of the thirty-three men in the Memphis office, nineteen died.

With the frosts of October 18 and 19, and a simultaneous decrease in the mosquito population, the rate of yellow fever infection dropped rapidly. The epidemic was declared over on October 29. Refugees came home to seek the graves of lost friends and relatives. On Thanksgiving

FIGURE 5.3 *The conquerors of yellow fever. (Left) A painting of Carlos Finlay with the members of the Yellow Fever Commission, Walter Reed, James Carroll, Jesse Lazear (all in uniform), and Aristides Agramonte (not shown). Both Carroll and Lazear were to become infected by yellow fever, with Lazear dying from the disease. (Right) Max Theiler, who developed the 17D yellow fever strain vaccine that conquered the epidemic form of the disease. Photo of Max Theiler courtesy of the National Library of Medicine.*

day, the city of Memphis held a mass meeting to praise the heroes of the epidemic, to thank the rest of the nation for its help in sending assistance, and to mourn the dead. There were fewer than 20,000 who remained in the city, and of these over 17,000 had gotten yellow fever. Of the 14,000 African Americans, roughly 11,000 got the fever and 1,946 died. Of the 6,000 Caucasians, nearly all got yellow fever and 4,204 died. Although the epidemic of 1878 hit Memphis most severely, throughout the Mississippi Valley over 100,000 had the fever from which 20,000 died (25).

In the fight to control and prevent yellow fever, several groups of microbe hunters stand out. The first group, represented by Dr. John Erskine, serves to memorialize those health-care workers who gave their lives caring for infected patients. There were 111 known physicians in Memphis, of which seventy-two came from other states in the country. All were fully aware of the risks involved, but they were determined to stay. Most had not had yellow fever before and so had no immunity to the disease. More than 60 percent gave their lives caring for patients during this epidemic. The second group comprised Jesse Lazear, James Carroll, Aristides Agramonte, and Walter Reed of the U.S. Army Yellow Fever Commission, who were appointed in 1900 and led by Reed. Within this group, Lazear, Carroll, and Agramonte risked their lives by self-experimentation, documenting that yellow fever was a transmissible agent passed by the *Aedes aegypti* mosquito from patient to patient. The third group was characterized by Max Theiler, who successfully attenuated the yellow fever virus and developed a strain (17D) used for the vaccinations that prevent this disease.

John Erskine was born in Huntsville, Alabama, in 1834 and became a Memphis Health Officer. At the height of the plague, when the city was one of silence and death, Erskine's fearlessness, his abundant energy, and his tireless work to treat victims were noted by his contemporaries. During those weeks when only doctors, nurses, relief workers, undertakers, and grave diggers were active, he was considered a model of the best medical professionals. A graduate of New York University Medical School in 1858 and a Confederate surgeon during the American Civil War, he returned to Memphis in 1865 and played an active role in the yellow fever epidemics of 1867, '73, and '78. He was chosen Health Officer of the city in 1873, '76, and '78. It was in his capacity as Health Officer in 1878, while treating sufferers of yellow fever, that he became infected and died. In spite of the raging plague, fifty leading citizens united and provided a tribute to his memory (18,23). Simultaneously, local and national newspapers eulogized him and his work. In 1974, the city of Memphis named one of its libraries for him and filled its shelves with accounts of the city's health disasters and triumphs. In 1990, St. Jude's Hospital in Memphis and the city of Memphis established an annual lectureship in his honor. I had the privilege of being the recipient of that award in 1993.

Twenty years after the death of John Erskine, during the last years of the nineteenth century, Reed, Lazear, Carroll, and Agramonte, under the auspices of the U.S. Yellow Fever Commission, performed experiments on human volunteers in Havana to identify the source of yellow fever (26–30). Their results demonstrated clearly that the blood of patients with yellow fever was infectious during the first three days of fever, that *Aedes aegypti* mosquitoes feeding on that blood by biting the patient during those three days could then transmit the infection after an interval of about twelve days, and that the infectious agent in the blood's serum fraction passed through a Berkefeld filter, indicating it was a virus, not a bacterium. These experiments also proved that yellow fever was not transmitted by fomites (inanimate objects or materials capable of conveying disease-producing agents) and that disinfection of clothes and bedding was unnecessary because this disease was not passed by patient-to-patient contact. From this work, Walter Reed and his coworkers are credited with establishing that the agent of yellow fever is a virus. Mosquitoes ingest the viruses when they bite and draw blood from an infected human and then, after a lag period, expel these viruses into the blood of new victims while biting them.

Walter Reed was born in 1851 in rural Belroi, Virginia, where his father was a Methodist minister. At the age of seventeen, he became the youngest graduate of the University of Virginia Medical School. He continued his medical education at the Bellevue Medical School (now New York University Medical School) from which he received his medical degree. After several years of work in various New York hospitals, he joined the U.S. Army and was commissioned in 1875 as an Assistant Surgeon. After the next fifteen years spent at various Army posts, he took a sabbatical leave and went to the newly established Johns Hopkins Medical School in Baltimore. During that time, Reed became acquainted with William Osler, considered the most illustrious physician in North America, and trained in pathology and bacteriology with William Welsh. Welsh had earlier studied in the newly emerging bacteriology laboratories in Europe established in response to the observations of Koch and Pasteur. In 1893, Reed was appointed curator of the Army Medical Museum and also Professor of Bacteriology at the recently established Army Medical School.

In stark contrast to Reed, James Carroll was a free spirit who described himself as a "wandering good-for-nothing." He was born in England and left at age fifteen for Canada. There he lived as a backwoodsman until enlisting in the U.S. Army. He decided to become a physician while serving as a hospital orderly at Fort Custer, Montana. With encouragement from Reed, he studied initially at Bellevue Medical College in New York and received his medical degree from the University of Maryland School of Medicine in Baltimore. He then also trained in bacteriology and pathology at the Johns Hopkins Hospital with William Welsh. In 1897, Carroll became Reed's laboratory assistant. In this same year, at the urging of George Sternberg, then Surgeon General of the Army Medical Corps, Reed formed and headed a Commission to do research on yellow fever, and Carroll became second in command.

The two civilian physicians, Jesse Lazear and Aristides Agramonte, attended Columbia University Medical School in New York but came from very different backgrounds. Jesse Lazear was born in 1866 to a wealthy family in Baltimore. Trained in art as well as medicine, he also traveled to Europe where he studied modern bacteriologic techniques. After receiving his medical degree in 1892, he became the first Chief of Clinical Laboratories at the Johns Hopkins Medical School and joined the Yellow Fever Commission in that position. He was described as "quiet, retiring, and modest." The other civilian physician was Aristides Agramonte. He was born in Cuba and brought to New York City as an infant after his father was killed in an abortive revolt to free Cuba from Spain. Described as "energetic and nosy," he worked as a bacteriologist for the New York City Health Department after obtaining his medical degree. He joined the Yellow Fever Commission as a civilian pathologist in charge of laboratories at Military Hospital #1 in Havana and was Chief Physician on the yellow fever ward.

Yellow fever was endemic in Cuba and thus endangered all countries with which Cuba traded. In 1898, with the outbreak of the Spanish-American War, yellow fever became a primary concern of the U.S. Army. Therefore, the Yellow Fever Commission was sent to Cuba in 1900. Interestingly, at that time, none of the four members had actually observed a case of yellow fever. Their first aim was to confirm or refute the claim that yellow fever was caused by a bacterium, namely *Bacillus icteroides*, as first proposed by Guiseppe Sanarelli, an Italian pathologist who injected the bacteria into five South American subjects of whom three died from jaundice. Although the conclusion that bacteria caused yellow fever brought Sanarelli notoriety and awards, the Yellow Fever Commission proved the idea untrue. The bacillus had simply been a contaminant, a passenger in patients with yellow fever; it was not the cause. The Commission then turned their investigation to the hypothesis of Carlos Finlay (31–33) that a mosquito was the transmitter of yellow fever.

Carlos Finlay, born in Camaguey, Cuba, was the son of Scottish and French parents. He entered the Jefferson Medical College in Philadelphia in 1853, a year in which yellow fever caused a troubling amount of disease in that city. This episode, in addition to the multiple cases occurring in Cuba, focused his interest and laid the foundation for his life's work in the investigation of yellow fever. He graduated from Jefferson Medical College in 1855 and, in 1857, began the practice of medicine in Havana. In 1881, Finlay formally presented his thesis, "The Mosquito Hypothetically Considered as the Agent of Yellow Fever" (31, 32). In that report, he concluded that, since yellow fever affected vascular endothelium, a blood-sucking insect might be an intermediate host responsible for transmission. He described three events necessary for the transmission of yellow fever:

> 1) The existence of a yellow fever patient into whose capillaries the mosquito was able to drive its stinger and impregnate it with virulent particles, at an appropriate stage of the disease. 2) That the life(cycle) of the mosquito be spared after it bites a yellow fever patient and so it has a chance of biting the patient in whom the disease is to be reproduced. 3) The coincidence that some of the persons whom the same mosquito happens to bite thereafter shall be susceptible of contracting the disease.

Consistent with other discoveries throughout the course of medicine and science, the concept that a mosquito causes yellow fever had earlier been suggested by many but proven by none. For example, in 1807 John Crawford of Baltimore published a paper stating that the mosquito was responsible for malaria, yellow fever, and other diseases, and in 1848 Joshua Nott from Mobile, Alabama, reiterated this concept. An interesting sideline is that Dr. Nott, in his function as an obstetrician, delivered William Gorgas, who in the 1900s would virtually eliminate the *Aedes aegypti* mosquito from Cuba and other areas throughout the Americas including the site where the Panama Canal was to be built. In 1853, Louis Beauperthuy, a French physician working in Venezuela, also incriminated the mosquito in spreading yellow fever and malaria. However, none of these physicians provided any experimental evidence to confirm the hypothesis. To the contrary, Finlay undertook realistic experimentation. First, he trapped wild mosquitoes and allowed them to bite yellow fever patients and then bite healthy individuals who had no previous history of yellow fever. However, the results were inconclusive. Although four of the five healthy individuals became feverish and mildly ill, classic yellow fever did not occur. Indeed, the Army Surgeon General, William Sternberg, one of the premiere microbiologists in North America and the organizer of the Yellow Fever Commission, totally rejected Finlay's experiments and the mosquito theory. Having worked directly with Finlay in Cuba during the first Yellow Fever Commission of the late 1870s, Sternberg respected the work of Finlay but believed that mosquitoes did not inject anything harmful into humans. Unfortunately, Sternberg's position of power was sufficient to dampen support for Finlay's hypothesis. Nevertheless, evidence was mounting that insects could indeed transmit disease to humans (33). In 1878, Patrick Manson found that a mosquito infected humans with the parasitic disease filariasis. Theobald Smith in 1892, along with Frederick Kilbourne, showed that ticks spread the parasitic disease of cattle called "Texas Fever." In 1894, Manson showed that the tsetse fly caused human sleeping sickness or trypanosomiasis, and in 1896, Ronald Ross of the British Army showed that mosquitoes transmitted malaria.

The Yellow Fever Commission members differed in their opinions as to whether the mosquito could cause yellow fever, with Lazear being the only one among the four who strongly believed so. No animal except man was known at that time to be susceptible to yellow fever. Therefore, to test the mosquito transmission hypothesis, members of the commission decided to engage in human experimentation. None were enthusiastic about taking the risk of catching yellow fever, but Carroll, Lazear, and Agramonte directly participated. Reed did not. To control these studies, they reared the mosquitoes from eggs provided by Carlos Finlay so as to rule out the mosquitoes' previous exposure to humans or to any human disease. In the first set of experiments, Lazear and eight other volunteers were bitten by mosquitoes almost immediately after they had bitten patients with yellow fever. As described by Agramonte:

> Each insect was contained in a glass tube covered by a wad of cotton, the same as is done with bacterial cultures. As the mouth of the culture is turned downwards, the insect usually flies towards the bottom of the tube (upwards), then the bottom is uncovered rapidly and the open mouth placed upon the forearm or abdomen of the patient; after a few minutes the mosquito drops upon the skin and if hungry will immediately start operations; when full, by gently shaking the tube the insect is made to fly upward again and the cotton plug replaced without difficulty.

None of the nine individuals came down with yellow fever.

Next, Carroll volunteered for experimentation: "I reminded Dr. Lazear that I was ready, and he at last applied to my arm an insect that had bitten a patient with a severe attack 12 days previously . . . . I was perfectly willing to take a soldier's chance." That night Carroll wrote Reed, who had returned to Washington, "I remarked jokingly, that if there were anything in the mosquito theory I should have a good dose, and so it happened."

Two days later Carroll experienced the earliest vague symptoms of yellow fever, and four days later the symptoms became severe, marked by weakness, chills, and a temperature of 102°F. No malaria parasites were found in the blood that came from Carroll, ruling out the possibility of malaria. Agramonte wrote:

> Not finding any malaria parasites, he (Carroll) told me he thought he had caught a cold at the beach; his suffused state, bloodshot eyes and general appearance in spite of his efforts at gaiety and unconcern, shocked me beyond words. Having yellow fever did not occur to him. Lazear and I were almost panic stricken when we realized that Carroll had yellow fever.

Carroll's life was in the balance. He was delirious with fever fluctuating between 103°F and 104°F, severe headache, back pain, swollen gums, and yellowing of his eyes and body. However, he did not bleed severely and within several days his temperature was normal.

The relief in Carroll's survival from yellow fever is dramatically recorded in the letter sent to him from Walter Reed, who was in Washington at the time of Lazear's and Carroll's illness:

Sept. 7, 1900
1:15 pm

My Dear Carroll:

Hip! Hip! Hurrah! God be praised for the news from Cuba today— "Carroll much improved—Prognosis very good!" I shall simply go out and get boiling drunk!

Really I can never recall such a sense of relief in all my life, as the news of your recovery give me! Further, too, would you believe it? The Typhoid Report is on its way to the Upper Office! Well, I'm damned if I don't get drunk twice!

God bless you, my boy.

Affectionately,

Reed

Come home as soon as you can and see your wife and babies.
Did the mosquito do it?

Carroll's attack left him so weak that two weeks later he could not stand or change position without assistance. However, Carroll had been in contact with yellow fever patients a few days immediately preceding his illness, so it was not clear whether the mosquito bite alone had caused the yellow fever or had been an incidental factor. For that reason, the next experiment was done on a volunteer who had no previous exposure to yellow fever, Private William H. Dean. On the day that Carroll became sick, Lazear applied to Dean's arm, in addition to three other mosquitoes, the same mosquito that had bitten Carroll, to provide the greatest chance of transmitting the disease. But Dean developed only a mild case of yellow fever. So, on September 13, 1890, Lazear let himself be bitten again. Five days later he began to feel ill. As the disease progressed, Lazear developed jaundice, vomited blood, and became delirious. Just twelve days after the experiment began, Jesse Lazear died.

James Carroll wrote, "I shall never forget the expression of his eyes when I last saw him alive on the third or fourth day of his illness."

Washington D.C.
September 26, 1900

My Dear Carroll:

Major Kean's cable, telling of poor Lazear's desperate condition, was quickly followed by the one announcing his death—I cannot begin to express my sorrow over this unhappy termination of our colleague's work!

I know that your own distress is just as acute as my own—He was a brave fellow and his loss is one that we can with difficulty fill. I got the General to cable yesterday about securing Lazear's notes which he wrote that he had taken in each case bitten by mosquitoes.—Examine them carefully and keep all.

I will leave here in the morning for New York—and will ask you to meet me with a conveyance at the foot of O'Reilly Street or at the Navy yard dock if you can find out from Quartermaster where passengers will land on the arrival of the Crook, which should be Wednesday, October 3.

If your observations are such as you and Lazear have intimated, we must publish a preliminary note as soon as it can be gotten ready.

Affectionately,

Reed

The evidence was now substantial. Yellow fever was transmitted by mosquitoes, and a lag time was required between the insect's acquisition of infected blood and biting of a susceptible individual to induce disease. This latter point accounted for the failure of Finlay's experiments and of Agramonte's first attempt to become infected. This time lag after the mosquito first feeds on the blood of a subject with the yellow fever virus is twelve to twenty days, during which the virus travels from the insect's gut to its salivary gland, a position where the virus is available to infect the next susceptible individual. This timing agrees with that observed by Henry Carter, a U.S. Public Health Service physician who in 1898 conducted epidemiologic studies of yellow fever in two Mississippi villages. He concluded that an extrinsic incubation period of approximately two weeks was required for the induction of new cases of yellow fever.

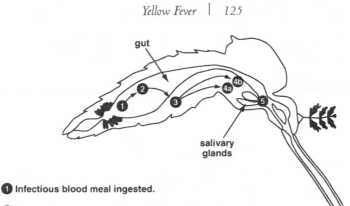

① Infectious blood meal ingested.

② Virus infects and multiplies in gut epithelial cells.

③ Virus released (escapes) from gut epithelial cells.

④ⓐ Virus infects salivary glands after secondary amplification in other cells/tissues.

④ⓑ Virus infects salivary glands without secondary amplification in other cells/tissues.

⑤ Virus released from salivary gland epithelial cells and is transmitted by feeding.

FIGURE 5.4 *Schematic of the lifecycle of the yellow fever virus in the mosquito.*

Thus, of the four Commission members who undertook the study of yellow fever in Cuba, one died and another barely survived. Their conclusion that the mosquito served as an intermediate host for the agent of yellow fever and that disease was propagated through the bite of this insect was not universally accepted, however. For example, the *Washington Post* on November 2, 1900, in publishing the mosquito hypothesis reported, "Of all the silly and nonsensical rigmarole of yellow fever that has yet found its way into print—and there has been enough of it to build a fleet—the silliest beyond compare is to be found in the arguments and theories generated by a mosquito hypothesis."

Shortly thereafter, on November 20, the Yellow Fever Commission members established another experimental camp in Cuba. Strict quarantine was enforced and experiments conducted only on subjects never previously exposed to yellow fever. Named Camp Lazear, the facility was created to include only residents who were judged to be susceptible to yellow fever and with no previous exposure to the disease. Of five volunteers tested, four contracted the disease, but all recovered. The one volunteer who did not get sick was bitten by a mosquito later found incapable of transmitting the infection. The irrefutable conclusion was: "The precision with which the infection of the individuals followed the bite of the mosquito left nothing to be desired."

To fulfill the exacting requirements of scientific experimentation, additional research was performed and clearly showed that yellow fever was not spread by human-to-human contact or through fomites but was transmitted by the injection of blood taken from infected patients into susceptible humans. Further, when the infectious blood was passed through a filter designed to retain bacteria, it still transmitted disease, indicating it was not bacterial in origin.

One consequence of these studies was that William Gorgas, Chief Sanitary Officer in Havana, introduced antimosquito measures that decreased the number of yellow fever cases in Havana from 1,400 in the year 1900 to none in 1902. The second consequence was the building of the Panama Canal. Results from the U.S. Yellow Fever Commission deserve much of the credit for preventing this disease in the large labor force needed to build a ship route across the tropical isthmus of Panama, joining the Atlantic and Pacific Oceans. The third and lasting consequence was that the days of ignorance, superstition, and controversy about yellow fever and its transmission were over.

The building of the Panama Canal was first conceived and undertaken by Ferdinand de Lesseps, born in 1805 into a family of wealth and national service (34,35). His interest in canal building is believed to have begun in Egypt in 1830. His drive to build two great ship canals through the isthmus of Suez and the isthmus of Panama was attributed more to his almost religious desire to achieve great events for France and the welfare of humanity than to any prospect of financial gain.

To undertake the challenge of building the Panama Canal (34–37), the Compagnie Universelle du Canal Interoceanique raised funds for the "La Grande Entreprise," the biggest financial venture ever attempted at the time. French engineers of the nineteenth century were an exceptional breed and took the task of building the canal as a matter of French pride and destiny. At the beginning of 1881, some 200 French or European engineers and about 800 laborers began making test moorings on the isthmus, also building barracks, hospitals, and roads. They actually began chopping a pathway across Panama. Lacking knowledge of the cause of yellow fever and the breeding habits of mosquitoes, they used large pots with stagnant water in gardens and under the legs of barracks and hospital beds to retard crawling ants. These water vessels provided an exceptionally good milieu for the breeding of mosquitoes. By the end of 1881, over 2,000 men were at work and the digging of the great trench began. In 1882, approximately 400 deaths were reported, and in the next year 1,300 from yellow fever and malaria. Approximately 200 laborers died each month. Reports of the death rate in Panama were so frightening that they were suppressed to assure French investors of the project's financial stability and to continue raising funds by bond issues for building the canal. However, reports began filtering back to France as sons who participated in the Panama challenge died there. Engineering schools soon began advising their graduates against going to Panama. Nevertheless, graduating engineers continued to answer the call for this grand adventure in Panama, "as officers hastened to the battlefield and not as cowards who flee from the sorrows of life." However, the project became more difficult and hazardous as unexpected earthquakes and landslides added to the deaths from yellow fever. For example in 1885, of seventeen newly graduated French engineers arriving in Panama, only one survived the first month.

To stem the rumors of death from yellow fever, Jules Dingler, in charge of the Panama Canal operation, brought his entire family to Panama. This move was designed to provide the best possible proof of the Director General's confidence in Panama. But within several months, his only daughter contracted yellow fever and died within a few days. His wife wrote to Charles de Lesseps:

> My poor husband is in despair which is painful to see—my first desire was to flee as far as possible and carry far from this murderous country those who are left to me. But my husband is a man of duty and tries to make me understand that his honor is the trust you have placed in him that he cannot fail in his task without failing himself. Our dear daughter was our pride and joy.

A month later Dingler's remaining child, a son of twenty-one, showed signs of yellow fever, and in three days he too was dead. Dingler wrote to de Lesseps:

> I cannot thank you enough for your kind and affectionate letter. Mme. Dingler who knows that she is for me the only source of affection in this world, controls herself with courage, but she is deeply shaken . . . . We attach ourselves to life in making the canal our only occupation; I say "we" because Mme. Dingler accompanies me in all my excursions and follows with interest the progress of the work.

Shortly thereafter their daughter's fiancé died in Panama, also of yellow fever, and by summer forty-eight officers of the canal company were also dead. In Paris the fearful death toll was no longer secret. Engineers, physicians, nuns, and laborers sent to work on the canal were developing yellow fever. Patients were dying so swiftly and so desperate was the need for bed space that in the final minutes of life, a dying man saw his own coffin brought in. For the sick who never made it to the hospital—the vast majority—the end was frequently more gruesome:

> Sitting on your veranda late in the evening you see the door of a little adobe house across the way open. The woman of the house, who lodges two or three canal employees, peers cautiously out in the street, reenters the house, and when she comes out again drags something over the threshold, across the narrow sidewalk, and leaves it lying in the dirty street. When she closes the door again there is no noise but the splash of the tide.... Soon it grows lighter. A buzzard drops lazily down from the roof of the cathedral and perches on something in the street. The outlines become more distinct. You walk down, drive away the bird who flies suddenly back to his watchtower, and stand looking in the quick dawn of the tropics at what was yesterday a man—a month before a hopeful man, sailing out of Le Havre. He is dead of yellow fever.

So wrote a visitor from the *Herald Tribune*, S. W. Plume. He would recall, "It was the same way—bury, bury, bury, running two, three, or four trains a day with dead all the time. I never saw anything like it. It did not matter any difference whether they were black or white, to see the way they died there." The rate of sickness was not determined accurately, but a conservative estimate was that about one-third of the total work force at any given time was infected with yellow fever. Thus in a year such as 1884, with more than 19,000 at work, probably 7,000 were sick.

By December 1888, the news of continued sickness and death associated with yellow fever, coupled with rising costs, led to a financial crash. Publicity about these overwhelming risks prevented the company formed to dig the canal from raising new capital, and it dissolved by February 1889. Within a few years, the U.S. government, led by Theodore Roosevelt, reinstated the challenge to connect the Atlantic and Pacific oceans (6,35–38). By this time the Yellow Fever Commission

FIGURE 5.5 *A cartoon from the early 1900s indicating a principal challenge to Theodore Roosevelt and the U.S. government on building the Panama Canal.*

report was known, and the success of William Gorgas in controlling both yellow fever and malaria in Havana through mosquito eradication well established. By overcoming the disease, medical scientists paved the way to success for this engineering project.

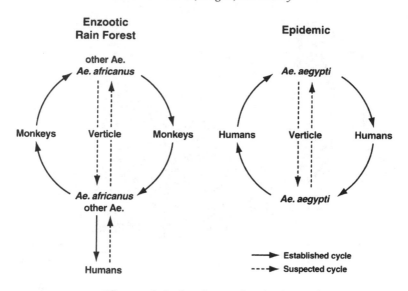

FIGURE 5.6 *The spread of yellow fever: various host–mosquito life cycles.*

World Distribution of Anopheles Aegypti- 1995

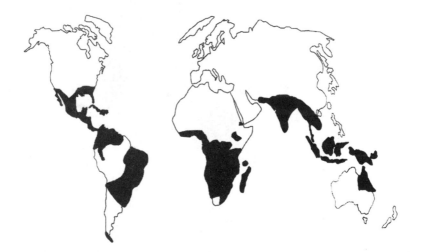

FIGURE 5.7 *World distribution of* Anopheles aegypti—*1995. The theoretical danger of yellow fever epidemics today is depicted on this world map that displays (in black) the current habitat of the mosquito vector of yellow fever, the source of its potential spread. Illustration courtesy of Brian Mahy, Centers for Disease Control and Prevention, Atlanta, Georgia.*

Although the *Aedes aegypti* mosquito clearly transmitted yellow fever throughout the Americas, researchers soon learned that other mosquitoes could transfer disease in jungle populations (8,9). Further, experimentation showed that monkeys could be infected and were susceptible hosts of yellow fever, so instead of being conquered and eliminated, this disease continues to pose a considerable and permanent threat. With rapid travel by air and other transportation, the possibility of bringing yellow fever into urbanized areas remains real, especially since the *Aedes aegypti* mosquito still lurks on the borders of the southern United States and is prevalent throughout Mexico and the Caribbean. Thus, in still another way, the story of yellow fever is not yet complete.

A third and more recent group of microbe hunters were those at the Rockefeller Foundation (8,39–43). For over half a century, they have mounted a comprehensive and broad attack on yellow fever that led to the discovery of a yellow fever vaccine called 17D. This group, guided by Wilbur Sawyer, included Wray Lloyd, Hugh Smith, and Max Theiler. It was Theiler who built on the discovery of the yellow fever virus, attenuated its effects, and developed a safe vaccine. For this innovation, he was awarded the Nobel Prize in 1951 (44).

The research on yellow fever can be divided into two periods. During the first, Walter Reed and his coworkers in Havana, as described above, successfully used human volunteers to attain proof that the causative agent of yellow fever was a filterable virus and that the virus was transmitted by the bite of a common urban mosquito. Then Gorgas showed that interrupting the habitat and breeding of these mosquitoes could control so-called urban yellow fever.

The second period began nearly thirty years after the U.S. Army Commission's work in Havana when, in 1928, Adrian Stokes, Johannes Bauer, and N. Paul Hudson (39) of the Rockefeller Foundation found that rhesus monkeys were susceptible to yellow fever virus, thus providing the first animal model of this disease. Later, the first strains of the yellow fever virus family were isolated—the Asibi and the French Dakar strains. Despite the accumulated knowledge about yellow fever, this disease continued to kill by infecting even those scientists working with the viruses. Stokes, Hideyo Noguchi, and William Young, members of the Commission, subsequently died from yellow fever.

Eventually scientists realized that, although urban yellow fever could be controlled by elimination of the *Aedes aegypti* mosquito, they could not exterminate the so-called jungle yellow fever carried by mosquitoes in the canopies of tropical trees along with the virus's natural host, the monkey. Unfortunately, this life cycle of yellow fever viruses in mosquitoes and monkeys could be and was occasionally expanded when man entered the habitat, contracted yellow fever, and brought it to the outside world. This remains so today.

In the laboratory, Max Theiler developed a small animal model of yellow fever infection that was easier to work with than the rhesus monkeys formerly used. He found that intracerebral inoculation of Swiss white mice with the yellow fever virus caused disease. This discovery simplified study of the disease and eventually its control. Mice could be protected from a lethal injection of yellow fever if they first received sera from humans or monkeys that were immune to the disease. Theiler then established a method of testing for antibodies to the virus in the bloodstream, charted the epidemiology of the disease, and finally provided the framework for attenuating or disarming the virus, a necessary requirement for the development of a successful vaccine.

Beginning in 1927, when yellow fever virus was isolated from a patient named Asibi in the African Gold Coast, scientists recorded the movements of this virus in monkeys and intermittently in *Aedes aegypti* mosquitoes. Later they tracked its passages in embryonic cultures. At some point in the culture passages, the virus mutated and lost its ability to produce fatal encephalitis, a disease of the central nervous system, when injected into rhesus monkeys and later even into mice. Eventually, infected monkeys made antibodies to this virus within five days after inoculation. These antibodies protected them so that later injection with the virulent Asibi strain of the yellow fever virus did not cause the disease. The next step was the vaccination of laboratory personnel working with yellow fever. Afterward, although the vaccinees experienced mild side effects, they made antibodies that neutralized the virus—the basis of immunization. The end result was production of the 17D strain of yellow fever virus (42–44). Thereafter, over 59,000 people were vaccinated with 17D, and 95 percent of these showed immunity against yellow fever. Subsequently, millions have been vaccinated, with successful results. Recently molecular biology techniques used to identify the amino acid sequences of this virulent Asibi and the 17D vaccine strains located differences in only thirty-two amino acids of the two strains. Exactly what has mutated in the virus to cause its attenuation is not known but may be in a protein of its outer layer.

Max Theiler's background positioned him uniquely to work with the yellow fever virus. He was born in January 1899, one year after the formation of the U.S. Army Commission on Yellow Fever. As a child in Pretoria, South Africa, under the influence of his family, he became an observer of the animals and plants around him. He received his medical training at the Universities of Basel and Cape Town but completed his studies at St. Thomas' Hospital in London. Thereafter, he took a short course in tropical medicine and hygiene at the London School of Tropical Medicine. This experience focused him on an area of biomedical research that held his interest for the rest of his scientific career. While still in London, he met Dr. O. Teague of Harvard Medical School, who recruited Theiler to join a group there under the direction of Andrew Sellards. In 1930, Wilbur Sawyer induced Theiler to leave Harvard and join the Rockefeller Foundation in New York, where in 1937 he developed the 17D strain of yellow fever vaccine. In 1951, he was awarded the Nobel Prize for "discoveries concerning yellow fever and how to combat it."

Despite the effectiveness of the vaccine, yellow fever still lurks in any area frequented by the *Aedes aegypti* mosquito. With the introduction into a susceptible population of just one person infected with yellow fever, the disease could once again emerge as a terrifying plague. Further, yellow fever is unlikely to be completely exterminated as smallpox has been and measles and poliomyelitis may perhaps be because the virus remains part of a monkey–mosquito life cycle in the world's jungles. Rapid human travel to and from those jungles makes it possible that yellow fever may revisit civilization. Since World War II, outbreaks of yellow fever have been documented in Western Panama, with a spread through Central America to the Southern borders of Mexico. Yellow fever afflicted Trinidad, Ethiopia, Senegal, Nigeria, and the upper Volta region in Sierra Leone, Ghana, and elsewhere. The 1960–62 outbreak in Ethiopia alone involved an estimated 100,000 persons and caused 30,000 deaths in a population of one million. Thus, the problems of circulating viruses in Africa combined with the failure to implement sustained vaccine programs because of poverty, civil war, and inaccessibility to rural areas ensure the continuation of this disease. Similarly, yellow fever virus remains established along the river basins of South America, the Amazon, Araguaia, and Orinoco. Although mass vaccination reaching at least 90 percent of a population should be able to control outbreaks, yellow fever remains endemic in countries adjacent to the equatorial forests of the Amazon basin in South America. The *Haemagogus* mosquito, which also transmits yellow fever, lives in this jungle region, and the *Aedes aegypti* mosquito still dwells throughout parts of south-central Latin America, Mexico, and along the southwestern and southeastern borders of the United States. Yet, now that we have a more perfect understanding of the disease, its route of transmission, and methods to control its epidemics, the unrelenting fear of yellow fever that was present a hundred years ago is no longer with us. Of course, this infection can still recur, especially when mandatory vaccination is ignored and records of vaccination are not checked at ports of entry. Even now, to grasp the hysteria of that time, one needs only an awareness of Ebola and Lassa fever viruses (see Chapters 9 and 10), the "new" viral hemorrhagic fevers, which kill at a high rate in Africa.

6

Measles Virus

Measles is one of the most contagious of viruses passed among humans and can cause a severe disease (1,2). Before extensive vaccinations began throughout the United States, even as late as the 1960s, over 500,000 individuals a year were infected, and more than 400 of them died. Included annually were over 48,000 hospitalizations, 4,000 cases of brain infection (encephalitis) resulting in 7,000 patients with seizures, and over 2,000 children with severe brain damage requiring hospitalization in mental institutions. By the mid-1970s, when immunizing vaccination became routine, measles virus infections decreased by 90 percent as did its sequela. However, during 1977, a severe outbreak in Los Angeles underscored the difficulty of achieving universal vaccine coverage in some urban areas. After that onslaught, primary immunization followed by a secondary inoculation of vaccine became compulsory for school children. The result was an interruption of circulating measles viruses in the United States so that, by the year 2000, measles was no longer an epidemic in this country. The handful of cases that appeared after that time came from foreign travelers who brought the virus with them. Infection then occurs in those infants exposed prior to being eligible for vaccination or in other children/adults who resisted or escaped vaccination. Such unvaccinated individuals provide a source to further spread measles and its complications. For example, in February 2008, measles virus broke out in San Diego, California. The index case was a 7-year-old returning from Switzerland. Measles infection then spread to children in schools, those visiting doctors' offices, and one on an airplane. In the San Diego Unified School District in which the first three cases broke out, 10 percent of the 350 students were not vaccinated while in other schools in the city and state of California one-tenth less or roughly 1 to 2 percent of children in public school skip vaccination. California is one of twenty states in the United States that allows personal exceptions of avoiding vaccination. Although vaccines have saved countless lives and negated countless human tragedies, they are not without risk. The benefit-to-risk ratio is extraordinarily in favor of benefit, yet some parents with libertarian views, misinformation about side effects, etc., are not impressed. Regarding the San Diego outbreak, the *New York Times* quoted one parent who refused to vaccinate her child in the school where the outbreak occurred: ". . . I refuse to sacrifice my child for the greater good" and "I cannot deny that my child can put someone else at risk." (3). At risk and at discomfort. For within a few weeks, 12 children were known to be infected, thousands of children and adults were exposed at schools, grocery stores, theaters, entertainment events at the regional Del Mar fairgrounds, in doctors' offices, and 250 passengers on an airplane bound from San Diego to Hawaii. Of the 12 ill children infected, 9 had not been vaccinated because their parents objected while the other 3 were too young to be vaccinated. Due to the relatively high measles virus vaccination rate in the San Diego population, a large epidemic was averted. But could the measles virus return to epidemic proportions in this country, and is the eradication of this virus possible throughout the world?

This chapter on measles virus explores the origin and infectivity of the virus in the course of human history and ends with a discussion about purported evidence that measles virus vaccines may be harmful. Such misinformation is often propagated for personal reasons yet greatly affects public health and individual lives.

Humans are the only natural host for measles virus, and recovery from the infection results in lifelong immunity. The vaccine, especially when given twice, provides long-term protection, although some humans have a genetic profile that makes them unresponsive or poorly responsive to the vaccine and, thus, not protected from the infection. However, so-called herd immunity may offset their vulnerability; that is, immunity arising when the virus no longer circulates because vaccine coverage exceeds 95 percent of the population. Prohibiting the circulation of measles virus is also important in the vaccinated population because vaccine-stimulated immunity eventually wanes.

Both arms of the immune system provide protection or immune memory. These two "arms" of immunity are the humoral components (antibodies circulating in the blood) and cellular constituents subdivided into (thymus-derived) CD8 T cells, which have cytotoxic and cytokine functions, and CD4 T cells, which help CD8 T cells and also B cells, cells that differentiate into plasma cells that make antibodies. According to recent studies, CD8 T cells and antibodies that react specifically with measles virus or measles virus-infected cells generally maintain their levels and activities over several decades; in contrast, virus-specific CD4 T cells slowly but significantly decline over that time frame (4).

Although less of a problem in countries with strong vaccine schedules, elsewhere, primarily in Third World countries with inadequate vaccine coverage, measles remains among one of the ten most important causes of death from infectious disease. Currently, of the approximately 20 million cases per year of measles on our globe, over 500,000 persons die, a shameful figure considering the availability and low cost of effective vaccines. Problems that should be readily solved arise because of the virus's great infectivity, difficulty in administering vaccine in certain areas, need for two vaccine doses to achieve the protection now called herd immunity, as well as the ambivalence, indifference, and refusal of some to take the vaccinations. Consequently, susceptible individuals in the local community and in the world made ever-smaller by rapid transportation are endangered by infected persons who carry measles from areas where the virus is active to places where it is not. Take, for example, another outbreak of measles, this time in Indiana in the United States during 2005 (5). As background, the vaccine to prevent measles virus infection was licensed in 1963 (6). Since that time, it has been clear that this vaccine (live attenuated virus) should be given for the first time to an infant at age nine to fifteen months. The result is an immune response that usually prevents the infection in 80 to 95 percent of those vaccinated. Vaccination earlier than nine months of age is rare because antibody to measles virus contained in mother's milk neutralizes (kills or deactivates) the live attenuated virus in the vaccine. To obtain the 95 percent or greater immunity to measles in a population, a second vaccine dose is required. This second dose also boosts the immune response of poor responders to the first vaccination. This two-step schedule is mandatory for children attending public schools, and its strict enforcement has prevented epidemics of measles virus infection. The rub is that for either religious or individual reasons, those doing home schooling can by design escape this regimen of vaccination. An additional stumbling block is misinformation that attributes disorders like autism to the administration of measles virus vaccine. Regardless of the reason, refusal of protective vaccination encourages a breeding ground of susceptible people primed for the infection and spread of measles virus whenever or wherever they are exposed—even though 95 percent coverage of the population they enter has interrupted the circulation of measles virus.

In just such a setting, a severe outbreak of measles virus infection erupted in west and northwest Indiana, mainly in Tippecanoe and Clinton counties (5). There, a group of folks refused vaccination for multiple reasons. Some were simply apathetic from not witnessing anyone with measles for years; others could not understand scientific information or reconcile it with personal experience. Religious beliefs or strong individual concerns that government should not be trusted with decisions about vaccination deterred still others. Some thought that children receive too many vaccines, and inaccurate advice from alternative health-care providers to not vaccinate was convincing. Thus, many had opinions but few the facts. Preceding the Indiana epidemic, a group of unvaccinated church members, many of whom home schooled their children to avoid mandatory vaccination, sponsored among their charitable works a visit to a Romanian orphanage. Joining them was an unvaccinated seventeen-year-old girl from a missionary group. Although measles vaccine coverage in Indiana was 98 percent, measles virus infection was epidemic in Romania. The girl became infected in Romania and incubated the virus on the airplane that carried her back home to Indiana. There, the virus she bore attacked and infected thirty-four susceptible individuals gathered in church to hear a report of the missionary work. These thirty-four cases constituted the largest epidemic of measles in the United States since 1996. Genetic profiling of the virus substantiated that it originated in Romania. Thus, a virus from outside the United States transported rapidly across several countries and an ocean soon infected citizens of an otherwise measles-free region. The first victim was a six-year-old girl who was hospitalized in Cincinnati fourteen days after attending the church gathering attended by 500 congregants. Of the thirty-four cases, thirty-two (or 94 percent) had not been vaccinated, and the vast majority infected were under twenty years of age (88 percent). Of those afflicted, 71 percent belonged to just four families. Three patients were severely sick enough to require hospitalization. Two previously vaccinated persons were infected; one had been vaccinated only once, but the reason for the second's failed protection is currently unknown. The cost of containing the disease was over $167,000, including $113,647 in costs for a hospital employee who was unnecessarily infected as a consequence of the outbreak. Practical, philosophical, or legal questions that arise concern the individual's right to avoid vaccination balanced against the welfare of a community. What is the responsibility of that person when he/she serves as a vehicle for spread of a potentially devastating illness to others?

History reveals that when measles viruses attack people who have been sequestered from such exposure, even for several generations, nearly everyone becomes infected and many die. By this means, whole native tribes have been nearly obliterated. An example is populations in the Fiji islands, which were placed under administrative rule by the British Colonial government in the last half of the nineteenth century. To participate in signing the Colonial Treaty, the Chief of the Fiji people, Thacombau, traveled to Sydney, Australia. During the voyage home aboard his Majesty's ship Dido, on January 6, 1875, one of Thacombau's sons and a native attendant became ill and developed measles. Treatment followed the isolation procedures of the time, so the two patients were kept separate from the crew by quarantine in a temporary house built on the ship. By January 12, when the boat arrived at the native city of Levuki, both patients recovered and went ashore. But on January 14 and 15, another of Thacombau's sons came down with measles. Yet with festive plans already in place, on January 24 and 25, the other native chiefs, their retainers, and their relatives from all the nearby islands met in a great assemblage to learn of the treaty and to pay their respects to Thacombau. After two days of celebration, they returned to their separate villages. Just thirteen days later, on February 12, an epidemic of measles erupted. By February 25, the British authorities enforced quarantine regulations throughout the islands. However, all the chiefs and subjects throughout their villages were now ill. According to William Squire (7), a physician in the area, "All the Chiefs who attended the meeting have it and it is spreading rapidly."

By March 13, "The attacks have been so sudden and complete that every soul in the village is down with it at once, and no one able to procure food or if procured cook it for themselves or others. . . . People have died of starvation and exhaustion in the midst of plenty." In the ensuing four months, there were more than 20,000 deaths from measles, and the native population was depleted by over 40 percent.

Seventy-seven years later, with the availability of precise laboratory tests to complement clinical observations that documented the presence of measles, an epidemic was recorded in Southern Greenland (8). The attack rate of measles virus in this virgin population was 99.9 percent, with a mortality corresponding to that seen earlier in the Fiji islands. The vaccine to conquer measles was still eleven years in the future, and the only treatment available then as in the past was supportive therapy, providing nourishment, fluids, and food in a quiet environment.

Measles virus is transmitted through the air (1,2). Infected droplets are released by talking, coughing, and sneezing. These measles viruses sprayed into the air reach cells lining the mouth, throat, nose, and eyes of potential victims. The lower respiratory tract (lungs and bronchi) are more susceptible to infection than the nose-to-throat canal, which is in turn more susceptible than the mucous lining of the mouth. During the initial two to four days after infection, the virus replicates in local areas of the respiratory cells and spreads to draining lymph nodes where viral production enters a second round. The virus then enters the bloodstream carried within white cells of the blood (leukocytes and peripheral mononuclear cells). The end result is viruses circulating in the blood (viremia) and carrying infection to many parts of the body. The infected person feels well; during this time there is little obvious clinical evidence of viral infection, although the viruses permeate the body. Thus, the initial measles virus infection and incubation periods are silent.

The next (prodromal) phase of measles begins after the eight- to twelve-day incubation period and is heralded by fever, weakness, and loss of appetite. This is followed within a few hours by coughing, tearing eyes, and running nose. Along with this phase is a second interval of viremia, greater in magnitude than the first, that spreads infection to tissues throughout the body. These viruses are again carried primarily within lymphoid cells, and it is the further replication of viruses in these cells together with development of the host's specific attack against the viruses (immune response) that is responsible for the signs and symptoms of disease. These signs and symptoms reflect involvement of cells lining the respiratory tract, the gastrointestinal tract, and the eyes. In addition, as cells in small blood vessels become infected and interact with components of the host's immune response (antibodies and T cells), the

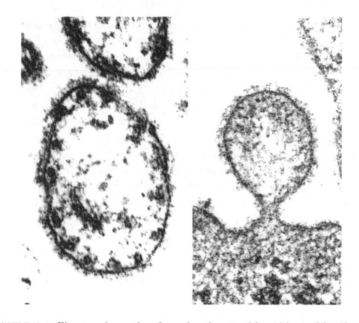

FIGURE 6.1 *Electron micrographs of measles virus particles (virions). Magnification, 120,000×. (Left) The complete virion is composed of an envelope covered by a fuzzy outer coat (virus glycoproteins) and lined on the inside by fuzzy nucleocapsids. The nucleocapsid contains the viral RNA. When cut in cross-sections, the measles virus matrix protein, which is located under the plasma membrane, has a donut appearance. (Right) A virion budding from the plasma membrane of an infected cell. Studies and photomicrographs by Michael B. A. Oldstone and Peter W. Lampert.*

characteristic measles rash begins on the face and spreads rapidly over the body, arms, and legs.

The cough increases in intensity as does the fever, reaching their peaks on about the prodromal fifth day. The rash begins after the third or fourth day and consists of small 3- to 4-mm red maculopapular (flat to slightly raised) lesions that blanch on pressure. Characteristically the rash appears first behind the ears and on the forehead at the hairline, then spreads downward over the face, neck, upper extremities, and trunk, and continues downward until it reaches the feet by about the third day after its first appearance. Soon it begins to disappear.

However, the immune system is often crippled during this phase (1,2,9–13). The intense inflammation of lymphoid tissues and cells that comprise the immune system suppresses the ordinarily vigorous immune function required to control nonmeasles infections. Other microbial diseases normally held in check by a functioning immune system are now able to rage in some patients. It is this virus-induced suppression of the immune system, first recognized in the late 1800s (11), that is responsible for many of the deaths during measles virus epidemics, although measles viruses by themselves, as a consequence of inducing infection, are also capable of causing death.

Measles virus was the first infectious agent known to abort the immune response, leaving humans susceptible to other microbial agents. This ominous picture is all too familiar today as redefined by the human immunodeficiency virus (HIV), and the acquired immunodeficiency syndrome (AIDS) epidemic that HIV continues to cause (9).

Once measles virus infection was accurately identified, several interesting consequences followed. During the nineteenth century, tuberculosis was rampant. Observers of the disease recognized that infected persons could progress to the terminal stage and die, or enter a stage of arrested illness only to have full-blown tuberculosis recur at a later time. In the absence of antituberculosis drugs, which were not developed until around the mid-twentieth century, the usual therapy was simply rest in the countryside or in a sanitarium located in a quiet place, preferably at high altitude. Near the end of the nineteenth century, clinicians attending these patients recognized that, following a measles virus infection, previously arrested tuberculosis became active and spread rapidly through the body (10). Patients with syphilis reacted similarly; measles caused reactivation and rapid spread of the formerly inactive disease.

The Austrian pediatrician Clements von Pirquet developed a cutaneous (skin) test for tuberculosis and commented (11): "A positive reaction to the tuberculin test signifies that the individual has been in contact with tubercular bacillus. . . . It is not possible, however, to conclude directly from that finding in which stage of tuberculosis that the individual is; the disease may be either active and progressive or inactive." However, this reaction to tuberculosis can be transiently lost, as von Pirquet noted: "the cutaneous reaction in tuberculosis that had been present can disappear following measles virus infection" (11). Von Pirquet recognized that measles virus infection suppressed the host's immune response, as evident by loss of the immune response to tuberculin. This loss of immunity allowed the reemergence of clinically active tuberculosis. At the beginning of the twentieth century, many medical practitioners knew that measles virus infection could suppress the immune system and that a secondary or other microbial infection, either newly involved in infecting the host or one that was maintained in an inactive stage, would then become rampant. Another interesting observation of von Pirquet's was that patients with active kidney disease (nephrosis) who would ordinarily die from kidney failure were protected, and the clinical disease temporarily halted after they became infected with measles virus (12). Although why this occurred was not fully understood, similar and multiple observations with measles virus and nephrosis led some physicians to treat nephrosis by purposely infecting the patients with measles virus (13). In fact, in patients with autoimmune kidney disease, the immune system was aggressive against the body's own tissues, and after suppressing the immune response by use of measles virus, the process of nephrosis ceased. With the invention of cortical steroid hormones to suppress the immune system, this viral therapy was discontinued.

Suppression of the immune system induced by measles virus infection, especially in undernourished and genetically susceptible individuals, left the patients open to continuing reinfection by any of several passing bacteria. Affected sites were primarily the lungs, producing pneumonia, and the intestinal tract, causing diarrhea, both of which contributed to a high death rate. Such events decimated the Native American tribes of North, Central, and South America (14,15). A graphic example is the deaths of Aztecs and Peruvian natives during the Spanish conquest of South and Central America; measles along with smallpox slaughtered these populations, as described in Chapter 4. Another example is the Yuman tribes of the Gila River in Southern Arizona. This community of Native Americans recorded significant events in their lives by marking sticks with scratches and dots between dashes that denoted the year (16). Selected elderly people of the tribe made these records. From such artifacts, their history has been traced from 1838, with references to measles in 1878–79 and 1883–84 (16). Although other illnesses undoubtedly struck them over this timespan, only measles is recorded, presumably because of its devastation among the tribes.

There is no treatment that arrests measles virus infection, once begun. To control its spread to others in a susceptible population before the 1960s, quarantine (17) to segregate infected persons was the only protection known. Until the vaccine to curb measles arrived in 1963, this virus continued to wreak havoc on peoples throughout the world. In

FIGURE 6.2 *Measles virus victim in this sixteenth-century Aztec drawing from the Códue Florentino.*

some instances the infection leads to a chronic, progressive neurologic disease in which loss of brain function eventually ends in death, usually within seven to ten years (1,2). This disorder named subacute sclerosing panencephalitis (SSPE) invariably necessitated chronic hospitalization.

1871-72	The Pima fought among themselves.	
1873-74; 1874-75	The Yavapi were all captured. This year they killed all the Yavapai in the cave.	
1875-76	The Yavapai were concentrated at Fort McDowell.	
1876-77	Halchidhoma at Sacate lost a race to the Pima.	
1877-78	"About" fifty-two Maricopa and Pima went to the Mohave. Eclipse of the sun.	
1878-79	Measles killed many children.	
1882-83	Raced with the kicking-ball against the Pima.	
1883-84	Measles again.	
1887-88	Earthquake. Established the boundary of the present reservation.	

FIGURE 6.3 *Sticks/stone messages of different dates from the Yuman tribes of the Gila River and the role measles virus infection played in their lives. From Leslie Spier,* Yuman Tribes of the Gila River *(Chicago: University of Chicago Press, 1933).*

Normally, recovery from measles virus infection produces a lifelong protection from reinfection (18). This conclusion was reached by a young Danish medical officer, Peter Panum, while studying the outbreak of measles virus infections in the Faeroe Islands in 1846 (19). In March of that year, a carpenter to be employed in the Faeroes left Copenhagen, Denmark, shortly after visiting friends ill with measles. He arrived eight days later in the village of Thorohavn. On April 1 he developed measles. Before the year's end, 6,000 cases were documented amongst the 7,782 inhabitants. Because the Faeroes were under Danish control, Peter Panum, in his capacity as a Medical Health Officer, was dispatched from Denmark to assist in the fight against this epidemic. He noted that the measles virus infected only individuals younger than sixty-five years of age (19). The high attack rate in all others from early infancy to sixty-five years matched closely the data from a previous outbreak of measles in 1781. Thus, he reasoned, persons who were resistant to the current Faeroes epidemic of 1846 had been exposed to measles virus sixty-five years earlier. Panum based his firm conclusion on three facts. First, the Faeroe Islands were isolated. Second, quarantine of all ships before they were permitted to dock or furlough their crews to come ashore was strictly enforced. Third, the number of ships landing in the Faeroes over that sixty-five-year span was limited. Panum was able to accurately define the incubation period between the previous and current attacks of measles virus, the infectiousness of the illness in newly afflicted individuals, and the duration of immunity among individuals who had earlier contracted measles virus. This observation of lifelong immunity after infection, coupled with the fact that humans were the only host for measles virus infection—that is, no animals carried the virus—would be an important guide and stimulus to John Enders and his colleagues who 100 years later created the measles vaccine. This vaccine, by preventing the disease, eventually provided the means for controlling and then perhaps eliminating measles.

When introduced into isolated, relatively small communities, measles viruses attacked with disastrous consequences. Such infections of rural populations not previously exposed to childhood illnesses ran wild, especially during times of war and with the forced migration of people fleeing their enemies. The American Civil War was the last large-scale military conflict fought before the germ theory of disease was developed by Louis Pasteur, Robert Koch, and Joseph Lister. Two-thirds of soldiers who died in that war, 660,000 in all, were killed by uncontrolled infectious diseases. Of these, over 67,000 members of the Union Army had measles, and more than 4,000 died.

In the early years of the Civil War, the strategy of Abraham Lincoln and his war cabinet focused upon the rapid seizure of Richmond, Virginia, led by George McClellan in the Peninsula Campaign. However, disease attacked McClellan's army along the Chickahominy River, reducing his troop strength by over one-third. Several hard-fought battles against the Confederate Army of Northern Virginia, led for the first time by Robert E. Lee, stalemated the Union Army's efforts, forcing McClellan to abandon the project and retreat (20–22). During this first year of the war, 21,676 cases of measles and 551 related deaths were reported in the Union Army alone. Deaths were primarily from respiratory and cerebral (brain) involvement. A written record indicates, "This infection is always serious, often fatal either directly or through its sequelae. The prognosis therefore should be guarded" (22).

Measles also ravaged the Confederates with over 4,500 sick at Winchester, less than three weeks after the battle of Antietam. Lee wrote to the Secretary of War:

> They are principally, if not altogether, the conscripts and recruits that have joined since we have been stationary. They are afflicted with measles, camp fever, etc. The medical director thinks that all the conscripts we have received are thus afflicted, so that, instead of being an advantage to us, they are an element of weakness, a burden. I think, therefore, that it would be better that the conscripts be assembled in camps of instruction, so that they may pass through these inevitable diseases, and become a little inured to camp life.

And to his wife:

> We have a great deal of sickness among the soldiers, and now those on the sick-list would form an army. The measles is still among them, though I hope is dying out. But it is a disease which though light in childhood is severe in manhood, and prepares the system for other attacks. The constant rains, with no shelter but tents, have aggravated it. All these drawbacks, with impassable roads, have paralyzed our efforts (23).

At this time America was primarily a rural society. Newly formed regiments with many susceptible soldiers from the countryside had their first exposure to the contagious diseases of childhood in the camps of assembly. Measles virus was the chief offender. Because of the solid immunity following an attack, most knowledgeable commanders "seasoned" their troops before sending them as reinforcements for battle. "Well-seasoned troops" were soldiers who had survived the epidemics that struck most recent enlistees. Typical was the response of General M. Lovell to a request from Richmond that he forward new troops from New Orleans in January 1862 (20). He would send them, "as soon as [he] can have them put through the measles; a process which they are now undergoing—one-half of them now being sick" (24).

It was the crowding together of so many susceptible individuals that promoted measles virus outbreaks in the Civil War. Measles virus was and is primarily a disease of large cities. Urbanization brings into close contact masses of people and is, in fact, a requirement for maintaining the measles virus pool. Aggregations of people permit the continuous circulation of viruses and provide a balance between an abundance of the virus and a continuous supply of susceptible individuals. Epidemiologic studies suggest that a population of 200,000 is required to sustain measles virus infection (25,26). With increasing urbanization, measles virus shifted away from an illness of adults to primarily a disease of children—now the most susceptible targets of this infection.

Undoubtedly the great river valley cultures, dominant over 6,000 years ago in Mesopotamia and along the Tigris-Euphrates Valley, were the first to suffer measles virus epidemics. Indeed, some have conjectured that the plague of Athens in 4 B.C., in Antonine of the Roman world in the second century A.D., in China in 162 and 310, and in Tours in Southern France in the sixth century were associated with or consequences of measles virus infections (14). The formation of these urbanized centers as large, complex, organized, and densely populated cities brought together diverse people, some with resistance and others with susceptibility to the measles virus.

How measles first came to infect humans is not clear. Perhaps the source was animal herds brought together in close proximity with large groups of people. The similarities between measles virus, canine distemper virus (1,2) of dogs, and rinderpest virus (1,2) of cattle make the latter viruses suspects in the development of measles virus infection. This concept has long been fancied but never proven. Definitive proof is hard to come by, since measles virus infection was once nearly impossible to distinguish from smallpox virus infection. Consequently, both had been lumped together as a single entity. In as early as the tenth century, the Arab physician Abu Becr (also called Rhazes) first attempted to distinguish between smallpox and measles (27). But not until the seventeenth century did the English physician Thomas Syndenham (28) actually document the clinical entity of measles infection. From that time forward, accurate records of the disease and its effect on populations accumulated. The movement to cities of large populations attracted by job opportunities of the industrial revolution ensured the continuous presence of measles virus and cycling of the disease. The disease was identified as a virus in 1911 (29), when respiratory secretions of a patient with measles virus were passed through a filter designed to retard bacteria but allow the passage of viruses. Inoculation of the passed fluids into monkeys then caused a measles-like disease. Many observations indicate that the natural host for measles virus is mankind, and among the animal species only certain primates are susceptible to this infection. Interestingly, monkeys are not infected by measles virus in their natural habitat. They become infected only when they come in contact with humans incubating the virus. Perhaps the small tribal social structure of monkeys allows this susceptible population to avoid measles virus infection in nature.

Once it was understood that infection with measles virus confers life-long protection from the disease and that humans are the natural host, interest turned toward developing a preventative vaccine (30). The principles of growing bacteria in culture had been defined in the mid- and late-nineteenth century by Robert Koch and Louis Pasteur. Such cultivation techniques allowed the isolation in pure cultures of bacterial agents identified as the cause of certain diseases. Then, investigators could readily manipulate, purify, and study bacteria for their biochemical and biological properties. For example, the ability to grow bacteria in the culture dish and in the test tube was instrumental in the discovery of antibiotics, which have reduced bacterial infections dramatically. In addition, therapeutic materials such as inactivated toxins, antibodies to toxins, and vaccines were produced in this way. Thus, devastation by the bubonic plague, cholera, typhoid, diphtheria, sepsis, endocarditis, and meningitis was largely prevented by the products of laboratory research. Such products reduced deaths from bacterial infection by over 99 percent.

The situation was different for viruses. Viruses, unlike bacteria and other microorganisms, replicate only inside living cells. Therefore, the inability to grow viruses in culture became the main limitation to controlling infections by measles, poliomyelitis, and others. In the first decade of the twentieth century, Alex Carrel had developed a procedure for growing cells in culture. Interestingly, Carrel worked with Charles Lindbergh, the aviator who was the first to fly across the Atlantic Ocean, on the development of the artificial heart and was awarded the Nobel Prize in 1912 for his work on "vascular suture and the transplantation of blood vessels and organs." However, it was Carrel's pioneering work with tissue culture (31) that was to be of more interest. Unfortunately, his methodology was burdensome, difficult, and impractical. Then in the 1920s, S. Parker, Jr., and R. Nye showed that viruses could grow and multiply in cultured tissue. Several years later, Hugh and Mary Maitland simplified this technique and found a way of keeping cell fragments alive in culture for short periods of time (32).

Hugh Maitland was born in Canada and, after training in bacteriology at the University of Toronto and in Germany, worked at the Lister Institute on the first animal virus isolated, foot-and-mouth virus. In 1927, he was appointed to the Chair of Bacteriology at the University of Manchester, England. There, with Mary Cowan Maitland, he succeeded in growing vaccinia viruses in a simple tissue culture system, later known as Maitlands' medium. This suspended cell technique of the Maitlands was applied extensively by multiple investigators to the study of viral growth.

Then in 1936, Albert Sabin and Peter Olitsky attempted to grow poliomyelitis viruses in Maitland cultures of tissues from chick, mouse, monkey, and human embryos. However, they found that only in human embryonic brain tissue would the virus replicate. Their conclusion, that the virus was strongly neurotropic (attracted to nerve cells) and that growing of poliovirus was not practical or possible in other cell types, as we will see in Chapter 7, was incorrect but quite reasonable at the

FIGURE 6.4 *John Enders, whose group at Harvard developed the effective attenuated live measles virus vaccine.*

time. For their studies, Sabin and Olitsky used a poliovirus obtained from Simon Flexner of the Rockefeller Institute that was likely already adapted for and restricted to growth in nerve cells because of its multiple passages through the monkey nervous system. The faulty conclusion was reversed by Thomas Weller, Frederick Robbins, and John Enders, who had already used human embryo cultures to isolate varicella virus (a DNA virus that causes chickenpox) and diarrhea-causing viruses of kittens. They tried a different source of poliovirus and successfully infected these embryonic cells (33,34). John Enders was destined to develop the measles virus vaccine (30).

John Franklin Enders was born in 1897 to a family of means in West Hartford, Connecticut. Beginning in a graduate program of English at Harvard, he focused on English and Celtic literature. However, impressed by a lecture and teachings of Hans Zinsser, Chairman of Bacteriology and Immunology at the Harvard Medical School, Enders decided to change careers and pursue a Ph.D. course in microbiology. Three years later, at age thirty-three, he received his doctoral degree in bacteriology and immunology and became an instructor at Harvard Medical School. Like most microbiologists of his generation, he worked on techniques to control tuberculosis and pneumococci infections. A devastating disease of kittens that rampaged through the animal quarters at Harvard in 1937 grabbed Enders's attention and changed the direction of his future field of study. Enders, with William Hayman, showed that the cats had a disease caused by a filterable agent and that this agent could transmit the disease. These observations on what proved to be panleukemia virus of cats provided Enders with his first real experience in virology, led to his first publication in this field, and focused the remainder of his career on this discipline. It was also at this time that Enders, working with the tissue culture techniques of the Maitlands, realized their unsuitability and returned to Alex Carrel's approaches for growing cells in tubes that slowly rolled (roller tubes). In spite of this method's complexity, he was successful by the 1940s in growing large amounts of vaccinia virus in cultured cells and obtaining high titers of virus. He was also able to prolong the lives of grown chick embryo cells in culture. This work was interrupted by the Second World War, after which Enders returned to Harvard where a research division of infectious disease was established at the Children's Hospital for his continued work. The major theme of his endeavors was to be the application of tissue culture techniques to virology and the extension of his findings to diagnosis and vaccination. With his newly improved techniques, he repeated the Sabin–Olitsky studies in 1946 but used tissue culture cells. He showed that poliomyelitis viruses grew not only in brain tissue but also in cultured cells from the skin, muscles, and intestines. He then proved that viruses produced in this way caused recognizable cytopathology (cell destruction) and that serum from the blood of individuals who were immune to poliovirus could block such cell destruction. Now Enders was able to supply virologists with a tool as important as the one Pasteur and Koch had provided for bacteriologists by developing defined culture media. Viruses could be grown in culture, isolated, purified, and attenuated (30).

Fifty years before Edward Jenner (35) showed that cowpox inoculation protected humans against smallpox and introduced the concept of vaccination, and thirty years after Lady Mary Montagu had her son variolated in Constantinople (36), a Scottish physician, Francis Home (37), drew on the same idea and attempted to produce mild measles by mimicking the variolation process. Similarly, by taking blood from an infected patient and inoculating it through the skin of an uninfected recipient, Home was able to transfer measles to ten of twelve patients. This experiment clearly demonstrated the presence of measles virus in human blood nearly 100 years before Frosch and Loeffler described the first animal virus (38). With the availability of a roller tube culture system and knowing of Home's results, Enders and his student Thomas Peebles obtained viruses from the blood and throat washings of a youngster, David Edmonston, who had an acute measles virus infection. Next, they grew these viruses in epithelial cells obtained from kidneys of humans and monkeys (39). Subsequently, the same viruses grown in human kidneys, human amnionic fluid, fertile hen eggs, and chick embryo cell cultures became the progenitors for the vaccines used today. For recognizing and adapting the culture method of replicating viruses, mainly poliomyelitis virus, Enders, with his colleagues Frederick Robbins and Thomas Weller, received the Nobel Prize in 1954 (30).

The safety of cultured and attenuated viruses in producing immunity but not disease was demonstrated first in monkeys. Viruses passed in cultured cells were selected for their diminished ability to harm recipients while still inducing an immune response upon inoculation. Monkeys injected with the tissue culture–passed live viruses soon developed protective antibodies. When these viruses were inoculated into monkeys intracerebrally (into the brain), no disease or tissue damage occurred. By contrast, monkeys not first immunized developed severe measles virus infections when exposed to the virus. After this success, the attenuated virus was tested in humans, first by inoculating the vaccine into immune adults in whom it was safe. The next step was a bigger clinical trial using children in several American cities. The results were dramatic. In 1961 Enders and his colleagues reported that measles virus infection could be prevented through vaccination (6).

Shortly thereafter, in September 1961, an editorial appeared in the *New York Times* enthusiastically complimenting Enders on his accomplishment in developing the vaccine for measles and his work leading to the development of the poliomyelitis vaccine (40). Enders's response, published on October 1, 1961 (41), epitomizes what is the best in and of science:

To the Editor of the *New York Times*:

Editorial reference was made to our work on measles and poliomyelitis in your edition of Sept. 17. I wish to express my deep appreciation of these favorable comments on our work.

For the sake of accuracy, however, I would emphasize the fact that whatever may have been accomplished represents the joint product of many co-workers supported by several institutions. In the studies on measles virus and vaccine, essential contributions were made by Thomas C. Peebles, Milan V. Milovanovic, Samuel L. Katz, and Ann Holloway. In the researches on the growth of poliovirus the role of Thomas H. Weller and Frederick C. Robbins was as important or more important than my own.

Without the generous provision of financial aid and physical facilities not only by Harvard University but also by the Children's Hospital Medical Center, Boston, the National Foundation, the Armed Forces Epidemiological Board, the U.S. Public Health Service and the Children's Cancer Research Foundation, in which a large part of our laboratory is situated, nothing could have been done.

To me it seems most desirable that the collaborative character of these investigations should be understood, not solely for personal reasons but because much of all modern medical research is conducted in this way.

John F. Enders
Professor of Bacteriology and Immunology at the Children's Hospital
Harvard Medical School
Boston, Sept. 20, 1961

Two items are added for readers' interest. First, Edmonston and his wife, owing to their personal philosophy, resisted any vaccination of their own children. Second, a favorite toy of children around the globe is called Thomas the Tank Engine. Thomas' story was invented by Wilbert Awdry and appears in a book about the fictional Island of Sodor, where train cars with unique faces and personalities go about their own work. One train running too fast or pulling too much load ends up in a mess that seriously disturbs Sodor's tranquil equilibrium. Awdry wrote the story in the 1940s, with publication in 1945, while caring for his son Christopher who was laid up with the measles.

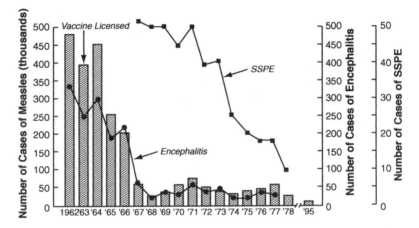

FIGURE 6.5 *The effect of vaccine in controlling cases of acute measles virus infections (hatched bars). Acute brain (encephalitis) and chronic brain (subacute sclerosing panencephalitis [SSPE], a chronic progressive degeneration of the brain) complications are shown.*

Nevertheless, despite the stance of Edmonston and others of like opinion, the widespread vaccination of children in the United States and around the world has dramatically decreased the incidence of measles virus and its sometimes severe complications. A single exposure to the measles virus vaccine results in the production of antimeasles virus antibodies in greater than 80 to 85 percent of susceptible individuals. However, an unsolved problem remaining has been those infants infected with measles virus before their ninth month of age (6). This early infection occurs in a number of countries where the virus continues to circulate widely, particularly in the sub-Saharan African nations. The nine-month period is a window of susceptibility between the time those children lose protection afforded by passage of the mother's antibody through the placenta to the fetus and the time when attenuated viruses in the vaccine successfully replicate. The mother's antibody obtained by breast feeding, although protective to the newborn, inactivates the vaccine. Whether this dilemma will be overcome by immunization of all susceptible children and adults, thereby reducing the circulating virus pool, or design of a new vaccine that can provide protection but avoid neutralization by maternal antibody, remains to be determined. This conflict is currently being hotly debated among experts on measles virus infection (in favor of developing new vaccines that are not neutralized by maternal antibody) and epidemiologists (mainly in favor of using the current vaccine only). The outcome will have an important impact on the goal of possibly eradicating the measles virus.

In addition to the large numbers of infants under a year of age who are susceptible to infection, a considerable population of children and adults lack immunity to the measles virus. The virus circulates in a community until its chain of transmission is broken by a massive vaccination program. Unless this occurs, global control is not likely to be achieved. However, as documented in Gambia from 1967 through 1970, such control is possible. In that small country, a year before the onset of mass vaccinations, 1,248 cases were recorded, but in 1969 and 1970 that number dropped to zero following a series of universal vaccinations done each year. What is clear from such examples is that a commitment by all nations to enforce universal immunization with the current vaccine will clearly reduce or potentially eliminate the presence of circulating virus in virtually every area of the world.

Another problem still remaining is the low but significant number of vaccine recipients who fail to respond to the initial inoculation. To counteract this difficulty, many countries have instituted a two-dose schedule, with a second dose given at varying times after the first one. With such a strategy, measles has been eliminated entirely in Finland, Sweden, and Cuba, and the annual number of reported cases in the United States decreased from more than two million per year to now less than a handful. However, this highly contagious virus still travels beyond the borders of countries where vaccination is universal to those where it is not widely practiced, and measles viruses continue to infect those who remain susceptible. Other countries have made vaccination voluntary instead of mandatory. In Japan, despite some difficulties experienced with the side effects of a Japanese-manufactured measles virus vaccine, the vast majority of their people have been vaccinated and, until recently, outbreaks of the infection numbered less than a few thousand per year. However, within three years of abolishing the mandatory requirement for taking measles virus vaccinations, over 200,000 cases of measles developed in Japan during 1995–1997.

In Third World countries, measles has been more difficult to eliminate than in developed countries because the contact rates as well as reproduction rates are higher and the infrastructure is less well organized to provide vaccinations. Nevertheless, the determination and will to overcome the obstacles in such areas, as demonstrated by the "Mothers of Nepal," has achieved amazing results (42). Organized by mothers and supported by the government of Nepal, the first national campaign to vaccinate in 2005 cut by 90 percent that country's deaths due to measles infection from 5,000 to 500. However, although the cost of the vaccine is $0.15, deaths from measles infection still occur, for example, in India with over 100,000 per year. India currently has more measles-related deaths than any other country and yet, at the time of writing this book, has not made measles vaccination a national priority.

Even in highly industrialized European countries or the United States, measles has not been eliminated. The causes are inadequate vaccination coverage in preschool-age children, the approximately 5 percent primary vaccine failure rate, apathy, and concern that individuals not government agencies should decide whether to vaccinate. Further, objections that children are receiving too many vaccines and that the measles vaccine is often harmful, even a major cause of autism, although untrue, nevertheless block some vaccinations.

The backdrop of this misconception was claims from several parents of autistic children in Britain asserting that the combined measles, mumps, and rubella (MMR) vaccine caused the condition. Shamefully, some physicians supported that claim (several of whom later proved to have received payment from plaintiffs' attorneys), as did a few news reporters and British government officials. Over time, vaccinations to prevent measles sank to 85 percent of the population or below in the United Kingdom in the late 1990s and early 2000s (reviewed in 43,44). As one would predict, soon afterward, outbreaks of measles followed with some devastating aftereffects.

Autism, first recognized as a distinct disease in the 1940s, results in children who cannot relate to themselves or to other people and situations. Although its cause was not known in the 1990s and still is not completely understood, the initial reports clearly indicated that autistic children frequently had parents who were highly motivated and career oriented. Further, the incidence of autism increased at the same time that mandatory vaccinations were initiated for infants. In 1998 *The Lancet*, a usually respected medical publication with Richard Horton as Editor, published a paper by gastroenterologist Andrew Wakefield and colleagues at the Royal Free Hospital in London that linked autism with the MMR vaccine (43,44). According to the paper, of twelve children who had autism and chronic enterocolitis (bowel disease), eight had been given the vaccine and one had a measles virus infection before the onset of autism. No virologic evidence was provided for the measles virus infection, nor was there any stringent epidemiologic evidence to link the infection or other events to autism. Importantly, no control group of children was included for comparison. Two unsavory and unfortunate events followed. First Horton, despite the doubts of his reviewers, published the measles-autism article presumably to increase reader interest in *The Lancet*. Second, some of the authors of the article and parents of autistic children went to newspapers and other communication outlets, citing the article as proof of a connection between MMR vaccination and autism. This publicity sparked a public movement against vaccination that quickly grew out of control not only in the United Kingdom but also in the USA and elsewhere.

Later, the financial conflicts-of-interest of some authors of *The Lancet* paper along with questions over lack of informed consent for the children were uncovered and resulted in most, but not all, of the authors retracting the paper six years after its publication. Horton, the editor of *The Lancet*, in his book *MMR Science and Fiction: Exploring a Vaccine Crisis* (44) laments his own responsibility in this sad affair, stating that if he knew in 1998 what he knows now (2004), "*The Lancet* would not have published the part of the paper relating to the MMR vaccine." As a barrier to prevent the future spread of such misguided and faulty information, he recommended that ombudsmen groups of scientists and laymen should evaluate controversial submissions to the journal. Horton further advocated obtaining financial and conflict-of-interest statements from all authors, which one would consider an absolute condition for any scientific publication.

Shortly before the retraction of *The Lancet* paper, I had the pleasure of meeting and dining with Liam Donaldson, Britain's Chief Health Minister at his Pall Mall Club in London. He was involved in the measles virus–autism affair and willing to discuss those issues. A few years later Donaldson said, ". . . if the paper had never been published, then we wouldn't have had the controversy, we wouldn't have had the seed of doubt sown in parent's minds, which has caused false loss of confidence in a vaccine that has saved millions of children's lives around the world."

Although the cause of autism is still under vigorous investigation, new genetic evidence indicates that the defect resides at the synapse—the cleft separating cells of the nervous system (neurons) that transmit the chemo-electrical signals (45). Such synapses are junctions across which neurons communicate, and they are required for sensory perception, movement, coordination, learning, memory, and likely social interaction.

The World Health Organization (WHO) estimates that in the 1980s and early 1990s, as many as 2.5 million children died annually from measles, primarily because of the failure to vaccinate susceptible individuals. With prodding from WHO and other health organizations, 78 percent global coverage by measles immunization was achieved, so that reported cases dropped significantly and deaths were reduced by over 70 percent to an annual rate of approximately one million. By 2004, the enhanced number of vaccinations reduced the death rate to 500,000.

The WHO in 1990 set the goal of "reduction by 95 percent in measles deaths and reduction by 90 percent of measles cases compared to pre-immunization levels by 1995 as a major step towards the global eradication of measles." Eradication is planned by the second decade of the twenty-first century. Since humans are the only reservoir for measles virus, immunity provides lifelong protection, and immunity can be induced by vaccination, WHO is justified in proposing global eradication of measles viruses. Measles, once the scourge of all lands, is now controlled in most countries, although it still kills millions in developing countries. The strategy for elimination of this virus depends on the dedication of every government to do so. The will to save these 500,000-plus lives per year rests solely on the dedication, responsibility, and commitment of the more fortunate nations, of all citizens on this planet, and, in turn, on the politicians and legislatures positioned to set the necessary priorities. Whether measles-related deaths will continue for over 100 years after the development of the measles virus vaccine, as was true for the smallpox vaccine, will largely be determined by the kind of society present in the twenty-first century.

7

Poliomyelitis

The book *Viruses, Plagues, and History* was published in 1998, two years before the date set by the World Health Assembly in Geneva for the worldwide eradication of poliomyelitis as a virus and a disease. At that time, tens of millions of dollars donated by the World Health Organization (WHO), the United Nations Children's Fund (UNICEF), the U.S. Centers for Disease Control (CDC), and Rotary International utilized by a dedicated team of public health and medical doctors led to the decrease of poliomyelitis by over 98 percent. At the time of the World Health Assembly declaration of intent in 1988, more than 1,000 people per day developed polio. One hundred and twenty-five countries worldwide reported cases of poliomyelitis, among the oldest and most ferocious of maladies. Eradication of this dread disease was deemed possible due to successful development of the effective vaccines against polio: the inactivated killed vaccine of Salk in 1955 and the oral attenuated live virus vaccine by Sabin in the early 1960s. The United States, and then most other Western countries, discontinued use of the Sabin vaccine in 2000 because no new cases of poliovirus appeared spontaneously (wild-type). However, vaccine-induced polio developed in some geographically scattered individuals whose attenuated poliovirus inocula reverted to a virulent form. The WHO's program's plan for eradication relied on the oral Sabin vaccine because of cost (the Sabin vaccine was much cheaper to produce than the Salk vaccine) and ease of administration (oral versus sterile needle/syringe inoculation). The plan was, first, to interrupt wild-type polio transmission and, second, to stop using the oral vaccine three years after elimination of polio.

Although the goal of eradication was not met by the year 2000, the approach appeared to be on target. Dramatically, by the year 2003, fewer than 800 cases of poliomyelitis were recorded per year worldwide compared to the over 1,000 cases a day in 1988 when the global initiative program began. In parallel, during 2003 only 6 countries, India, Pakistan, Afghanistan, Egypt, Niger, and Nigeria, reported cases of poliomyelitis in contrast to 125 countries documenting the disease in 1988. Then, things became unglued in 2003. A mostly uneducated Muslim population in Nigeria, encouraged by religious and political leaders as well as distrust of the vaccine and the West, spoke against vaccination. Instances of polio increased in northern Nigeria, and the poliovirus likely infected pilgrims going to and returning from Hajj in 2004. By 2005, 264 persons newly infected with poliomyelitis received care, and the epidemic spread initially in countries bordering Nigeria then crossed the Red Sea and moved along the shipping routes to many other areas, predominantly the Muslim country, Indonesia. The use of genetic profiling techniques classified the viruses isolated from the Indonesian patients and several distant countries as identical to the poliovirus circulating in Nigeria. These widespread new cases of poliomyelitis along with an outbreak in Hispaniola in 2002 and another in the United States (Minnesota) in 2005 raised speculation that the elimination of poliomyelitis virus might be impossible.

The issues of how polio was first discovered and then controlled, the problems of elimination, and argument for continued vaccination to ensure control constitute the body of this chapter.

On April 12, 1955, church bells pealed throughout the United States. Employees of the National Foundation for Infantile Paralysis beamed, and thousands upon thousands of volunteers for the lay organization the March of Dimes celebrated a job well done. These volunteers had walked throughout their communities, apartment houses, cinema theaters, and even grocery stores soliciting contributions, and millions of adults and school children had made large and small donations. Not since the Second World War had the fabric of America been woven together more tightly in a single cause. That cause was the conquest of poliomyelitis. The ringing of the bells was testimony to the announcement that the clinical trial of the polio vaccine showed it to be effective in preventing disease. The Associated Press dispatch of that day read: "(Advance) Ann Arbor, Mich. (AP)—'The Salk polio vaccine is safe, effective and potent it was officially announced today.'"

Diseases, in general, have no respect for the boundaries of any one nation or region. However, with polio, two countries made it their own challenge. Epidemics in the late nineteenth and early twentieth centuries in Scandinavia, where outstanding clinical investigations and epidemiologic studies by Karl Oskar Medin, Ivor Wickman, Karl Kling, and others took place, led to a lasting commitment by Sweden toward the understanding and treatment of polio. The second country to make such a stand was the United States. A major epidemic in New York City and surrounding cities during 1916 riveted attention on this disease. Five years later, the man who was to be the thirty-second President of the United States, Franklin Delano Roosevelt, became paralyzed from the waist down after infection with the poliomyelitis virus in midlife. Formation of the National Foundation for Infantile Paralysis, primarily by Basil O'Connor and other friends of Roosevelt, coupled with the mounting concern of parents that their children would become victims of this crippling disease and the belief that infantile paralysis might be conquered, led to an American crusade to fight polio. With missionary zeal throughout all parts of the United States, dimes and dollars were raised to alleviate the suffering and tragedy polio inflicted and to wipe out the infectious virus that was responsible. It was one of the rare times, outside of war, in which the citizenry of a nation was united. The result was one of medicine's greatest technical and humanistic triumphs, indicating what is possible when public support, science, and technology are directed to the good of humankind.

Unlike other viral diseases that began waning or remained constant in the twentieth century, poliomyelitis was on the increase. In the United States, it blighted lives with ever larger epidemics that peaked in 1952, during which time nearly 58,000 became sick, 21,000 were paralyzed, and over 3,000 died. In 1954, just one year before the pealing of the bells, more than 38,000 individuals were infected (1,2). The impact of poliomyelitis was felt not only in the United States but worldwide. The epidemics were common in Asia, South America, Europe, and elsewhere. In fact, in the early 1950s polio was the fifth major killer of young children in Sweden (3). For as long as any parent or child could remember, each summer brought fear that a poliomyelitis epidemic would sweep through and indiscriminately kill the young and healthy or cripple survivors, leaving them a legacy of withered limbs and destroyed ambitions. Not until the National Foundation for Infantile Paralysis proved successful in its quest for a vaccine to prevent poliomyelitis did vaccination in the United States cause the number of cases to drop below 1,000 in 1962, below 100 in 1972, and to fewer than five by 1992. The natural virus has not caused a single case of poliomyelitis in the United States during the last decade and up to 2005. The few cases (five to ten) recorded per year are the result of a side effect from using a live vaccine.

The stories of poliomyelitis and of three main personalities who were fundamental in developing the vaccine for its conquest, Jonas Salk, Albert Sabin, and Hilary Koprowski, are also the subjects of this chapter. Jonas Salk and his colleagues chemically inactivated the poliomyelitis virus with formaldehyde and provided a vaccine that produced immunity and dramatically lowered the incidence of poliomyelitis (2,4). Salk became the people's hero in the war on polio. But immunity, in terms of antibody quantities produced by the inactivated vaccine, waned over time. Additionally, administration by needle made vaccinations of large populations difficult. For these and other reasons, Koprowski, Sabin, and others independently worked on the development of vaccines with live attenuated (weakened) viruses, following the successful examples of Jenner's smallpox vaccine and Theiler's yellow fever vaccine. The attenuated vaccines developed by Sabin and Koprowski also proved highly effective in large clinical trials on humans (2,5–7). The Sabin vaccine was chosen over the Koprowski vaccine and in most countries initially replaced the Salk vaccine. Sabin never enjoyed the popular glory that Salk received but obtained the scientific respect that Salk never got. Koprowski's achievements in the development of the polio vaccine, for the most part, were forgotten. Yet, all three played important roles in the victory over the plague of poliomyelitis. Of course, many others made seminal contributions. Without such combined efforts, the vaccine would never have materialized. To mention but a few, of these contributors, the best known are innovations with the monkey model by David Bodian, Isabel Morgan, and colleagues, epidemiologic and clinical studies by John Paul, Dorothy Horstmann, and William Hammon, tissue culture studies by John Enders, Thomas Weller, and Frederick Robbins, and the immunologic observations of Macfarlane Burnet.

FIGURE 7.1 *The earliest known illustration of a suspected case of poliomyelitis. An Egyptian stele dating from the eighteenth dynasty (1580–1350* B.C.*).*

Paralytic poliomyelitis epidemics first became known in the nineteenth century. Whether or not sporadic outbreaks of paralytic poliomyelitis occurred earlier is less certain and a matter of disagreement (2,6). The description of Ramses' withered limb as a child in ancient hieroglyphic records is inadequate to associate the deformity with an infection, but poliomyelitis virus was certainly a possible cause. Similarly, the withered leg of a priest pictured on an Egyptian stele of the fifteenth to thirteenth century B.C. is characteristic and reminiscent of a deformity caused by poliomyelitis infection but, of course, could have originated from trauma, birth defect, vascular insufficiency, or other afflictions. Numerous other examples of withered limbs were known in antiquity and throughout the Middle Ages (2,6). However, polio, which could have been responsible, was not defined as a specific disease entity until the late seventeenth century. It was at that time and through the efforts of Thomas Syndenham (8), an English physician who lived from 1624 to 1689, that symptoms described by patients and signs documented by their doctors were correlated and classified with specific diseases. On occasion, such correlations came only at autopsy. This early devotion to charting clinical details was the basis for sorting fevers, rashes, and so on, into defined clinical entities and diseases. Therefore, if poliomyelitis did occur before 1800, its incidence was sporadic and not in the epidemic forms of the nineteenth century.

The late eighteenth century and early nineteenth century provide us with good examples of what was probably paralytic poliomyelitis. The great Scottish writer and poet, Sir Walter Scott, who was born in Edinburgh in 1771, developed an attack of fever in infancy that left him permanently lame, as in the following description of his own illness:

I showed every sign of health and strength until I was about 18 months old. One night, I had been often told, I showed great reluctance to be caught and be put to bed, and after being chased about the room, was apprehended and consigned to my dormitory with some difficulty. It was the last time I was to show much personal agility. In the morning I was discovered to be effected with the fever which often accompanies the cutting of large teeth. It held me three days. On the fourth, when they went to bathe me as usual, they discovered I had lost the power of my right leg. My grandfather, an excellent anatomist as well as physician, the late Alexander Wood, and many others of the most respectable of the faculty, were consulted. There appeared to be no dislocation or sprain; blisters and other topical remedies were applied in vain.

When the efforts of regular physicians had been exhausted, without the slightest success, my anxious parents, during the course of many years, eagerly grasped at every prospect of cure which was held out by the promise of empirics, or of ancient ladies or gentlemen who considered themselves entitled to recommend various remedies, some of which were of a nature sufficiently singular.

The impatience of a child soon inclined me to struggle with my infirmity, and I began by degrees to stand, to walk, and to run. Although the limb effected was much shrunken and contracted, my general health, which was of more importance, was much strengthened by being frequently in the open air, and, in a word, I who was in a city and probably being condemned to helplessness and hopeless decrepitude, was now a healthy, high-spirited, and, my lameness apart, a sturdy child.

The lameness, coming on suddenly and unexpectedly in a child, after a short bout of fever, makes this a suspected instance of poliomyelitis. Similar cases may have also been frequent at this time, but most often doctors were not called early enough and, when called, were consulted only after the child had been lame for weeks or months.

Providing a factual description was left to Michael Underwood (9), who in 1789 wrote one of the earliest known, accurate accounts of clinical paralytic poliomyelitis: "debility of the lower extremities, usually attacks children previously reduced by fever . . . when both [limbs] have been paralytic, nothing has seemed to do any good but irons to the legs, for the support of the limbs, and enabling the patient to walk."

Underwood refers not to any epidemic but only to isolated individuals. Later, in 1840, the German physician Jacob Heine (10) wrote the first review that described several patients with the disease and its clinical characterization. By 1870, Jean-Martin Charcot (11) applied microscopic study to tissues obtained from patients with poliomyelitis, noting the shrinking and loss of substance in the anterior horn of the gray matter of the spinal cord—the area containing the large motor neurons that control the limbs.

Charles Bell was a Scottish physician whose unique feats of observation were well appreciated by many, including Arthur Conan Doyle, who used Bell, in part, as his model for detective Sherlock Holmes. Bell wrote what is probably the first description of an epidemic of poliomyelitis depicting events in 1844 on the island of St. Helena (12):

A lady whose husband was the English clergyman at St. Helena consulted me about her child, who had one leg much wasted. In conversing about the illness, which preceded this affliction in her little girl, she mentioned that an epidemic fever spread among all the children in the island about three or five years of age; her child was ill of the same fever. It was afterwards discovered that all the children who had the fever, were similarly affected with a wont of growth in some parts of their bodies or limbs! This deserves to be inquired into.

From the time of Bell's recorded observation, reports of poliomyelitis epidemics were confirmed and on the increase. Numerous Swedish investigators contributed significantly toward the characterization of poliomyelitis. Oskar Medin characterized poliomyelitis as an acute infection, and Ivor Wickman, his student, published several studies of poliomyelitis epidemics.

The first documented epidemic of poliomyelitis in the United States occurred in the Otter Valley near Rutland, Vermont, in 1894. There, Charles Caverly of the Vermont State Department of Public Health reported 123 cases. Eighteen of those patients died, and fifty were permanently paralyzed. Among the victims, 68 percent were children under the age of six. In 1905, Ivan Wickman, a pediatrician from Stockholm, Sweden, reported 1,200 cases. The worldwide epidemic had come to light. The horror of a poliomyelitis epidemic can be illustrated by events that occurred in San Angelo, Texas, in 1949. In that city, with a population of roughly 50,000, a report of poliomyelitis infection surfaced on May 20th. As the numbers afflicted increased, the city's swimming pool, bowling alleys, theaters, and camp grounds were closed. Entry of migrant workers was curtailed. Yet, by mid-June, 50 percent of the 160 beds in San Angelo's hospitals were filled with patients sick from poliomyelitis. By the end of the epidemic, 1 of every 124 inhabitants, or 420 total, actually a little more than 1 percent of the population, was affected. Of the more than 400 total cases, 24 died and 84 were permanently paralyzed. By comparison, the number of cases in the United States at this time was 40,000 or one of every 3,775 persons. Questions were several; most are still unanswered. Why were the attacks seasonal, with about thirty-five times more in August than April? Why were children so susceptible? Why within one family was the disease so much more severe, that is, bulbar paralysis and death, whereas in other families during the same epidemic in the same geographical location, the patients recovered? Why the discrepancy in a single family cluster between a severe and a mild course? Why more disease in boys than girls? Why a twentieth century epidemic? Why do only 1 or 2 become paralyzed out of 200 individuals infected? What is the genetic marker(s)?

The modern push to solve the poliomyelitis problem described by Medin and Wickman had its origins during the last third of the nineteenth century. Revolutionary concepts formed by Louis Pasteur and Robert Koch, their students, and a host of eager disciples established the foundation of bacteriology, immunology, and virology. Those scientists dispelled the then current doctrine of "spontaneous generation," which held that many lower forms of life arose in some mysterious way directly from materials in which they were usually found, for example, maggots from rotting flesh. The intellectual revolution of that time resulted in the discovery and isolation of infectious agents and their assignment as the sources of specific diseases. These early bacteriologists made culture media in which to grow isolated bacteria and used microscopes to identify the microbes that grew in the media. Fluids obtained from such cultures or samples garnered from patients, animals, or plants were passed through a porcelain-type filter connected to a hand pump to collect their contents. These first filters, known as Pasteur-Chamberland-Berkefeld-type filters, contained several standard pore sizes, the smallest of which excluded bacteria from passing through. The bacteria collected on such a filter could be grown in culture, studied, and analyzed. However, in contrast, certain infectious materials did pass through the filters. Although these minuscule materials were invisible under the microscopes of the time and would not grow in culture media, they did multiply when reinoculated into appropriate laboratory or domestic animals. This was the first method of isolating viruses.

The infectious agent that causes foot-and-mouth disease in cattle was the first virus to be isolated from an animal. Friedrich Loeffler and Paul Frosch passed fluid obtained from blisters on cows with an unknown disease into the Pasteur-Chamberland filter. Whereas bacteria were retarded by the filter, the infectious agent causing foot-and-mouth disease passed through (13). This material would not grow in culture medium. However, when inoculated into infection-free cows, it reproduced foot-and-mouth disease. Four years earlier Dmitri Ivanovski observed a filterable agent obtained from the tobacco plant known as tobacco mosaic virus. From the turn of the twentieth century until the outbreak of World War I, filtration devices were actively applied to the isolation of viruses.

As the polio epidemics of the early 1900s took hold, their cause, whether from an infection or not and, if so, by what kind of agent, was unknown. However, the events of Karl Landsteiner's career in the laboratory moved polio research toward its successful conclusion. After graduating from the Medical School at the University of Vienna in 1891, Landsteiner spent five years studying chemistry in several laboratories outside of Austria, including that of the great German chemist, Emil Fischer, in Wurzburg. Landsteiner returned to Vienna to assume a junior faculty position, the same year that Loeffler and Frosch discovered foot-and-mouth virus. In 1908, during an epidemic of poliomyelitis in the city of Vienna, Landsteiner, along with Edwin Popper, obtained spinal cord material from a nine-year-old boy who had died of the disease. Landsteiner then tried to infect a series of animals with this material. Inoculations of rabbits, guinea pigs, and mice did not result in any illness. But fortune smiled on these two experimentalists. They wanted to test their material on monkeys because of the animals' physiologic similarity to humans, but then, as now, monkeys were expensive and available only in limited numbers. Two Old World monkeys were offered to Landsteiner and Popper for transmission studies because the monkeys were so-called "damaged goods," since they had been used previously for other experiments. These monkeys were deemed expendable. In contrast, unused New World monkeys were on hand but reserved for higher ranking professors and more important projects. Landsteiner and Popper injected the Old World monkeys with the spinal cord material. Both monkeys developed a disease that clinically and microscopically closely resembled that of the boy from whom the tissue was taken (14,15). The ultimate irony came later. New World monkeys, like those forbidden to Landsteiner and Popper, are not susceptible to poliomyelitis, but Old World monkeys are. By a quirk of fate, these junior investigators became the first to isolate poliomyelitis virus from the nerve system tissue, then pass the virus into the appropriate experimental animal. As a follow-up to these observations, Landsteiner next showed that a virus caused poliomyelitis and that the virus infected the nervous system. In this way, an experimental model for the study of poliomyelitis became established.

In the following year, Landsteiner teamed up with Constantin Levaditi of the Pasteur Institute and reported the successful filtration of the material through a newer filter, the Berkefeld V type (16,17). This outcome established the final proof of the viral origin of poliomyelitis. Within several months, the scientific team of Landsteiner, Levaditi, and Mihail Pastia was able to detect poliovirus in tissues other than the nerves. They recovered the viruses from tonsils, membranes lining the throat, nasal

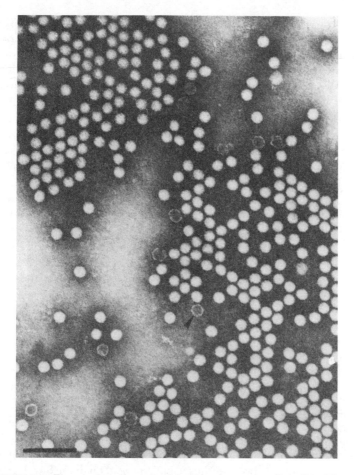

FIGURE 7.2 *Electron photomicrograph of the virus that causes poliomyelitis. The arrow points to a particle that has no RNA genome (empty). The symmetrical icosahedral pattern is evident. Bar, 100 μm. Photomicrograph from E. L. Palmer and M. L. Martin,* An Atlas of Mammalian Viruses *(1982), courtesy of CRC Press, Inc., Boca Raton, FL.*

secretions, and lymph nodes of the intestine taken from polio patients who had died. Results showing the viral cause of poliomyelitis were shortly confirmed by Simon Flexner and Paul Lewis at the Rockefeller Institute for Medical Research (18). Thus, by 1909, the groundwork was laid to develop a vaccine for poliomyelitis. The agent was known, tissues of the nervous system and other sites where the virus replicated were recorded, and an animal model was available. However, despite predictions in the early 1900s of the vaccine's imminent appearance, over forty-five years passed before an effective vaccine actually took form. The reasons were in some part the scientific complications still to be resolved, but in larger part the politics and scientific attitudes of those working on the problem.

The excitement created by Landsteiner's discoveries that a virus caused polio and that monkeys could be used for the necessary research offered the promise of controlling polio with a vaccine. At this time in 1909, Pasteur's earlier striking success in developing vaccines against a variety of infectious diseases of animals and humans was well known. Pasteur had established the principle of attenuation for the viruses that cause fowl cholera and rabies. Further, the vaccine to control smallpox had proved successful and was widely used (see Chapter 4). With these events fresh in the minds of many, hopes of equal and rapid success for poliomyelitis were high. The time required to obtain such success was estimated to be short. The scientific mood was optimistic. In the spring of 1911, Simon Flexner at the Rockefeller Institute reported in the *New York Times*, "We have already discovered how to prevent the disease, and the achievement of a cure, I may conservedly say, it is not now far distant" (19).

When Flexner died in 1946, a vaccine to prevent poliomyelitis was still far from real. The long delay in producing a vaccine stemmed from a sad combination of circumstances. First, those who were making clinical observations of the disease were too widely separated from those working with the experimental model. This led to overemphasizing the leads obtained from experiments and not paying close enough attention to the actual course of poliomyelitis in patients. Although the Swedes had collected significant epidemiologic data indicating replication of viruses in the gut and their possible passage into the blood, this information was virtually ignored compared with the work of Americans primarily engaged in experimental research. Rhesus monkeys preferentially replicated the virus in the respiratory area and not in lymphoid tissues of the gut, as patients did. Therefore, the experimentalists believed that the virus passed through nerves linking the respiratory tree to the brain. Second, not suspected until the late 1930s, and proven only in the 1940s, was the fact that more than one type of poliomyelitis virus was capable of causing disease.

While in Australia, Macfarlane Burnet, who in 1960 was to receive the Nobel Prize in Medicine for his discovery of immunologic tolerance (control of the immune response and elimination of immune response cells [clones] that are harmful), became interested in the work of Jean Macnamara. The latter's plan was to evaluate serum obtained from convalescent poliomyelitis patients as a potential therapy for the disease. With that possibility in mind, Burnet began to compare the Rockefeller Institute's standard polio strain MV with a recent isolate (the Melbourne strain):

We had two strains of virus, which in those days meant that we had in the refrigerator two sets of small bottles containing, in a preservative mixture of glycerin and saline, small pieces of spinal cord from monkeys that had been paralyzed by the appropriate type of virus. We knew that one of those pieces, ground up with saline, would give an extract capable of paralyzing the next monkey inoculated. One of these strains was isolated from a fatal case of polio in Melbourne, the other was obtained from the Rockefeller Institute and was a very virulent strain called MV. First experiments showed that the pooled convalescent serum could neutralize both viruses. Then Dame Jean [Jean Macnamara] and I found we had two monkeys that had been typically paralyzed but recovered, apart from their residual paralysis. One was paralyzed with the local strain, L, the other had been given MV with serum. The antibody had not been fully effective but the virus was weakened sufficiently to allow the monkey to survive. In order to obtain just a little more information, we tested them each with the opposite strain of virus. To our surprise, both were again paralyzed and died of polio. Recovery from infection with virus L therefore did not protect against MV nor previous infection with MV against L. We had only a few monkeys left but we were able to show that the two strains were antigenically different (20).

The impact of Burnet's finding was enormous, since an effective vaccine would need to contain the three strains of polio that were later identified.

But without a vaccine, without any control, poliomyelitis virus infection and the epidemics it caused struck terror in parents' hearts as each summer approached. Powerless to alter the progression of epidemics caused by the virus, state and local communities undertook quarantine measures in an attempt to isolate acutely infected patients and seclude them from contact with susceptible individuals.

FIGURE 7.3 *The concern and suffering from poliomyelitis are depicted in these two pictures. (Top) The isolation and forcible quarantine of a child newly infected with poliomyelitis during the 1916 epidemic in New York. Photo courtesy of the* American Legion Magazine. *(Bottom) An iron lung like those required to keep alive polio victims with paralysis of respiratory muscles that control breathing. Without such temporary support, many of these patients would have died and some eventually did.*

In New York during 1916, children were dying and being crippled from poliomyelitis virus infection. Many parents believed that sending their children to a hospital housing infected patients was tantamount to condemning them to death or lifelong paralysis. But regardless of parents' protests, some sick children were forcibly taken into isolation wards, initially by police officers (21). Nurses were soon substituted because they were more successful than the police in persuading parents to let their children go to the hospital. However, parental fears continued unabated. As reported by a social worker:

> The mothers are so afraid that most of them will not even let the children into the streets, and some will not even have a window open. In one house the only window was not only shut, but the cracks were stuffed with rags so that "the disease" could not come in. Babies had no clothes on, and were so wet and hot they looked as though they had been dipped in oil. I had to tell the mother I would get the Board of Health after her to make her open the window, and now if any of the children do get infantile paralysis she will feel that I killed them. I do not wonder they are afraid. I went to see one family about 4 p.m. Friday. The baby was not well and the doctor was coming. When I returned Monday morning there were three little hearses before the door; all her children had been swept away in that short time by the virus. The mothers are hiding their children rather than giving them up (22).

Under the sway of panic, people looked with skepticism and suspicion on government health offices. The selectmen of many villages, whose doctors were struggling with the impossible and failing to stop the epidemic or save patients from paralysis, resorted to homemade martial law. Movie theaters were closed to children under sixteen years of age. Swimming pools were closed. Children exposed to polio infection, or in an area where a case was found, were to be isolated for two weeks at home. Isolation could be best controlled in middle class and wealthy families, but poor children unable to be isolated were often forcibly taken to hospitals.

The 1916 panic precipitated by poliomyelitis virus infection in New York closely resembled the panic of yellow fever–stricken Memphis in 1878. On July 5, the *New York Times* depicted the wholesale exodus from the city of children from homes of the well-to-do "... 50,000 of them had been sent out of New York ... to places considered safe by their parents.... Reports of persons fleeing from town continue to come in" (23).

Similar to that earlier yellow fever exodus was the panicky response of several neighboring states and communities. The *New York Times* reporting on Hoboken, New Jersey, taking action against unwanted intruders stated: "Policemen were stationed at every entrance to the city—tube, train, ferry, road, and cowpath—with instructions to turn back every van, car, cart and person laden with furniture and to instruct all comers that they would not be permitted under any circumstances to take up their residency in the city" (24).

In response to the continuing epidemic, Haven Emerson, the New York Commissioner of Health, announced on August 9 the postponement of the opening of New York City's public schools. As the summer continued, deputy sheriffs, hastily appointed and some armed with shotguns, patrolled roads leading in and out of towns, grimly turning back all vehicles in which were found children under sixteen years of age. Railways refused tickets to those younger than sixteen. Ignorance, arrogance, and despair were evident. The notion was firmly held that below the magic age of sixteen there lurked the dread disease, whereas above it no menace existed either for the individual or the community.

But of course those over sixteen were not uniquely privileged to avoid poliomyelitis. Franklin Delano Roosevelt (FDR), later President of the United States, was infected with the virus in his fortieth year:

> I first had a chill in the evening which lasted practically all night. The following morning the muscles of the right knee appeared weak and by afternoon I was unable to support my weight on my right leg. That evening the left knee began to weaken also and by the following morning I was unable to stand up. This was accompanied by a continuing temperature of about 102° and I felt thoroughly achy all over. By the end of the third day practically all muscles from the chest down were involved. Above the chest the only symptom was a weakening of the two large thumb muscles making it impossible to write. There was no special pain along the spine and no rigidity of the neck (25).

As observed by his family, "Below his waist he cannot move at all. His legs have to be moved often as they ache when long in one position" (26).

FDR went to great lengths to hide his paralysis from the waist down. He could not stand or walk on his own. He wore heavy leg braces and leaned against a wall, a podium, or another person to give the impression of walking on his own. For all practical purposes, he was confined to a wheelchair.

His disability was attacked by both Republicans and those Democrats seeking to replace him as their party's nominee for the country's presidency in 1932. Articles were written on the theme; "Is FDR physically fit to be President?" questioned an article in *Liberty Magazine* in 1931 written by Earl Looker, a Republican. At the Democratic National Convention, Massachusetts Governor Joseph Ely, the nominator for Roosevelt's main rival for the nomination, Al Smith, said: "...we as Democrats will find it difficult to impress a nation with the advisability of change unless our nominee is a man of action, virile and rugged personality—to win requires a man who can take blows both physically and mentally..." (27).

Roosevelt's comments to these and other attacks suggesting weakness and disability from poliomyelitis was: "...I find that there is a deliberate attempt to create the impression that my health is such as would make it impossible for me to be president. To those who know how strenuous have been the three years I have passed as Governor of this state (New York) this is highly humorous but is taken with great seriousness. I shall appreciate whatever my friends may have to say to dispel this silly source of propaganda." Roosevelt went on to be a vigorous president, elected four times and one of the great statesmen and movers of the twentieth century. Although his disability was obvious, the fact that his weakness did not affect his strenuous performance in the White House as he led the United States out of the Great Depression and through the Second World War did much to dispel the notion that disabled persons are unfit or lack the strength to perform their duties. How ironic it is that FDR, who tried to avoid being seen in a wheelchair during his life, was sculpted sitting in a wheelchair and will be viewed that way for eternity at his memorial in Washington, DC.

The polio epidemics returned each summer and seemed to increase in severity. Reports from Sweden stated that one of every five children who died succumbed to acute infectious poliomyelitis (3). Others were crippled. Not uncommon was the experience of Leonard Kriegel, who, while eleven years old and attending summer camp, shared a cabin with four other boys. Two of the four got poliomyelitis; one died and Leonard survived but was told he would never walk again without braces and crutches:

> I started to scream and cry and bang my fists on the window, I remember. There was nobody in the house, thank God. But right after that I very methodically sat down and thought, "What do I have to do?" It was a month before my seventeenth birthday and I decided that what I had to do was to build up my arms. I realized I had to walk on my shoulders (21).

Josephine Walker also contracted poliomyelitis, the same year as Leonard Kriegel did. She was six years old at the time:

> It was the most profound thing that happened in my young life. I remember the night I got sick. I remember my father returning from a business trip and coming up to say good-bye to me. I remember the ambulance coming and taking me off alone to the hospital. We were all put in quarantine for about two weeks, when nobody was allowed to see us.
>
> My parents did everything for me that was needed physically—I was held and carried around by my mother for many years. They were in total denial about the fact that there was an emotional component to this. And so they pretended, after a while, like it didn't happen, other than the fact that I needed—you know—a little bit of medical help. People didn't talk about it; they didn't talk about the implications of it for my life. They just kind of let me go (21).

These stories were repeated many times throughout the world. No hope seemed in sight even though it was known that a virus caused the disease and that virus infection could, in some instances, be controlled through vaccination. A turning point finally came through the influence of Franklin D. Roosevelt, when his law partner Basil O'Connor and other associates committed time and resources to forming the National Foundation for Control of Infantile Poliomyelitis, dedicated to overcoming this disease. This organization publicized the effect of polio on children and, with posters of crippled children, induced masses of people throughout the United States to join a money-raising crusade toward seeking a cure.

The National Foundation revolutionized charities in the United States. Building around the earlier poliomyelitis attack on President Roosevelt, the Foundation cleverly singled out an attack on polio as a disease of American children. Instituting a President's Ball at the Waldorf-Astoria Hotel in New York City on Roosevelt's birthday in

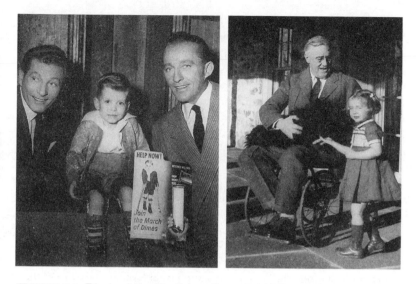

FIGURE 7.4 *Friends of Franklin Delano Roosevelt initially organized the crusade to prevent poliomyelitis virus by forming the National Foundation for Infantile Paralysis. This organization sponsored the March of Dimes, a fundraising effort by mothers and other volunteers who walked city and rural neighborhoods and solicited funds at homes, theaters, and sports events. Fear of an illness that indiscriminately killed and crippled children brought together the diffuse fabric of American society. (Left) Hollywood stars Danny Kaye and Bing Crosby, who actively participated in the crusade. (Right) Franklin Delano Roosevelt and a child, both stricken with polio.*

1934 with the motto of "We dance so others will walk," corresponding birthday balls spread throughout the country with the proceeds from the sale of tickets going to the foundation. There were over 6,000 such balls from waltzes, to fox-trots, to square dances in hotels, union halls, barns, and restaurants, with over one million dollars raised in the first year. Metro-Goldwyn-Mayer movie studio sent some of its biggest stars: Jean Harlow, Ginger Rogers, Robert Taylor, and others, to glamorize the festivities. By this means, and for years to come, a celebrity pipeline turned out to raise funds and publicize the cause. Politically, to overcome the complaints of Roosevelt's antagonists who objected to holding the benefit on Roosevelt's birthday, a nonpartisan National Foundation for Infantile Paralysis was formed in 1938 with Basal O'Connor as director. This foundation became the largest voluntary health organization of all time and re-defined the role and methods used by private philanthropy.

One of the celebrities, the entertainer Eddie Cantor, suggested calling this fund raiser the "March of Dimes," a takeoff of the news feature, "March of Time," shown at film theaters of that era. Contributions were requested and sent to the president or the foundation. The March of Dimes in one year received over 2,680,000 dimes and thousands of dollars in checks. The scope of fund raising was so great that from 1938 to 1955 the National Foundation raised over $350 million of which $233 million was used for patient care. The National Foundation founded the vast majority of research on polio including clinical trials for the Salk polio vaccine.

Americans now over the age of fifty recall the National Foundation's Mother's March of Dimes because of the likelihood that their own mothers participated. Begun in 1950 by a local chapter in Maricopa County, Arizona, the march assembled on January 16 at 7 P.M. in the city of Phoenix when women appeared carrying jars, containers, and shopping bags. They canvassed private homes, apartments, and hotels. Earlier, radio stations and newspapers and posters spread the word of the Mother's March announcing, "Turn on your porch lights, help fight polio tonight." On that night in Phoenix the mothers marching to support and prevent polio collected $44,890 from roughly 42,000 donors. The next year the March proceeded throughout the United States and, between 1951 and 1955, succeeded in raising over $250 million. Just as important, an enormous population became directly involved in a personal commitment and effort to fight polio both as collectors and donors. Of course, preventing polio by obtaining a vaccine to protect their children and grandchildren was the driving force because every community had local children stricken with poliomyelitis and crippled.

Similarly, the challenge to understand and prevent poliomyelitis attracted many dedicated scientists who sought to unravel the puzzle of its prevention.

A major factor delaying vaccine production was that a few authorities with political power essentially controlled the field and its scientific direction (2). Simon Flexner, director of the Rockefeller Institute, remained convinced throughout his life that poliovirus was exclusively neurotropic, that is, grew only in nerve cells of the brain and spinal canal. His rigidly held belief was that the virus causing poliomyelitis invaded the respiratory system and from there moved straight to the central nervous system. This view was partially based on study of the rhesus monkey, which is highly susceptible to infection with poliomyelitis but only by way of the respiratory system, not the alimentary canal. With the prestige of the Rockefeller Institute behind him, Flexner's conviction became the prevalent, although wrong, opinion for many years. Unfortunately, the weight of esteem for Flexner and his followers successfully dampened, if not drowned out, the voices of Karl Kling and other Scandinavians whose systematic analysis of tissues obtained from humans dying of the disease enabled them to recover the virus not only from the expected respiratory areas, in the pharynx and trachea, but also from the intestinal wall and intestinal contents. Kling and his group had also studied healthy carriers. They isolated poliomyelitis virus from the stools of healthy members of the families of patients infected with poliomyelitis virus as well as from other healthy individuals (28). But it was not until 1937–38 that Paul N. Trask finally confirmed the Swedish results. His evidence finally established, beyond any doubt, that poliomyelitis virus could reside in the intestinal tract, proof that Flexner had resisted for so long.

The agent causing polio is widespread and exists in most inhabited areas of the world. Usually the virus causes only a mild infection (98 to 99 percent incidence), a form that far outweighs that of the severe crippling disease that infects the nervous system (1 to 2 percent incidence) (29). The portal of entry for poliomyelitis viruses is the alimentary tract via the mouth. The time from viral exposure to the onset of disease is usually between seven and fourteen days but may range from two to thirty-five days. After migrating inward from its oral doorway, the virus likely binds to and enters a special cell in the gut called the M cell. It travels from there to an area heavy in lymphoid tissues called Peyer's patches, where it undergoes initial and continuing multiplication (29). This replication of the poliovirus in the lymphoid tissues of the gut is responsible for passage of the viruses into the feces, which can subsequently contaminate swimming pools (or a city's water supply) and continue the cycle of infection. The oral route of transmission presumably facilitates the passage of poliomyelitis to susceptible adults who lack immunity to the virus but care for infants given the oral polio (living attenuated) virus vaccine. Although initially attenuated, the virus can revert genetically to a more virulent form during only a few days of replication in the infant's gut, thus leading to its presence in the infants' stools and diapers.

A connection between the summertime spread of poliomyelitis and bathing in public swimming pools was made long ago by several public health officials but never fully proven. For example, following the outbreak in Britain in 1911, a public health worker in London's East Side wrote in the *British Medical Journal*:

> I have for some considerable time interested myself [in bathing-water purification] at Poplar, where I have endeavored to give every bather a clean and sterile bath.
>
> I pointed out to the Baths and Waterhouses Committee of Poplar Borough Council the horrible dangers of public swimming baths, inter alia mentioning how quickly swimming-bath water changes its pristine sweetness even after being used only by a few bathers . . . and becomes after use by a number of bathers nothing more nor less than diluted sewage, and this condition exists often before the first day's use is finished. As it is during the months of July, August, and September that swimming baths are mostly used . . . it would possibly be of considerable interest to bacteriologists to take into consideration the possible connection of polluted swimming-bath water . . . and the disease and possible determination of one of the causes of poliomyelitis (30).

After infecting its victim, poliomyelitis virus is usually passed in stools for several weeks, replicates, and is present in the gut and pharynx one to two or three weeks after infection. Consequently, the quarantine procedure was and is foolhardy unless maintained for the several-week period when poliovirus is being excreted (29).

Once the virus multiplies sufficiently in lymphoid tissues of the gut and pharynx, it travels into the blood and probably through nerve routes to reach the central nervous system. Poliomyelitis virus has been detected in the blood of patients with the mild abortive form (which does not produce central nervous system illness) and also several days before obvious clinical signs of central nervous system involvement in patients who later develop paralytic poliomyelitis. The strategy of vaccination is to allow replication of the viruses in the alimentary and respiratory tracts, their original site of entry into the would-be patient. The replicating viruses then stimulate an immune response and thereby prevent the transport of virus into the blood and to the central nervous system.

Poliomyelitis virus infects only certain subsets of nerve cells and in the process of its multiplication damages or destroys these cells. The large so-called anterior horn cells of the spinal cord are the most prominently involved. Since these cells relay information that controls motor functions of the arms and legs, it is not surprising that poliomyelitis virus infection becomes visible as weakness of the limbs preceding paralysis. In severe cases, other neurons are involved including those of the brain stem where breathing and swallowing are controlled. Usually, though, the neurons in the cortex, the area of the brain associated with learning, are spared so that intelligence and cognitive functions remain intact. In the most frightening form of polio, involvement of the lungs and throat is uncommon, and was so even during the worst epidemics. When it occurred, the only option was to place the patient in the infamous iron lung to force the exchange of air into and out of the lungs. Without such a device, death was the alternative. If the paralyzed respiratory muscles recovered and the time in the iron lung was short, survival was possible.

The first mechanical respirator in wide usage was developed in 1929 by Philip Drinker, an engineer, and Louis Shaw, a physiologist working at the Harvard School of Public Health. Experimentally, air was pumped in and out of a box in which a cat whose respiratory muscles were paralyzed was kept alive. With commercial assistance, Drinker then constructed a man-sized respirator. The Drinker respirator, or iron lung, was a rigid cylinder in which the patient was placed, and at regular intervals negative and positive pressure was applied within the chamber. But during a severe epidemic of poliomyelitis in Copenhagen in 1952, with an attack rate of 238 polio patients per 100,000 individuals, the number of patients who could not breathe or swallow far exceeded the iron lungs available. This emergency necessitated finding a more easily accessible and manageable solution. The approach was to apply the principles used in anesthesia, positive pressure ventilation—pumping air into the paralyzed lungs through a tube inserted directly into the trachea—essentially adapting a technique of the surgical operating room to the polio ward. The subsequently designed mechanical positive-pressure respirators eventually replaced the iron lung tanks. However, even in 2007, some thirty to forty patients in the USA were still dependent on the iron lung. One, Dianne Odell of Jackson, Tennessee, who developed poliomyelitis at age three, has been in an iron lung for fifty-seven years, tethered to the machine twenty-four hours a day. The cost is $1,000/week and, outrageously, was disapproved for Medicare reimbursement. The cost for maintaining Ms. Odell's survival is borne by the West Tennessee Health Care Foundation and private contributors.

By far the most common consequence of viral poliovirus infections in humans is an asymptomatic, usually mild, and short-lived disease. However, during even this relatively short time span, the virus can replicate and spread widely. Of those actually infected by the poliomyelitis virus, fewer than 1 to 2 percent become paralyzed. The most common aftermath (>98 percent of individuals so-infected) is that the patient develops fever, weakness, drowsiness, headache, nausea, vomiting, constipation, or sore throat in various combinations. These infected individuals recover within a few days. Alternatively, a much smaller number suffers troubling stiffness and pain in the back of the neck that lasts for two to ten days. For in fewer still (less than 1 percent), the disease advances to paralysis of the limbs and sometimes involves brain centers that control respiration.

The knowledge that poliomyelitis viruses infected the alimentary tract and multiplied there before spreading into the nervous system overcame a major stumbling block in controlling the disease. Yet, two other barriers had to be removed before an effective vaccine was developed. The first involved the unusual complexity of poliomyelitis virus, compared, for example, with smallpox or yellow fever virus from which successful vaccines had been made. Immunity to smallpox or yellow fever is dependent on protection against a single virus strain. By contrast, poliomyelitis viruses comprise three distinctly different strains. Thus, any successful vaccine would need to include all these three strains. But this realization did not surface until the 1930s with the work of Macfarlane Burnet. Further, his discovery was not initially accepted. The painstaking work of the Typing Committee set up by the National Foundation for Infantile Paralysis in the United States finally resolved the issue of the three polio strains in 1949. This they accomplished by typing over 195 different poliomyelitis virus isolates collected from near and far. These tests were done primarily on monkeys because no one then had the ability to grow viruses in cultured cells. The final barrier was the actual production of a vaccine. The seminal contribution of Enders, Weller, and Robbins was their development of an easily manipulatable tissue culture system in which poliomyelitis virus could be grown (31). Finding that they did not need to use nerve cells, which are hard to manipulate and keep alive in culture, but could substitute nonneuronal cells in which poliomyelitis viruses readily replicate, was the turning point in formulating their successful culture system and led to their Nobel Prize in 1956. Once these three conditions were met, it was possible to make a vaccine.

But which kind of vaccine was to be developed? Two approaches were considered. The first involved chemical inactivation of the virus. The idea was to purify the viruses grown in culture, then inactivate them with a chemical that would kill them, thus destroying their virulence (ability to cause disease in a host) while retaining their antigenicity (the ability to generate an immune response). Objections to the chemical inactivation approach were several. One objection was that the inactivated virus would enter the body by needle into the skin and muscle, as opposed to the gut and alimentary tract. Because the virus normally enters its host through the mouth and digestive tract, providing live attenuated virus vaccine that mimics the usual site of infection would be better for achieving optimal immunity. Further, attenuated live viruses had been the most universally successful vaccines, as witnessed by their ability to protect against smallpox and yellow fever. An additional argument was that, although the chemically inactivated vaccine might lead to immunity, this immunity was limited in time so that booster vaccinations would be required. Others argued that an infectious viral particle might escape the killing procedure and cause acute infection. This argument echoed a chemical inactivation approach that had been tried earlier. Maurice Brodie inactivated poliomyelitis virus by using formaldehyde. Soon afterward, in 1936, over 3,000 children were inoculated with this chemically killed virus with tragic results: some of them developed paralytic polio (2). It was and is still not clear whether these incidents of polio resulted because no one knew at that time that the virus was subdivided into three strains or because the virus was not sufficiently inactivated.

After discovery of the separate strains of poliomyelitis virus, the test of chemical inactivation was pursued in the early 1950s by Jonas Salk at the University of Pittsburgh (2,4,32,33). He successfully prepared a vaccine containing all three strains of poliomyelitis that had been killed with formaldehyde. To conduct the Herculean task of field testing the Salk vaccine, the National Foundation for Infantile Paralysis selected Thomas Francis, Jr., of the Rockefeller Institute. He organized and administered this study of 650,000 children, of whom 440,000 received the vaccine and 210,000 a placebo, all administered by needle inoculation. An additional 1,180,000 children served as unvaccinated controls. This clinical trial is still the largest in history.

Two years later, the foundation's report indicated that the Salk vaccine was both safe and effective. It was at this announcement that the church bells pealed across the American landscape. Richard Mulvaney, a physician from McLean, Virginia, gave the first inoculation of the Salk vaccine to six-year-old Randy Kerr of Falls Church, Virginia. As Dr. Mulvaney related years later, "So when this vaccine came out; people were overjoyed. This was wonderful because instead of having thousands of cases every year, there were practically none."

The vaccine was licensed several hours after the report. Yet difficulties remained. Although millions of doses from five manufacturers licensed in the United States, Canada, and Denmark proved effective, with no hazardous effects, seven of seventeen lots made by Cutter Biologicals contained live, virulent viruses instead of killed viruses. This vaccine caused polio in 204 polio recipients of whom 75 percent, 153, were paralyzed and 11 died. The Cutter incident was a tragedy. What went wrong with their inactivation procedure was not clear. The results that followed were dramatic. Dr. Leonard Scheele, Surgeon General of the United States, withdrew the Cutter vaccine from the market. The Division of Biological Standards, located within the National Institutes of Health (NIH), was removed and created as a separate agency to ensure appropriate manufacturing standards and controls for medical compounds. Oveta Culp Hobby, Secretary of Health, Education, and Welfare in President Eisenhower's administration, resigned, although it was said for the purpose of spending more time with her family. Dr. William H. Sebrell, Jr., stepped down as director of the NIH and was replaced by Dr. James Shannon, who insisted on more effective safety measures. Dr. Victor Haase, director of the Allergy and Infectious Disease Institute of the NIH, where the Division of Biological Standards was formerly housed, was also replaced. Lastly, one child paralyzed as a result of the Cutter incident was Josephine Gottsdanker. A lawsuit brought against Cutter (Gottsdanker vs. Cutter), coupled with pressure released by media reporting, revolutionized popular and legal views of vaccine safety. Yet, the effectiveness of the Salk vaccine was evident. In the period of 1946 to 1955 preceding vaccination, the incidence of poliomyelitis per year in the United States was 32,890 cases with 1,742 deaths. By contrast, after administration of the Salk vaccine, and before institution of the Sabin vaccine, the number of cases dropped to 5,749 with 268 deaths per year, although universal coverage for all susceptible individuals had not been achieved. In Sweden, where only the inactivated vaccine was and is used up to the present, poliomyelitis was eliminated.

FIGURE 7.5 *Three leading figures in the drive to make a vaccine to conquer poliomyelitis: (Top left) Albert Sabin, (top right) Jonas Salk, and (bottom) Hilary Koprowski. Salk worked on a chemically killed vaccine; Sabin and Koprowski worked independently on developing a living attenuated vaccine. Photo of Albert Sabin courtesy of the National Library of Medicine; photo of Jonas Salk courtesy of the March of Dimes; Koprowski photo courtesy of Hilary Koprowski.*

Nevertheless, research on attenuated virus polio vaccines continued. Such attenuated viruses had been used for vaccination previously with dramatic effects. For example, Max Theiler isolated yellow fever virus and passed it through animals and tissue culture to develop the 17D strain of yellow fever vaccine, which was successful in the control of yellow fever. Theiler now began attenuation of poliomyelitis virus, showing in 1940 that Type II poliovirus of the Lansing strain passed through mice infected them but was not virulent for monkeys and presumably not virulent for humans. Interestingly, at the Rockefeller Foundation's Yellow Fever Laboratory in Brazil, Hilary Koprowski became aware of and impressed by Theiler's work on the attenuation of yellow fever virus. After Koprowski moved from Brazil to the United States to his job as Head of Research at Lederle Laboratories, he spent many hours discussing with Theiler the problem of immunization against poliomyelitis virus (6). From these discussions, he became convinced that the living attenuated vaccine would be the best choice. Beginning with Type II poliomyelitis virus, Koprowski adapted the virus to rats and then, in 1950–51, fed the resultant attenuated vaccine to twenty human volunteers (6). No side effects followed, and all those vaccinated made good antibody responses, proving their immunity. These results, representing the first demonstration of the attenuation of a poliomyelitis virus and its success in immunization, were presented at a closed meeting called by the National Foundation for Infantile Paralysis (2,6). Koprowski next attenuated Type I poliovirus, again through passages in mice and rats, and eventually also Type III virus. With the live attenuated viruses of all three types on hand, immunization trials were begun in 1956, with more than 1,000 children vaccinated orally (6). Of those vaccinated, over 91 percent showed significant antibody responses to all three poliomyelitis virus types, and none of these children became sick with polio during subsequent epidemics. In 1956, Ghislain Courtois, director of a laboratory in Stanleyville, Belgian Congo, approached Koprowski about vaccinating chimpanzees in his chimpanzee camp. Later, when Courtois feared a poliomyelitis epidemic, he requested mass vaccination for local natives. In 1958, some 244,000 children of the Belgian Congo were vaccinated within six weeks, and 67 percent achieved protection from the disease (2,5,6,32). An infamous false claim popularized in large part by Edward Hooper in his book *The River: A Journey to the Source of HIV and AIDS* asserted that the polio vaccine made in monkey kidney cells was contaminated with simian immunodeficiency virus, a close relative to human immunodeficiency virus, and that these simian (monkey) viruses caused the modern AIDS epidemic. Reinvestigating the lots of virus used and review of the data by the United States National Academy of Sciences and by the Royal Society of Medicine in the United Kingdom has totally refuted this claim. Despite the overwhelmingly conclusive evidence, a small but vocal group continues that erroneous theme undoubtedly for economic and political gain. In part, this misinformation was the allegation used by Muslim legal/political authorities in temporarily stopping the polio vaccine campaign in 2003.

Independently, Albert Sabin began attenuation of the three poliomyelitis virus strains selected through tissue culture. By 1956 he had prepared a vaccine and had tested it in monkeys and in 113 human volunteers with excellent results (2,7,32,34). By then, Andre Lwoff at the Pasteur Institute showed that the best poliomyelitis virus variants were temperature-sensitive mutants selected from the now routine tissue cultures. The success of Lwoff and Koprowski spurred Sabin along in his quest for a more effective attenuated virus vaccine. By the end of the 1950s, the live attenuated polio virus had been clinically tested as an oral vaccine in numerous countries. The keystone of this effort was the successful mass vaccination of children in the USSR by Mikhail Petrovich Chumakov using the Sabin oral vaccine (2,7,32).

With completion of the main field trials and mass vaccination campaigns, all of which demonstrated both the safety and efficiency of oral poliomyelitis vaccine, it was time to decide which of the vaccines would be licensed. Accordingly, the U.S. Public Health Service called for the establishment of a committee to make that decision. The committee was composed primarily, but not exclusively, of scientists whose work was supported by the National Foundation for Infantile Paralysis. It seemed likely that the vaccine chosen would be a live attenuated one, and it would replace the chemically fixed Salk vaccine as the vaccine of choice. On August 24, 1960, the surgeon general announced that the attenuated strains developed by Albert Sabin were recommended for licensing by authorities in the United States. Such a vaccine was easily administered, via a sugar cube, and could be given orally, the natural route by which poliomyelitis virus entered the body. This vaccine might best focus immunity locally in the alimentary canal where the virus attached to and entered M cells and then replicated in lymphoid cells. The attenuated live virus given as a vaccine at that site would then replicate and shed virus and viral variants, thereby allowing the immune system to be primed and to generate a diverse and protective immune response. Further, the vaccine had proven effective in massive field trials in Russia (2,7,32).

The committee decided on the attenuated strains developed by Albert Sabin over those by Hilary Koprowski. Overall, there seemed to be little difference between the two preparations, although several believed the Sabin vaccine slightly safer. Others suggested that the decision was based not on scientific facts or any advantage in one group of strains over another, but on political considerations (2,6). In his recent article on "A Visit to Ancient History" (6), Koprowski wrote that the decision was based simply on support for a member of the "coterie" as opposed to an outsider:

> My suspicion was confirmed at Christmas of the same year when Joseph Smadel, a member of the Committee, told one of my friends at a party that the Committee knew that there was no difference between the strains of all investigators but Sabin is an old boy and, since we decided only one set of attenuated strains will be licensed, we have chosen his strains.

John Paul, in his book, *A History of Poliomyelitis* (2), wrote:

> Koprowski remained one of the leaders, he was later to lament the fact that the vaccine against poliomyelitis which he had discovered should have been named the Sabin vaccine. Salk also saw himself . . . "as a young Turk fighting the establishment."

Such political positioning, disappointment, and resentment with the development of the poliomyelitis virus vaccine were no different than for the earlier smallpox and yellow fever vaccines. Benjamin Jesty and his supporters petitioned the House of Commons and the Royal Society to disallow Jenner's claim and substitute theirs in its place for the discovery of the smallpox vaccine. Wilbur Sawyer of the Rockefeller Institute never overcame his exclusion from the Nobel Prize awarded to Max Theiler for development of the yellow fever virus vaccine.

Regardless of whose poliomyelitis virus was chosen for the polio vaccine, all the personalities involved took great satisfaction when paralytic poliomyelitis was eliminated from Canada as well as North and South America by 1992. By 1996, the World Health Organization reported fewer than 2,200 poliomyelitis cases per year and by 2003 fewer than eighty persons with poliomyelitis for the first time since such epidemics were recorded in the nineteenth century. With the commitment of every country in the world, the eradication of poliomyelitis disease was planned for the year 2000, some 200 years after Jenner's description of the cowpox vaccine and the successful eradication of smallpox, although eradication is not still complete in 2009, the time of writing this chapter. Nevertheless, the success in control of poliomyelitis has been outstanding. In 1995–96 alone, over half of the world's children under five years, 400 million children, were immunized against poliovirus. Clearly, vaccination of all susceptible persons is needed if the disease is to be contained; its elimination is still considered by some as a possibility but with enormous difficulties.

What precisely are the difficulties in the elimination of poliovirus? First, poliovirus circulates invisibly. That is, the great majority of those infected, >98 percent, show no distinct clinical sign, such as a rash. The specific manifestation of polio infection, the paralytic disease, represents but one out of one hundred or two hundred persons infected. Second is the problem of accessibility. For example, significant parts of the Congo, Pakistan, and Afghanistan are extremely difficult to enter. For vaccination to succeed, near universal vaccination is required. Further, in these and some other countries, roaming soldiers impair the safety of health workers needed to administer the vaccine. Fourth, thirty to forty healthy individuals have been identified who are constant shedders of infectious polio virus. These carriers are a continuing hazard to unvaccinated or poorly immune individuals, and their steady shedding of virus into sewage is the main danger. Fifth, in some countries with poor hygiene and numerous persons who are chronically infected with other viruses that cause diarrhea and gastrointestinal problems, such as some areas in India, several administrations of vaccine (six or seven repetitions) may not be sufficient either due to rapid removal of the oral vaccine or to competition with other infectious agents in the gut. Whether this infectious state can be overcome by killed vaccine, which is difficult to administer because of sterility issues, cost, challenge of inoculation, and so forth, is yet to be determined. A sixth and last problem is the conflict between culture and science. The Nigeria problem is illuminating.

Nigeria is a heavily populated African country with religious divisions between the largely Christian south, where vaccination is relatively acceptable, and the Muslim north, which questions the need for vaccination. Many of the northern Muslims voice suspicion that vaccination is a vehicle to be used by political enemies in Nigeria or by the West to spread HIV or to sterilize Muslim females (reviewed 35). The HIV fantasy is attributed to contamination by monkey viruses leading to AIDS, which is not true. The sterility issue is based on a real trace contamination of the female hormone estradiol in the polio vaccine that once occurred. Although the levels of the hormone are too low to be harmful to children, nevertheless it was present. The Governor of Kano in the Muslim North Nigeria, Ibrahim Shekarean, stated ". . . it is a lesser of two evils to sacrifice two, three, four, five, or even ten children (to polio) than allow hundreds or thousands or possibly millions of girl-children (Muslim) to be infertile." Comments of Dr. Datti Ahmed, President of The Supreme Council for Shari'a in Nigeria, "We believe that modern day Hitlers have deliberately adulterated the oral polio vaccines with antifertility drugs and contaminated it with certain viruses which are know to cause HIV and AIDS." Thus, mistrust spread through much of Muslim Nigeria. Some in the population questioned: why push the polio vaccine when that is not our problem (major health problem), but other infections like measles and malaria are? When culture and science clash, culture always wins. Therefore, although the polio vaccination effort has partially resumed after mediation and pressure by a number of Arab countries and the government of Nigeria, the repercussions of errors on both sides are remembered.

A problem with polio occurred even in the United States as recently as 2005. In a secluded Amish village in Minnesota, five children contracted vaccine-derived poliomyelitis. The original case is believed to be an eight-month-old baby with a genetically impaired immune system who was hospitalized with diarrhea. This child contracted polio and then transmitted the virus by shedding to susceptible neighbors who for perhaps social or religious reasons were not vaccinated.

These difficulties suggest that elimination of poliovirus would at best be difficult and perhaps impossible. Nevertheless, containment and reduction, if not elimination, of infections through continuous vaccination of the emerging population are likely to succeed.

Of the innovators who virtually defeated poliomyelitis viruses, Albert Sabin made many other significant contributions to virology. His work on sandfly fever, dengue fever, and herpes B virus, all preceding his study of poliomyelitis virus, produced significant discoveries. After the Sabin vaccine was licensed, he played a prominent role in its usage in many countries and devoted his energies in the Pan-American Union and the World Health Organization toward the control and eventual eradication of many childhood illnesses in addition to poliomyelitis. Jonas Salk, throughout his life, continued to lobby for inclusion of his killed virus vaccine for usage in the United States. His vaccine was used in Sweden, India, and several other countries, but never again in the USA during his lifetime. An interesting addendum is that, after the deaths of Sabin and Salk, a program that gave both vaccines to an individual as a preferred course was proposed and recommended by the U.S. Commission in 1995, approved in 1996 by the American Academy of Pediatrics, and recommended in January 1997 by the Advisory Committee on Immunization Practices of the U.S. Department of Health and Human Services. With that plan, the Salk vaccine was to be given early in life (to prevent attenuated virus-induced poliomyelitis while providing good neutralizing antibody titers) along with the Sabin vaccine, which provides wider coverage, more lasting immunity,

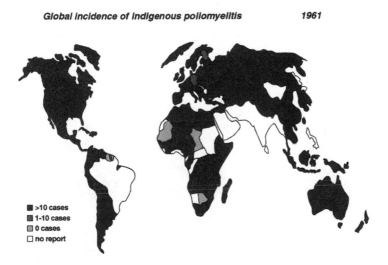

Global incidence of indigenous poliomyelitis   **1961**

■ >10 cases
■ 1-10 cases
▨ 0 cases
□ no report

FIGURE 7.6 *Control of poliomyelitis from 1961 to 2007 is shown according to the World Health Organization and Centers for Disease Control and Prevention. Incidence of indigenous poliomyelitis in 1961, 1988, and 1993 (dotted areas = more than ten cases; hatched areas = one to ten cases; solid areas = zero cases; open areas = no report). Bottom portion of figure shows reported cases of poliomyelitis—worldwide, 1995; and recent incidence of poliomyelitis, 2006–2007. The goal of the World Health Organization was the total elimination of poliomyelitis by the year 2000. The map dated 1995 is courtesy of the Centers for Disease Control and Prevention, Atlanta, Georgia; the map dated 2006–2007 is reprinted by permission of the World Health Organization, http://www.who.int/ith/maps/polio2008.jpg.*

Global incidence of indigenous poliomyelitis   *1988*

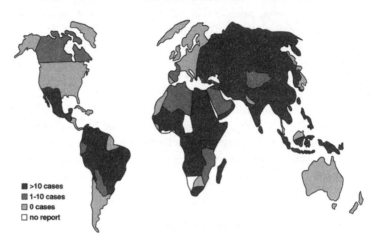

■ >10 cases
■ 1-10 cases
▨ 0 cases
□ no report

Global incidence of indigenous poliomyelitis   *1993*

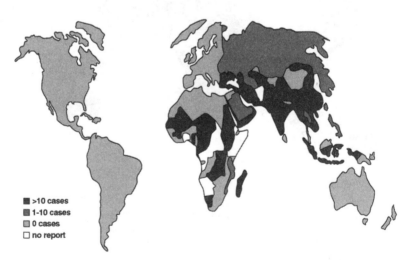

■ >10 cases
■ 1-10 cases
▨ 0 cases
□ no report

FIGURE 7.6 *(continued)*

Reported cases of poliomyelitis — worldwide, 1995

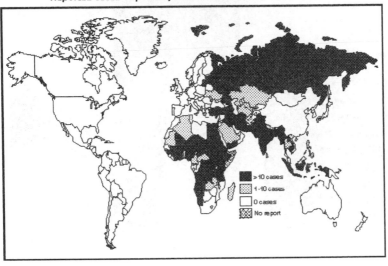

Poliomyelitis, 2006–2007

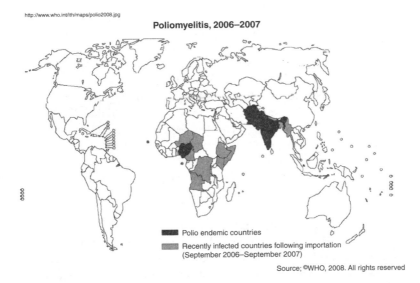

FIGURE 7.6 *(continued)*

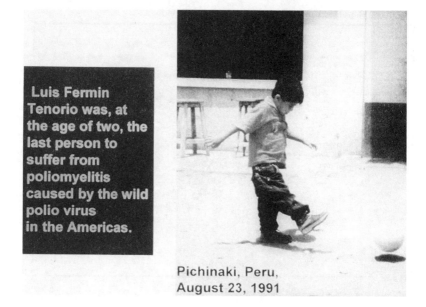

Luis Fermin Tenorio was, at the age of two, the last person to suffer from poliomyelitis caused by the wild polio virus in the Americas.

Pichinaki, Peru, August 23, 1991

FIGURE 7.7 *The last case of wild-type poliomyelitis in the Americas.*

and both humoral and cellular immune responses. However, by 2000 the Salk vaccine, after recommendations from the same committees, replaced the Sabin vaccine and is now exclusively used in the United States and most Western countries. Hilary Koprowski went on to make major medical contributions to the development of the rabies vaccine, which is currently in use throughout the world. He additionally developed monoclonal antibodies to type and segregate individual strains of rabies arising in different geographic areas, and with his colleagues developed the first human monoclonal antibody for therapy of nonvaccinated individuals exposed to rabies. He has also been a major contributor to cancer research and the development of human vaccines made from plants.

Finally, the ascendance and contributions of Salk, Sabin, and Koprowski reflect a telling change in biomedical research in the United States. Sabin and Koprowski came to the United States as immigrants, and Salk was the son of immigrants. All came from the minority Jewish religious faith that, prior to the 1940s and in some instances until the 1960s, were a group whose members were largely excluded or under quota restriction from medical schools, residency programs, or work in premiere research institutes. The "Old Boys Club" lamented by Koprowski was already being dismantled at this time. Instead, admission to join the great adventure of medical research was becoming available to those of talent, regardless of race, religion, gender, or national origin. Thus, the story of the conquest of poliomyelitis and the participation of Salk, Sabin, and Koprowski, in addition to recounting scientific accomplishment, also reflects a changing American culture and a continuing evolution toward a more just and democratic society.

Part Three
Present and Future Challenges

8

An Overview of Newly Emerging Viral Plagues: The Hemorrhagic Fevers

Six of the best studied, newly emerging viruses are the topics of chapters that follow. Of the first three, Lassa fever, Ebola, and Hantaviruses, little is known except that they exist and cause frightful diseases. More is known about the other four, SARS, West Nile virus, chikungunya virus, and human immunodeficiency virus (HIV).

Lassa fever virus, Hantavirus, and Ebola virus—all equally lethal infectious agents but members of different viral families—share the ability to cause hemorrhagic fever (1). Once infected with any of these viruses, the victim soon suffers profuse breaks in small blood vessels, causing blood to ooze from the skin, mouth, and rectum. Internally, blood flows into the pleural cavity where the lungs are located, into the pericardial cavity surrounding the heart, into the abdomen, and into organs like the liver, kidney, heart, spleen, and lungs. Eventually, this uncontrolled bleeding causes unconsciousness and death. We currently have no effective vaccines to prevent these potential plagues, although several are undergoing various stages of development. Once hemorrhagic fever strikes, it is relentless and devastating.

The agents of hemorrhagic fevers can be placed into two groups. First are the killer viruses that are endemic in remote areas. These viruses lie unendingly in wait of transport to introduce them into highly susceptible and distant urban populations. Representatives of this group are Lassa fever virus and Ebola virus, both of which are endemic in Africa. As in the sixteenth through nineteenth centuries when transoceanic ships brought not only goods to trade but also diseases like yellow fever, small-pox, and measles to infect residents of the New World (2), presently—in the twenty-first century, airplanes provide transit for infectious agents. The only difference is that planes move viruses faster and further. Now, a formerly secluded individual incubating a potentially lethal infection, but showing no outward signs of illness, can board a flight and quickly carry an infectious agent to the Americas, Europe, Asia, and Australia. The second group of hemorrhagic fever viruses is endemic within the United States and is represented by Hantavirus. Although this virus has infected only a few hundred known humans in American states of the West, South, and North, the carrier (vector), the deer mouse, is found throughout the country (1). Riding aboard the deer mouse, Hantaviruses, like yellow fever viruses, can be transported by their nonhuman hosts to cities and suburbs far from their customary habitat in much the same way that human travelers, already infected but in the incubation stage, bring their diseases from tropical forests of the Americas or Africa to other continents.

As impressive and of marked concern is that new infectious diseases have continuously emerged at an increasing and alarming rate over the last few decades. The recognition of such diseases correlates directly with the intensification of related scientific research and of international mon-itoring by public health services. Furthering the spread of these diseases are the increase in human mobility via airplanes, ships, and trains and the migration of humans into new areas of forests and jungle habitats where animal viruses lurk. Moreover, the number of individuals who are susceptible to these diseases has swelled markedly because of the ever-growing populations who take immunosuppressive drugs or are infected by such pathogens as HIV, measles virus, malaria, and tuberculosis, all of which suppress the immune system. Since 1969, thirty-nine new pathogens have emerged including SARS, HIV, and Ebola. Other seri-ous but previously known viral infections have spread to new territories and continents. West Nile virus was first isolated in 1937 from an infected patient in the West Nile province of Uganda and subsequently appeared in Africa, West Asia, the Middle East, and parts of Europe. Previously unknown in the United States, West Nile virus entered North America in 1999 and now presents a major problem of morbidity and mortality to this region.

Yet another formerly obscure viral infection, Chikungunya, is transmitted by the Asian tiger mosquito. Since its discovery in 1953 in Tanzania, the disease it causes was limited to developing countries in Asia and Africa. However, in 2005–2006 a massive outbreak of Chikungunya disease scoured the island of La Reunion, a geographic entity located off the coast of Madagascar and under French mandate. Of the 785,000 population on La Reunion, over 40 percent became infected with this virus, which caused severe headaches, muscle and joint pain, and rash, leading to immobility and a number of hospitalizations. Chikungunya then rapidly spread to the surrounding islands in the Indian Ocean, Comoro, Seychelles, Mayotte, Mauritius, and to India where about one and a half million people were infected. With the popularity of those Indian Ocean islands for vacations and rapid air transport to and from Europe and the Americas, the disease soon broke out in Italy and France and was imported to North America and the Caribbean. The explosive outbreak was tied to two factors. First, during the initial outbreak in 2005, the virus underwent a point mutation of a single amino acid that allowed it to replicate more efficiently in its mosquito host. This newly selected form of the virus multiplied to about 100-fold larger numbers in the mosquito's salivary gland, thus greatly enhancing the spread of its infection after 2005. Second, the Asian tiger mosquito vector was able to reach new sites throughout Europe, North America, and the Caribbean.

If a satisfactory vaccine were developed against these infectious agents, its greatest potential benefit would likely be in limiting the spread of the virus. Take measles virus as an example of controlling a highly infectious agent. Even with about 98 percent coverage by measles virus vaccine in the United States, a formidable number of persons remain susceptible to this infection (2 to 3 percent in a population of 260 million, or roughly 5 to 8 million persons). Further, even though the measles virus vaccine is effective and efficient, the immunity it produces may wane two or so decades after vaccination, thereby adding to the number of individuals at risk especially when the circulating virus in the population has been removed with the result that subclinical infections no longer abound. When a virus circulates in a population, it causes boosting or such low-level infection to those immune and is similar to and more effective than revaccination. Travelers from an area where an epidemic of measles occurs, like that currently flourishing in Africa or Japan, may carry the incubating virus into the United States. In the event of resulting outbreaks, massive vaccination of people in surrounding areas would likely be undertaken. With such blanket vaccination, virtually everyone would become immune, and the epidemic would be controlled.

Unfortunately for the victims of Lassa fever virus, Ebola virus, or Hantavirus, no such vaccine is available to contain the diseases they cause. Even if there were, it is unlikely that the vaccine would be used in countries with a low incidence of these diseases. Nevertheless, the exotic viruses from Africa have made their way into the United States and elsewhere, although infrequently. So far, neither they nor the indigenous Hantavirus has caused a massive epidemic, although West Nile virus has done so.

How do such new viruses surface? There are five major paths. First, viruses can modify their behavior and increase their virulence as they evolve through changes in their genetic material. Such genetic evolution can occur through reassorting of viral genes, recombination of a viral gene, or mutation within a viral gene. Reassorting occurs when a virus has multiple gene segments and swaps one or more of its segments with those from a different virus to form a new virus.

Studies in the laboratory show that a "new virus" created by such alterations can be much more virulent than the "parent" viruses, changing a mild and usually controlled infection into a lethal one. For example, the lymphocytic choriomeningitis virus, which infects rodents, is a member of the family that includes Lassa fever virus. The former virus contains two pieces of RNA (a so-called segmented virus), and each RNA piece contains two genes. The several strains of lymphocytic choriomeningitis virus are called Armstrong, Traub, or WE, named after their discoverers (Charles Armstrong and Eric Traub) or place of isolation (Walter and Eliza Hall Institute of Research, Australia). In experiments, none of these strains caused disease when injected into two- to three-day-old mice of the Balb strain. Yet, if the genes undergo reassorting so that the small RNA piece of Armstrong becomes joined to the larger RNA piece of Traub or WE, the newly generated Traub strain kills 88 percent of the mice it infects, and the new WE strain kills all of them (3). In fact, many viruses swap segments of genes to become disease producers (4,5). For humans, swapping of an influenza gene from birds or pigs with an influenza gene of man resulted in a new form of influenza virus that wreaked havoc on a human population (see Chapter 16) (6).

Another way in which viral genes change from a benign to a lethal form is recombination, the swapping of a gene within a single segment to form a new virus. Still another gene alteration process involves a single point mutation or several mutations during which just one or several amino acids replace those normally present and, thereby, create a new virus. The processes of reassortion, recombination, and single point mutation are shown in Figures 8.1, 8.2, and 8.3.

Such point mutations usually occur once per 10,000 to 100,000 base replications with most RNA viruses like Lassa, Ebola, or Hanta. During continuous replication of viruses, a large population of mutants form that differ from their parent viruses. The few mutants that survive may grow better than the parent virus, may be attracted to and replicate in different cells, and may have greater disease-producing abilities. This is what occurred with the Chikungunya virus.

The second way that new viruses surface is when their hosts undergo an increase in susceptibility to their harmful effects. This can occur via certain behavioral or social practices or through weakening of the immune system, for example, by taking immunosuppressive drugs.

Reassortment
(movement of whole gene[s])

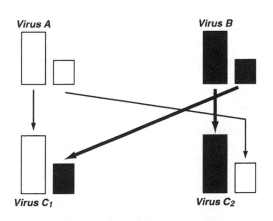

FIGURE 8.1 *The reassortment of viral genes. Each of the boxes represents a separate piece of nucleic acid that may encode one or several genes.*

Recombination
(within a single gene)

Virus A

genes: 1 2 3 4̲ 5̲

mutated Virus A

genes: A B C D̲ E

genes: 1 2 3 D 5

mutated Virus C

FIGURE 8.2 *The recombination process. In this scenario, gene D from mutated virus A replaces gene 4 of virus A to form new mutated virus C.*

Point Mutation
(change within a single gene)

Virus A

genes: 1 2̲ 3 4 5

mutated Virus A

genes: 1 2m̲ 3 4 5

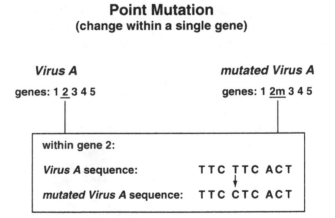

within gene 2:

***Virus A* sequence:** T T C T T C A C T

mutated *Virus A* sequence: T T C C T C A C T

FIGURE 8.3 *The generation of a new virus due to a mutation in a single nucleotide within a gene. Nucleotides depicted: (T) thymine; (C) cytosine; (A) adenine. Three nucleotides form (triplet) codons that encode specific amino acids. Amino acids are the building blocks to make proteins. The example shown is from real observations published from studies with lymphocytic choriomeningitis virus (7,8). Virus A (which represents part of the sequence from Armstrong strain) has a mutation at base pair 855 of a TC. The TTC codon represents the amino acid phenylalanine, whereas the mutated CTA encodes the amino acid leucine. This single amino acid change allows the virus to infect adults, cause immunosuppression, and establish a persistent infection (CTA leucine). Upon infecting an adult host, the original virus (TTC phenylalanine) is cleared from its host, and neither persistent infection nor immunosuppression occurs.*

The third route of viral emergence is when people increase their contact with vectors or humans that carry virulent viruses. As the need for more farming or grazing lands increases, humans penetrate the rain forests or enter new environmental niches and come in contact with rodents and other vectors that carry viruses. An example of behavior that encourages infection among humans is the African custom of staying in direct contact with sick relatives. In Zaire (renamed the Congo Republic in 1997), during the 1995 Ebola outbreak, healthy relatives shared hospital beds with the ill, and in one hospital, seventeen of the twenty-eight who had been healthy contracted Ebola and died. In contrast, none of the seventy-eight persons who visited Ebola patients in the hospital, but did not touch them or share their beds, got Ebola. A fairly recent modification in human behavior that has spread infection is the accessibility of rapid and frequent travel to distant areas.

The fourth origin of new viruses is simply an increase in their recognition and classification as biomedical and research technologies advance. For example, hepatitis viruses, which infect the liver, were categorized not long ago as hepatitis A virus, hepatitis B virus, and non-A/non-B hepatitis virus. With newer molecular techniques for identifying viruses by cloning, hepatitis viruses D through G have now been isolated, more than doubling just this one group of pathogens. The fifth source of new viruses is referred to as the mystery source because the cause is completely unknown. For example, the recent Ebola virus outbreak in Kikwit, Zaire, was traced to an index case, a charcoal worker/supplier. Before the outbreak was identified, he died but had infected thirteen of his relatives who also died. The social custom among his people of touching the dead was probably responsible for this instance of spreading infection. Those taken to the hospital infected hospital personnel and others, until the Ebola spread to 316 individuals, of whom 244 died. But how did the index case—the charcoal worker—get Ebola? Investigators are still evaluating insects, rodents, other wild life, and so on, in concentric rings outward, like circles made when a stone drops in water, from the charcoal pit where he worked and the house where he lived. Still, the original source of his Ebola remains nameless. In February 1996, thirteen individuals died in Gabon, West Africa, from Ebola after feasting on a chimpanzee. How the chimpanzee got Ebola is unknown.

Ebola outbreaks with high lethality have continued. In 2007, the Bundibugyo district in the Congo hosted an Ebola infection. This outbreak was unusual because, since several of the classic signs associated with Ebola infection were missing from the patients, their disease was hidden even while rapidly being transmitted to doctors, nurses, and other health-care workers who cared for them. Of 217 people infected, at present 103 have died. The native custom of washing the body of those who have died no doubt caused the disease to spread so robustly.

By August of 2007, the first evidence that fruit bats were likely reservoirs of Ebola and Marburg viruses was recorded (7, 8). Viral RNA and virus-specific antibodies were found in these bats. Now, bats are considered the probable reservoir not only of Ebola and Marburg viruses but also of SARS, NIPAH, and rabies virus infections. Thus, in the wild, fruit bats are believed to be a (the) vector of numerous diseases, whereas infections of Ebola travel by direct contact of those who are not infected with lingering viruses in sick or dead infected persons. The person-to-person contact occurs through mucous surfaces, skin abrasions, contaminated needles or blood/blood products.

The source of Ebola is not the only mystery involving newly emerging viruses. A new virus (morbillivirus), believed to be related to the measles family, caused an outbreak of acute respiratory disease in horses at a stable in Brisbane, Australia, in 1994. Then, two humans became infected, a stable hand who recovered after several weeks and a horse trainer who died one week after becoming ill. In 1995, a farmer in Queensland, Australia, died from a similar infection.

How many other mystery viruses will surface? How devastating will they be to humans? How do they form? This Pandora's box of mysteries and misery seems limitless. The historic struggle between viruses and humans described in the chapters on smallpox and measles and the more recent twentieth and twenty-first century battle with polio continue today and into the future.

Lassa Fever

The family name of Lassa fever virus, the arenaviruses (1), stems from *arenosus*—Latin for sandy—because of the virus's characteristic fine granules seen by electron microscopy. Like its relatives, Lassa fever virus causes persistent infection in the host, that is, a long-term infection that does not directly kill. Persistent infection, in general, does little harm to its animal host because the two have evolved a near-symbiotic relationship, usually over the host's lifespan. The natural host of an arenavirus is often restricted to a single kind of rodent. The rodent host carries these viruses in its blood and passes them in its urine. It is by contact with such excretions from the rodent that humans become infected. Although no chronic or persistent arenavirus infections have been found in humans, Lassa fever virus has been isolated from the urine of patients as late as one month after the onset of acute disease. Since no insects are known to transmit this disease, its spread to humans occurs only when humans come in close contact with the infected rodents in their natural habitat.

Lassa fever was first recognized in West Africa in 1969 but likely has existed in that region for much longer. The natural carrier is the rodent called *Mastomys natalensis* (multimammate mouse). In Africa, Lassa fever has struck natives, travelers on business, missionaries, and tourists. However, the cases that have provoked international fear are the several explosive hospital outbreaks. An example of the direct and continuous transmission of Lassa fever to five health-care workers is the following initial report of the disease by John Frame and colleagues in 1970 (2–4):

> Ms. Laura Wine, a nurse working in the small mission hospital, Church of the Brethren, in Lassa, Nigeria, was in good health until about January 12, 1969, when she complained of a backache. On January 20th, she reported a severe sore throat, but the physician who examined her found no signs to account for her discomfort. The next day, she complained that she could hardly swallow; she had several small ulcers in her throat and mouth, an oral temperature of 100°F, and bleeding from body orifices and hospital-induced needle puncture wounds. By January 24th, she was suffering from sleepiness and some slurring of speech; late in the day she appeared increasingly drowsy. On January 25th, she was flown to Bingham Memorial Hospital in Jos, Nigeria. She died on January 26th after several convulsions.
>
> A 45-year-old staff nurse, Ms. Charlotte Shaw, at the Bingham Memorial Hospital in Jos, Nigeria, was on night call when Ms. Wine was admitted on January 25th. Ms. Shaw had cut her finger earlier picking roses for another patient. As part of her nursing care, Ms. Shaw used a gauze dressing on that finger to clear secretions from the patient's mouth. Only afterward did she wash and apply antiseptic to the small cut on her finger. Nine days later Ms. Shaw had a chill with headache, severe back and leg pains and mild sore throat, a clinical picture similar to that of Ms. Wine who died eight days earlier. Over the next few days, Ms. Shaw had chills with fever to 102°–103°F, headache and occasional nausea. Seven days after the onset of symptoms, a rash appeared on her face, neck and arms and spread to her trunk and thighs. The rash appeared to be petechiae (small hemorrhages), and blood was oozing from several areas of her body. Her temperature was 104.8°F. By February 12th, her face was swollen; she had shortness of breath, a rapid, weak pulse ... became cyanotic [bluish] ... had a drop in blood pressure. Nurse Shaw died on the eleventh day of illness. Autopsy showed the presence of fluids in each pleural (chest) cavity and in the abdomen.
>
> A 52-year-old nurse, Ms. Lily Pinneo, working at the same Nigerian hospital, Bingham Memorial, had nursed both these patients and had assisted in autopsy of the second patient. She collected blood and tissue samples. On February 20th she too developed a temperature of 100°F ... followed two days later by weakness, headache, and nausea. After another three days, she had a sore throat and petechiae and was admitted to the hospital. Since this was the third case in progression, the physician decided to send the patient to the United States for diagnosis

and treatment. She was flown to Lagos, Nigeria, where she lay for four days in an isolation shed, and then to New York attended by a missionary nurse . . . She was admitted to Columbia University Presbyterian Hospital (New York City) . . . was placed in isolation with full precautions attended.

Pinneo continued to be acutely ill with a temperature of 101.2°F. The first night after admission, her temperature rose to 107°F. . . . She became extremely weak during the next six days. . . . Specimens from Ms. Pinneo were carried to the Rockefeller Foundation Arbovirus Laboratory at Yale for study. Even so, the patient recovered strength slowly, became fever-free and was discharged from the hospital on the 3rd of May.

About one month later, Dr. Jordi Cassals of the Yale University Arbovirus Research Laboratory, who was working with specimens from Ms. Pinneo, felt unwell. Because he had developed symptoms like those of the other three patients, he was admitted to the Columbia University Presbyterian Hospital. The medical team decided to give the deteriorating Dr. Cassals blood from Ms. Pinneo, the blood containing antibodies to protect against Lassa fever. Within twenty-four hours, his temperature was normal. During his slow convalescence, virus was isolated from his urine. In keeping with the practice of arbovirology at the time, the virus was assigned a name from the first geographical community where it had been isolated—Lassa, after the area in Nigeria. Other tests confirmed that all four patients had been infected with Lassa fever virus.

A few months later, in the autumn of 1969, Dr. Cassals was well enough to resume his studies in the Yale Arbovirus Laboratory. By November, work began on the live virus isolated from patients and passaged in mouse brains. Shortly thereafter, a laboratory technician, Juan Roman, near to but not in Dr. Cassals's laboratory, began to feel sick just before visiting his family in Pennsylvania. On the day after Thanksgiving, he entered a local hospital and died from Lassa fever before blood from an immune donor (such as Dr. Cassals or Ms. Pinneo) could be transfused. The Yale Arbovirus Laboratory decided not to perform any more experiments with live Lassa fever virus. The *New York Times, Time* magazine, and other publications reported that the virus was "too hot to handle."

Today in Africa, as in 1969, the scenario is that patients ill with fever of an unknown source are brought to medical stations or hospitals. Most are suspected of having malaria, an extremely common disease in that area also accompanied by fever, or of having a bacterial or viral infection.

Patients infected with the Lassa fever virus similarly have a high temperature along with throat and muscle pain. Invariably, their contact with the virus has been as short as five or as long as twenty-one days earlier. After an additional week of progressively worsening sore throat, diarrhea, and cough, pain surges through the chest and abdomen. Frequently red lesions erupt inside the mouth; the patients become anxious and appear deathly ill as their faces swell and their eyes redden. Blood leaks from small blood vessels, called capillaries, and from needle punctures made during hospital care. As internal bleeding worsens, the patients become delirious or confused, and many convulse before dying.

Lassa fever virus is constantly present in portions of West Africa, particularly in Guinea, Liberia, Sierra Leone, and Nigeria. An estimated 100,000 to 300,000 residents incur these infections each year with approximately 5,000 to 10,000 deaths. For about 80 percent of those infected with the virus, the disease is mild, although the remaining 20 percent suffer severe involvement of multiple bodily systems that, during epidemics, can reach a 50 percent or more level of fatality. Additionally, 15 to 20 percent of patients hospitalized for Lassa fever die from the illness. The death rate is extraordinarily high for women in the third trimester of pregnancy, and close to 95 percent of fetuses die in utero when the mothers have been infected. Of those who recover, deafness frequently follows, occurring in approximately one-third of the subjects. Estimates are that fewer than 10 percent of African patients with Lassa fever appear at medical care stations; the vast majority stay in their homes or in the bush. Those who do come to medical clinics or hospitals, once they begin to bleed, have the potential to infect nurses, orderlies, and physicians through blood contamination because their blood contains high levels of infectious virus. The death rate among hospital workers varies from outbreak to outbreak; the worst reported is about 60 percent and the least 10 percent. As the infection spreads, attending personnel and families of the patients sicken and die. Despite its virulence, Lassa fever has yielded but few of its secrets to those studying tissues from the victims. Little has been found to help in understanding the pathogenesis, or cause, of the disease (1). Although the liver is the most consistent site of disease, only a modest number of liver cells are destroyed, probably accounting for the absence of jaundice in these patients. Damage to the spleen is common, as is the loss of white blood cells such as T lymphocytes and macrophages in that organ. But many areas of the body become swollen, and, occasionally, T cells and other lymphocytes infiltrate a variety of tissues. The most significant fact is that so little tissue is actually destroyed—just enough to cause a lethal disease.

The reservoir for Lassa fever virus is rodents, which can retain a long-term, persistent infection with the virus. Secretions of urine or feces from infected rodents then contaminate humans who come into contact with them. The rodent-to-human transmission is augmented by human-to-human transmission, which spreads the viruses via contaminated blood, excreta, or saliva. Sadly, the African custom of nursing patients in homes and hospitals where relatives sleep in close quarters with the infected patient helps to spread the disease during both the incubation period and acute infection. Home nursing care nearly always involves direct contact with infected or dead persons through mucosal surfaces, skin abrasions, and contaminated needles/syringes/blood supply. After the virus enters its host, a four- to twelve-day incubation period passes, then the symptoms of disease suddenly begin. Usually, a flu-like syndrome of fever, chills, and malaise with muscle and headaches is followed by abdominal pain, nausea, and vomiting. The terminal stage adds poor coagulation, increased vascular permeability, hemorrhage, and neurologic symptoms. Those progressing to death have extremely large amounts of virus in their blood but little evidence of a functional (innate or adoptive) immune response.

Most of our understanding of the pathogenesis (disease causation) of Lassa fever virus is by analogy with lymphocytic choriomeningitis virus, the prototype Old World arenavirus. Like Lassa fever virus, lymphocytic choriomeningitis virus utilizes a molecule called alpha-dystroglycan as its receptor for attachment on and entry into cells (5). Dendritic cells are the players of the immune system that are essential for initiating the innate and adaptive immune response. Among various cell populations that constitute the immune system, dendritic cells express the greatest amounts of the viral receptor alpha-dystroglycan on their surfaces (6,7). That is, greater than 99 percent of the total amount of alpha-dystroglycan found in the immune system is on dendritic cells with less than 1 percent on T and B lymphocytes. As carefully worked out and well established during intensive research, we know that those strains of lymphocytic choriomeningitis virus that bind at the highest affinity (most tightly) to alpha-dystroglycan preferentially infect dendritic cells and alter their ability to initiate effective and efficient immune responses (6,8). The consequence of suppressing such innate and adaptive antiviral immune responses is that the viruses are free to replicate unchecked.

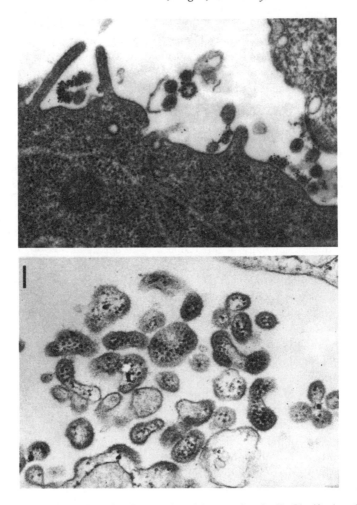

FIGURE 9.1 *Lassa fever virus is a member of the arenavirus family. Identification of the virions is useful for diagnosis because of the variation in size (polymorphism) and electron-dense ribosomes within virions. The electron photomicrographs here are of lymphocytic choriomeningitis virus, a member of the arenavirus family that looks identical to Lassa fever virus. These related viruses are distinguishable on the basis of chemical, nucleic acid, and immunologic assays. (Top) Virus; (bottom) virus budding from cell. Both show the polymorphism and ribosomes.*

Photomicrograph (top) from E. L. Palmer and M. L. Martin, An Atlas of Mammalian Viruses *(1982), courtesy of CRC Press, Inc., Boca Raton, FL.; (bottom) courtesy of Peter W. Lampert and Michael B. A. Oldstone.*

A similar scenario, although not yet proven, is thought to occur in Lassa fever virus-infected individuals who fail to develop an effective adoptive (antivirus T cell [cytotoxic CD8 T cell, helper CD4 T cell] or B cell [antiviral antibody]) response. This failure, coupled with the elevated virus titers that result from unchecked replication, lead the host to succumb from overwhelming infection. By contrast, those Lassa fever virus-infected individuals who mount adequate immune responses most often survive the infection. Recent biochemical analysis of the alpha-dystroglycan molecule found that a cellular glycosyltransferase enzyme, LARGE, is essential for adding a sugar unit to alpha-dystroglycan (9), thereby changing its conformation to promote binding to Lassa fever virus (10). A subject of great interest and current speculation concerning this observation is the result from a genomic survey that identified a polymorphism (more than one form) of LARGE in the western part of Africa where Lassa fever is endemic (11). In theory, as is still being tested, the polymorphism in LARGE may partially account for host factor(s) that determine susceptibility in one person but resistance in another to infection by the Lassa fever virus (12).

Could Lassa fever infection enter the United States unexpectedly? The answer is "yes." In 1990, a resident of Chicago, Illinois, went to Nigeria to attend a family funeral. While in Ekpoma, Nigeria, he unknowingly became infected with Lassa fever virus. When he returned to his home in Chicago, he became sick and was admitted to the hospital for a fever of unknown origin. The specific cause of his illness was not diagnosed or understood during the short remainder of his life. He died of Lassa fever (13). Fortunately, the infection did not spread among the other hospital patients, the medical and technical staff, his friends, or family.

Currently, a very modest amount of research is under way in the West African countries where Lassa fever virus is endemic. Monitoring of the disease is underreported, so understanding of its epidemiology and spread is limited. Yet, the introduction of Lassa fever from Africa into Europe, the United States, and other densely populated countries remains a continuing concern. The classification of Lassa fever virus as a highly dangerous biowarfare (terrorist) weapon also calls for more vigorous research in this area of virology.

10

Ebola

The Ebola virus first struck humans living in northern Zaire (in 1997, renamed the Congo Republic). Of the 318 persons infected with Ebola virus in that outbreak of 1976, 88 percent died (1–4). The responsible strain of this virus, called Ebola Zaire, surfaced again a year later in southern Zaire, but only one person died. The reason for the difference in the virus' virulence or the host susceptibility between the two outbreaks is not understood. The virus then lay quiescent until 1995, when it erupted to cause another epidemic in Southern Zaire.

In that year, the world's attention focused on Kikwit, Zaire, whose population is approximately half a million. There, the Ebola virus is known to have infected 316 persons, and in its wake over 244, or 77 percent, died. But certainly the numbers were greater, since no one could count individuals infected and dying in the bush. Most of those infected were young adults, on average about thirty-seven years old, although the range was from two to seventy-one years of age.

In the virus-stricken city of Kikwit, there was panic. The army sealed off roads and prevented anyone from leaving, a situation reminiscent of the yellow fever panic along the Mississippi River in Memphis 117 years earlier and of the barricades around parts of New York City seventy-nine years earlier during the outbreak of poliomyelitis. Similarly, the Ebola virus began to move toward the city of Kinshasa, about 250 miles away from Kikwit, despite the blockades. Like the Ebola outbreak in 1976 in villages along the Ebola River, 500 miles to the North of Kikwit, when nine of every ten residents who became infected died, the Ebola virus again made its mark along the Kinshasa Highway.

At the beginning of May 1995, a large number of patients with hemorrhagic fever entered the hospital in Kikwit, Zaire. In short order, the patients hospitalized for treatment, their families accompanying them, and many nurses and doctors who treated these patients died of severe hemorrhages. Ebola was suspected by local physicians who had observed similar cases nineteen years earlier (2). As reported in the weekly magazine *Newsweek* (5):

> When a 36-year-old lab technician known as Kinfumu checked into the general hospital in Kikwit, Zaire, last month, complaining of diarrhea and a fever, anyone could have mistaken his illness for the dysentery that was plaguing the city. Nurses, doctors and nuns did what they could to help the young man. They soon saw that his disease wasn't just dysentery. Blood began oozing from every orifice in his body. Within four days he was dead. By then the illness had all but liquefied his internal organs.
>
> That was just the beginning. The day Kinfumu died, a nurse and a nun who cared for him fell ill. The nun was evacuated to another town seventy miles to the West where she died—but not until the contagion had spread to at least three of her fellow nuns. Two subsequently died. In Kikwit, the disease raged through the ranks of the hospital's staff. Inhabitants of the city began fleeing to neighboring villages. Some of the fugitives carried the deadly illness with them. Terrified health officials in Kikwit sent an urgent message to the World Health Organization. The Geneva-based group summoned expert help from around the globe: a team of experienced virus hunters composed of tropical-medicine specialists, virologists and other researchers. They grabbed their lab equipment and their bubble suits and clambered aboard transport planes headed for Kikwit.
>
> Except for a handful of patients too sick to run away, the hospital was almost abandoned when the experts arrived. While the team went to work, the Zairean government tried to cordon off the city to prevent more inhabitants from spreading the contagion across the countryside—possibly even to the sprawling slums of Kinshasa, the capital, where most of its 4.5 million people live. The quarantine was mostly a hollow announcement; it had been years since there was a functioning government in Zaire. The international doctors sent people with bullhorns through the streets pleading with residents to stay home. And they managed to get a preliminary death toll—at least fifty-eight of seventy-six confirmed sufferers had now died.

Specimens were collected and forwarded via the Belgian Embassy to the Institute of Tropical Medicine in Antwerp for evaluation. But they could not be tested there for diagnosis of Ebola because that institute no longer had the appropriate containment laboratory for such studies. In Belgium, as elsewhere including the United States, short-term political considerations had reduced funding for surveillance as well as research into infectious diseases. The samples then traveled from Antwerp to the Communicable Disease Center in Atlanta, Georgia, where tests proved that most of the patients were infected with Ebola virus.

At that time, public health officials sought travelers to Europe or other countries who had been in the Kikwit region during the time of the outbreak and who might be incubating the Ebola agent. One such family quarantined in England was front-page news. The quarantine lasted until blood samples could be obtained and analyzed to show that they were not carriers of the Ebola virus.

Undoubtedly, the reports of 280 cases of Ebola in Kikwit and its surrounding areas were gross underestimations of the true tragedy that had occurred. Why? First, the stigma of disease prevents many victims from coming into the city, so they die in their rural villages. Second, an epidemic is frequently underreported or denied because of the fear that prospective tourists would cancel their visits. Zaire, like other African countries, depends on tourist travel for a major portion of its budget. Nevertheless, teams of international scientists arrived and searched for plants, animals, or insects in which the virus might reside when not ravaging humans. They failed to turn up leads until 2007, twelve years after outbreak in Kikwik, when the fruit bat was implicated as a reservoir (1).

Ebola virus can spread either through the air or by exposure to contaminated blood of infected humans. Relatives and family, who usually accompany African patients to the hospital and stay with them to administer nursing care, as well as medical and technical staff, are at high risk of contamination by coming into contact with blood or breathing infectious particles from these patients. The clinical course of Ebola virus infection is that of a severe hemorrhagic fever (2,3). During an initial incubation period, usually six to ten days (ranging from two to twenty-one days), the virus replicates in infected individuals. An abrupt onset of fever, frontal headache, weakness, muscle pain, slow heart rate, reddening of the eyes (conjunctivitis), and abdominal pain follow. Lethargy and lack of facial expression are common, with eyes having a sunken look. Two to three days later, the patients experience nausea, vomiting of blood, bloody

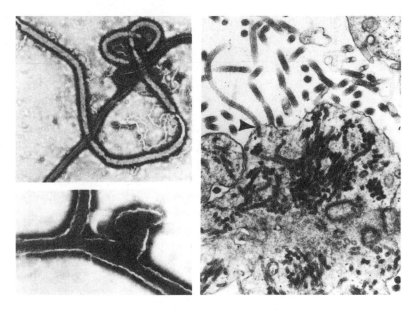

FIGURE 10.1 *Ebola virus morphology. (Left) Electron photomicrograph of a specimen from cell (tissue culture) passage. Human blood specimen from the 1976 epidemic. (Top) Magnification: 35,000×; (bottom) magnification: 63,000×. (Right) Ebola virus (arrow) budding from the plasma membrane of an infected cell. Magnification: 28,000×. Pictures courtesy of Fields' Virology (Philadelphia: Lippincott-Raven, 1996).*

diarrhea, and hemorrhage in the mouth and nasal passages, followed by prostration. A rash then appears, and death usually follows six to nine days after the symptoms start. For those few who survive, convalescence usually takes two to five weeks and is marked by profound exhaustion and weight loss. Spontaneous abortions are common consequences of this infection, and infants born of mothers dying of the infection become fatally infected. The terminal state consists of coagulation disorders, disseminated intravascular coagulation, increased vascular permeability, hemorrhage from mucosal surfaces, and death (2,3).

Because the disease process moves with such rapidity and devastation, systematic study of pathophysiologic changes has been difficult. Still not clear is how the terminal shock syndrome unfolds nor how the body chemistry makes holes in tiny blood vessels, causing the patients' profuse bleeding. There is no treatment for Ebola virus infection except rest, nourishment, and fluids. The only antiviral drug with potential benefits, ribavirin, has not been tested enough to evaluate its effectiveness. Those who die show little evidence of an adoptive T cell response, whereas those recovering display an antiviral CD8 T cell response and antiviral antibody response. However, since administering (passive transfer) antibodies to ill patients is not effective, it is questionable whether antibodies play a protective role. Within the immune system, infection settles in dendritic cells, monocytes, and macrophages. At present, researchers who seek to understand how the Ebola/Marburg group of viruses infect and destroy tissues focus on the involvement of endothelial blood vessels, the coagulation system, and the suppression of T and B cell antiviral immune responses, likely a consequence of dendritic cell infection. The Ebola virus bears an enclosing coat of glycoprotein that is thought to increase viral replication and even kill (cause apoptosis of) several types of cells where the virus replicates. As to the source of this virus, the fruit bat (1,7) was recently identified as its first-known nonhuman vector.

Unanticipated outbreaks of Ebola continue. A total of sixty cases with forty-five deaths (fatality rate 75 percent) occurred in Gabon between mid-July 1996 and January 1997. As recently as August 2007, reports from the southeastern Congo documented 217 people who were afflicted with the virus, of whom 103 have died (fatality rate of 47 percent).

Has Ebola escaped to the Western world? Again, yes. In 1989, in Reston, Virginia, a suburb located less than twenty miles from Washington, DC, at least four humans became infected during an outbreak of Ebola in monkeys. The infection caused by airborne Ebola virus was from cynomologous monkeys brought from the Philippines (6). Of the 161 monkeys imported, more than half died over a two-and-a-half-month period. Luckily, and for unknown reasons, the virus failed to spread to other humans, even though the airborne route of transmission was available.

Ebola virus is classified as a filovirus (*filo*, Latin for worm) because its structure seen under the electron microscope resembles that of a worm (1). Another member of this group of viruses is called Marburg, for the city of Marburg, Germany, where the virus caused an outbreak of infection. In Marburg and unaware that monkeys carried Marburg virus, technicians and researchers used such monkeys as a source of tissue culture materials in their laboratories. At the initial outbreak in 1967, thirty-one persons came down with an acute illness and fever, and seven of them died before the virus was identified. The Marburg virus enjoys a

TABLE 10.1 Proven Filovirus Infections

Virus	Year	Location	Cases	% Mortality
A. In the 1960s–1990s				
Marburg	1967	Germany and Yugoslavia	31	23
Marburg	1975	Zimbabwe	3	33
Ebola (Zaire)	1976	Northern Zaire/Congo	318	88
Ebola (Sudan)	1976	Southern Sudan	284	53
Ebola (Sudan)	1976	England	1	0
Ebola (Zaire)	1977	Southern Zaire/Congo	1	100
Ebola (Sudan)	1979	Southern Sudan	34	65
Marburg	1980	Kenya	2	50
Marburg	1987	Kenya	1	100
Ebola (Reston)	1989	Virginia, USA	4	0
Ebola (Reston)	1992	Siena, Italy	0	0
Ebola (Ivory Coast)	1994	Ivory Coast	1	0
Ebola (Zaire)	1995	Southern Zaire/Congo	316	77
Ebola (Zaire)	1996–97	Gabon	60	75
B. Recent Outbreaks				
Ebola	2007	Uganda	149	25
Ebola	2007	Congo	249	74
Marburg	2007	Uganda	1	100

near symbiotic relationship with the monkeys it infects so does not harm them. But when man as an interloper comes into contact with fluids from an infected monkey, potentially fatal disease follows.

Ebola virus remains endemic in parts of Africa. Of over 5,000 blood samples collected from individuals in central Africa, nearly a quarter (25 percent) tested positive for prior infection with Ebola. Whether the fruit bat is the only natural reservoir for such viruses, how Ebola is transmitted, and where it lurks, all remain unknown.

Ebola—with its high fatality rate in humans, the lack of information about its natural history, origin of its periodic outbreaks, or mode of its transportation, and the inability to prevent or stop the disease once it begins—conjures up fears of a spreading disaster. These human responses to Ebola are reminiscent of events in the past associated with outbreaks of yellow fever and polio. The fear and fascination attached to Ebola infection come from our ignorance of how to treat, prevent, or contain the disease, and our helplessness in its wake. The possibility of terrorist groups using Ebola as a biological weapon amplifies the fearfulness of this situation.

11

Hantavirus

Hantaviruses are among the infectious agents currently found in the United States with the potential of causing plagues (1,2).

In 1993, a man and woman living on the Navajo Reservation in Muerto Canyon, New Mexico, suddenly experienced high fever, muscle pain, headache, and cough. Their lungs soon filled with fluid, and death from respiratory failure followed, first the woman and five days later the man. Public inquiries by the New Mexico Department of Health revealed twenty similar cases of acute respiratory distress in the region where the four states of New Mexico, Arizona, Utah, and Colorado join, the so-called "Four Corners" area. As with the initial two cases, all had been healthy young adults. Their mean age was thirty-four years. Of the twenty afflicted, half died.

Evaluation of these patients' medical histories and analysis of samples taken from their blood and tissues at autopsy by virologists at the Communicable Disease Center in Atlanta, Georgia, indicated that a single infectious agent was the cause. This agent was identified as a Hantavirus (3), a member of the Bunyaviridae family (4). Next, scientists using molecular techniques for study of the viruses' genes reported that the Hantavirus recovered was quite different from previously isolated strains, all of which were known to cause hemorrhagic fevers and kidney disease, but not acute lung injury. The newly observed disease was termed Hantavirus pulmonary syndrome (1–3). By March 1995,

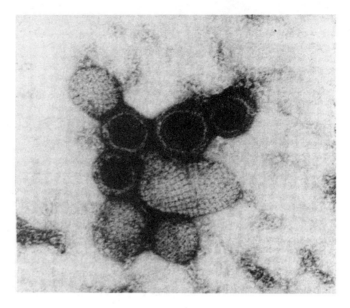

FIGURE 11.1 *Electron photomicrograph of Hantavirus. Magnification: 128,000×. Photomicrograph from E. L. Palmer and M. L. Martin,* An Atlas of Mammalian Viruses *(1982), courtesy of CRC Press, Inc., Boca Raton, FL.*

some 106 patients with Hantavirus pulmonary syndrome had been identified in twenty states and more than half of those afflicted died. Generally symptoms were fever, muscle pain, cough, nausea, vomiting, and headache lasting about four but up to fifteen days and eventually requiring hospitalization of the patients. At admission, most patients were feverish with low blood pressure and low platelet counts (the cells required for clotting of blood), and they had abnormalities (specifically, infiltrates) of the lungs visible in chest X-rays. Thereafter, the patients developed pulmonary edema, a condition in which the lungs progressively fill with fluid. To this day, no one knows exactly how the Hantavirus causes disease, although recent evidence suggests that the release of certain proteins, possibly the cytokines and chemokines that are such prominent moderators of immune response, are responsible. During the inflammation that results from this infection, a so-called "cytokine storm" plays an important role in the pathogenesis of the disease. No treatment other than supportive therapy and prevention is available to alleviate the symptoms of Hantavirus infection. As in Zaire and other sites of epidemics, the southwestern United States suffered a decline in tourism once the outbreak of Hantavirus became public knowledge, causing economic hardship. Consequently, the original name of the virus, Four Corners virus, which depicted the geographic site where the disease emerged, was changed. Because of the political and economic outfall, the virus is now called Sin Nombre virus, Spanish for "no-name virus" (1,5). This is the first politically correct virus.

Hantavirus as a cause of hemorrhagic fever is not new (4). Evidence from Chinese medical tests suggests its existence over 1,000 years ago. In 1951–53 during the war in Korea, this virus made news when hemorrhagic fever developed in over 2,000 United Nations troops. The transmissible nature of the disease was first documented after serum and urine taken from patients, then inoculated into human volunteers, produced the infection. Epidemiologic evidence suggested that wild rodents or ectoparasites carried the viral agent, which in 1976 was identified in

Distribution of known rodent hosts for Hantavirus and location of HPS cases, as of May 17, 1995.

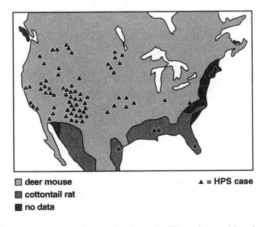

□ deer mouse   ▲ = HPS case
▨ cottontail rat
■ no data

FIGURE 11.2 *Distribution of known rodent hosts for Hantavirus and location of Hantavirus pulmonary syndrome (HPS) cases, as of May 17, 1995. Known distribution in the United States of the rodent vectors that carry Hantavirus and the locations where human HPS has been recorded. (Hatched area) Peromyscus maniculatus (deer mouse); (dotted area) Sigmodon hispidus (cottontail rat). Data courtesy of Brian Mahy, Centers for Disease Control and Prevention, Atlanta, Georgia.*

the lungs of field rodents in Korea. Four years later the virus was isolated, grown in tissue culture, and used to develop a diagnostic test. Although the virus is named for the Hantaan River in Korea, Hantaviruses had infected victims in Japan, Russia, Sweden, Finland, and several other European countries preceding the outbreak in the United States.

The deer mouse (*Peromyscus maniculatus*), a natural carrier for Hantavirus, was trapped and examined in the Four Corners area of the United States (1,5). Later, several hundred of these rodents were trapped in other areas where the Hantavirus pulmonary syndrome erupted, and the animals had antibodies to the virus in their blood and also RNA sequences specific for Hantavirus in their tissues. This viral RNA in the deer mice matched viral RNA sequences found in lungs of patients dying with disease. Clearly, the disease spread from the mice to humans interloping into their territory.

P. maniculatus rodents live throughout the North American continent from northern Canada to Mexico and across South America. These carriers of virus present a potential hazard to many large populations and probably have been responsible for cases of acute pulmonary disease occurring widely. The latest studies of *P. maniculatus* rodents outside the Four Corners region indicate that the Hantavirus they now carry is a newly mutated form. Additionally, several other rodent species also bear the virus. For example, investigation of viral pulmonary disease in a Florida resident led to the isolation of Hantavirus in *Sigmodan hispidus* (cottontail) rats. Later, the fatal pulmonary syndrome of a patient in Rhode Island was attributed to Hantavirus carried in the *P. leucopus* (white-footed) mouse. Similar isolates have been located in the northwestern part of the United States, in Canada, and as far south as Brazil. In only two years since its description in 1993, over 100 cases of Hantavirus pulmonary syndrome disease have been noted. Moreover, the mortality rate is above 50 percent. The rodent populations widely ranging throughout the Americas capable of carrying Hantaviruses, coupled with humans at risk for exposure to such rodents in rural and urban areas, signal a potential health disaster. At present, neither an effective antiviral therapy nor a vaccine is available. The best strategy now is rodent control and avoidance of close contact with rodents or their excretions. But in winter, rodents frequently leave the open fields for the warmth of cities and their homes, possibly to deliver disease directly to our doorsteps.

The status quo of these viral infections for which no cure exists is bad enough, but even worse is the fact that Lassa fever virus, Ebola virus,

Hantavirus, and other RNA viruses like SARS, West Nile virus, HIV, and influenza virus frequently mutate. RNA viruses lack the fidelity that DNA viruses (such as smallpox) have to maintain the stable genetic information that programs their nucleic acid structure. The enzyme (DNA polymerase), which makes DNA for DNA viruses, has the capacity to proofread what it has made. If a mistake occurs, DNA polymerase corrects the error often by removing the incorrect sequence. By contrast, the enzyme for RNA viruses (RNA polymerase) lacks this ability and cannot correct errors. Consequently, RNA viruses have relatively high mutation rates because they lack good editing devices. The high level of mutations that RNA viruses frequently undergo provides them with a great potential for adaptability. Through a process of mutation and selection in a new host, more virulent or easily transmitted viruses may arise.

12

Severe Acute Respiratory Syndrome (SARS): The First Pandemic of the Twenty-First Century

Severe Acute Respiratory Syndrome (SARS) represented the first new viral pandemic of the twenty-first century. Beginning mysteriously in southern China during November of 2002, it was brought under control by 2004 but only after spreading to thirty-three countries on five continents and infecting over 8,000 humans, 774 of whom died (1). Then as mysteriously as it came, it disappeared.

Following the original epidemic in 2002–2003, a new outbreak occurred in 2003–2004. During this second attack, the city of Toronto in the province of Ontario, Canada, was the world's most affected city. Because of the 375 SARS cases and forty-four deaths (2–4) there, the World Health Organization (WHO) advised staying away from Toronto. Their tourism industry suffered a loss of 260 million Canadian dollars, and layoffs of employees in related businesses reached double digits. The total financial loss for the province of Ontario was $1.13 billion (5,6).

What SARS is, how it originated and became a pandemic, and how it was recognized are the principal ingredients of this chapter. Telling those stories accents the danger SARS evoked in the world community, the Chinese government's initial denial that the disease existed, and a reversal of that claim by a courageous whistleblower, Dr. Jiang Yanyong. Finally, how the disease spread to and through Toronto exemplifies the speed and breadth of viral migration today.

SARS is caused by a member of the coronavirus family; therefore, the virus's full name is SARS-CoV (7). Corona refers to the crownlike appearance of coronavirus, a circular core with spikelike projections of the surrounding glycoproteins, as viewed by electron microscopy. Coronaviruses infect a wide variety of animals as well as humans. The first coronaviruses isolated included an infectious bronchitis virus of animals identified in 1930 (8), a transmissible gastroenteritis virus of pigs noted in the mid-1940s (9), and an encephalitis virus of mice recorded in 1949 (10). By the 1960s, coronaviruses were isolated from humans, primarily from their upper respiratory tracts, and were associated with modest respiratory disease and minimal mortality (7). All that changed in 2002/2003 with the birth of SARS-CoV and the severe clinical disease it caused in humans (1,11–14).

SARS-CoV infects not only the upper airway, as do the other human coronaviruses, but also cells lining the lungs, that is, the alveolar epithelium in the lower respiratory tract (7). As a result, these patients have severe difficulty in breathing, causing shortness of breath, respiratory distress, and poor transfer of oxygen from the lungs to the blood. The smallest units of the lungs are the pulmonary alveoli or air cells that form the lung's alveolar ducts and sacs. In this area, the exchange of gases (intake of oxygen and exit of carbon dioxide) between the lungs and blood takes place. The alveolar lining is composed of epithelial cells that become infected with SARS-CoV. In addition to infecting the lungs, SARS-CoV also nests in the small intestine, liver, and kidneys. The mechanism(s), or pathogenesis, of injury to tissue infected by the virus is not clear. For example, as the clinical disease worsens, the amount of virus present (virus titer) decreases, while the number of infiltrating macrophages and T cells increases greatly. This scenario suggests that a major mediator of this tissue injury and disease may be the host's own immune response to the virus. Further support for the concept of immune-mediated injury is the heightened levels of proinflammatory chemokines and cytokines, which are factors made primarily by infected macrophages and T cells (7) but known to cause injury. The significant elevation of these inflammatory products suggests that a "cytokine storm" plays an important part in the disease of SARS.

The lower respiratory track's involvement in this disease is often serious enough to require the victims' hospitalization. Of those admitted to the hospital, over 20 percent are so sick that confinement in an intensive care unit is necessary. The fatality rate is about 10 percent, over half of whom are the elderly and/or those having preexisting heart or pulmonary problems. The course of disease after exposure to SARS-CoV is short; within four to six days the infected individuals develop the general symptoms of fever, weakness, muscle pain, and loss of appetite. After a few more days, respiratory symptoms emerge including a dry nonproductive cough and shortness of breath. Thereafter, the disease either resolves or progresses to ongoing respiratory failure within several days, weeks, or occasionally months. For those who recover, complete remission may take months, and for some of these patients, respiratory difficulties remain permanent.

The coronaviruses per se are RNA viruses and contain the largest genome of any RNA virus, as much as 27–32 kb. By comparison, other RNA viruses like Lassa fever virus is 10.7 kb and poliovirus 7.5 kb. The RNA of coronaviruses is of a positive strand type; that is, their RNA is infectious and serves as a virus messenger RNA. Organizationally, the various RNAs of coronaviruses contain seven to fourteen open reading frames and usually encode five structural proteins.

The original outbreak of SARS began in November 2002 in Guangdong, southern China. Because the characteristic symptom was respiratory distress without identifiable bacteria, the cause was provisionally attributed to a virus (reviewed 15). Epidemiologic studies showed that about half the patients examined early in that epidemic were food handlers in markets where live animals were sold or processed for meat or in restaurants (1,16,17). Others were health-care workers or family members taking care of SARS-infected patients. Laboratory study of viral RNA obtained from such patients revealed a similarity to coronaviruses but also a uniqueness. Further, RNA genetic mapping of the SARS-CoV isolated from patients indicated a structure almost identical to that of coronaviruses isolated from animals in the marketplace, primarily the masked palm civet (catlike animals used in Chinese cuisine). Serologic (blood) studies supporting the unique properties of this new infection and the relationship to civet animals defined a distinctive pattern. First, market traders whose blood was sampled during 2002–2003 had higher antibody titers to the coronavirus than did the general population; second, patients infected with SARS had high antibody titers to SARS-CoV, and third, retrospective surveys failed to document antibodies to SARS-CoV prior to 2002 in the South China area. Further, the earliest bearers of SARS viruses were more often persons who lived close to the animal market than those further away. The first evidence that infected animals sold or processed in the markets might have transmitted the disease to humans occurred in 2003. Of twenty-five animals studied, a virus closely related to SARS-CoV was isolated from three masked palm civets and one raccoon (1,15). Unfortunately, no further epidemiologic surveys were done at that time as follow-up on animals traded in the markets. Experimental studies were performed and revealed that ten mammalian species could be infected with SARS-CoV isolated from humans. One of these was the masked palm civet. When further sequence analysis proved a close match between viruses isolated from the civets and humans, an association of civets with the human disease was inferred. However, still not clear was whether the civets only spread the disease through primary infection and/or were also a natural reservoir of the virus. Even so, evidence suggested that civets could transmit and thereby spread SARS. A primary example was an incident of a waitress who became infected while working in a restaurant where a sick civet was housed in a cage (18).

However, this was obviously not the complete answer. Part of the puzzle was missing, since epidemiologic studies also revealed that many animal handlers in close association with civets did not get the disease, whereas a number of humans who got SARS and were positive in tests for SARS-CoV had no contact with civets. However, suspicion that the masked palm civets transmitted SARS and the desire to prevent its spread led to the removal of civets from Chinese markets.

Later investigations cast doubt that civets were the reservoir for SARS viruses. First, there was no compelling evidence for widespread SARS-CoV infections of civets either trapped in the wild or raised on farms. Second, animals that serve as vector for transmitting a disease usually have coevolved with the pathogen and are rarely ill from the infectious agent they harbor. Examples of such host/microbe interactions are the mosquito that carries and spreads yellow fever, the rodent that harbors and spreads Lassa fever virus, or the bat in which Ebola and Marburg viruses travel. Yet, when civets not previously exposed to SARS-CoV were experimentally infected with the virus, they developed overt disease. This result strongly suggested that, although civets could have initially infected humans, civets themselves had also become infected from another source and were not the natural reservoir for maintaining the infectious agent. What then could the natural reservoir be?

A number of investigators then evaluated the possibility that bats might be the natural reservoir for SARS-CoV (reviewed 15,19–22). Bats are the known carriers of several viruses that infect humans— the so-called zoonotic viruses; these include rabies, Ebola, Hendra, and Nipah viruses. Additionally, bats and bat products frequent the foods and medicine markets throughout southern China. To test this hypothesis, over 400 bats in their natural habitat were trapped and sampled. The results showed a high prevalence of antibodies to SARS-CoV. The polymerase chain reaction (PCR) assay of genome sequences soon provided molecular evidence of SARS-CoV in bats. Nearly 80 percent of the bats sampled had antibodies to SARS-CoV, and 39 percent had SARS-like genetic sequences in fecal swabs. The fact that bats were not sick from the SARS-CoV they carried further indicated that they were its natural reservoir. At present, three distinct species of horseshoe bats have been implicated as natural reservoirs for maintaining SARS in the communities they occupy.

But how does the SARS-CoV spread from bats to civets and then to humans? Bats have a high energy requirement, and they meet that need by eating fruit. However, instead of swallowing, bats chew the fruit they eat to extract sugars, proteins, and other needed compounds then spit out the partially digested residue. Presumably, bat saliva contains SARS-CoV, and the extruded infected material is then available on digestion to cause infection of other animals. Eating such processed and expelled fruits, civets would become infected. Moreover, fecally or orally passed material from bats likely infects civets. Subsequently, by ingesting civet meat or by drinking a fruit drink expelled from bats' partially digested fruit, which is a popular beverage in China, humans could be infected. However at the time of writing this chapter, infectious SARS-CoV had not yet been isolated from bats, although those tested contained the viral genetic material. An additional issue still to be resolved is that the genomic sequence of SARS-CoV of humans differs significantly from SARS-CoV of bats. Since viruses usually cannot jump from one species to another without adaptation, and bat SARS-CoV fails to grow in cell cultures that support the growth of both human and civet SARS-CoV, another yet to be discovered animal reservoir(s) may exist. Although bats are a likely candidate as the SARS-CoV reservoir, they probably are not the only one. Most important to the spread of SARS virus among humans is the transmission from one person to others, which spreads the infectious agent and resulting disease.

A still vital but incompletely answered question is, how did SARS become a global pandemic? After the initial outbreak in 2002, the disease was contained in southern China by 2003. The Chinese government reported to the international community and the World Health Organization that containment was almost complete and that no new or very few cases of SARS had materialized. However, this report was untrue, a purposeful deception by members of China's government. In fact, SARS infections continued to arise and spread throughout China. Soon nongovernmental reports leaked to the outside world from individuals who reported that SARS was not controlled but, instead, repeatedly broke out in China during 2003. As evidence of new cases emerged and as international pressure mounted, the Chinese government changed its course of denial and took drastic steps to curtail the epidemic and reverse its image of public health negligence and irresponsibility. After an internal investigation, criminal charges were brought resulting in the death penalty for Chinese officials, doctors, and public health workers who had hidden the SARS outbreak. In addition, the mayor of Beijing and the minister of public health were ousted from office. The spark that ignited international awareness that SARS remained unchecked in China despite official government denial came from a courageous Chinese doctor, Jiang Yanyong (23), who supplied documents to the outside world proving his claim. Yanyong was a military physician posted in hospital 301 near Tiananmen Square. After the discovery that he had passed information about SARS infections to Western journalists, Yanyong was initially placed under house arrest and forbidden to talk to strangers. However, once the SARS outbreak was acknowledged by the Chinese government, Yanyong rose to international prominence for his disclosure that at least 100 patients were undergoing treatment in Beijing hospitals for severe cases of SARS. The embarrassed Chinese leaders were forced to acknowledge that false information about the epidemic had been provided to the world's health community. As the whistle blower, Dr. Yanyong was then hailed as a national hero of China (23), and, remarkably, he used that platform to press China's ruling Politburo standing committee to admit not only their lies about the country's SARS epidemic but also their error in ordering military troops to shoot unarmed civilians and students in Tiananmen Square's massacre. This admission had special meaning for Yanyong, who had been deeply involved in the 1989 massacre as a physician treating wounds of injured demonstrators. In 2007, this brave man was selected to receive The Heinz R. Pagel Human Rights of Scientists Award given by The New York Academy of Sciences (23), but he was prevented from receiving this award when the Chinese government removed his status of national hero and placed him under house arrest.

China is a powerful country whose ancient culture provided the world with such inventions as paper, gunpowder, and pasta. However, its governing style has been and continues to be dominated by a strong ruling body controlling a populace that is completely subservient. As a government with absolute power whose members are not elected by its citizens, the rulers feel no need for responsiveness to its people or compliance with international law. This scenario played out during the SARS epidemic when the Chinese government shed its responsibility and failed to participate in global cooperation. For disease control, especially in this era of mass movement of people/businesses throughout our world and the rapidity of transportation to every geographic area, the cooperation of all the world's governments is an urgent necessity. Without universal cooperation in public health, continued fatal epidemics must prevail.

In 2003, a Canadian woman on a visit to Hong Kong became exposed to SARS-CoV and incubated the virus as she traveled by airplane on her return home to Toronto, Canada (2,13,14). She developed fever and respiratory distress, was cared for at home, and died. Her son assisted with her care soon felt ill, found breathing difficult, and went to the hospital emergency room to seek help. The waiting room where he sat for hours was, as usual, crowded with others, so this son of the mother who died from respiratory failure and was later diagnosed as having SARS infected two more people. Those two communicated the disease to many more until the contamination of patients, health-care workers, and visitors resulted in 375 cases of SARS-CoV infection (7,15,24). Among them, 45 percent, or 169 of the individuals infected, were health-care workers; two nurses and one doctor died (2,24). This episode was a catastrophe in the handling of human disease, during which one country's government failed to curtail its spread causing severe overloading of the medical and hospital facilities and a substantial financial loss in another country, which then suffered a lethal epidemic. The World Health Organization responded with an advisory quarantine that, within three months after the first incident of SARS in Toronto, was discontinued when local authorities declared the crisis over. Nevertheless, a second and larger outbreak followed, likely due to the political and business pressures to lift the WHO advisory warning, the removal of local emergency restrictions, and a decrease in the surveillance system.

What are the lessons to be learned from this first pandemic of the twenty-first century? The first is a responsibility of all nations to maintain surveillance for known lethal diseases, to exchange blood and tissue samples from infected humans and lower animals, and to be prepared with sophisticated new molecular assays such as gene chip analysis, PCR, cloning, and amino acid sequencing that allow rapid diagnosis. In this context, no man is an island; we are all connected on this one planet. Second, local and national politics as well as government control to protect any nation's image, business, or economy must be secondary to international health concerns. Third, unrelenting surveillance that applies the established tools of epidemiology must be utilized to control disease and quarantine sites of infection when necessary to protect the common good. Fourth, extreme care must be exerted in working with newly emerging and established human pathogens. For example, in 2004, thirteen laboratory workers became infected with the SARS virus while working under improper containment conditions. Fifth, the accessibility of rapid transportation to most every corner of the globe requires an international vaccine and quarantine program where appropriate. Sixth, emergency plans should be devised and adopted in national and/or local areas where a new pandemic threatens. The SARS outbreak in Toronto serves as a blueprint for the difficulties and workload involved and emphasizes what should and should not be done. At that time, public health workers investigated 2,132 potential cases of SARS and identified 23,103 individuals who required quarantine because of contact with SARS patients. Over 315,000 phone calls were logged on a hotline for those concerned about the infection. SARS spread to eleven of Toronto's acute care hospitals, dramatically overburdening the health-care system of that city. Of the 225 patients who met the criteria for a SARS diagnosis, all but three infections originated from the single index case initiated in Hong Kong.

13

West Nile Virus: Deaths of Crows and Humans

As recently as 1999, West Nile virus made its first appearance in North America, and the target it struck was New York City. This chapter tells of the detective work that identified this virus as the cause of a formerly unknown disease whose path through America was a trail of dead birds and dead people. The initial concern and later panic embodied the possibility that this country was witnessing its first bioterrorist attack, one that threatened to overshadow even the events of 9/11/2001. In just a few years, West Nile virus and the disease it caused spread geographically south, north, and west from New York City to the majority of states in the United States. By early 2008, this disease had been identified in over 28,000 individuals of whom one-third suffered inflammation/infection of the brain (encephalitis) or cells lining the brain (leptomeningitis) and about 3 percent died from the infection (1–5). West Nile virus is currently the most common and severe of the mosquito-borne encephalides in North America.

In late June of 1999, the Bayside Veterinarian Clinic located in the borough of Queens in New York City examined several birds with an unusual disorder of the nervous system. Many had died, but the survivors were released. By July and August, more dead birds were found in the area. Nassau County highway crews brought bags of dead crows picked up along roads in Queens to the city's Department of Environmental Conservation. At the Bronx Zoo, keepers discovered dead birds in their cages and others in the wild. These birds were also sent to the New York Department of Environmental Conservation. Then still more birds died at the Queens Zoo. A wildlife pathologist who was enlisted to perform autopsies on several of the birds failed to identify the cause but ruled out common problems that could have killed so many of the creatures. Examiners at the New York State Department of Environmental Conservation could not identify any of the known toxins or parasites like bacteria or fungi in samples sent to them for testing.

That summer the New York City area was hot and dry. In mid-August, Flushing Queens Hospital admitted a feverish, seriously ill elderly patient whose symptoms affecting the central nervous system (CNS) included headache, confusion, and muscle weakness (6). Five days later two other patients with similar symptoms (indicators of illness that the patient describes) and signs (indicators that the doctor sees) (6) were admitted to the hospital. One of these patients then developed heart failure. By the end of August, the hospital physician specializing in infectious diseases noted that his department had admitted more patients with brain infections (encephalitis/meningitis) than the expected number and that their condition involved an unusual association of CNS disease with muscle weakness. About the time a fourth patient with CNS disease and muscle weakness was admitted, the infectious disease specialist became aware that excessive and increasing numbers of cerebral spinal fluid (CSF) samples had been sent for diagnosis of CNS disease compared to the usual few drawn each year. Unable to find a cause for these infections and muscle impairment, the specialist contacted the Bureau of Communicable Diseases within the New York City Health Department, which advised sending the CSF samples to the virology laboratory of The New York State Health Department and The Centers for Disease Control and Prevention (CDC). The CDC, which is the federal government's agency that evaluates disease outbreaks, is administered by the Department of Health and Human Services. Furthermore, the CDC is the lead agency for investigation of bioterrorism.

At the hospital in Queens at the end of August, a seventh patient was admitted. One of the previous patients with the mysterious infection died, and an autopsy was performed (6,7). Meanwhile, the New York City Health Department sent epidemiologists to investigate the disease outbreak in Queens. The epidemiologic field investigator located numerous mosquito breeding sites and mosquito larvae in and around the hospitalized patients' backyards and surrounding neighborhoods, all pointing to a mosquito-borne disease as the possible culprit. At the same time, reports of bird deaths continued to increase, especially crows in New York City and as far as Buffalo. Again, the Bronx Zoo found dead birds in and outside their caged facilities. By the second week in September, when the head pathologist of the Bronx Zoo had recorded the deaths of over 400 birds, samples were sent to the U.S. Geological Survey at the National Wildlife Center, a federal government facility that assesses and diagnoses disease outbreak in birds and other animals.

Meanwhile, the New York State Health Department reported evidence of flavivirus infection in the patients' samples they had received. Flaviviruses are a group of small positive-strand RNA viruses that includes the yellow fever virus (see Chapter 5) (1,2). After being bitten by a mosquito bearing this virus, the victim develops an infection that reaches the brain, most likely by traveling in circulating blood, although spread via the peripheral nerves is also possible. Flavus is the Latin word for yellow. Several members of the flaviviral family are mosquito borne, have birds as their natural hosts, and cause encephalitis. Antibodies to specific flaviviruses are usually used to identify these pathogens in patients' blood or tissues but often cross-react among various sub-species in the viral group. Therefore, positive diagnosis of a specific family member rests primarily with distinguishing its genetic sequence and unique differences therein.

Along with its many responsibilities, the CDC also maintains laboratories that identify unusual or exotic viruses and other pathogens. One such laboratory, and the one actively involved in this investigation, is the Division of Vector-Borne Infectious Diseases at Fort Collins, Colorado. This unit deals with viral and bacterial diseases transmitted by mosquitoes and ticks and provides laboratory services for diagnoses of such vector-borne pathogens. Evaluating methods to prevent, treat, and control vector-borne outbreaks is also the work of this division.

By early September 1999, samples of the blood and cerebrospinal fluid previously drawn from hospitalized patients and sent to The New York State Laboratory as well as the CDC had been tested by serologic assay. The results showed strong reactivity for St. Louis encephalitis virus, a member of the flavivirus group but never before reported in New York City. However, St. Louis encephalitis virus had caused most of the mosquito-borne virus outbreaks of this nerve disease in the United States. The lower forty-eight states are home to this virus, which induces, on average, thirty to forty cases of encephalitis per year.

The saga continued. Virtually equaling the entire country's usual caseload, the number of patients with suspected encephalitis approached forty in the New York City area alone, and the eighth patient was admitted to the Flushing Queens Hospital. Again, the CNS symptoms and muscle weakness were prominent. The CDC Division of Vector-Borne Infectious Diseases using an ELISA antibody test reported positive identification of St. Louis encephalitis virus and ruled out several other viruses. For the ELISA, an investigator isolates the antigens (proteins that stimulate an immune response) of several viruses. These antigens are placed on a plate along with the serum portion from the patient's blood. On the basis of reactions produced during these tests, news releases stated that the CDC had confirmed an outbreak of St. Louis encephalitis in New York City. The New York Health Department initiated a mosquito control program for the city, disseminated public information about the disease, and established a hotline. The Federal Bureau of Investigation (FBI) was alerted about the unusual infection in New York City to evaluate whether this was a potential bioterror attack. Public hotlines now overflowed with reports that large numbers of birds continued to die. At the CDC headquarters in Atlanta, an antibody used as an immunochemical stain disclosed that brain samples from the patient who had recently died contained the flaviviral antigens. Bird deaths increased further in the Bronx Zoo, throughout New York City and surrounding areas. The first human outside of Queens who tested positive for this virus was reported in Brooklyn, and a third patient died in the Flushing Queens Hospital. As the number of patients with suspected flavivirus infections grew throughout New York City, *The New York Times* reported that public health officials were investigating additional cases over those already reported. Eight more patients died of encephalitis, and fifteen more infected people in New York City and Westchester County were suspected of hosting the St. Louis encephalitis virus (4).

Nevertheless, the relationship between these infections and the St. Louis encephalitis virus was not entirely clear. The uncertainties fell into five categories. First, as mentioned earlier, St. Louis encephalitis virus had never before visited New York City. Second, questions remained unanswered about diagnoses issued by investigators using a newer assay, the polymerase chain reaction (PCR) test, whereas others used antigen/antibody reactions for diagnosis. Third, the St. Louis encephalitis viruses had been identified by their reaction to antibodies, but those antibodies sometimes cross-reacted with several other members of the flavivirus group. Fourth, the St. Louis encephalitis viruses that were known generally were not toxic for birds; however, large numbers of birds were dying. Finally, the clinical picture of human illness from St. Louis encephalitis virus infection did not usually include muscle weakness, yet muscle weakness was prevalent among infected patients in the current outbreak. It was against this backdrop that, on the thirteenth of September in Albany, New York, The New York State Department of Health and CDC convened a meeting to discuss encephalitis of unknown causes. Attending this conference were investigators from The New York State Health Department, CDC, and academics from medical schools or related institutions. One of the attendees was Ian Lipkin, a professor of neurology and microbiology at The University of California Medical School in Irvine, who was head of a laboratory studying emerging diseases.

Several years earlier, upon concluding his medical and neurology training, Ian applied to work with me in the Viral-Immunobiology Laboratory at The Scripps Research Institute (at that time called Scripps Clinic and Research Foundation) in La Jolla, California. His research training was negligible; however, he showed a keen intellect and desire to learn what research was about and how to do it. On that basis, I accepted Ian into my laboratory. His interest was to develop new assays for detecting infectious agents, primarily viruses that might be responsible for human diseases whose cause was unknown. The most serious, like multiple sclerosis, diabetes, amyotrophic lateral sclerosis (Lou Gehrig's disease), and schizophrenia, were his special area of concern. His desire was to become a modern microbe hunter, a term coined for the earliest seekers of pathogens that kill and maim humanity. In 1984, when Ian trained in my laboratory, the scarcity of MDs going into basic research was evident. In my laboratory alone, the number dropped from 80 to 90 percent of my research staff in the 1970s to roughly 50 percent during his time with me to less than 5 percent for the last decade. This deficiency in persons trained broadly in normal human biology and its diseases is more than a national concern; it is a disaster. Such individuals are needed to complement the gifted PhDs and doctors of veterinary medicine (DVMs) who are the main research population today. Together, they provide a thirst for understanding the current issues of human diseases in biomedicine with a balance between clinical and laboratory training. Only with this full set of skills is the ultimate goal of establishing causes, understanding mechanism(s) of disease, and devising therapies to cure and prevent human diseases likely to succeed. There are many causes why medical physicians are not entering the investigational research pool, and this crisis in biomedicine urgently requires correction.

It was a gathering of researchers and clinicians from The New York State Health Department, CDC, and medical school staff members who attended the Albany Conference of September 13 to discuss evidence for or against designating St. Louis virus as the cause of so many human and animal deaths from encephalitis. At this point, virologists at the National Wildlife Health Center had isolated viruses from birds but were not convinced they were St. Louis encephalitis virus. The Albany conference had also been designed to discuss new methods of detective virology for the rapid identification of disease-causing viruses. Lipkin, after leaving my laboratory to begin his own at The University of California, Irvine, had devised and set up rapid molecular biologic assays to screen for just such an infectious agent as that being sought in the New York City encephalitis outbreak.

From contacts he made at the Albany meeting and following a lecture he gave about his rapid assays, participants recommended sending brain samples from infected patients to Lipkin for testing. State health officials also wished to evaluate Lipkin's assay because they had failed to obtain positive results for St. Louis encephalitis by PCR testing. Repeated testing for St. Louis encephalitis virus at the CDC was too inconclusive to rule out another flavivirus as the cause of the expanding outbreak. Soon after the conference ended, the virology section of the New York State Department of Health sent samples to Lipkin's laboratory. A few days after receiving samples, members of Lipkin's team purified RNA from the human brain samples, synthesized reagents, performed PCR testing and began genomic sequence studies. Six days later, Lipkin's staff identified flavivirus sequences in the brains of three patients. Genomic sequencing and aligning the materials obtained from the three human brains indicated to Lipkin that the infectious agent was not St. Louis encephalitis virus but was, instead, most closely related to West Nile virus, a virus that had never before been seen in the United States, and to Kunjin virus. These results were then relayed to the New York State Department of Health and CDC. Independently, the CDC and National Veterinarian Service Laboratories designed PCR tests for West Nile virus, which they then identified in samples from infected birds (8–15). West Nile virus is toxic for several species of birds, and crows are highly susceptible (15–17).

In our current world of rapid communication, many findings like these are disseminated on the Internet or by Pro Med. When the reports linking West Nile virus with encephalitis reached Vincent Deubel of the Pasteur Institute in Paris, he replied that he had in his laboratory genomic sequences of West Nile virus that had never been published in the medical literature. Moreover, he was willing to provide those sequences to assist in uncovering the cause of New York City's outbreak of deadly viral infection. Alignment of sequences from Deubel both by Lipkin's laboratory and CDC laboratory confirmed that the virus in question was West Nile-like but definitely not St. Louis encephalitis virus. The time was by then the last week in September, just a little more than two weeks after the Albany Conference, when the source of blood from more than 50 percent of the infected birds surveyed were positive for West Nile virus. Simultaneously, the U.S. Department of Agriculture reported that a horse in Long Island was infected with what looked like West Nile virus.

By the end of that same week in September, sixty-two cases of West Nile virus infection were verified in humans, and seven had died. The New York City Department of Health reported an additional 622 suspected cases. There were 17,000 dead birds, one third of which were crows. One hundred and thirty of the dead birds were confirmed as infected with West Nile virus as were twenty-five horses. By October, dead crows were found in Baltimore, other counties of New York State, Massachusetts, Connecticut, Rhode Island, and New Jersey. Over 25,000 mosquitoes were collected and put into 1,500 test pools; 15 of those pools tested positive for the virus. The mosquitoes involved were *Culex pipiens*, a type that inhabits polluted water and is active at night, and *Aedes vexan*, which occupy natural areas and are active during the day. Both can carry West Nile virus.

The *New York Daily News* reported in the first week of October 1999, "Ancient Disease is on The Move." The second week in October the *New Yorker* magazine published an article suggesting that the West Nile virus outbreak could have been a deliberate bioterrorist attack by a Middle-Eastern country. In July 2000, the U.S. congressional committee investigating the outbreak released this statement: "Expect the Unexpected: The West Nile Virus Wake-up Call."

West Nile viruses were first isolated in the West Nile provenance of Uganda from a patient presenting with a syndrome of muscle aches, fever, and headache (1,18). However, very little activity by West Nile viruses was documented until a substantial outbreak in Israel during the 1950s. At that time, evidence of the virus was also noted in Egypt and India. However, until the West Nile virus surfaced in New York City in 1999, the geographic distribution of this infection was limited to countries bordering the Mediterranean, the Middle East, Africa, and West Asia. But despite its stealthy entrance into New York City, the virus spread rapidly throughout the region involving the majority of American states (3,19, Table 13.1), Canada, Central and South America, Mexico, and the Caribbean. So far, this virus has now been isolated from all the

TABLE 13.1 2008 West Nile Virus Activity in the United States: Provisional Data

State	Encephalitis/ Meningitis	Fever	Other Clinical/ Unspecified	Total	Fatalities
Alabama	11	10	0	21	0
Arizona	62	43	9	114	7
Arkansas	7	2	0	9	0
California	290	147	3	440	15
Colorado	17	54	0	71	1
Connecticut	5	2	1	8	0
Delaware	0	0	1	1	0
Florida	2	0	0	2	0
Georgia	4	3	1	8	0
Idaho	1	30	6	37	1
Illinois	11	4	4	19	1
Indiana	3	0	1	4	0
Iowa	3	0	3	6	1
Kansas	14	17	0	31	0
Kentucky	3	0	0	3	0
Louisiana	18	31	0	49	1
Maryland	7	6	1	14	0
Michigan	11	4	2	17	0
Minnesota	2	8	0	10	0
Mississippi	22	41	0	63	2
Missouri	12	3	0	15	1
Montana	0	3	2	5	0
Nebraska	5	44	0	49	0

TABLE 13.1 (*continued*)

State	Encephalitis/ Meningitis	Fever	Other Clinical/ Unspecified	Total	Fatalities
Nevada	9	5	2	16	0
New Jersey	6	4	0	10	2
New Mexico	5	3	0	8	0
New York	32	14	0	46	6
North Dakota	2	35	0	37	0
Ohio	14	1	0	15	1
Oklahoma	4	5	0	9	0
Oregon	3	13	0	16	0
Pennsylvania	12	2	0	14	1
Rhode Island	1	0	0	1	0
South Carolina	0	1	0	1	0
South Dakota	11	28	0	39	0
Tennessee	12	7	0	19	1
Texas	40	24	0	64	1
Utah	6	18	2	26	0
Virginia	0	0	1	1	0
Washington	2	1	0	3	0
West Virginia	1	0	0	1	0
Wisconsin	4	3	1	8	1
Wyoming	0	8	0	8	0
TOTAL	674	624	40	1338	43

(Reported to CDC as of February 13, 2009)

Earth's continents except Antarctica. This coverage represents the largest arbovirus epidemic of human encephalitis in history. The disease is transmitted in enzootic cycles involving a variety of mosquitoes, but primarily the *Culex* species, and birds (1,2,20). The virus moves with infected migratory birds as well as being maintained locally by resident birds (15). At present, the West Nile virus has been isolated from over 300 species of birds. The infected birds fall into two major groups: those that carry the virus and are asymptomatic and those that develop an often fatal neurologic disease. Crows, jays, magpies, and house finches, upon infection, develop high virus loads and rapidly infect the mosquitoes that prey on them (21–24). These birds, which are highly susceptible to the deadly neurologic disease, are sentinels of virus activity whose deaths should be considered an alarm that West Nile virus has infested the community. House sparrows are also reservoirs for high titers of West Nile virus and play a role in the virus's transmission in city areas. The current depletion of certain bird populations in North America, for example, the robin, is related to their infection by West Nile viruses (25).

Humans are incidental/accidental hosts in the natural mosquito–bird cycle of this viral infection. In addition to humans, domestic and wild animals can intrude into the mosquito–bird cycle; some known examples are horses, cats, dogs, sheep, goats, rodents, bats, and even alligators (22). Most humans who become infected have received bites from mosquitoes carrying the West Nile virus. The viruses then replicate at the bite site and likely spread to specialized cells, dendritic cells, that act as processors of foreign antigens (in this case, the viruses). Subsequently, these viral antigens initiate both the rapid (innate) and adoptive (T cell [killer cells] and B cell [antibodies]) immune responses. Dendritic cells then carry processed virus material and probably infectious virus as well to the lymphoid system, from there to blood and then to other tissues. Viruses may also travel directly from the bite site into and through the blood. Since West Nile viruses travel in blood, they can also spread from human to human by transfusion, from mothers to their fetuses through the placenta and from organ donors to recipients of transplants (26,27).

The clinical picture following West Nile virus infection is an asymptomatic incubation period of two to fourteen days followed by mild symptoms, or none at all, in the majority or at least 80 percent of infected persons. For the remaining 20 percent, the story is different. That group experiences severe headaches, backaches, muscle pain, fever, and fatigue; half develop a rash. One percent will go on to develop a severe neuroinvasive disease. The portrait of the CNS infection includes mental disorientation, aseptic (nonbacterial) meningitis, encephalitis, poliomyelitis-like disease, and tremors. Of those patients surveyed, one-half have permanent disabilities. From studies in mice, the pattern of damage to the CNS involves receptors on dendritic cells that sense the virus's molecular structure, whose involvement with West Nile virus leads to increased permeability of the barrier between the blood and brain allowing the virus to reach nerve cells (28). These observations were made in mice whose toll-like receptor 3, which is normally present, was genetically removed (28). The observation is that mice without toll-like receptor 3 were more resistant to lethal infection with West Nile virus and had larger loads of virus in the periphery than the brain. In contrast, mice with the toll-like 3 receptors had smaller viral loads but inflammation and tissue damage in their brains following West Nile virus infection. The idea is that TLR3 is required for the generation of certain cytokine molecules like TNF-α, which allow increased permeability of the barrier surrounding the brain (blood–brain barrier: BBB). The leakiness of the BBB facilitates the entry of the virus from the blood into the brain. Thus, West Nile virus infection initiated peripherally after a mosquito bite led to a breakdown of the blood–brain barrier due to high cytokine and chemokine production followed by enhanced brain infection in mice possessing toll-like receptor 3. However, mice with or without the toll-like receptor 3 were equally susceptible to the lethal effects of West Nile virus when the virus was inoculated directly into their brains, thereby bypassing the virus's travel from the periphery through the BBB into the brain.

Since the 1999 outbreak in New York City, West Nile virus has been responsible for major epidemics of neurologic disease throughout the United States in 2002, 2003, and thereafter. Over 2 percent of residents in the Queens borough of New York City, the epicenter of the outbreak, were infected. As of March 2008, throughout this country, over 28,000 cases of West Nile virus infection have been recorded; of these, over 11,000 individuals suffered neurologic involvement and over 1,000 died (3).

Just as canaries have been used in mines to detect gas leakage, crows can warn that West Nile virus is present. The unique susceptibility of crows to North American strain(s) of West Nile virus (14,15) and the birds' close association with human habitation in almost all areas except the Southwestern desert make them an excellent indicator for the active presence of West Nile virus. But why the excessive susceptibility? We now know from the work of Brault et al. (29) that a change in a single amino acid of a threonine to a proline in the NS3 helicase gene of West Nile virus at amino acid position 249 allows for positive selection of a mutant virus with a dramatically enhanced virulence in susceptible birds. This mutation of a single amino acid allows selection for a strain of West Nile virus that replicates with such robust vigor in susceptible birds that the amount of virus in their blood is nearly 10,000- to 100,000-fold greater than that of the nonmutated West Nile virus. The heightened level of virus in the blood not only for crows but for other susceptible birds as well provides the best opportunity possible for a mosquito to become infected when biting that bird. In turn, the opportunity for human infection is maximized.

The emergence of West Nile virus in North America correlates directly with the large-scale decline of the North American bird population (30). Utilizing twenty-six years of breeding bird survey data to determine the impact of West Nile virus on avian hosts in North America, the Smithsonian Migratory Bird Center and The National Zoological Park in Washington DC reported that, since the 1999 New York City outbreak, the nation has experienced a 45 percent loss of the crow population along with other highly susceptible birds like the American robin, house wrens, chickadees, Eastern blue birds, and blue jays. Populations of birds that are resistant to West Nile virus like the mourning dove, downy woodpecker, Northern mockingbird, wood thrush, Baltimore oriole, Eastern towhee, and the white-breasted nuthatch remain undiminished. Flocks of birds with moderate or intermediate susceptibility to West Nile virus like the common grackle, Northern cardinal, and the song sparrow have been reduced somewhat in size but not as greatly as the most susceptible bird populations. Thus, this recent redistribution in the bird population is not caused primarily by changes in local environment, bird habitat, land usage, or climate, since these variables were taken into account when the numbers of birds in each group were calculated. For no other reason than the epidemic of West Nile virus infection, the bird communities and populations most commonly associated with humans in towns and suburbs where the mosquito–bird/mosquito–human cycle flourishes have undergone drastic changes.

How the West Nile virus first traveled to New York City and began its spread through North America, Mexico, Central and South America, and the Caribbean remains unknown. All we do know is that the earliest outbreaks of encephalitis caused by infection with West Nile virus centered around the two international airports in Queens. This suggests strongly that the virus arrived by air travel either by import of an infected bird(s), a mosquito, or a human incubating the virus (4). Any of those three possibilities could begin the bird–mosquito cycle in which the West Nile virus was initiated and maintained, although a scenario of human transmission may be less likely due to lower titers of virus carried when compared to birds. We know that from September 13 to 23, 1999, samples obtained from 430 birds of eighteen different species in Queens and surrounding counties indicated that 33 percent were positive for West Nile virus by serologic assay. Included were crows, domestic geese and chickens, house sparrows, Canadian geese, and rock doves. Similar surveys of domestic mammals showed that two of seventy-three horses, 10 of 189 dogs, but none of twelve cats contained West Nile virus neutralizing antibodies. These results suggest that domestic mammals, horses, and dogs could also act as reservoirs of the virus (31). However, studies of dead and dying birds, especially crows, were reported three or more months prior to reports of human cases. Therefore, a mosquito–bird cycle that increased to involve large numbers of birds presumably emerged before the human–mosquito cycle occurred. Some believe (4,32) that the virus was brought in by bioterrorists, but there is no evidence, as yet, to support that claim. The genomic sequence of the West Nile virus isolated in New York City most closely resembles that of a West Nile virus strain isolated from a goose in Israel and also present in other Middle Eastern areas (4,8,9,33,34). However, recent studies indicate that closely related West Nile virus strains were also circulating in Romania, making the Middle East area somewhat more tenuous. Once established in a migratory bird population, West Nile virus spread from its origins throughout North America, Mexico, Central and South America, and the Caribbean as the birds reached destinations where the appropriate mosquito vectors and closeness to human population continued to extend the disease.

The events and lessons surrounding the outbreak of this new plague in North America soon indicated the need for a rapid exchange of information among experts in various areas of public health and epidemiology, infectious disease, biomedical research, avian and vector research, control, and epidemiology at all levels of the federal, state, and local health departments coupled with private academic expertise and input. The history of this plague is chronicled in a report to the minority staff, U.S. Government Affairs Committee of 24 July 2000 entitled "Expect the Unexpected: The West Nile Virus Wake-Up Call":

CDC issued an official statement on September 24 that implicated a West Nile-like virus in several bird deaths. CDC also announced that it would perform additional lab tests to determine if human patients who were diagnosed with St. Louis encephalitis, or who had encephalitis symptoms but whose illnesses were not confirmed as St. Louis encephalitis, might be suffering from a West Nile-like virus instead. On September 27, CDC formally reclassified the St. Louis encephalitis outbreak as a West Nile virus-like outbreak. This reclassification process for human cases was as circuitous as the bird diagnosis.

There had been some reservations about the identification of St. Louis encephalitis almost from the beginning. Although most factors pointed to St. Louis encephalitis as the disease in the humans, there were signs that something else might have been responsible. As mentioned, the first unusual signal was that large numbers of birds were dying, yet birds had never been known to show signs of St. Louis encephalitis. Second, no striking example of clinical St. Louis encephalitis had been experienced earlier. Third, the outbreak was unique from an epidemiological viewpoint. There had never been a case of St. Louis encephalitis recorded in New York City, and only nine cases of St. Louis encephalitis were reported in New York State over the past thirty-five years. In past outbreaks, St. Louis encephalitis had typically advanced northward along the Ohio and Mississippi river valleys and had left a trail of cases in its wake. There was no national outbreak of St. Louis encephalitis in 1999. Finally, laboratory tests on the humans suggested St. Louis encephalitis in some cases, but in others, results were harder to interpret. Furthermore, the tests run through most of September had not been specific enough to confirm a case of St. Louis encephalitis or to disprove a competing hypothesis.

"It was the uncertain lab results that prompted New York State Health Department officials in mid-September to ask Dr. Ian Lipkin, the Director of a University of California-Irvine (UC-Irvine) Emerging Diseases Lab, to examine tissue samples from five of the fatal human encephalitis cases. The lab began its studies on September 21 and three days later Lipkin was virtually certain that the viral genetic material present was not from the St. Louis encephalitis virus but from one of two closely related viruses, either Kunjin or West Nile virus. On the 24th and 25th, the lab communicated these findings to the New York State and City Health Departments, CDC-Atlanta, and CDC-Fort Collins."

"Tipped off by the bird cases, CDC-Fort Collins used similar genetic fingerprinting techniques to independently confirm that a West Nile-like virus was responsible for at least 25 human cases of encephalitis. CDC officially reported its findings on September 27. The CDC-Fort Collins lab director, Dr. Duane Gubler, called the sudden appearance of West Nile virus the most significant development in North American arbovirology in the past 50 years."

"By October (1999), West Nile encephalitis had conclusively killed thousands of wild birds and seven people, though the full extent of the outbreak had yet to be determined. On October 8, a USDA Emergency

Response Team detected 25 cases of West Nile virus infection in horses on Long Island. Horses in Connecticut and New Jersey were also tested for West Nile, but no positive cases were found. During this time, the European Union banned horse and poultry imports from affected areas in New York, New Jersey, and Connecticut."

The Russian poet Yevgeny Yevtushenko published in *20th Century Russian Poetry* "That poets can be a noisy, quarrelsome lot who continue to howl at one another" and "Oh Lord when will we at last understand that writers are not race horses competing for first place, but work horses pulling in common harness. The common cart of literature (35)." Indeed, what Yevtushenko said for poets can be a similar refrain for science and scientists. Yet, despite a few bumps in the road and disturbed egos, the search to identify the West Nile virus as a killer was a magnificent effort by many that led to solving the mystery of dead crows and sick and dying humans in the borough of Queens, New York City, in 1999.

At the local level, the infectious disease specialist's suspicion was aroused that a new epidemic of human encephalitis was occurring. The events she observed in the Flushing Hospital in Queens were used to alert the Bureau of Communicable Diseases of the New York City Department of Health. The city Department of Health then sent epidemiologists to investigate and arranged for the hospital's Chief of Infectious Disease to send CSF samples from ill patients to the New York State Department of Health for evaluation. The city Department of Health contacted health officials within CDC's arboviral and viral special pathogens branch to request assistance and alerted State Health Department of New York and Connecticut. The New York State Department of Health began testing samples. Epidemiologic studies suggested that the neurologic disease they saw was mosquito borne, and the New York State Department of Health sent blood and CSF samples to the CDC Division of Vector-Borne Infectious Disease. Similarly, the CDC Infectious Disease Pathology Laboratory received for analysis brain samples drawn from a patient dying in Flushing Hospital. The Bronx Zoo contacted wildlife pathologists at New York State of Environmental Conservation who sent samples from dead birds to the U.S. Geological Survey National Wildlife Health Center. Samples were also sent to Animal and Plant Health Inspection Services and the U.S. Department of Agriculture. The U.S. Army Medical Research Institute of Infectious Diseases, which has long played a monumental role in identifying mosquito-borne infectious diseases, was brought in. Conclusions at a conference on the rising number of hospitalized patients with encephalitis resulted in a recommendation to send viral materials for analysis to another laboratory (Emerging Disease Laboratory at the University of California, Irvine, Medical School) with expertise in using molecular probes for diagnosis of infections and diseases of unknown etiology. The universality of the approach for these new epidemics was quite magnificent. The following studies were undertaken by Federal agencies:

Research (October 1999–January 2000)

Centers for Disease Control and Prevention
Mosquito surveillance in New York City area
Confirmatory West Nile testing in humans and animals
Sequencing of West Nile virus genome
Standardized laboratory testing protocols
Serological survey in Northern Queens
Vertebrate serological surveys
Sentinel bird studies
West Nile Workshop
Development of West Nile surveillance, prevention, and control

United States Department of Agriculture
Screening and, later, confirmatory West Nile testing in animals
Pathogenicity studies in domestic poultry
Sequencing of West Nile virus genome
West Nile infection study in horses
Bird serological surveillance in Atlantic region
West Nile Workshop
Development of West Nile surveillance, prevention, and control

National Wildlife Health Center
Necropsy, screening, and later, confirmatory West Nile testing in birds
Wild bird and small mammal serological survey in New York City
Bird serological surveillance in Atlantic region
Bird vaccine studies

United States Army Medical Research Institute of Infectious Disease
Vector studies
Pathology studies of Bronx Zoo birds
Serological survey of birds and mammals
Sequencing of West Nile virus genome

Since its emergence in 1999, West Nile virus caused the largest outbreak of arbovirus encephalitis ever recorded in the United States. Further, the West Nile virus outbreaks in North America are the largest encephalitis outbreaks ever recorded for this virus. In my area of San Diego, which is relatively insect and mosquito free, and despite a cool summer, San Diego County as of August 2008 reported 318 dead birds, 8 chickens, 1 horse, and 7 human illnesses from West Nile virus. One thing appears certain, West Nile virus is here to stay in the USA.

Human Immunodeficiency Virus (HIV): AIDS, the Current Plague

A plague as horrifying as any ever known now afflicts us, and the cause is a virus, the human immunodeficiency virus (HIV). In the twenty-five years (1983–2008) since the initial case report of Acquired Immunodeficiency Syndrome (AIDS), this disease caused by HIV has afflicted over 60 million people, and nearly one half of them have died. Not only the victims of this infection but also their families, communities, countries, and even continents endure years of suffering as AIDS proceeds on its long course of physical destruction. Today the enormous advance in antivirus drug therapy has reduced the death rate by two-thirds compared to that in the United States during the 1990s. However, worldwide, for every four newly infected persons, only one receives therapy. Furthermore, HIV therapy is a lifelong commitment. Despite an outlay of a billion dollars per year for AIDS research, no vaccine is on the horizon for preventing this medical catastrophe.

The United Nations estimates that, today, over 34 million humans are infected with HIV worldwide, but the real number is likely closer to 39 million. In Africa alone, the estimated HIV infection rate is 3 percent of the adult population. In the United States, according to the Centers for Disease Control (CDC), roughly 40,000 persons are newly infected annually. Because of this high infection rate, coupled with the belief that over 250,000 individuals are infected but not yet aware that they are carriers who spread HIV infection, the CDC and multiple health groups recommend that all teens and adults (ages thirteen to sixty-four) in the United States have tests to detect HIV as part of routine medical care or emergency room visits. Additionally, annual testing is recommended for those with high-risk behavior such as multipartner sexual intercourse. The tests are to be voluntary with the individual being tested told the reason and result. Also recommended is that pre-legal counseling and signed consent forms be abolished. Unfortunately, many lobbyists for groups of people with AIDS, libertarians, and civil liberty groups oppose even this nonjudgmental testing, which is regrettable, since an estimated 25 to 50 percent of those newly infected do not know they are. They pose risks to themselves because the earlier treatment begins, the better the prognosis. Delaying treatment until one develops the symptoms and signs of AIDS has a much poorer outcome. Too often, patients with AIDS do not seek medical care for as long as ten years after the initial infection, when they already have a compromised immune system and are seriously ill. Thus, a longer life expectancy correlates directly with the shortest time interval between HIV infection, diagnosis, and start of antiviral medical therapy. Of course, the privacy of these individuals must be protected so that their health insurance and job security remain intact, particularly if HIV testing is mandatory. Universal testing for HIV would enable those who know they are infected but remain symptom free to protect their sexual partners. Further the numbers of HIV-infected children resulting from passage of virus from mother to child would be markedly lessened. Currently, individual states in the USA have different laws governing informed medical consent counseling before testing for HIV and for informing parents of minors both for their consent and reporting of test results.

The first description of HIV-infected patients appeared in the *New England Journal of Medicine* in 1981. The report stated that four previously healthy homosexual men developed pneumonia from an infection caused by *Pneumocystis carinii* (1). The men also suffered fungal infections in the mouth and had multiple viral infections. This scenario of disease in persons with a low resistance to infection was consistent with the broad picture of an acquired deficiency of the immune system. The patients' infections by a variety of bacteria, fungi, and viruses produced prolonged fever and a marked reduction of cells now called the CD4$^+$ subset of T lymphocytes (1–6). These CD4$^+$ T cells function primarily to provide help to CD8$^+$ killer cells, the cells that are responsible for killing virus-infected cells. CD4$^+$ T cells also work with B cells to form antibodies. Since medical observations indicated that the immune system had broken down in these multiply infected patients, the name "acquired immunodeficiency syndrome" (AIDS) was coined to designate this pervasive disease state (2–8). Later reports described cases involving heterosexual and homosexual transmission of infections, transmission by blood and blood products, transmission by contaminated needles of intravenous drug users and from improperly collected and stored blood, and spread by nursing. By 1995, only fourteen years after the original report of the four AIDS patients, CDC and the World Health Organization (WHO) estimated that, in the United States, 1 of every 70 males and 1 of every 700 females was infected with the virus. As of October 31, 1995, a total of 501,310 persons with AIDS had been reported to the CDC by state and territorial health departments; 311,381 (62 percent) had died. From 1993 through the present, among men that are twenty-five to forty-four years of age, AIDS is the leading cause of death. For women, it is the third leading cause of death. These numbers are an underestimate of AIDS in the United States. Even worse, in Africa over one of forty persons, both male and female, is infected. The incidence in Asia, India, Latin, Central and South America, the Caribbean, Eastern Europe, and Russia is not fully known but is increasing to astronomical proportions. Figure 14.1 displays the counts of adults and children living with HIV infection in 2007. Although a few, scattered individuals have remained healthy for ten to fifteen years or more despite infection with HIV, to date not a single spontaneous cure of HIV infection has been confirmed. Those infected have either died or remained continually infected.

Patients infected with HIV now or for the last several years are living longer with fewer disease symptoms (6,9) than those infected during the first two decades of the epidemic. The reason is the development of anti-HIV medications now formulated so only one pill a day is needed. Drugs are also available that attack different aspects of the virus's life cycle. With the introduction of protease inhibitors in the mid-1990s, and within two years of their licensing, combination drug therapies have now lessened deaths of HIV-infected individuals by over 67 percent. The scientific revolution in molecular biology and genomics now allows the

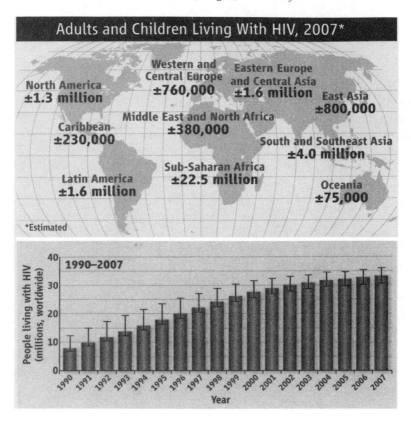

FIGURE 14.1 *Chart depicting the adults and children throughout the world still alive but infected with HIV in the year 2007. This large number partially results from the success of antiretroviral drug therapy, which prolongs survival.*

typing of viruses dominant in an infected patient and selection of the best three drugs designed for combination therapy for that individual. Owing to the high mutation rate of HIV and selection of its drug-resistant forms, the use of this triple therapy reduces the opportunity for a virus to escape. Monitoring patients' viral load and CD4 T-cell levels are useful medical guides. During infection, mutation, recombination, and adaptation, new forms of HIV can be "selected" for survival and resistance to therapy. Therefore, when a patient no longer responds well to previously helpful drugs, genotyping of newly isolated viruses follows, and the medications are replaced accordingly. The result for those fortunate enough to receive such therapy, especially early in the course of HIV infection as is usual in westernized countries, is often a nearly normal life in terms of working and participating in daily events. The eventual death of a patient whose HIV infection is in remission because of drug therapy will come from the usual factors, for example, heart failure, cancer, or accidents, rather than AIDS. However, there are complications. Despite being "healthy," HIV-infected individuals still shed virus in their semen. Therefore, continuous education is needed to avoid risky sexual behavior and, thereby, prevent the spread of HIV to other individuals. The enhanced life expectancy of those infected with HIV and on medication leads to an estimated medical cost per individual throughout his/her predicted lifespan of approximately twenty-five years after HIV diagnoses of $600,000 to $650,000, the average cost of $25,000 per year for drugs and medical visits (10). As the virus hides and remains latent in certain body sites, current drugs are unable to provide eradication but are effective in suppressing viral volume. This dilemma for public health, public/government, and individual/insurance financing has led to the vigorous push to develop vaccines both to prevent the disease as well as to curtail its effects in those already infected, a so-called therapeutic vaccine. The purpose of therapeutic vaccines is to recover CD8[+] killer cells' and CD4[+] T helper cells' activity, the loss of which is a direct effect of HIV infection. Resurrecting the function of these T lymphocytes is required to control the infection. Trials using conventional forms of vaccine have failed (11–14). However, new experimental findings in animal models of infections have promise. There, negative regulators of the immune response have been found; that is, long-term (persisting) viruses induced the production of factors that compromised CD8 killer and CD4 T helper function, which would otherwise rid the body of infection. The identification and removal of these factors resurrected T-cell functions (15–23). Such restored and functioning T cells purged viruses and controlled infection. Although these intriguing results have been limited to experimental animals used as living models of persistent virus infection (15–19), this success has been reproduced in cultured cells infected with HIV (20–23). Whether these findings can be extended to humans remains to be determined. Theoretically, blocking the actions of molecules that suppress the immune system in combination with therapeutic vaccination (18,19) may offer a unique opportunity for combating HIV infection.

The first trial in humans for HIV vaccination using conventional approaches was in 1987, but in over twenty years of clinical testing of several vaccines, no AIDS/HIV vaccine has been sufficiently successful to be recommended for use. However, one should recall that it took forty-seven years to develop a successful vaccine to protect us from poliomyelitis and forty-two years to find a vaccine that conquered measles virus infections.

Infection by HIV is characterized by two major events. First, the victim makes a vigorous immune response against the virus (6). This is noted by the presence of antibodies to HIV (proteins in the blood that are induced by viral proteins [antigens] and react specifically with the inducing HIV proteins) and cytotoxic T lymphocytes (CTLs, cells responsible for cellular immunity). The CTLs arise during the early stage of infection and often remain to some degree throughout its course (6,24,25) during which the patient is either clinically well or only minimally to moderately ill. The initial presence of CTLs directly correlates with a dramatic reduction in the amount of virus present (viral load). Subsequently, the loss of CTL activity but retention of antibodies marks the phase of AIDS that culminates in terminal illness and death (24,25). Infectious virus and viral nucleic acid sequences are continuously present throughout the infection even in the face of a continuous anti-HIV immune response (6,24,26). Viruses or viral sequences are found primarily in monocytes and CD4$^+$ T cells in the blood (26–28), in lymphoid tissues (such as the spleen, lymph nodes [27], and gut [29–30]) as well as in microglia (31) (a form of macrophage), endothelial cells of the brain (32), and other organs (reviewed 6,33).

The emergence of resistant HIV forms that are untouchable by anti-HIV drug therapy and the concurrent development of AIDS have resulted in flare-ups of previously treatable and curable tuberculosis, due to coinfection with HIV. Tuberculosis is now the most opportunistic infection occurring in HIV-positive individuals. The result is three major health problems. First, difficulties arise with dual therapies designed to treat HIV and tuberculosis because of overlapping drug toxicities. Second, suppression of the immune system caused by HIV also suppresses the immune system's ability to restrict and control tuberculosis. The outcome is a widespread systemic presence of the tuberculosis bacteria, reminiscent of the effect observed by von Pirquet with measles virus in the 1890s (see measles virus chapter). Third, the selection and evolution of drug-resistant strains of tuberculosis bacteria put not only HIV-infected

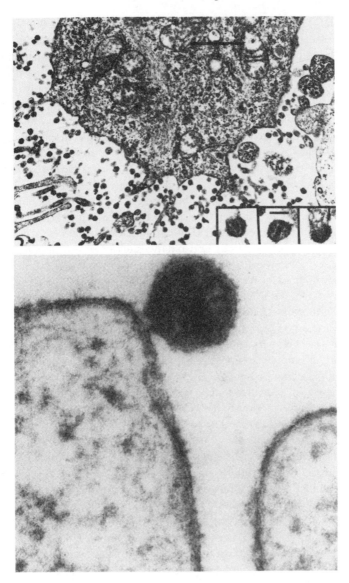

FIGURE 14.2 *The virus that causes AIDS. (Top) An infected CD4⁺ T lymphocyte that is producing virus. The insert is an enlargement of viral particles found in culture fluids. The virion is approximately 110 μm. (Bottom) The HIV budding from a cell's surface. Magnification: 180,000×. Note the bar in the virion that is characteristic of HIV. Photomicrographs courtesy of Robert Gallo.*

individuals but also entire populations at risk. Indeed, since 2006, over 400 incidents of humans infected with drug-resistant tuberculin bugs have been found. The Bacille Calmette-Guerin (BCG) vaccine contains a live attenuated form of the tuberculosis bacillus developed over eighty years ago. Although not fully effective, the BCG vaccine is the only tuberculosis vaccine in existence and is used in most countries of the world. The vaccine is a weakened live attenuated form of the *Mycobacterium bovis* strain, which is related to *Mycobacterium tuberculosis*, the disease-causing strain, and has shown significant protection for some but not all children during their first fifteen years of life. Now it is clear that HIV-infected children are especially susceptible to side effects from the BCG vaccine ranging from a strong local reaction at the site of inoculation to a disseminated BCG infection that can be life threatening.

Similarly, dual infection with HIV and malaria or measles virus fuels the spread of both infections and often results in severe diseases. For example, a one- to two-log (log = 10-fold) jump in the blood's content of HIV accompanies febrile malaria episodes, and susceptibility to malaria increases during HIV infection. In Kenya, since the late 1980s, roughly 200,000 adults have had both malaria and HIV infections.

HIV usually enters the host via fluids (blood or semen) or within infected cells. The persistent infection that results remains intact in spite of an early immune response that coexists with the virus. All the experiences with vaccines for smallpox, yellow fever, measles, and poliomyelitis have focused on using an attenuated virus that could replicate in the host initially, would not seriously harm the host, yet would provide enough stimulus for the host's immune system to combat and clear the viral infection. This experience has been useless for HIV.

For a vaccine to be successful, it should mimic the immune response elicited by the pathogen during a natural infection. Further, the vaccine must be milder and less injurious than the natural infection yet should provoke immunologic memory. Immunologic memory is the rapid and specific viral immune response programmed by previous virus infection or immunization. Thus, vaccines prime the immune system and program it to anticipate and resist future infection by that specific pathogen. To provide a robust immune response and subsequent immune memory that prevents or at least controls infection, three approaches have been used for developing successful vaccines. The first and overall the most successful is to use an attenuated or weakened virus whose composition closely resembles that of the virus to be overcome. This is the strategy used for the most effective vaccines, those that prevent measles, mumps, yellow fever, and smallpox, and for one of the poliomyelitis vaccines (Sabin). A second way is to use a killed virus preparation as is done for the Salk poliomyelitis vaccine. A third method utilizes recombinant viral protein(s), that is, a subunit vaccine, and is represented by the one that successfully prevents hepatitis B virus infection. The challenges that have thwarted manufacture of a successful vaccine for HIV are several, stemming from the following issues. The first is that HIV has enormous diversity in its amino acid sequence. The causes are the virus's reverse transcriptase that is not correctable by RNA proofreading, a high degree of virus recombination, and a very high turnover of virus in vivo. Therefore, the rates of mutation, selection, and adaptation of HIV are so huge that making a vaccine directed against only one or a few species of virus has little chance for success. Globally, HIV is classified by sequence analysis into three different groups named M, N, and O. These groups are further subdivided. For example, there are nine distinct subtypes for group M and, within a subtype, the virus's envelope glycoproteins can vary by up to 35 percent. A second major problem is that HIV directly infects cells of the immune system, specifically CD4 T cells. Within days of the initial infection, a massive number of CD4 T cells are lost (30), and these cells function primarily to help CD8 cytotoxic T cells and antibody-producing B cells eliminate pathogens. Third, some HIV proteins, mainly those designated Nef, down-regulate molecules of the major histocompatibility complex that are crucial for presenting virus antigens for recognition by cytotoxic T cells, which would otherwise kill foreign invaders (34–36). Fourth, although neutralizing antibodies are made to viral glycoprotein on the surfaces of virions, HIV can make alterations to limit and avoid antibody recognition (37,38). Fifth, HIV rapidly establishes a latent reservoir of infected lymphocytes by integration of its genetic material into the host's chromosome (33,39). This is an irreversible process that occurs immediately after infection and lasts until the cell in which integration takes place is eliminated. This reservoir is stable over the life of the infected individual, is immunologically silent, and, if the cell becomes activated, it can produce new infectious viruses. Sixth, HIV induces host molecules that are negative regulators of the immune system (20–23). These molecules persist during the lifelong infection and restrict/abort antiviral CD8 and CD4 T-cell function.

HIV causes AIDS and is associated with cancer (Kaposi's sarcoma). The discovery that a viral infection can have links with a cancer has a long history. Nearly 100 years ago, the search for a viral source of cancer began, and for the past forty-five years the focus has been on a specific viral group, the human retrovirus. Scientists now know that viral infections cause at least 20 percent of all cancers. Hepatitis B virus and hepatitis A and C viral infections are associated with liver cancer, Epstein-Barr virus infection with nasopharyngeal cancer, papillomavirus with certain cervical and penile cancers, and HIV and herpes simplex virus-7 with Kaposi's sarcoma. Papillomaviruses were among the first viruses defined as filterable agents (40) and shown by Harold zur Hausen and colleagues in the late 1970s (41) to be associated with human epithelial cancers including human cervical cancer. For this observation and subsequent follow-ups, zur Hausen was awarded the Nobel prize in Physiology and Medicine for 2008. In 2006, a vaccine to prevent human cervical cancer became available (42,43). Further, over one-quarter of the six hundred-plus known animal viruses have oncogenic potential, that is, the capacity to initiate in animals or cultured cells the kind of cellular division and growth that promotes the development of tumors.

Transmission of cancers among animals had been attributed to viruses since the early part of the twentieth century. Many of these cancers arose from retroviruses, a family of viruses in which the replication of the viral nucleic acid is unique. By the rules of molecular biology, genetic information flows from DNA to RNA to protein. This is the pathway for DNA viruses like smallpox and for the products of human genes. Other viruses contain their genetic knowledge in RNA (yellow fever, polio, measles, Lassa, Ebola, and Hanta are RNA viruses). They do not go through a DNA stage, but from RNA to protein. However, unlike other RNA viruses, retroviruses essentially reverse the process, since their viral genetic material is RNA, but the RNA serves as a template (blueprint) for the synthesis of viral DNA through the action of a virus-specific enzyme, reverse transcriptase. This sequence results initially in a DNA–RNA complex, but the RNA piece is digested, leaving the DNA to carry out the replication process. In addition, the retroviral DNA becomes integrated into the host DNA. With HIV, like all retroviruses, information goes from RNA to DNA to RNA to protein. To replicate in the host it infects, HIV must integrate its DNA into the DNA of host cells, a strategy that poses an extraordinarily difficult problem when the host's immune system or antiviral drug therapy attempts to remove cells containing this foreign infectious agent.

A progression of events led to the concept that a virus could cause cancer. At the close of the nineteenth century, the first virus that infected animals had been reported by Froesch and Loeffler (44). By the first decade of the twentieth century, viruses were being isolated and manipulated as physical entities through the use of Pasteur-Chamberland-Berkefeld filters and experimental animals. It was during this time that the first retroviruses were shown to be transmissible agents that could cause cancers.

Vilhelm Ellermann and Oluf Bang (45), working in Copenhagen, Denmark, described the first true cell-free transmission of cancer. They showed that cancer induced by an agent "smaller than a bacterium," "an ultravisible [not seen by the microscope] virus," caused erythromyeloblastosis (a leukemia) in fowl. Filtered extracts of leukemic cells and blood transmitted the virus. However, at that time leukemia was not considered a cancer, and so this discovery lacked impact. Three years passed and then Peyton Rous reproduced solid tumors (sarcomas) in fowl by injecting them with filtrates of a tumor obtained from a hen. Working at the Rockefeller Institute, Rous, after examining Plymouth Rock hens brought to him by farmers, identified their malignant tumors as spindle cell sarcomas (46). He then demonstrated that these tumors could be transmitted to closely related animals. He prepared a cell-free, bacteria-free filtrate of such tumors and inoculated it into a healthy chicken; as a result an identical sarcoma grew in that second chicken (46).

By the 1930s, breast carcinomas and other cancers were noted in mice. Active research on breast cancers transmitted from the mother to her offspring via breast milk focused on determining whether the cancer came from a virus as opposed to a milk factor. The research results showed conclusively that the cancer originated from a retrovirus, later called mammary tumor virus. Despite these accumulated findings that associated cancer with viruses, the investigations failed to achieve major scientific recognition. For example, when the National Cancer Institute of the United States was created in 1937, the committee of leading scientists who advised the newly created institute on "various lines of work which merit investigation" came to this conclusion regarding tumor virus research (47):

It has been definitely shown that the animal parasites and bacteria which may incite malignancy in other organisms play no role in the continuation of the process [in humans]. The present evidence tends to indicate that the same may be true of viruses. As causes of the continuation of the malignant process, many microorganisms which may have been described as specific etiologic agents may be disregarded.

In spite of this advice, fifty years later the first human retroviruses were isolated by workers at the National Cancer Institute and shown to cause cancers (48,49).

From the 1950s through the 1970s, a plethora of discoveries were made regarding retroviruses. Many could cause tumors in mammals, and these could be transmitted vertically (into the fetus) as well as horizontally (from one individual to another after birth). In addition to their use of reverse transcriptase to begin replication from an RNA to a DNA form, many but not all retroviruses infect cells of the immune system. Such infections often harm the immune system, most frequently by immunosuppression (suppressing its function). For example, a number of retroviruses can live in lymphocytes and macrophages and stop their activity as members of the immune system. A critically important development was a test to detect reverse transcription and to identify retroviruses, thus facilitating the study of retroviral infections.

The 1970s ushered in frantic activity in a large number of laboratories housing the search for a retrovirus that could infect humans. Although many candidates were found, careful investigation showed that these retroviruses were not of human origin but rather were contaminants of nonhuman retroviruses. The most common examples were retroviruses that contaminated cells originally from subhuman primates or other mammals and later used for culturing human materials. Another complication was the presence of host-dependent polymerases (enzymes important in making DNA) that, in many instances, were difficult to distinguish from the viral reverse transcriptase.

Numerous medical scientists were at this time engaged in the HIV problem. Early on, the two best known were Robert Gallo, formerly of the National Institutes of Health and currently the founder and director of the Institute for Human Virology at the University of Maryland Medical School in Baltimore, and Luc Montagnier of the Pasteur Institute in Paris and cofounder of the World Foundation for AIDS Research and Prevention. Both investigators and the workers in their respective laboratories were catalysts in the initial investigation and identification of the virus causing AIDS (50). However, as we will see, others have also played roles in establishing the importance of retroviral infections.

FIGURE 14.3 *The two microbe hunters most identified with the isolation of HIV from patients with AIDS—Robert Gallo (right) and Luc Montagnier (left). Montagnier received the 2008 Nobel Prize in Medicine along with Françoise Barré-Sinoussi for this work but, quite depressing, Bob Gallo was left out. Photographs courtesy of Robert Gallo and Luc Montagnier.*

As reflected in other chapters of this book, not one or two but many researchers contribute to defining and understanding each viral disease, as is true of HIV and AIDS. Many more will participate in its eventual control.

Robert Gallo was born and grew up in Waterbury, Connecticut. He was imprinted early in life by the sickness and death of his only sibling, his sister Judith, from leukemia at age seven (8): "I saw her emaciated, jaundiced, covered with bruises. . . . When she smiled I saw only caked blood over her teeth. . . . It was the last time [Gallo was 11] I would ever see Judy. . . . It remained the most powerful and frightening demon of my life."

This traumatic experience strongly influenced Gallo to choose a career devoted to understanding the biology of blood cells and leukemia. Initially, he trained in virology at the National Institutes of Health, where he became immersed in the study of retroviruses. As a result, his work joined together the fields of retrovirology and blood cell biology. Gallo's great contribution followed when he and his associates devised a method to grow lymphocytes (white blood cells) in culture and defined a growth factor required to maintain them (51). This, combined with a technique to detect viral reverse transcriptase developed by Howard Temin and David Baltimore, for which they shared a Nobel Prize in 1975, positioned Gallo to look for human retroviruses. First, tests had to be perfected that distinguished viral reverse transcriptase from cellular reverse transcriptase. With such tests and the use of T-cell growth factor to grow lymphocytes from patients with leukemias, Gallo and his colleagues isolated the first human retrovirus, human T-lymphotropic virus (HTLV-I), identified from a patient with cutaneous T-cell lymphoma (48,49). Independently, investigators from Japan isolated a similar virus causing acute adult T-cell leukemia (52). One year later the second human retrovirus was isolated, HTLV-II, from a patient with hairy-cell leukemia.

The isolation of these first human retroviruses was made possible by finding reverse transcriptase activity in the fluid of cultured T cells taken from patients with leukemia. When Gallo and associates categorized the cancerous cells containing reverse transcriptase, by use of several techniques, the cells proved to be $CD4^+$ lymphocytes. Additionally, this reverse transcriptase was virus specific, not a component of human cells, and was distinctly different from that of human DNA polymerase. Under an electron microscope, the virus looked like a C-shaped particle, just like retroviruses found previously in nonhuman mammals. The genes of this virus were mapped and their relative positions to each other in the genome determined. A great many subsequent studies showed that HTLV-I was transmitted through blood products, during gestation from an infected mother to her fetus, and through sexual intercourse. HTLV-I, HTLV-II, and HIV proved to be human retroviruses.

In December of 1981, Michael Gottlieb and colleagues in the Department of Medicine at the University of California, Los Angeles, examined four homosexual males who had been hospitalized for prolonged bouts of fever and multiple bacterial, fungal, and viral infections—signs of a faulty immune system and low $CD4^+$ T-cell levels (1,5). All four patients developed *Pneumocystis carinii* pneumonia, and one had a rare tumor, Kaposi's sarcoma.

A 30-year-old previously healthy homosexual male (Patient 3) was admitted to the UCLA Medical Center with a one-month history of pain on swallowing, oral thrush [fungal infection], leukopenia [low peripheral blood white blood cell count] and a weight loss of 12 kilograms [about 26 pounds].

Virus was not recovered from the initial biopsy sample. The patient was discharged . . . but readmitted five days later with fever, dyspnea [difficulty in breathing], and dry cough . . . A chest film showed bilateral interstitial [lung] infiltration . . . biopsy specimen revealed abundant *Pneumocystis carinii.* . . . Cytomegalovirus was cultured from the urine [four months later] . . . the patient was readmitted [three months later] because of progressive cachexia (weakening and wasting). . . . A nodule which had not been present on previous examination was noted on the left wall of the chest . . . three similar lesions were located in the esophagus . . . biopsies revealed Kaposi's sarcoma.

Medical reports like this one of an acquired immunodeficiency syndrome with multiple infections and, sometimes, Kaposi's sarcoma soon appeared in numerous places (5,6). Clearly a new and dangerous disease had emerged not only in the United States but also in Europe and Haiti. Characterizations of patients from many medical centers all indicated a condition of prominent defects in the T lymphocyte arm of the immune system, especially the CD4$^+$ T cells, an association with pneumonia caused by *Pneumocystis carinii* bacteria, other infections, and, on occasion, the rare cancer Kaposi's sarcoma. The fatality rate exceeded 90 percent. Although the causative agent was not known, epidemiologic evidence suggested an infectious one, probably a virus.

This new disease became an epidemic by 1983. But how could such a disease suddenly appear? The history of other infectious agents that have caused epidemics in the past indicates that they frequently accompany major changes in social and/or economic conditions. The first epidemics of measles and smallpox infections likely developed as people left isolated villages and entered new, more densely populated cities along river basins. With measles, a new relationship between humans and the animals they domesticated probably also played a role, considering the similarity (amino acid sequence homology) between the human measles virus, the distemper virus of dogs (38 percent similarity), and the rinderpest virus of cattle (60 percent similarity). Migrations in ocean-crossing ships bore a clear-cut link with the initial epidemics of yellow fever in the New World. Still another factor was the exposure of remote populations to a novel infectious agent, for example, the natives of Fiji, who had never come in contact with measles virus, or the Native Americans, who lacked prior experience with smallpox and measles viruses. These populations were not only isolated but were relatively inbred, so their gene pool lacked the extensive polymorphism of multiple genes seen in larger cosmopolitan areas. Inhabitants of such segregated communities would undoubtedly possess "susceptibility" genes that had not been deleted (through deaths) owing to the lack of exposure to the specific infectious agent.

The origin of HIV and AIDS was decoded in 2006 (53–57). Evidently, contaminated blood from two simian (monkey) species contained the infectious agent that jumped the species barrier and entered humans who butchered the animals for food. HIV came from the African chimpanzee *Pan troglodytes*, and the source of HIV-2 was the Sooty mangabey. Investigator Beatrice Hahn and colleagues studied antibodies and nucleic acid sequences in fecal samples from *Pan troglodytes*, troglodyte apes living in the wilds of southern Cameroon, and analysis established a relatedness to human HIV. Although these infected chimps were not ill, their blood contained large amounts of the virus and represented the natural reservoir for HIV. Eventually, by positive selection, mutation, and recombination in human hosts, the viral agent became highly virulent for other humans. The infected chimps are relatively resistant to developing AIDS despite their large viral load (as in humans), but, unlike humans, they are not confronted with immunopathologic events that affect the function and health of lymphoid cells. Although more than 30 species of African primates carry SIV, the simian form of HIV, chimpanzees are the only apes that harbor a form of the virus that is closely related to HIV. When chimpanzees and gorillas in remote forest regions of Cameroon were assayed for HIV cross-reactive antibodies and sequence closeness to HIV, only 40 of 232 *Pan troglodytes*, troglodytes species, but none of 55 *Pan troglodytes*, vellerosus species, were positive for this cross-reactivity; additionally, 6 of the 213 gorillas tested were positive. From this animal pool, the virus that became HIV jumped species to infect humans an estimated fifty to seventy-five years ago, although recent genetic analysis in October 2008 pushed back the estimated origin of HIV to between 1884 and 1924, with a likely date around 1908. The HIV pandemic began near Kinshasa in the Democratic Republic of Congo; at least, this was the site for the earliest known HIV infection, which was documented there in 1959. From southern Cameroon, Gambon, and the Congo Republic where the *Pan troglodytes* troglodytes lives, the Sangha River flows into Kinshasa. Perhaps this river and its shoreline inhabitants carried this new disease that, within a decade, would reach epidemic proportions in many parts of equatorial Africa. Numerous traditional ceremonies and practices form the culture of those areas, and gatherings there readily enhanced transmission of the virus throughout Africa. For example, Cameroon has a naming ceremony for newborns during which babies are breast fed not only by the mother but also by virtually all lactating women in the tightly knit community. An example of disease transmission during a ceremony for ethnic identification calls for the mixing of body fluids after participants receive three short cuts—one on each wrist and one on the back—from knife blades used repeatedly. Fruit is then placed in the cut/wound to draw out evil influences. In several areas of Cameroon where polygamy is legal, the chieftain or wealthy persons frequently have up to forty wives, and the cultural norm is to marry wives of male relatives who have died, another form of disease spread. Again, wives often nurse each other's infants, thereby sharing body fluids and diseases.

Shortly after this newfound virus was identified, humans infected with HIV appeared in the United States, Europe, and Haiti. Factors contributing to the spread were the increase in international travel by airplane, increased sexual promiscuity with multiple partners, increased use of blood and blood products for medical purposes, and, finally, increased intravenous drug use. Along the way came a suspicion that AIDS resulted from contaminated poliomyelitis vaccine, but this allegation has been refuted by multiple international commissions. Further, direct evidence proved that the type of virus isolated from chimpanzees whose tissues were used to grow the polioviruses made into vaccine is phylogenetically distinct from all strains of HIV (58) and that the cultured cells originally used for poliomyelitis vaccine did not contain HIV.

Along with the rise in HIV-positive patients, reports of unexpected infections associated with pneumocystic pneumonia (bacteria), cytomegalovirus and other herpes viruses, as well as skin conditions related to Kaposi's sarcoma were becoming more prevalent by 1980–81. Physicians had observed similar infections earlier but usually in patients with suppressed immune systems. However, Kaposi's sarcoma had been extremely rare, and when diagnosed, the usual victims were elderly men in and around the Mediterranean area or in Africa among Bantu tribes. By 1980, a few young males in the United States were afflicted with Kaposi's sarcoma and swollen lymph glands; instead of progressing slowly their cancers grew rapidly. The patients often proved to be homosexuals. But how to put the parts of this puzzle together?

The late 1970s and early 1980s were a dramatic period in the social acceptance of homosexuality. Initially hiding the truth of their sexual preference from themselves and others, gays began identifying themselves as such and becoming politically active by the 1970s. They constituted a major voting block in San Francisco, comprising an estimated one in four registered voters and providing 70,000 votes in a city of 650,000. The promise of sexual freedom in San Francisco led to a migration of nearly 20,000 homosexual males to San Francisco from 1974 to 1978, with approximately 5,000 every year thereafter. An estimated 5 to 7 percent of the blood donated in San Francisco came from gays. As is well known now, HIV, the cause of AIDS, occupies the blood of infected carriers, and an AIDS-like disease was soon seen in children born of AIDS-infected mothers, in patients given blood transfusions during surgical procedures, and in hemophiliacs requiring regular blood transfusions or blood product therapy. Then, other large metropolitan cities housing gays reported similar situations.

With social legitimacy came political and sexual freedom. Commercialization of gay sex spawned bathhouses and sex clubs that soon became over a 100 million dollar business. With unlimited and unrestrained sexual freedom, regardless of gender preference, came blood diseases like hepatitis B, enteric diarrheal diseases like amebiasis and giardiasis, as well as long-known, sexually transmitted diseases like gonorrhea and syphilis. Shortly, increased numbers of patients were diagnosed with pneumocystis pneumonia infections, Kaposi's sarcoma, lymphoid swelling, and fatigue. Although bathhouses were breeding incubators for disease, few if any in the gay community seemed to care; few physicians, public health officers, politicians, or gay leaders were concerned. The first few random cases leading to the tidal wave of a full epidemic are described in a riveting story by Randy Shilts (59), then a reporter for the *San Francisco Chronicle*, who followed gay activities. His book *And the Band Played On* (59) chronicles the Castro Street happenings, the bathhouses, and the beginning and relentless spread of AIDS among a community and persons he knew:

> The timing of this awareness [of the spread of AIDS] reflected the unalterable tragedy at the heart of the AIDS epidemic. By the time America paid attention to the disease, it was too late to do anything about it.
>
> From 1980 when the first isolated gay men began falling ill, years passed before all these institutions of public health, federal and private scientific research establishments, the mass media and the gay community leadership mobilized sufficiently to fight the disease.

People died while the gay community leaders played politics with the disease, putting political dogma ahead of preservation of life. Local public health viewed the disease as a political problem.

People died and nobody paid attention because the mass media did not like covering stories about homosexuals and several clergy, senators, congressmen, and leaders in the Reagan government saw it as a political and public relations problem that would not be supported by the majority of the voting public.

The HIV epidemic is unique. Unlike measles or smallpox infections, which cause acute illnesses followed by immunity or death, HIV inserts its viral material (genome) into a host's cells where the infection persists without an immediate effect. Consequently, HIV infection most often progresses very slowly compared with the rapid infection of measles, smallpox, yellow fever, poliomyelitis, and the hemorrhagic viruses. Because individuals are infected with HIV for many years, each carrier has many opportunities to transmit the disease. With the current increase in longevity for HIV-infected persons due to antiviral medication, the risk becomes greater. Incidentally, HIV is poorly transmitted; fewer than 5 percent of exposed humans are estimated to develop the infection. In comparison, measles and smallpox viruses infect more than 98 percent of susceptible humans. However, one similarity between HIV and measles virus is that both viruses attack and infect cells of the immune system. The result is immunosuppression, leaving the victim at the whim of other infectious diseases, a situation called opportunistic infection. However, in the case of measles virus, the host immune system usually overcomes the infection and clears the virus. Exceptions are rare; as few as one in one hundred thousand to one in a million individuals infected with measles virus develops a chronic disease called subacute sclerosing panencephalitis. In contrast, once it infects, HIV is unforgiving. The virus persists throughout the life of its victim.

HIV inserts its viral material (genome) into a host's genetic material thereby allowing the infection to persist. HIV infection sets off a cascade of events that disseminates the viruses to multiple lymphoid tissues. The immune response generated against HIV effectively lowers the host's viral load but does not remove all of it. The remaining viruses hide and cause a low-grade persistent infection. As the persistent viruses replicate, their offspring become trapped and/or infect a variety of lymphoid organs, causing chronic activation of cells of the immune system and secretion of products (cytokines) made by lymphocytes and macrophages. The cytokines activate other lymphoid cells, allowing further viral replication until the ultimate destruction of lymphoid tissues results in AIDS—breakdown of the immune system. Both the virus and the virus in combination with an antiviral immune response (immunopathology) are considered responsible for disabling the lymphoid tissues and cells. Quickly, just days after the initial infection, a massive involvement of memory CD4$^+$ T cells occurs followed by their loss, particularly within the gut-associated lymphoid tissues (60–63). The result is twofold. First, the loss of CD4 T cells compromises the generation of an effective immune response during the early phase of HIV infection and, second, bacteria migrate across the intestinal mucosa (64). Some hypothesize that translocated bacterial products, like lipopolysaccharide, activate CD4 T cells, thereby enhancing their infection by HIV while also causing the release of cytokines and chemokines. The ensuing cytokine storm acts to augment not only the infection but also the associated disease. In addition, the number of CD4 T cells decreases due to several other factors. These include the killing of T cells by other T cells specialized for that purpose, the induction of apoptosis (killing) of uninfected T cells by HIV glycoproteins, and incitement of autophagy, a form of cell suicide. Other immunopathologic events are likely fueled by virus antigen/antiviral antibody immune complexes, by overactivity of T cells, and by the involvement of dendritic cells.

HIV was first defined as a clinical disease in American homosexuals living in or near New York City, San Francisco, and Los Angeles (5). The early symptoms are weakness, chills, enlarged and painful lymph glands, and occasionally, purple skin blotches characteristic of the slowly progressive cancer (5,6), Kaposi's sarcoma. As HIV infection progresses, or even initially, effects on the brain become evident. Loss of concentration and poor mental function are common, especially with respect to solving puzzles or playing chess, which require a good attention span and ability to analyze new information. Many who are infected remain relatively healthy during the early phase of disease and may do so for years. For others, death is rapid, in just one to a few years. The common thread for rapid progression of disease leading to death is the lowering of the CD4$^+$ T cell count usually below 100.

The notably rapid effect of HIV was its invasion of the heterosexual community in the form of AIDS. As new cases of AIDS increased to frightening proportions, scientists in several laboratories searched for the agent involved. Lessons learned from earlier work that led to the successful isolation of HTLV-I indicated the strategy to follow and the difficulties to avoid. First, cultured T cells from AIDS patients were grown with T-cell growth factor. Second, an assay for reverse transcriptase activity was needed that would be unique to this new human retrovirus and would exclude host DNA–dependent RNA polymerase or the previously described HTLV-I or II.

In 1982, several French scientists—mainly Jean Claude Chermann, Françoise Barré-Sinoussi, and Luc Montagnier—obtained lymph node tissue from an AIDS patient, identified by Willy Rozenbaum, a clinician at the Hopital Bichat in Paris. The patient was Frederick B. and the isolated virus, the Bru HIV strain. The scientists cultured lymphoid cells from Frederick B., identified their content of viral reverse transcriptase, and then infected healthy cells with materials from the culture. Chermann had been trained previously in the retrovirology of laboratory mice, and Barré-Sinoussi had experience in growing human T lymphocytes. Montagnier had worked with DNA viruses, interferons, and arenaviruses like lymphocytic choriomeningitis virus.

Simultaneously, in America at the National Institutes of Health (NIH), Robert Gallo had also obtained blood samples from patients with AIDS. Members of his laboratory had been the first to grow human T lymphocytes in culture using their newly discovered T-cell growth factor. They had also been involved in isolating the first human retrovirus, HTLV-1. In 1982, they detected reverse transcriptase in lymphocytes from patients with AIDS.

These simultaneous research discoveries led to the back-to-back publication in 1983 by the French group (3) and the NIH group (2), both of whom presented data concerning the isolation of a retrovirus from patients with AIDS, and this virus's attack on T lymphocytes. In the same issue of the publication *Science* where these two articles appeared, Max Essex (4) and his colleagues in Boston reported on antibodies to cell-membrane antigens that were associated with human T-cell virus in patients with AIDS.

Despite the excitement generated by these initial reports, several issues still needed resolution. For example, it was not clear whether the newly isolated virus was a variant of HTLV or a separate and new human retrovirus. In the report by Essex (4), 35 percent of the blood samples obtained from AIDS patients also reacted with HTLV-I infected cells. Further, some of the virus particles seen by electron microscopy were interpreted by a panel of experts as being not retroviruses but arenaviruses (8). However, subsequent studies rapidly and conclusively showed that this entity was indeed a new virus, now called HIV, not a variant of HTLV-I or II. The initial confusion occurred because some of the early cultures were infected with both HTLV and HIV (8). A characteristic profile of HIV soon became clear and ruled out an arenavirus as the agent of AIDS.

As recalled by one of the earliest workers on AIDS, Jean-Claude Gluckman (7):

> I have been working on AIDS since the first case of the disease was diagnosed in France [December 1981].... We adopted the hypothesis that the disease was caused by a retrovirus and defined what we considered to be the most propitious experimental conditions for the isolation of this hypothetical virus. Our idea was that the virus would be isolated more easily from patients with an AIDS-associated syndrome (essentially a generalized lymphadenopathy [enlargement of lymph nodes]) than from patients with AIDS itself. Because we thought it was likely that the lymph node hyperplasia was evidence of a localized immune response, which suggested the presence of a virus in the lymph nodes, we decided to search for the virus there, rather than in the peripheral blood of the patients. Rozenbaum and the virologist Françoise Brun-Vezinet contacted Luc Montagnier's group at the Institute Pasteur and brought them a lymph node specimen. That it was not a mere blood sample attests to the study group's contribution to the isolation of the virus. Montagnier, Jean-Claude Chermann, and Françoise Barré-Sinoussi went on to successfully isolate LAV, now known as HIV, early in 1983.

Robert Gallo (8) remembered:

> Our earliest detections of reverse transcriptase [RT] activity in an AIDS patient dated to May 1982 with the cells of [patient] E.P. These cells were clearly positive for HTLV-I proteins (or very related proteins) and we worked on this isolation for a number of months. Our next set of detections occurred between November 1982 and February 1983, with at least five positives, but none of these samples were as vigorous as E.P. and most showed at best low level RT viral activity. Nevertheless, they appeared significant to us and they were negative for HTLV proteins; therefore they were suggestive of a new retrovirus. Our cell culturing was now speeding up ... cells from both the symptomatic baby and the asymptomatic mother were positive for reverse transcriptase.
>
> That was one of the earliest detections Phil[lip Markham] and Zaki [Salahuddin] [Gallo's associates] had and probably provided the first

indication that the AIDS virus could, in fact, be transmitted either by intravenous drug abusers [as the mother was] and/or by heterosexual routes, and also to babies of infected mothers . . .

It was not until one year later, in 1984, when Gallo and his colleagues used a test they had developed to detect antibodies to HIV, along with epidemiologic data, that they firmly established HIV as the cause of AIDS.

Today we know that HIV has a narrow host range (6). It is a disease of humans, although certain subhuman primates can be infected by inoculation with either patient's tissues, cells infected in culture, or cell-free virus. Even before HIV was isolated, its routes of transmission in humans were well established (5). HIV enters its hosts by sexual transmission, transfusion of blood and blood products, or prenatal transmission from mother to fetus. The virus can travel during both homosexual and heterosexual activities, and, as with other sexually transmitted infections, the likelihood of infection is related to the number of sexual partners as well as to sites of sexual contact. In the United States, homosexual anal intercourse had been the major mode of transmission, whereas in Africa and the Caribbean, heterosexual vaginal intercourse is the dominant mode. With the increasing incidence of HIV infection in American women, heterosexual intercourse has now become a prominent means of infection and has increased dramatically. The virus has been isolated from semen and female genital secretions.

The HIV saga also mirrors social thought and conflicts of the 1980s and 1990s. Although HIV can pass through contact with contaminated blood or blood products, which involves a small but significant group of unfortunate individuals, the major route of transmission is sexual intercourse. Yet, since its discovery and for too long, HIV was one of the only sexually transmitted diseases that did not require reporting to health authorities in the United States. AIDS is now reported to local health boards by physicians, and sexual partners are to be informed that they are at risk for developing and spreading the disease. However, twenty-five years after the first outbreaks of HIV, roughly 40,000 new cases emerge each year and an estimated 250,000 persons in the United States have HIV infections but do not know it. To close this public health gap, the CDC has recommended that every patient seen in the emergency room aged from thirteen to sixty-four years should be offered an HIV test. The test is not invasive, simply a swab of the gums. Results are available in about twenty minutes. However health insurers have almost universally refused to pay for testing. Their reason is that they pay for an emergency room visit based on the final diagnosis of admission. Thus, no reimbursement or payment is available for a test(s) not related to admission. Nevertheless, having the test is good public health policy for the patient and for anyone he/she might infect. The test costs about forty dollars, but the return in monies recovered by limiting HIV spread is likely in the hundreds of millions of dollars since antiretroviral therapy per person over his/her lifetime is estimated from $600,000 to $650,000. Some hospitals, but not all or even most, offer the test and are funded by city or state governments or private foundations. In one such hospital, Dr. Jeremy Brown (65) found that slightly over 60 percent of emergency room patients accepted the offered HIV test, and a significant number were identified who had no idea they were infected. These individuals then received antiviral drug therapy.

Along similar lines, a court in California ruled on July 3, 2006 that individuals who lead high-risk sexual life styles are responsible for knowing whether or not they are infected with HIV and for informing their partners about possible exposure. A similar ruling was written in 1993 by Justice Marvin Baxter of a Federal Court in Michigan: "negligent transmission of HIV does not depend solely on actual knowledge of HIV infection and would extend at least to those situations where the actor, under the totality of the circumstances, has reason to know of the infection." Clearly, we in America still need a more rigorous public health policy for the states and leadership by state and federal governments.

The principal source of HIV infection in newborns is infected mothers (6). Although the virus can be transmitted across the placenta before birth, infection also occurs at the time of delivery through exposure to an infected genital tract or after birth through breast feeding. An estimated 30 to 50 percent of infants become infected when the mother is an HIV carrier. Mothers requiring blood transfusions during delivery have been infected with HIV as have their babies. This transmission of HIV is now preventable with antiretroviral drug treatment.

Whole blood, blood cell components, plasma, and clotting factors have all been shown to transmit HIV infection. Even the transfusion of a single unit of blood from an HIV-infected person almost uniformly transmits HIV to the recipient. Errors and overt transmission that occurred in the past were unacceptable then and are unacceptable and outrageous today. As we will subsequently discuss, greed and local politics mixed with a country's nationalism even today have allowed the spread of HIV via the blood supply and blood equipment.

The spread of HIV through blood products is dramatic and tragic. First, the past: In Great Britain, roughly 6,287 hemophiliacs were registered between 1977 and 1991. During the period from 1979 to 1986, when blood products in Britain were contaminated by HIV, a total of 1,227 people were infected or about one-fifth of those on the register. HIV in blood products is highly infective; as evidence, hemophiliacs who have not developed disease received no contaminated blood, but many others have. For example, in Japan, half of the 4,000 transfused hemophiliacs developed HIV infection from contaminated blood products Moreover, because donated blood is often pooled, a single infected source can taint other "clean" products. Therefore, ratios of infected to noninfected persons are at best very rough guides of the proportion of blood infected with the virus.

Fortunately, a test is now available to detect HIV in donated blood and has markedly reduced, although not eliminated, HIV transmission through transfusions in the United States and other industrialized countries. In the course of their research, Gallo and his associates developed the initial test to detect HIV contamination in blood as long ago as 1985. For the United States in 1984, a year before the test, 7,200 people were infected with HIV through blood transfusions, compared to fewer than fifty people in 1996 after the test was available. Sadly, and criminally, French health authorities purposely chose not to use this test primarily for nationalistic reasons, that is the Montagnier Pasteur Laboratory was developing a French test similar to but competing with that from the NIH Gallo laboratory. In France, the result of that governmental choice was the deaths of several hundred hemophiliacs and others transfused during surgery. Thousands more became infected with HIV from that blood. The delayed use of the "American" test in France evidently stemmed from two rationales. First, the French wanted to develop their own test and directly obtain the commercial benefits. Second, they wanted to sell blood products previously collected, since their loss might inhibit French dominance of the European blood product market (66). Subsequent investigations and criminal trials led to the conviction and jailing of four health-care workers but did not trace how high in the French government the scandal penetrated.

Even worse, France was not alone. Similar events occurred in Japan and in Germany; large supplies of blood products collected for commercial use but not screened for HIV by the Gallo test were sold for profit. For example, Dr. Günter Kurt Eckert, co-owner of the German drug laboratory Aproth, tried on some 6,000 counts of murder for selling blood products tainted with HIV. Elsewhere, other lawsuits have been settled including one in which over 300 HIV-infected hemophiliacs or their survivors contended that an American manufacturer continued marketing its blood-clotting products for two years after being informed in 1985 that the heating process used would not kill the AIDS-causing virus. Clearly, economic and political considerations have been more important to those in power and responsible for decisions in business and in government than the health of the public at large.

In February 1996, the Japanese Health Minister Naoto Kan publicly apologized for the government's failure to prevent transfusion of HIV-infected blood in the 1980s. Even though officials learned of the risk in 1983, diseased blood was nevertheless used and infected about 2,000 people. The consequences of a criminal investigation into this act led, in October 1996, to the arrest of Akihito Matsumara, who from 1984 to 1986 headed the Ministry of Health's Biologics and Antibiotics Division; of the two former presidents of Green Cross Corporation, the pharmaceutical house that had Japan's largest market share of blood products; and of Takeshi Abe, former vice president of Teikyo University, who was in charge of the AIDS study group that recommended the continued use by hemophiliacs of unheated blood products in 1983 (heating kills HIV). The charge is murder due to professional negligence resulting in death.

Incredibly, the issue of contaminated blood still persists. In 2007, Dr. Gao Yaojie was placed under house arrest in the Chinese city of Zhengzhou. Gao, a doctor treating AIDS patients, had raised the alarm that transmission of HIV via blood was occurring in rural areas of Henan. Just as she was leaving China for America to receive an award for her work in public health, Dr. Gao was placed under house arrest. The idea was that stopping her from getting a visa in Beijing to travel outside of China would effectively prevent her from receiving the award and would also prevent the perception that China had/has an AIDS problem.

China went from initially denying the existence of an AIDS epidemic in the 1990s to actively confronting this plague in the 2000s by providing funds for medical research and public health. The government instituted free anti-HIV drug programs, educated the public, and allowed support from sources outside of China, the Bill and Melinda Gates Foundation and the Clinton Foundation among others.

However China's government is intolerant of any public dissent that would embarrass them. This is by no means a new government policy, but stands as a long-term tradition in China. From 1900 to the 1920s, the Chinese engaged in intense introspection trying to understand how their formerly great empire could have become so weak. They settled on the cause as, in part, a lack of democracy and, largely, a lack of science. Science then became a passion, and, by extension and expansion, scientism became the passion. Thus, a scientific venue was applied to a variety of traditional Chinese culture forms, including martial arts and Chinese medicine. Much of their focus was on the need to make a good impression in the area of public health and hygiene for the scientifically ordered West. Thus, the image of China became an essential component in health care so as not to be judged backwards. There were many Western-trained Chinese scientists, true believers in science, who were deeply concerned about transforming China's modes into what was/is considered a universally applicable system by those who had considerable economic, cultural, military power over the Chinese. This is the likely explanation for the SARS-Chinese fiasco described in Chapter 12, the HIV/AIDS event cited below, and related questions about the Chinese government's reporting of Asian (bird) flu mentioned in the chapter on influenza.

Dr. Gao Yaojie was instrumental in exposing the selling of HIV-infected blood, an operation that spread HIV throughout central China in the 1990s. Her crime was pinpointing official government corruption and mismanagement. Dr. Gao's history is that of a female admitted to medical school in the late 1930s–early 1940s, a rare event not only in China but even the West. She survived the Japanese bombing raids in the 1940s and delivered babies as an obstetrician in the 1950s. She subsequently became aware of and involved with HIV and AIDS by witnessing its spread throughout Henan province in the 1990s. The cause of this spread was a government sponsored and endorsed program for collecting and selling blood. This program led to the infection of thousands of farmers due to the usage of HIV-contaminated needles and instruments employed to collect blood. Dr. Gao travelled to villages in the province to provide medical care and information to people who had no idea why they had become sick and were dying. She spoke out forcefully against local government officials who were covering up the crisis, who benefited monetarily, and who were complicit in this shoddy affair. To be honored for her work in AIDS, Dr. Gao was to leave the city of Zhengzhou, travel to Beijing for a U.S. visa, and then leave for Washington DC to attend an event sponsored by Vital Voices. Vital Voices is a nonprofit, nonpartisan organization whose honorary chairpersons were then senators Hillary Clinton (Democrat, and U.S. senator from New York) and Kay Bailey Hutchinson (Republican, and U.S. senator from Texas). But in Zhengzhou, Dr. Gao's enforced house arrest was publicized by photographs of three high-ranking officials of Henan province seen beaming, clapping, and presenting flowers to Dr. Gao. The local paper denied she was under house arrest but rather had voluntarily expressed a desire to stay at home. Later, the Chinese AIDS activist Wan Yanhai was similarly detained and blocked from attending and participating in AIDS conferences.

Dissidents who have previously or currently spoken out against errors in Chinese governance in the Henan province or poor health-care in China are brutalized, jailed, or placed under house arrest on dubious charges. They are warned not to communicate with foreign journalists. In the case of Dr. Gao, police chief Yao Daixian went to her apartment and personally warned her to avoid journalists: "These people are liars and you must consider the negative influences it brings on our country. Love the country, the party, and the government." Such boundaries exist in China and you cross them at your risk. Dr. Gao did.

When scientific research interferes with politics, economics or culture, science is most often the loser. Thus, governments and businesses control health care for their personal gains or concepts and disregard or avoid factual knowledge and events. That unfortunate issue has been played out with HIV and contaminated blood products in France, Germany, and China as recorded here. With similar attitudes of denial, England avoids the possibility that contaminated beef causes a lethal degenerative disease of the brain, and the United States ignores its improper testing of beef for contaminants, as discussed in Chapter 15, "Mad Cow Disease and Englishmen: Spongiform Encephalopathies—Prion Disease."

Now the world must acknowledge that AIDS is a true plague in our midst. AIDS can be considered essentially an issue and crisis of governance; that is, what governments do or not do for their people. By contrast to South Africa's dismal record in controlling HIV and AIDS, other African governments have supplied education on safe sexual behaviors, testing for HIV, use of condoms and sterile needles, and have provided antiretroviral drug therapy. These measures have dramatically reversed the incidence of and deaths from AIDS. But cultural norms are difficult to change, and the practice of having unprotected sex with multiple partners remains, as do corruption and waste. Women in Africa are three to four times more likely than men to become infected. With unemployment over 60 percent in some areas, they become mistresses or fall prey to migrant workers for their basic survival. The cultural bonds of multiple women nursing of new babies as well as ritual cutting/scarification and blood mixing are long lived. Health-care providers are scarce, with roughly one physician for nearly 40,000 people compared to one traditional faith healer per every 400. Drug delivery is grossly inadequate, considering the lack of treatment for most of the 15,000 to 40,000 children in Cameroon estimated to have HIV infections in 2005; only 400 received the drugs they needed (67). Commentary on a similar sad event was chronicled by Nicholas Kristof (68):

> We met the family of Pascal Nttomba beside the fresh mound in the garden where he was buried two weeks ago. Mr. Nttomba was the breadwinner for the 20 people in the family.
>
> The Nttombas were relatively well off, living in a nice wooden house and sending their children to technical schools to learn vocations that would take them up a notch in the world. But then Pascal became sick.
>
> He could no longer work, and the family used all its savings to try to cure him—first paying a traditional healer and then a doctor. Neither did any good, although the doctor charged more.
>
> In theory, antiretrovirals are available here to control the disease. But they are mostly for middle-class victims in the cities, and as in most of Africa, an ordinary person in a remote area has next to no chance of getting the drugs. And so Pascal died, and now the family is destitute.
>
> "There's nothing to eat in the house, since this morning," said his father, Valeré. The women in the family were planning to scour the fields for cassava leaves to cook for dinner. They say they can also go into the forests to look for edible wild plants, but malnutrition looms.
>
> The children in technical school have dropped out, because there is no money. One of them is Hermine, a 19-year-old, who is now at risk of being approached by an older sugar daddy offering gifts in exchange for being his mistress, a common arrangement in Africa that has led to high infection rates among young women.
>
> "I'd do it," she acknowledged—after all, the family needs money.
>
> The family's predicament underscores how the virus not only kills people but also further impoverishes the world's poorest. And while the

hardest-hit countries in Southern Africa are doing a bit better against AIDS, others in the middle range like Cameroon or India have not yet realized the severity of the problem.

An essential challenge is that ninety percent of those with HIV world-wide don't know it, and you can't begin to tackle the disease when no one knows who has it. Here, for example, neither Pascal's wife nor any other member of his family has been tested.

Such events coupled with those in complete denial of reality make containment and treatment of HIV more difficult than it is already. Even today only about 25 percent or fewer infected or ill adults in Africa receive antiretroviral drugs, and less than 2 percent of children are treated.

Yet, perhaps the most grievous and shameful use of lies, denials, and misconceptions falls to South Africa, a country that has the highest inci-dence of AIDS in a continent where over twenty-five million are infected with HIV, over two million die each year, and over two and a half mil-lion become infected each year. As Stephen Lewis, Ambassador to Africa from the United Nations, stated in his keynote lecture at the 16th Inter-national AIDS Meeting, "South Africa is the only government in Africa whose government continues to propose theories (about the origin of HIV and AIDS) more worthy of a lunatic fringe than a concerned and compassionate state. The government has a lot to atone for . . . I am of the opinion they can never achieve redemption."

What has South Africa done to deserve such branding? Historically, Nelson Mandela, one of the twentieth century's great heroes and lead-ers, led his country from grievous apartheid to a democratic, nonvengeful democratic majority rule. He committed South Africa to diversity and tolerance and has been outspoken in his support for control of HIV and prevention of AIDS. Mandela's successor as president of South Africa, Thabo Mbeki, has failed to face up to this country's AIDS epi-demic. Mbeki insisted until recently that he knew no one with AIDS, although nearly 20 percent of South Africa's population is infected with AIDS, and millions have died from it. Mbeki has supported crackpot theories that denied AIDS was transmitted by a treatable virus infec-tion. He indicated that antiretroviral drug therapy was a toxin and encouraged the usage of herbal remedies as therapy. Mbeki appointed Dr. Tshabalala-Msimang as his health deputy. Tshabalala-Msimang's husband, a political powerhouse and an ally of president Mbeki, is the treasurer of the African National Congress, Mr. Mbeki's political party.

Tshabalala-Msimang has in the past and continues to promote lemons, beet root, and garlic as therapy against HIV and AIDS.

Into that tragedy of errors has come Nozizwe Madlala-Routledge, who exemplifies a true profile of courage not unlike Dr. Gao in China. Madlala-Routledge pursued a science degree in the early 1970s in South Africa at the University of Fort Haze, the same school that Nelson Mandela attended. While at the University, Madlala-Routledge joined a boycott against the then apartheid government's decree that black parents were prohibited from attending the graduation ceremonies of their children. As a student, she was required to apologize for participation in the boycott or be expelled from school. She refused and was expelled. Thirty-five years later, Madlala-Routledge was again discharged, this time from her post as South Africa's deputy health minister for refusing to apologize for her statements against the health department's anti-AIDS strategy of using herbal medicines in place of antiretroviral drug therapy. With over 1,000 South Africans infected with HIV every day and over 800 dying per day, Madlala-Routledge spoke out against the vegetable diet to cure AIDS and pushed for sufficient antiretroviral drugs to reach the majority (over 80 percent) of infected individuals by the year 2011. Accompanied by journalists on a visit to a rural hospital housing AIDS patients, she characterized the high death rates as a national emergency and endorsed the need for antiviral drug therapy. Again removed from office, this time by Mbeki's government instead of the white supremacists of the 1970s, she was offered possible reinstatement if she apologized for her words. President Mbeki called her "a lone ranger who fully ignored orders." Again she refused, saying "I didn't see what I had to apologize for."

President Mbeki and Tshabalala-Msimang are not alone in denying the cause and proper treatment of AIDS. In their company is Roberto Giraldo, a New York hospital technologist who preaches that AIDS is caused by a deficiency in the diet and not by a virus. He served as a consultant to Mbeki. There is David Rasnick who has written, "HIV cannot be transmitted between heterosexuals," and works in South Africa for a multinational vitamin company, The Rath Foundation, which advocates and sells vitamins to be used in place of antiretroviral drug treatment. In California, Christine Maggiore campaigns against the use of antiretroviral drug therapy to prevent transmission of HIV from mothers to babies, and Peter Duesberg at University of California, Berkeley, argues that HIV does not cause AIDS. Despite these naysayers, firm evidence supports the benefits of antiviral drug therapy, particularly the decrease in AIDS and related deaths from this treatment and its use to prevent mother-to-baby transmissions of HIV. Proof of these facts is the improved health of infected individuals.

Against the bleak side of this picture are some rays of light and hope in Africa. In June of 2007, the G-8 leaders of the world's richest industrial countries pledged $60 billion for the treatment of AIDS and other diseases in developing countries. Organizations like Doctors Without Borders are involved in providing health care as are several medical institutions. For example, Bruce Walker, a professor of medicine and expert in AIDS and director of the AIDS research program at Harvard (Massachusetts General Hospital) has received funding to work in Africa from the National Institutes of Health (USA), the Gates Foundation and other private supporters to actively engage in improving the understanding and treatment of AIDS in Durban, South Africa. These philanthropies have built facilities as well as training Africans to perform testing, treatments, and public health practices. Other foundations have similarly provided financial support, and personal commitments have come from physicians, health workers, and scientists to work in countries where HIV and AIDS are out of control. Such involvement is expanding and is exemplary. In the United States, the past paranoia that allowed exclusion of HIV-infected individuals from school or business employment, an illogical and shameful attitude, has diminished. In the past, frightened people faced with smallpox or other epidemics who attributed the disease to unfavorable constellations of stars, to the wrath of supernatural powers, or to poisoning of wells by Jews or other ethnic minority groups often paid for such superstitions with their lives. Today, most of the religious leaders, U.S. senators, and columnists who should have known better when they said, "HIV infection represents the wrath of God on unclean people," have publicly apologized. Such sad episodes remind us that history often repeats itself in the Westernized lands as well as elsewhere. Ignorance is not simply a relic of times past, unfortunately, but often remains viable, as does the frailty of humans faced with catastrophic events.[1]

---

[1] This year's Nobel Prize in Physiology and Medicine went to Françoise Barré-Sinoussi and Luc Montagnier for the discovery of HIV-1, the agent that causes AIDS. While both are deserving, the exclusion of Robert Gallo was noted with surprise and dismay by many in the scientific community (69,70). Currently much research is focused on host factors listed in Table 14.1 and inter-related with HIV.

TABLE 14.1 Human Genes Identified That Influence HIV Infection and Disease

Gene Products	Effect
Barriers to retroviral infection	
TRIM5α	Infection resistance
AB0BEC3G	Infection resistance
Influence on HIV-1 infection	
Coreceptor/ligand	
CCR5	↓ Infection
CCL2, CCL-7, CCL11	↑ Infection
(MCP1, MCP3, eotaxin), H7	
Influence on development of AIDS	
Coreceptor/ligand	
CCR5	↓ Disease progression
CCR2	↓ Disease progression
CCL5 (RANTES)	↑ Disease progression
CCL3L1 (MIP1α)	↓ Disease progression
DC-SIGN	↓ Parenteral infection
Cytokine	
IL-10	↓ Disease progression
IFN-y	↓ Disease progression
PD-1	↑ Disease progression
TGFβ	↑ Disease progression
Innate immunity	↓ Disease progression
KIR3DS1 (with HLA-Bw4)	
Adaptive immunity	
HLA-A, HLA-B, HLA-C	↑ Disease progression
HLA-B*5802, HLA-B*18	↑ Disease progression
HLA-B*35-Px	↑ Disease progression
HLA-B*27	↓ Disease progression
HLA-B*57, HLA-B*5801	↓ Disease progression
IL-40	↑ Disease progression
PD-1	↑ Disease progression
TGFβ	↑ Disease progression

Source: Modified from Heeney, J., Dalgleish, A., and Weiss, R. *Science* 313:465, 2006. For recent update of candidate genes using SiRNA screens, see Brass et al. *Science* 319:921–926, 2008.

Mad Cow Disease and Englishmen: Spongiform Encephalopathies— Prion Disease

Over 200 years ago, farmers in England, Scotland, and France noted that some sheep suffered progressive shaking, wasting, loss of balance, and severe itching that caused them to rub their hindquarters and flanks against any upright post. The name scrapie, or *tremblante* in France, was given to this disorder. Owners of healthy flocks recognized that their animals contracted scrapie only after introduction of new breeding stock later found to bear the disease. Eventually sheep exported from England infected herds in Australia, New Zealand, and South Africa. Only extermination of the affected animals stopped scrapie from spreading, but by then it was distributed widely throughout Europe, Asia, and America.

Nearly 100 years later, C. Besnoit (1) reported experimental transmission of the same disease by inoculating ewes with brain tissue from a sheep with scrapie. Then, in the 1930s, J. Cuillé (2,3) provided evidence for the first unequivocal transmission of scrapie from infected to healthy sheep and documented that the agent was in brain extracts taken from scrapie-infected sheep and passed through filters with pores small enough to retain all microbes but viruses and perhaps other yet-to-be identified agents.

In the 1950s and into the 1960s, a neurodegenerative disease among the isolated Fore tribespeople in the central New Guinea highlands, an area under Australian administration, was investigated by Drs. Vincent Zigas and D. Carlton Gajdusek (4,5), who wrote:

> In 1957, Dr. Vincent Zigas and I first described the rapidly fatal disease, kuru, a strong new subacute, familial, degenerative disease of the central nervous system (characterized by cerebellar ataxia and trembling) and restricted in occurrence to some 12,000 native Highland New Guineans of the Fore linguistic group, and to their immediate neighbors with whom they intermarry, and among whom it accounted for over half of all deaths.
>
> On first seeing kuru, we had suspected it to be a viral meningo-encephalitis, only to find very little in the clinical picture, laboratory findings, or epidemiology to support such a suspicion, and nothing in the neuropathology to suggest acute infection. The epidemiological pattern of kuru occurrence suggested some genetic determinant of disease expression and this was supported by the restriction of the disease in peripheral areas to those individuals genetically related to the population in the center of the region.
>
> We were unable to demonstrate any contact infections in people living in close association to kuru victims throughout the course of their disease. We had early considered association of the disease with extensive cannibalism, but soon dismissed this as unlikely when cases of the disease were encountered in individuals whom we did not believe had engaged in the ritual cannibalistic consumption of diseased relatives, the prevailing practice in the region. The hypothesis that the disease might be an autosensitization, perhaps provoked by early sensitization to human brain through cannibalism in infancy or early childhood, likewise was not borne out either by neuropathology or by the search for autoimmune antibodies to brain antigen in serum specimens (6).

Kuru, which means shivering or trembling in the Fore language, was originally characterized primarily as a disease of women and children.

However, the disease was common both in male and female children and in adult females, but rare in adult males. Those afflicted had tremors, poor balance, and an inability to form words, leading to a total loss of speech. Death followed usually in less than one year from the onset of obvious symptoms. Geographically, this mysterious disease was confined to the highlands of New Guinea. Anthropologic and epidemiologic investigations by Carlton Gajdusek suggested that the incubation period of kuru could be as long as thirty years or even more. Even though he had first discounted the possibility, Gajdusek went on to record that the disease was transmitted by the practice of ritual cannibalism, a rite of mourning and respect for dead kinsman during which several of their tissues, including what we now know was highly infectious brain matter, were consumed by women and small children of both genders. Boys over six years of age no longer took part in the ritual, and only 2 percent of adult males developed kuru. Estimates indicate that over 90 percent of children and women partaking in cannibalism or smearing of their faces with diseased brain tissue developed kuru. Igor Klatzo, a pathologist at the National Institutes of Health in Bethesda, Maryland, who examined Gajdusek's autopsied brains of patients with kuru noted a punched-out Swiss-cheese appearance of the tissue and attributed it to the dropout loss of neurons. But what was the cause of kuru? A toxin? An ingredient in the diseased tissue? The answer was not clear, but an infectious agent, such as a virus, was low on the list of probabilities. Lack of the usual hallmarks of infection— that is, fever, malaise, rash, cough, and inflammatory cells in the fluids that bathe the brain—along with the unusually long incubation period and, pathologically, the deficiency of inflammatory cells in the diseased brain, all disallowed a virus or any other ordinary infectious agent as the cause.

In those years, nothing more than a guess linked kuru with scrapie. William Hadlow, a veterinary pathologist at the Rocky Mountain National Laboratory of the National Institutes of Health in Hamilton, Montana, then entered the picture. He had broad experience in studying natural scrapie infection of sheep. This led him to report that the brain injury in kuru reported by Klatzo and colleagues resembled what he had seen in animals with scrapie (7). Hadlow published his theory in the British journal *Lancet*, describing the resemblance between both disorders. Seizing on Hadlow's report and knowing that scrapie was a transmissible agent, Gajdusek and his associate Joe Gibbs then promptly attempted to pass kuru to subhuman primates. As Gajdusek reported,

> In 1959, Hadlow brought to our attention the close similarities between the neuropathology, clinical symptoms, and epidemiology of kuru and of scrapie in sheep, a central nervous system degeneration known to be caused by a slow virus infection, susceptibility to which is genetically determined. Infection had before this seemed a very unlikely etiologic possibility for kuru. Now we were forced to reconsider the problem in the light of slow virus infections of the nervous system familiar to the veterinary virologists, of which scrapie and visna were the best elucidated examples (6).

With the realization that kuru (and possibly other degenerative diseases of the human central nervous system) could have resulted from a slowly progressing, long-lasting viral infection, Gajdusek recognized that the laboratory procedures he and his colleagues had used earlier and which failed to uncover an infectious agent were not suitable. So in 1959, he resumed his search for a transmissible agent in kuru but with a different strategy:

> The plan was for inoculation of unimpeachably adequate inoculum, i.e., human brain biopsy material or very early autopsy specimens containing viable cells, inoculated without delay, or, if not so promptly inoculated, frozen promptly to −70°C in liquid nitrogen (dry ice) and inoculated at a later, more convenient time. The program was planned to include inoculation of many species of primates, including the chimpanzee, and long-term observation of these primates for, at least, 5 years after inoculation (6).

This procedure proved successful but, as Gajdusek suspected, required an incubation period of many months to several years. The next step was to document continuous passage of the disease from one animal to others, and this he did by using brains from ill or autopsied subhuman primates to infect other subhuman primates. The results showed that scrapie and kuru were much alike in their ability to transfer disease and cause destructive lesions in the brain.

The pathologic similarity of kuru and scrapie to Creutzfeldt-Jakob disease (CJD), known previously as a chronic progressive dementia of humans tormented by tremors, led to the concept that a whole group of diseases involving slow progression and injury of nerve cells might be related. For his research on these lethal diseases, called spongiform

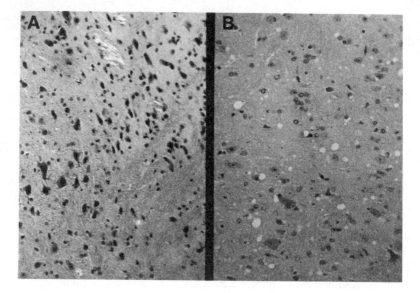

FIGURE 15.1 *Photomicrograph of (A) a normal brain and (B) a Swiss cheese–appearing brain representing that of a human or animal with spongiform encephalopathy. Photomicrographs taken from tissues studied by Michael B. A. Oldstone.*

encephalopathies, Gajdusek was awarded the Nobel Prize in 1976. As stated in his Nobel lecture on December 13, 1976:

> Kuru was the first chronic degenerative disease of man shown to be a slow virus infection, with incubation periods measured in years and with a progressive accumulative pathology always leading to death. This established that virus infections of man could, after long delay, produce chronic degenerative disease and disease with apparent heredofamilial patterns of occurrence and with none of the inflammatory responses regularly associated with viral infections.
>
> Kuru has led us, however, to a more exciting frontier in microbiology than only the demonstration of a new pathogenic mechanism of infectious disease, namely the recognition of a new group of viruses possessing unconventional physical and chemical properties and biological behavior far different from that of any other group of microorganisms. However, these viruses still demonstrate sufficiently classical behavior of other infectious microbial agents for us to retain, perhaps with misgivings, the title of "viruses".

Related to scrapie, kuru, and CJD is a rare condition, the familial disease, Gerstmann-Sträussler Scheinker (GSS) syndrome. These patients have ataxia (the loss of coordination) and eventually develop dementia and die. The symptoms are similar for familial fatal insomnia, which presents itself as an inability to sleep that progresses to loss of coordination, dementia, and death.

In the laboratory, these diseases of sheep and humans were transmissible by feeding or inoculation, showed a similar pathologic picture, and had incubation periods varying from a few months to years, depending primarily on dose and strain of inoculum and genetics of the host. The infectious factor had at least one aspect of a virus, that is, it passed through filters small enough to retain all organisms except viruses, but it differed from viruses by virtue of its resistance to inactivation by treatments known to kill viruses such as boiling, application of 70 percent ethanol, ionizing, ultraviolet radiation, autoclaving, and the lack of an identifiable nucleic acid.

Unfortunate accidents have proven that such diseases are transmissible. For instance, transplantation of corneas from CJD patients or reuse of needle electrodes in neurosurgery has resulted in the passage of this disease from one human to another (8–11). Similarly, growth hormone used for medical purposes and extracted from pituitaries obtained at autopsies produced CJD due to contamination by tissue from patients whose CJD had not been diagnosed. Comparable human-to-human transmission had occurred from ritual cannibalism causing kuru that killed thousands, growth hormone extracted from human cadavers that killed 180 children and young adults and, perhaps, nearly a hundred who died after the surgical procedures of transplantation or needle probing. Recently, transmission by transfusion was reported when blood from a human donor infected with and incubating variant CJD (vCJD) was infused into healthy recipients. Accidents of this kind are now largely eliminated: Ritual cannibalism is no longer practiced by the Fore people; corneas used for transplantation are screened by careful history taking so that those obtained from diseased patients are destroyed, and the same screening rules out the use of blood from donors who lived in England when mad cow disease was prevalent. Biotechnology companies now manufacture recombinant growth hormone so extraction from human tissues is no longer necessary, and electrode needles used to probe brain tissues are now disposable and used only once.

In 1985–86, bovine spongiform encephalopathy (BSE) was first identified in cattle of southern England, and within two years over 1,000 cases surfaced in more than 200 herds (11). This was clearly a new disease in cattle. Yet, by 1996, over 160,000 confirmed cases affecting 59 percent of dairy herds in the United Kingdom were reported by the British Government's Ministry of Agriculture, Fisheries, and Food. Overall, more than two million cows in the United Kingdom and Europe are believed to have had BSE (12). However, when those data became available from 1988 to 1996, they were sequestered by the British government and denied to nongovernment, independent researchers. When the information was finally accessible for analysis by others outside the ministry, reports (13–15) set the number of sick cows as considerably higher than previously acknowledged.

Epidemiologic investigations indicated that the addition of meat and bone meal as a protein supplement to cattle feeds was the likely source of that infection. Those studies also suggested that changes made in the rendering process during the early 1980s might be the cause. Why was the process changed? The high price and difficulty in buying oil because of OPEC policy and the Arab boycott were in part responsible. Suppliers who prepared the feed simply discontinued the use of petroleum-based products that inactivated disease agents. Thus, the sheep scrapie agent and/or possibly unrecognized BSE agents survived.

Epidemiologic studies indicated that the usual incubation period for cattle to develop the disease was four to five years, with a range of two and a half to over eight years. That interval coincides with the initial exposure of the cattle, presumably to the contaminated diet, from late 1979 through 1989, when feed without the disease inactivating agent was banned in the United Kingdom. Even so, by 1993 cases of BSE, or mad cow disease, peaked at over 1,000 per week (according to the Ministry of Agriculture, Fisheries, and Food; these figures may be too low). The total cases reached about 97,000 in Britain, 856 in Northern Ireland, 37 in Switzerland, and 5 in France. Cattle exported from England carried mad cow disease to areas as distant as Arabia, the Falkland Islands, and Denmark.

In spite of the ban on tainted feed, according to the Ministry of Agriculture, Fisheries, and Food, over 30,000 animals born after July 1988 have had BSE. Theoretically, these cattle should never have come in contact with contaminated feed. Nevertheless, either infected meat and bone meal are still entering the feeding process, although at a lower level, or the disease may be transmitted horizontally (animal to animal) and/or vertically (mother to baby) within herds.

In addition to controlling the BSE epidemic in cattle, measures were set up to gauge whether this disease was a human health problem and to safeguard the population from the potential risk of BSE transmission. As a defense measure, in 1990, a national CJD Surveillance Unit was established in the United Kingdom to monitor changes in the disease pattern of CJD that might indicate transmission of BSE to humans. The objective of this commission was to find out whether mad cow disease crossed species barriers to infect humans and manifested itself as CJD in people who had eaten infected beef and other cattle products (such as gelatin made from cattle bones) or had worked among diseased cows (e.g., dairy farmers, butchers, veterinarians). However, the long incubation period plus low incidence of CJD meant it might be many years before such surveillance yielded results.

A quicker route to obtain such answers seemed to be laboratory research. Since it was unethical to inject diseased cattle brains into humans, two alternative experimental approaches were taken to address the issue of whether mad cow disease might infect the human population. One approach was to process diseased cow brains into an inoculum to be used for widely diverse types of subhuman primates. The second was to genetically alter mice so that they carried the human prion protein, a protein implicated in and necessary for development of the spongiform encephalopathies, and then challenge such mice with diseased cow brains. Both types of experiments take time, so a worried country could not even predict when to expect results. The United Kingdom held its collective breath, and fortunately or not, the results soon arrived.

In 1993, the CJD Surveillance Unit reported that two dairy farmers who had been in contact with "mad cows" (that had BSE) developed CJD. One was a sixty-one-year-old male who suffered progressive loss of memory, loss of balance, and inability to talk, then died within four months after the initial diagnosis (16). The second, a fifty-four-year-old male, also died within four months after a medical examination for rapidly progressing dementia, tremors, and ataxia (17). Both farmers had the classical pathologic lesions and abnormalities in prion proteins—key indicators of spongiform encephalopathies and now CJD.

But were these actually cases of mad cow disease transmitted to humans? Although both dairy farmers had been exposed to mad cows and both displayed clinical courses and test results revealing CJD, they were only 2 of 120,000 individuals working in dairy farming and only 2 of about 51 million people in England and Wales where the expected incidence of new CJD cases is 30 per year.

Although CJD is the most common form of transmissible spongiform encephalopathies in humans, it is a rare disease with a uniform world incidence of about one case in two million persons per year. The disease most often strikes humans near age sixty-five (8–11), and its appearance is exceedingly unusual in persons under the age of thirty. Each year, approximately 85 percent of new cases appear randomly throughout the world for no known cause, so are called sporadic CJD. The remaining 15 percent are either inherited, associated with a mutation in the prion protein, or acquired. So-called "acquired CJD" comes from transplanted corneas, from cadaver tissues containing growth hormone, or, in the case of kuru among Fore tribes, from cannibalism of diseased tissue. Yet, the two British dairy farmers had no history or biochemical evidence for inherited or acquired CJD. Further, no cluster of the disease followed among local butchers or veterinarians. So this chance finding probably reflected the rare cases of sporadic CJD that occur.

Then, in 1995, CJD surfaced again in a fifty-four-year-old male dairy farmer in Britain. In the typical pattern, he had a three-month history of forgetfulness, altered behavior, slurred speech, difficulty in balance, and tremors (18). As this neurologic breakdown progressed relentlessly, analysis of his brain tissue led to a diagnosis of CJD. Again, since there was no evidence of familial or acquired disease, this case was considered to be sporadic CJD with no direct correlation to mad cow disease. At this time the European Committee Surveillance Project, while monitoring CJD in France, Germany, Italy, the Netherlands, and United Kingdom, found that the incidence of CJD in farmers closely approximated that in the general population and was not on the increase. So far, so good.

Unfortunately, this picture changed rapidly when, at the end of 1995, two additional cases of CJD emerged (19,20). The new complication was that the patients were sixteen and eighteen years old, not the usual sixty or so years of age. Previously, only four teenagers were known to develop CJD, a sixteen-year-old male in the United States in 1978, a nineteen-year-old female in France in 1982, a fourteen-year-old female born in England but living in Canada in 1988, and a nineteen-year-old female from Poland in 1991. No persons with CJD younger than thirty had been reported in the United Kingdom until these two.

The sixteen-year-old was a schoolgirl with worsening slurred speech, poor balance, and clumsiness. The eighteen-year-old boy's deteriorating memory showed up as a decline in school performance and an increase in confusion as his balance failed. Neither of these two teenagers had a history of familial dementia, and analysis of their brains failed to reveal the prion protein mutations that are associated with familial CJD.

Now the dilemma became acute. Was the world witnessing a new disease, perhaps associated with mad cow disease, or sporadic CJD? The small number of cases as well as the geographical separation suggested a sporadic nature; however, the patients' ages raised suspicion. As one might imagine, investigators considered the possibility that both patients had eaten contaminated beef or visited infected dairy farms.

One year later, in the first week of April 1996, the British journal *Lancet* published a report of not one or two, but ten cases of a new variant of CJD in the United Kingdom (21). These cases were still considered unusual because of the patients' youth, ranging from nineteen to thirty-nine. But even more deviations separated this disease pattern from previously recorded CJD. All these patients endured a relatively long period of symptoms—fourteen months (average)—compared with the average of four months for CJD. The brain wave features typical for CJD patients were missing, and the brain pathology revealed excessive amounts of abnormal prion protein lesions in the cerebrum and cerebellum, as opposed to the distribution found in older CJD patients whose lesions were located in the brain's basal ganglia, thalamus, and hypothalamus. These pathology reports from the recent cases were different from those of over 175 other patients with sporadic CJD. The CJD Surveillance Unit's proposal that Britain had a new variant of CJD (vCJD) raised an immediate alarm that the affliction could be linked to mad cow disease. As of today, 161 cases of vCJD have been documented.

However, at that time nearly fifteen years ago, and with less than a dozen known cases of vCJD, a combination of fear and anger fed uncertainty (13–15,22–25). The resulting paranoia embarrassed the country's conservative government and caused a huge economic loss as hundreds of thousands of cows had to be destroyed; several countries banned imports of British beef.

Was there or was there not a link between CJD and mad cow disease? Robert Will, a member of the British National CJD Surveillance Unit said, "I believe this is a new phenomenon." This was countered by the British government. Reassurance from the Prime Minister, the Health and Agriculture secretaries, the chief medical officer, and the Scientific Advisory Spongiform Encephalopathy Advisory Committee denied any increase in CJD or firm evidence that mad cow disease was transmissible to humans by eating British beef. However, John Pattison of the Advisory Committee said, "I would not feed [British] beef to my grandson."

The degree of danger, if any at all, could not be resolved with certainty at that time because of the limited number of cases. With no reliable independent data available (22–25), public debate quickly focused on inadequate government handling of the situation and the manipulation of facts for political purposes. That is, as the accusations mounted, expert committees appointed by the government met in private, then uncovered evidence and reached conclusions that were made public only to the degree and with the bias agreed upon by officials. Two basic issues surfaced. The first was two pronged: Who has access to the data, and do government interests and political spin conflict with the release of scientific test results? The second matter revolved around the balance between early release or publication of data, which on one hand would speed up understanding of the disease but on the other could create unnecessary panic if handled irresponsibly by the mass media.

The 1989 Southwood Report indicated that the incorporation of animal protein from sheep with scrapie into commercial cattle feed was the source of mad cow infection (10,11). The cause was changes in the preparation of cattle feed in the late 1970s and 1980s in the United Kingdom that allowed transmission of scrapie across species barriers from sheep into cows. The ban on such feed in 1989 was the good news, but the countering bad news was epidemiologic evidence that, if the disease again crossed the species barrier from cows to man, there was likely to be an incubation period of three to ten or more years. If all these steps actually transpired, then the cases recorded in 1996 might represent only the tip of a lingering iceberg. Because scrapie-contaminated feed was not banned until 1989, cases of CJD in the United Kingdom could be expected to increase markedly, perhaps into hundreds or thousands, for years to come. Alternatively, the CJD numbers might stay low, which would indicate a sporadic incidence of CJD and no relationship between the new CJD variant and mad cow disease.

Then in 2006, John Collinge and his colleagues from the Medical Research Council Prion (scrapie) Unit in London reported (26) that eleven patients were infected with kuru prior to the ban on ritual cannibalism and had incubated the disease for thirty-nine to fifty-six years. The implication was that newly discovered cases might represent those most susceptible genetically or exposed to higher doses of the disease agent and that an additional fifty years or so were required before one would know if these spongiform encephalopathies were limited to a few cases, say less than several hundred, or would run into the thousands or more. In a sense, the experiment to determine these results has included millions of people eating British beef from potentially spongiform encephalopathy-bearing cows from at least 1985, when the disease was first recognized, until 1989 at the earliest, when the ban on cattle feed was instituted or when infected cattle were subsequently removed from human food sources.

At present, over 200 cases of vCJD are on file. Genetically, all these unfortunates have (are homologous for) a methionine amino acid at position 129 of the prion protein. This protein, when folded into its abnormal beta sheath structure, confers CJD and its infectious transmissibility (8–11). However, the human prion protein can have either a methionine or valine amino acid at position 129. In the normal Caucasian population (i.e., humans without CJD), 40 percent are homologous for a methionine amino acid at position 129 of the prion protein, but all the vCJD cases also have this methionine homology. Ten percent of the normal population is homologous for valine, and the remaining 50 percent are heterologous, that is, they have methionine/valine residues at position 129. Experimental analysis of the role of these different amino acid residues can be achieved by using mice whose prion gene is removed (knocked out) and replaced (knocked in) with a human prion gene that expresses either methionine/methionine or methionine/valine or valine/valine at residue 129. When transgenic mice, laboratory animals bioengineered with this replacement, are inoculated with human CJD or vCJD tissue, the animals most susceptible to the disease symptoms are mice bearing methionine/methionine. In contrast, mice expressing valine/valine are resistant to this disease. Mice expressing heterologous methionine/valine at residue 129 develop brain lesions, so they are susceptible, but their disease begins later, and its course is more protracted and less severe than observed in mice expressing methionine/methionine. Thus, the single amino acid composition at residue 129 influences the incubation period for CJD and the severity of its eventual symptoms (26–31). Interestingly, ten of the twelve kuru patients with prolonged incubation periods proved to have methionine/valine at residue 129 (26).

The potential link between BSE and the new variant of CJD has been established by passage of infectious BSE into transgenic mice expressing human prion protein and by passage in subhuman primates. Time will tell if over 200 cases of vCJD end this saga or whether, like an emerging iceberg, those cases represent many more to come.

A particularly disturbing observation is that blood transfused from an individual incubating vCJD, although clinically healthy, has transferred vCJD into several recipients (10,32,33). Thus, the blood supply used for human therapy can be contaminated in this way, and no reliable test is available for its screening. As a consequence, anyone born in the United Kingdom before or during the outbreak of mad cow disease is restricted from donating blood. This excludes a sizable population, including youngsters born after 1996 who are now too young to be donors but could otherwise donate eventually. This massive exclusion severely limits the British blood and blood product supply. Therefore, the United Kingdom must import a large percentage of its blood and blood products for an unpredictable period of time. The United States has a similar dilemma, although not as grave. For current residents of the United States, anyone who lived in the United Kingdom from the mid-1980s to mid-1990s is prohibited from donating blood, a restriction that diminishes the country's available blood supply by approximately 10 percent. Further, the next question is what precautions or information must be given to residents of America who lived in the United Kingdom from the mid-1980s to 1990s, including travelers, government officials, members of the armed services, and their dependents who ate British beef during this period? That group may number close to a million.

Prions, only after modification to an abnormal structure, are associated with spongiform encephalopathic diseases like CJD and BSE. But in their normal configuration, prions are unique for each species, so for example, human prions differ from cow or mouse prions. To study whether "material" from the brains of mad cows or any other animal with a prion disease like chronic wasting disease of deer and elk (see below) could modify human prions and cause disease, experiments can be done in the laboratory where mice are genetically engineered to express normal human prion proteins and then given brain matter from the diseased animal under consideration.

In evolutionary terms, the animal available for experimentation that most closely resembles humans is the cynomolgus macaque monkey. These monkeys have prion proteins whose structures are 96 percent identical to human prion proteins. So to model prion infection of humans, such monkeys were inoculated with the CJD agent or its new variant and watched for disease transmission (34). When material from a cow with BSE was injected into the brains of three cynomolgus monkeys, two adults and one newborn, all three developed progressive central nervous system disease that included such abnormalities as depression, loss of balance, and shaking. These symptoms began within 150 days after inoculation and progressed in severity over the next ten to twenty-three weeks (34). After the animals' deaths, autopsies of brains from all three monkeys showed indications of spongiform encephalitis with special factors that more closely resembled brains from mad cows than brains from patients with sporadic CJD or from cynomolgus monkeys inoculated with brain tissue from CJD patients. The startling similarity of the clinical, molecular, and neuropathologic features found in these three cynomolgus monkeys with the CJD seen in young human adults or juveniles in Britain indicated to most of the research community that the agent of mad cow disease caused the recent outbreak in humans. Still, some disagree and argue that the association between mad cow disease and the new, similar disease of humans is less clear. They support an alternative hypothesis that a new variant of CJD, unrelated to BSE, has emerged or been newly recognized because of the recent focus on surveillance. To settle this question, two-part test results are required. First, BSE tissue must unequivocally transfer infectivity to monkeys and to transgenic mice expressing the human prion protein. Second, a distinctive chemical pattern must be proven for prion proteins (specifically, a high ratio of diglycosylated to unglycosylated forms) obtained from BSE-infected brain tissue, brains of animals inoculated with BSE, and humans with the new CJD variant (35–37), and those patterns must be clearly distinguishable from the pattern of sporadic CJD prions.

A major societal consequence of mad cow disease and vCJD was the loss of confidence in the British beef industry, concurrent with severe economic loss. On March 23, 1996, the (London) *Times* stated in a front-page article:

The British beef industry was staring ruin in the face last night as the world boycott spread and the European Commission has declared the unilateral bans by 11 EU [European Union] countries legal. As prices continued to plummet at cattle markets, the Consumers' Association gave the starkest warning yet to stop eating beef and supermarkets urgently reviewed buying and labeling policies. MPs alarmed by the fallout from the admission that "mad cow" disease might have caused fatal brain illness in people have set up an inquiry into the handling of the affair and summoned ministers to give evidence next week.

On this same day, a headline in *The Independent* read: "Should ours be the only children in the world to eat British beef?" It continued:

The 13 scientists on the independent expert BSE and CJD Advisory Committee meet today at 11 am to ponder one of the most urgent questions ever to face the nation: is it safe for our children to eat beef? Nobody knows for certain if we are on the brink of an epidemic of CJD that could kill 500,000 people, or a containable problem that might claim a few score lives a year. . . .

With British beef now banned worldwide, and the Consumers' Association advising against eating it, we wait for the committee to advise ministers on two crucial issues. Should parents ban their children from eating beef? And why might it be safe for adults to eat it but not children? Yesterday, Professor John Pattison, chairman of the committee, caused further confusion by saying that he would not feed beef to his three-month-old grandson who had never eaten meat but he would continue to give it to his nine-year-old granddaughter.

On March 24, the Sunday *Times* ran two front-page articles, one entitled "Scientists fear ban must now spread to lamb":

The safety of British lamb—so far untainted by BSE crisis—is in doubt as fears emerge that "mad cow" disease may have been passed on to some sheep. Although the government's scientific advisors admit they do not know the level of risk at present, they are considering taking the precaution of banning sheep offal. They argue that this would lessen the risk of the public being exposed to BSE agent from a second source. Such a ban would shatter confidence in British lamb, which has so far managed to escape the furor over beef.

The headline of the second front-page article read, "McDonald's suspends use of British beef in its burgers: McDonald's is dropping British beef from its 660 restaurants in Britain this morning because of the risks to customers from BSE, the company announced last night."

Further concerns arose when on July 18, 1997, the *St. Petersburg Times* reported:

St. Petersburg residents have just received another reason to stay awake at night worrying—the fear that the juicy steak they ate for dinner may have been contaminated with mad cow disease . . . meat (contaminated/banned British beef) was reportedly falsely labeled as Belgian, sold by the Belgian company Tragex-Gel to three French companies, imported into Russia and sold to companies in Moscow and St. Petersburg.

The problem is not just a British one. In September 1996, in an attempt to allay consumer and exporter fears concerning Swiss beef, a proposal reached the Swiss government to destroy 230,000 of its cows, thereby cutting the national herd by one-eighth hoping to eliminate all traces of BSE. Currently, several countries including Germany and Austria have banned imports of Swiss beef and beef products. By taking drastic measures of animal surveillance and testing, Britain has overcome most of its past difficulties although the psychology to the consumer may still be a problem.

Could the same fate that affected the British beef industry affect the cattle industry in the United States? In 2003, the first case of mad cow disease was reported in the United States. A cow imported from Canada into Washington state was the culprit. Several other cases arose when a total of seven mad cows were found in livestock from Canada. Then, in 2005, the first native cases occurred in the United States; the first was a cow in Texas followed a year later by one in Alabama. Quickly, political and economic interests in America came into play for control of the scientific issues as they had in Britain. After the sick Canadian cow was discovered in 2003, cattle prices in the United States dipped about 16 percent. The U.S. Department of Agriculture (USDA) tested more than 759,000 cattle over an eighteen-month period from 2004 to 2006 and found only two infected cows. Quoting a low prevalence of disease and bowing to pressure from the cattle industry, the U.S. secretary of Agriculture, Mike Johanns, cut surveillance to about 1 percent of the 35 million cattle slaughtered each year, this despite statements from the National Academy of Science, Institute of Medicine, that better and more rigorous testing was required, not less. Indeed, some companies like Creekstone Farms went to court to allow testing of each individual cow, a policy forbidden by the USDA. Michael Hanser of the Consumer Union, who was knowledgeable about the disease, retorted, "They're playing Russian roulette with public health." In fact, how many cattle are sick and not tested is unknown. Stanley Prusiner, a Nobel laureate honored for his work on prion disease and one of the most knowledgeable scientists in this specialty, testified before the U.S. Congress and wrote an op-ed piece stating that the testing used in this country is inadequate and that every cow should be tested. A *New York Times* editorial on August 13, 2005 stated:

> Fears of another case of mad cow disease in The United States have faded for the time being because tests on the most recent suspect animal came back negative. But that is no reason to feel confident about the American beef supply. American cows still eat food that can potentially infect them with mad cow disease. American meatpackers use dangerous methods that other countries ban. And The United States Department of Agriculture does not require enough testing to ensure that American beef is completely safe.
>
> USDA officials and spokesmen for the meatpacking industry argue that the public is protected by current safety procedures. The chance of human infection is indeed very low—but the disease that mad cow induces in human is always fatal, so extreme caution is warranted. The Agriculture Department is hamstrung by its dual and conflicting mission: to promote the nation's meat industry and to protect the consumer. It's clear which is winning.
>
> In April, Agriculture Secretary Mike Johanns suggested that the rules governing mad cow disease might even be relaxed to allow companies to sell some cows too sick to walk for use in human food. Instead of reacting to the confirmation of a case of mad cow disease in June by fixing the remaining loopholes in the system, Mr. Johanns announced that he had eaten beef for lunch.
>
> Boneless steaks and roasts are probably safe to eat. The riskiest meats are ground beef, hot dogs, taco fillings and pizza toppings – the things children love. These products can come out of "advance meat recovery" machines: rubber fingers that strip a carcass clean. These machines are banned in Europe and Japan, and some but not all American meatpackers have stopped using them.
>
> Still, there's no law against them, even though a USDA study in 2002 found that only 12 percent of the processing plants it examined consistently produced meat from these machines that was free of nervous system tissue. Regulations have been tightened, but they still allow the use of these machines to grind tissue from the nervous system for addition to meat products as long as it comes from young cows.
>
> Washington relies on its rules to keep mad cow disease out of the meat supply. But it doesn't test enough cows to know whether they work. America tests about one percent of the slaughtered cows, and recent

experiences don't inspire confidence in the testing regime. The Agriculture Department initially said its tests on one of the two American cows found to be infected had shown the cow was healthy. The positive result came out only after the USDA's inspector general required British tests that the USDA had said were unnecessary.

European countries test all animals over a certain age, and until recently, Japan tested every cow. More than sixty countries have completely or partly banned American beef, including Japan, the largest importer. Wider testing would probably open these markets. Creekstone Farms, a Kansas slaughterhouse, announced last year that it wanted to test all its cows. The cost of the test is about $20.00 per carcass and takes only a few hours. The USDA, which controls the mad cow testing kits, said 'no'; apparently major slaughterhouses thought that universal testing by Creekstone would create pressure on them to do the same.

The *Wall Street Journal* noted in June 2006 that the United States had fallen behind in measures to control mad cow disease (38). The USDA ruled out universal testing as not scientifically necessary, this in spite of testimony by scientists in the field. Further, no mandatory national identification system is in place that would determine the source of an infected cow and track its relocation. Of course, cattle have been identified for over 100 years by branding, but the Cattlemen's Association and USDA are currently concerned that any such national database could fall into the hands of militant animal rights activists or even be used to manipulate cattle prices. The association pressed for and the USDA agreed to voluntary identification. Not surprisingly, former members of the USDA, animal health experts, consumer watchdogs, and scientists in the prion field scoffed at both the voluntary system and current testing procedures. Even more compelling is the fact the largest commercial buyers, like the McDonald's Corporation, offered several cents per pound extra to U.S. producers who provided/used a cattle tracking system. National tracking systems of this kind are now used in many countries, for example, Australia, Canada, Britain, and Japan, but not in the United States.

Of equal or greater importance, scientific authorities found, in 2005, that the "gold standard" test used by the USDA was flawed and not as sensitive as tests used by other countries. Under pressure from many sources, a movement to provide better testing is now in place, but foot dragging continues because governmental administration in the United States still focuses primarily on economics, business influence, and politic favoritism, not on public health. This situation can be summed up by

Agriculture Secretary Johanns' statement, "I enjoyed beef this noon for lunch," or that of Ken Kramer from Cedar Creek, Texas, "This is supposed to be the land of the free, and pretty soon we'll be able to do nothing on our property without permission from the government."

This conflict between business interests/governmental policy controlled by lobbyists versus public health concerns continues to resurface. Paul Krugman wrote in the *New York Times* of June 13, 2008, an article titled "Bad Cow Disease," which started with the ditty:

> Mary had a little lamb
> And when she saw it sicken
> She shipped if off to Packing Town
> And now it's labeled chicken.

He compared the current policy of the Bush administration and its Department of Agriculture headed by Ann Veneman, a former food industry lobbyist, with the scandal of the meat packing industry in the early 1900s that was exposed by Upton Sinclair in his 1906 book *The Jungle*. Sinclair and other so-called muckrakers of that time helped then president Theodore Roosevelt and Congress pass the Pure Food and Drug Act and the Meat Inspection Act. However, over time and especially in the present political climate, the ideology has prevailed that market forces will control food and safety issues and that the relevant federal agencies should be replaced or disbanded. Concurrently, in June 2008, South Koreans rioted and pressured their government to prohibit the importation of American beef and cancel the trade agreement to receive such shipments made with the United States. The issue raised was the insufficient testing of American beef for mad cow disease. As a result, Korea, once the third largest importer of American beef, has closed its doors to acceptance of such shipments. The attempts of Korea's president, Lee Myung-bak, to reopen that market has caused protest demonstrations in Korea. How this will play out is not clear, although testing of individual cows would likely resolve the problem.

The medical and public health community's interest in transmissible spongiform encephalopathies has continued since the BSE epidemic and the emergence of vCJD in humans (21,39–45), particularly the reported cases, now four, of vCJD occurring in human recipients of blood transfusions (32,33,46). Whether these concerns about public health and safety will be sufficient to alter government and business policies remains to be seen.

Now another prion disease has arisen, that is, chronic wasting disease (CWD) of deer and elk, which is spreading throughout the United States (39,47–49). Public health interest has focused on CWD for two primary reasons. First, like the agent of BSE, normal deer/elk prion protein can be converted to an abnormal disease-associated form that is transmitted as an infectious, misfolded unit. In the laboratory, this abnormal prion protein (PrPres, PrP scrapie) can be duplicated by incubating normal prion protein from humans in a test tube with the abnormally folded deer PrPres (50,51). Although this experimental result indicates that deer PrPres could infect humans, at present no data exist to confirm the theory despite active surveillance systems. Second, deer scrapie is spread horizontally among herds and is a significant problem for those farming deer for human meat consumption. CWD is spreading among wild and captive deer and elk herds in several western states of the United States and to New Mexico, South Dakota, Illinois, New York, New England, and Canada (49). CWD was first described in captive mule deer during the mid-1960s at a research facility in Fort Collins, Colorado (47). By the 1970s the disease reached Wyoming and northeast Colorado from which it continued to spread. Unlike scrapie, kuru, and BSE, CWD can be transmitted from one animal to another by physical contact (horizontal spread) (49). The lack of understanding about how CWD spreads and whether it can cause a vCJD-like disease in humans lends urgency to the surveillance and investigation of transmissible spongiform encephalopathy.

What causes these spongiform encephalopathies? Originally the agent was thought to be a virus because of the clear-cut transmission of scrapie from sheep to sheep and then from sheep to mice. Similarly, kuru and CJD have been transmitted in the laboratory environment to subhuman primates, and spongiform encephalopathy from cow brains to mice, pigs, cats, marmosets, and healthy cattle. However, results from the extensive scientific investigations have been controversial and failed to identify the transmissible (infectious?) material (8–11).

Research to characterize the causative agent of spongiform encephalopathies not only continues but has accelerated. Like the arguments that swirl around this subject and its rising death rate, this chapter returns once more to the underlying medical science. Work pioneered by Stanley Prusiner (10,11,52) supports the assertion that a modified host protein—the prion—not a virus causes the mad cow-like diseases. Based on the inability to detect nucleic acids, which typify viral infection, the infectious pathogen capable of transmitting scrapie seems to be neither a virus nor a viroid (viroids are small RNA nucleic acid molecules of unique structure that can replicate and cause disease, primarily of plants). For this reason the term "prion" was introduced to distinguish the proteinaceous infectious particles that caused scrapie, CJD, GSS, kuru, mad cow disease, and CWD as entities quite separate from both viroids and viruses.

Experiments by Prusiner, Bruce Chesebro, Charles Weissmann (reviewed 11) and others have shown that, in the healthy brain, the prion protein exists in a form that is easily fragmented by certain proteolytic enzymes. In contrast, during the spongiform encephalitic disease state, the prion protein resists degradation by enzymes. This prion protein, which assumes an abnormally folded architecture, is associated with lesions in the brain and disease. Consequently, many if not most researchers working on this problem believe that conversion from the susceptible form (digested by enzyme) to the resistant form (resists digestion) of the protein is responsible for the disease. However, dissenting opinions remain. The Prusiner camp believes transmissible spongiform encephalopathies stem from a misfolded protein, an agent that lacks information programmed by nucleic acids (as required for all viruses and other microbes) but is presumably programmed by a protein structure. Therefore, this entity is unlike any other known infectious agent of disease. Further, Prusiner and his colleagues as well as other scientists have learned that patients with inherited diseases of human nerve tissues like GSS syndrome possess a unique (mutated) prion protein, unlike the prion protein present in the normal population. However, some medical scientists do not wholly accept the prion-only hypothesis as a possible cause of spongiform encephalopathies. For example, Chesebro is not totally convinced that a small virus or informational nucleic acid is excluded as the transmissible agent. The defining experiment requires synthesis in vitro (test tube) of the abnormally folded disease-producing protein, PrP scrapie, and proof that it can, by itself, transmit infection in a healthy animal. At present, many are attempting to do this experiment. Until they do, the controversy will rage among scientists engaged in one of the most interesting subjects in contemporary biology and biomedical research.

16

Influenza Virus, the Plague That May Return

In the spring of 1918, four years after declaring war, the German army again launched a massive attack on France, in anticipation of successfully concluding the First World War (1,2). Russia's withdrawal from the war enabled Germany to move more than one million experienced men and 3,000 guns to the Western Front, giving Germany vast numerical superiority there. This move gave the Germans thirty-seven infantry divisions in France and almost thirty more in reserve, their greatest assault force to date. In several sectors, it outnumbered those of the British and French by a ratio of four to one.

The French were desperate, and the allied British army had sustained serious losses at the battle of Passchendaele in Belgium. With her enemies so depleted, Germany's main hope of success depended on an early attack, before additional American forces could arrive.

At first, the Germans made substantial progress, gaining over 1,250 square miles of French soil within four months. By May, the German army reached the Marne River, and its heavy artillery was within range of Paris. More than one million people fled Paris during the spring of 1918.

Everything seemed to be in Germany's favor, yet the very speed of her advance coupled with an outbreak of influenza virus infection brought her armies to near exhaustion. In late June, Eric von Ludendorff, the German commander, noted that over 2,000 men in each division were suffering from influenza, that the supply system was breaking down, and that the troops were underfed (2). Infection spread rapidly, and by late July Ludendorff blamed influenza for halting the German drive (1,2). Even as the German's strength began waning, that of the Allies was increasing. Americans continued entering France in numbers that replaced the great losses of the British and French. As the Allies reorganized, the French Marshal Ferdinand Foch took command. Foch and General Henri Philippe Pétain then led a grand offensive that aggressively blocked the German advance and regained French ground. The result led to the armistice that ended the war.

Even though the casualties, both military and civilian, were massive during World War I, deaths from the epidemic of influenza virus in 1918–19 surpassed the war's toll: Some 40 to 50 million people died of influenza in less than a year (3–7). This was over four times the number of fatalities during the four years of war. An estimated one-fifth of the world's human population was infected, and 2 to 3 percent of those infected died. In comparison, the other two major influenza pandemics occurring in 1957 and 1968 were relatively mild with estimates of one to one and a half million deaths worldwide, an overall mortality rate of those infected about 100-fold less at 0.02 percent and 0.01 percent, respectively. But the 1918 pandemic differed in an important way from all previous ones of its kind and those to come because for the first time young, healthy adults succumbed. To the contrary, in past and subsequent influenza pandemics and epidemics, mostly the very young and the elderly died. Pandemic is derived from the Greek "pandemos" meaning "of all people" and indicates an outbreak of disease over a large geographic area. In contrast, epidemic refers to the involvement of a large segment that is regional but not global. Influenza is stems from the Italian word for "influence" and refers to "influence of the stars." The term flu is the shortened version and used by the poet W. H. Auden:

> *Little birds with scarlet legs*
> *Sitting on their speckled eggs*
> *Eye each flu-infected city.*

Although respiratory infection was a common companion of influenza during the 1918–19 pandemic, pneumonia in young adults has been rare before and since. Over 80 percent of current and past deaths related to influenza have occurred in people over the age of seventy who most often die from secondary bacterial infections. Yet the risk is almost as great for patients of any age who suffer from chronic heart, lung, kidney, or liver disease, for children with congenital abnormalities, or anyone undergoing transplant surgery or afflicted with AIDS.

The influenza pandemic of 1918–19 was lethal for healthy adults in the prime of life (3,6–8). The majority (nearly 80 percent) of U.S. Army war casualties were caused not by bullets, shells, or shrapnel but by influenza. From July 1917 to April 1919, this virus killed over 43,000 soldiers in the American Expeditionary Forces (7,8). In North America, the U.S. Bureau of Census recorded 548,452 deaths for the last four months of 1918 and the first six months of 1919 (4,8,9). In 1919, the American Medical Association reported that one-third of all deaths of physicians was caused by influenza-related pneumonia. Canada's death rate was proportionately high, with 43,000 deaths reported. In South and Central America, the devastation wrought by influenza virus was enormous. In the several Mexican states in which records were kept, over one-tenth of the population died; in Guatemala 43,000 deaths occurred in a total population of 2 million, and in Rio de Janeiro, with a population of 910,000, there were 15,000 deaths during the last three months of 1918. Chile lost 23,789 of her 3.6 million people in 1919.

Europe suffered as well; in England and Wales from June 1918 to May 1919, influenza killed 200,000, of whom 184,000 were civilians. Ireland and Scotland lost approximately 20,000 each. Over the same time frame in Denmark, with a population of slightly over 3 million, there was a mortality of 11,357, and Sweden, with a population of 5.9 million, had a mortality of 24,780 persons. Prussia's 7 million cases of influenza yielded 172,576 deaths. For the whole German population of over 60 million, there were over 230,000 deaths, while France with a population of 36 million recorded nearly 200,000 civilian deaths. In the French army, the mortality was three times higher than that reported for civilians.

In France, the American military forces taking part in the Meuse Argonne offensive of 1918 reported 69,000 sick with influenza. The infection was indiscriminate, afflicting soldiers, sailors, civilians, and leaders of many governments. Among the best known were the prime minister of Germany, Prince Max of Baden; the prime minister of

England, David Lloyd George; the prime minister of France, Georges Clemenceau; and Woodrow Wilson, president of the United States. Also included were Sir Mark Sykes and Georges Picot, the British and French representatives who agreed to separate Arab-speaking areas from Turkish-speaking parts of the Ottoman Empire in the infamous Sykes-Picot agreement of 1916.

In Russia 450,000 lay dead from influenza and in Italy well over 500,000. A British administrator traveling through villages in northern Persia noted that "in village after village there are no survivors." Japan reported 257,000 deaths, but in no part of the world did influenza exact a more crushing toll than in the islands of the South Seas. In western Samoa, the ship Talune, which sailed from Auckland, New Zealand, on November 7, 1918, introduced the disease into the islands of Upola and Savii. Within three months, over 21 percent of those populations died as did the Fiji islanders and Tahitians. As one government official noted: "It was impossible to bury the dead . . . Day and night trucks rumbled throughout the streets, filled with bodies for the constantly burning pyres."

Only when protective measures were taken to enforce a maritime quarantine in the South Pacific in 1918–19 did efforts to abolish the pandemic flu become effective. Four islands, American Samoa, Australia, Tasmania, and New Caledonia successfully delayed or excluded the arrival of foreign ships, which limited the pandemic's effect to less than 0.8 deaths per 1,000 islanders. Conversely, islands that failed to enforce a vigorous maritime quarantine were devastated. West Samoa lost slightly less than 23 percent of its population with a mortality rate of 225/1000, and 150/1000 or 15 percent of Tahiti's population died.

The total global mortality for the 1918–19 influenza epidemic is not fully known but likely exceeded 50 million people (4,6–10). At that time a large part of the world's population, especially in Africa and Asia, was not tracked by adequate death records. Where records were kept in those areas, the lists for a period of less than one year indicated that over 20 million died. This figure can be extended two- to threefold if one extrapolates from subsequent records, providing the generally accepted estimate of 40 to 50 million or more deaths.

Warren Vaughan of the Harvard Medical School, writing in the *American Journal of Epidemiology* in 1921, compared the mortality from influenza in the American army with that of other great plagues:

This fatality has been unparalleled in recent times. The influenza epidemic of 1918 ranks well up with the epidemics famous in history. Epidemiologists have regarded the dissemination of cholera from the Broad Street well in London as a catastrophe. The typhoid epidemic of Plymouth, Pa., of 1885, is another illustration of the damage that can be done by epidemic disease once let loose. Yet the fatality from influenza and pneumonia at Camp Sherman was greater than either of these. Compared with epidemics for which we have fairly accurate statistics the death rate at Camp Sherman in the fall of 1918 is surpassed only by that of plague in London in 1665 and that of yellow fever in Philadelphia in 1793. The plague killed 14 per cent of London's population in seven months' time. Yellow fever destroyed 10 per cent of the population of Philadelphia in four months. In seven weeks influenza and pneumonia killed 3.1 per cent of the population at Camp Sherman. If we consider the time factor, these three instances are not unlike in their lethality. The plague killed 2 per cent of the population in a month, yellow fever 2.5 per cent, and influenza and pneumonia 1.9 per cent.

The influenza epidemic became known as Spanish influenza, not because the disease began in Spain, but because Spain, neutral during the First World War, had uncensored reporting of influenza's wildfire spread through its population: "The whole of Spain was invaded by a disease sudden in its appearance, brief in its course and subsiding without a trace." Influenza killed 170,000 people there.

This epidemic is believed to have reached Europe, Africa, and Asia via three major seaports: Freetown in Sierra Leone; Brest, France; and Boston, Massachusetts (9). Freetown was one of the major ports in West Africa and an important coaling station. There, local West Africans mixed with British, South African, East African, and Australian soldiers going to and coming back from the war in Europe. Over two-thirds of the native population of Sierra Leone came down with influenza, propelling the virus onto troop transports traveling back and forth to the war zone and eventually to the servicemen's home countries. Brest, France, was the chief disembarkation port for the European allies, and Boston was a main port for transporting U.S. troops to and from Europe. In Boston, within just a few days thousands became sick and hundreds died.

Camp Devens, a U.S. Army camp, was located thirty miles west of Boston and housed 45,000 men. On September 14, 1918, thirty-six cases of influenza were reported, but by the end of September over 6,000 had

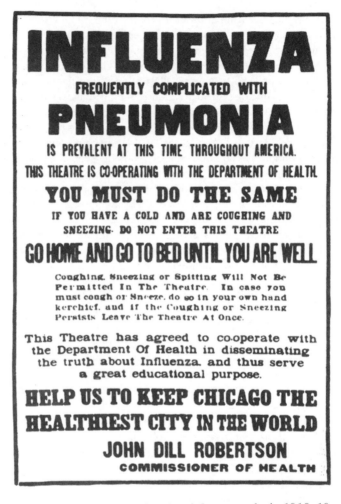

FIGURE 16.1 *Poster warning about influenza pandemic, 1918–19.*

been infected, with 60 to 90 dying per day. One camp physician noted, "Bodies were stacked like cord wood." By the end of October there were 17,000 cases of flu, or one-third of the total population.

Within a month influenza spread from Boston to Philadelphia, where there were 700 deaths in a day, then to other parts of the United States. A common rhyme sung by young school girls jumping rope was:

I have a little bird and its name was Enza
I opened the window and in-flew-Enza.

Perhaps the spread of influenza is illustrated best by a study done in San Francisco. The first new case of influenza in 1919 appeared on September 23, brought by a traveler from Chicago. One month later, over 75 percent of nurses in San Francisco hospitals were sick, and all hospital beds were filled with those ill from influenza. Schools and places of public entertainment such as cinemas and theaters were closed by city decree. The city's Board of Supervisors ordered the wearing of gauze masks by the entire population. Everyone who did not wear a mask paid fines or went to jail. On November 21, the sirens in the city shrieked to announce that masks could come off, but two weeks later the next wave of influenza began and struck 5,000 in December alone. The wearing of masks again became mandatory. By February, when masks came off for the second time, over 3,500 civilians had died.

Of course, public health officials attempted to deny suspected carriers of influenza entry to cities, as done for yellow fever, poliomyelitis, and Ebola. For example, J. W. Inches, Commissioner of Health of Detroit, notified commanders of all Army and Navy camps in the Midwest that Detroit, as of October 19, 1918, was off-limits to all military personnel except those in perfect health and traveling on necessary military business. They must carry a letter from a superior officer stating that these conditions were met, he decreed.

Just as the ships crossing on trade routes from Europe to the New World brought yellow fever, measles, and smallpox, so influenza traveled across the United States on routes once used by pioneers moving to the western United States. Railroad lines allowed the disease to move quickly to many localities, as did shipping lanes through the confluence of rivers and passage through mountain pathways. Influenza spread along the Appalachian Mountains, the Great Lakes, the Santa Fe Trail, the inland waterways, the Mississippi River, and across the plains and Rockies to Los Angeles, San Francisco, and Seattle.

Yet, as with the observations that quarantine was beneficial among South Pacific islands, so are public health measures and quarantines in American cities. Therein lies the tale of two cities, Philadelphia in Pennsylvania and St. Louis in Missouri, during the 1918 influenza pandemic. Philadelphia allowed public gatherings, open schools, churches, and assemblies. In fact, local authorities hosted a grand citywide parade

FIGURE 16.2 *During the pandemic of 1918–19, buses and sometimes streets were sprayed with disinfectant to stop influenza.*

in support of the World War I loan (bond) drive. Within four months of that gathering, over 12,000 Philadelphians had died from the infection. In contrast, physicians in St. Louis persuaded city officials to register influenza cases two days after the first illnesses were detected. The city government shut down schools, churches, theaters, and public gathering places then initiated strict quarantines with infected persons confined to their homes. Compared to Philadelphia, St. Louis had one half as many cases. However, three days after the armistice that ended World War I, St. Louis reopened schools and businesses and allowed public gatherings. Two weeks later a second and devastating wave of influenza struck St. Louis.

Although we know the origin of the word "influenza," it is not certain when the disease first manifested itself in the human population. A scientific colleague of mine at The Scripps Research Institute, a friend and biblical scholar, Professor Hugh Rosen, brought to my attention a description of the relationship between birds (quail) and disease, perhaps influenza, in the Bible's volume, Numbers 11:31–34.

11:31 God caused a wind to start blowing, sweeping quail up from the sea. They ran out of strength over the camp, and [were flying] only two cubits above the ground for the distance of a day's journey in each direction. 11:32 The people went about all that day, all night, and the entire next day, and gathered quail. Even those who got the least had gathered ten chomers. [The people] spread them out around the camp. 11:33 The meat was still between their teeth when [the people] began to die. God's anger was displayed against the people, and He struck them with an extremely severe plague. 11:34 [Moses] named the place "Graves of Craving" (Kivroth HaTaavah), since it was in that place where they buried the people who had these cravings.

Italians introduced the term *influenza* in about the year 1500 for diseases attributed to the "influence" of the stars (4,6,10,11). Another possible origin is *influenza di freddo*, the influence of a cold. In the eighteenth century, the French coined the term *grippe* for the same symptoms. The disease can be present as an asymptomatic infection or as a primary pneumonia (3,6,10,12). Either way, the infection spreads from one individual to the next through the air in droplets launched by coughing or sneezing. Bringing individuals in close contact helps spread the infecting viruses, which in many instances travel initially among school children and from them to adults. Once exposed to the infectious agent, the victim incubates the virus for at least twenty-four hours and up to four or five days before the disease becomes obvious. The first signs are headache, chills, dry cough, fever, weakness, and loss of appetite. Generalized fatigue and, in some, bronchitis and pneumonia follow. In general, the patient's recovery to full strength following influenza viral infection may take several weeks or longer. Although influenza is a distinct and recognizable clinical entity, many patients and, unfortunately, some physicians, tend to group most respiratory ailments under a blanket term of "flu."

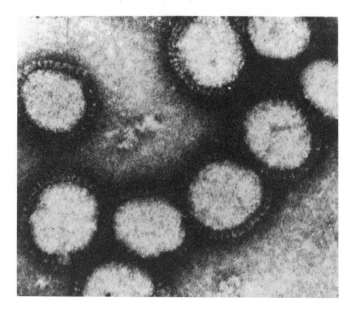

FIGURE 16.3 *Photomicrograph of influenza viruses.*

Knowledge about the details of viral structure and behavior is rather recent history; nevertheless, as long ago as 412 B.C., Hippocrates described what seem to be influenza epidemics. Later, in Rome, Livy mentioned a similar illness. From the Middle Ages, we have the following excerpt taken from a letter written by Lord Randolph in Edinburgh to Lord Cecil, dated 1562 (13,14):

> Maye it please your Honor, immediately upon the Quene [Mary]'s arivall here, she fell acquainted with a new disease that is common in this towne, called here the newe acquayntance, which passed also throughe her whole courte, neither sparinge lordes, ladies nor damoysells not so much as ether Frenche or English. It ys a plague in their heades that have yt, and a sorenes in their stomackes, with a great coughe, that remayneth with some

longer, with others shorter tyme, as yt findeth apte bodies for the nature of the disease. The queen kept her bed six days. There was no appearance of danger, nor manie that die of the disease, excepte some olde folkes. My lord of Murraye is now presently in it, the lord of Lidlington hathe had it, and I am ashamed to say that I have byne free of it, seinge it seketh acquayntance at all men's handes (13,14).

Although suspected influenza epidemics occurred during several decades of the 1700s, Robert Johnson, a physician from Philadelphia, is generally credited with the first description of influenza during the 1793 epidemic (15–17). With his description available and improved public health statistics, epidemics were documented in 1833, 1837, 1847, 1889–90, and 1918.

However, the identity of the infectious agent that caused influenza remained debatable. In Germany, Richard Pfeiffer discovered "bacteria" present in great numbers in the throats and lungs of patients with influenza. Because of this agent's large size, it could not pass through a Pasteur-Chamberland-type filter, causing many observers to speculate that influenza originated from a bacterium and not a virus.

Only by serendipity was the true nature of influenza as a virus discovered. This is a tale of pigs, hounds, foxes, and ferrets—all of which played decisive roles in the determination that influenza was a virus (18). Similar documentation that humans bore influenza viruses and the disease they caused did not surface until 1933.

The story begins with J. S. Koen of Fort Dodge, Iowa, an inspector for the U.S. Bureau of Animal Husbandry. In 1918, he observed in pigs a disease that resembled the raging human influenza plague of 1918–19:

> Last fall and winter we were confronted with a new condition, if not a new disease. I believe I have as much to support this diagnosis in pigs as the physicians have to support a similar diagnosis in man. The similarity of the epidemic among people and the epidemic among pigs was so close, the reports so frequent, that an outbreak in the family would be followed immediately by an outbreak among the hogs, and vice versa, as to present a most striking coincidence if not suggesting a close relation between the two conditions. It looked like "flu," and until proved it was not "flu," I shall stand by that diagnosis (19).

Koen's views were decidedly unpopular, especially among farmers raising pigs, who feared that customers would be put off from eating pork if such an association were made. Ten years later, in 1928, a group of research veterinarians in the U.S. Bureau of Animal Husbandry, led by C. N. McBryde, reported the successful transmission of influenza infection from pig to pig by taking mucus and tissue from the respiratory tracts of sick pigs and placing it into the noses of healthy pigs. However, these investigators were unable to transmit the disease after passing the material through a Pasteur-Chamberland-type filter. Therefore, no evidence was yet available that a virus caused influenza. That situation changed when Richard Shope, working at the Rockefeller Institute of Comparative Pathology at Princeton, New Jersey, repeated McBryde's experiments within a year of the negative report. By reproducing influenza disease in healthy pigs after inoculating them with material taken from sick pigs and passed through the Pasteur-Chamberland filter (20,21), Shope provided the first evidence that viruses transmitted influenza of swine.

But was the influenza of humans like that of pigs? Did viruses cause both diseases? In the late 1800s and early 1900s, English country gentlemen and gentlewomen engaged in running hounds and hunting foxes became increasingly concerned over deaths of their dogs from distemper infection. The canine distemper virus, which is in the same family as measles virus, causes a respiratory disease often complicated by severe infection of the central nervous system that cripples and then kills dogs. Banding together and acting through *The Field Magazine*, a journal that catered to fox hunters, subscribers raised enough money to support research on canine distemper infection. Their efforts contributed to funding the Medical Research Council's (MRC's) acquisition of a farm at Mill Hill in North London, where the sick dogs could be isolated and studied. The pharmaceutical company Burroughs-Wellcome joined this effort to find a cure and to prevent the disease. Thus, in the 1900s, those of sufficient wealth to afford fox hunting formed alliances with the government to set up the MRC and with a commercial company to find a vaccine. The alliance was successful; in 1928, the first vaccine became available to protect dogs from the canine distemper virus.

Initially, dogs were used for research on the virus and for studies to develop the vaccine, but problems soon surfaced. Among the difficulties was the issue that some dogs had become immune because of a previous encounter with canine distemper virus so did not contract the disease when exposed; additionally, antivivisectionists and some pet owners objected to using "man's best friend" as a research tool. These problems vanished when ferrets were substituted for dogs. Hound keepers on the English country estates had noticed that ferrets also developed distemper, presumably transmitted from dogs. Soon ferrets replaced dogs in canine distemper studies at both the Wellcome and the MRC laboratories.

In 1933, the first epidemic of influenza since 1919 struck London and, as before, spread quickly. Among the many humans infected were several members of the research staff at Wellcome and MRC laboratories. However, unexpectedly, ferrets kept at the Wellcome laboratory also became ill, with symptoms of wheezing, sneezing, and coughing reminiscent of human influenza infection. When Wilson Smith, a senior researcher at the MRC unit, recognized the situation, he infected ferrets with nasal washings from influenza-infected patients. As the ferrets came down with the influenza-like syndrome, both Smith and Christopher Andrewes examined them. A story soon told was that a sick ferret sneezed in Christopher Andrewes' face. A few days later, Andrewes came down with influenza. Smith obtained washings from Andrewes's throat, passed the material through a Pasteur-Chamberland-like filter, then injected the filtrate into healthy ferrets. Soon they too began sneezing and coughing, discharging phlegm from the nose and eyes and spiking a temperature. Here was the first evidence that a virus caused human influenza, at the same time fulfilling Koch's postulates (22).

Following his studies with tuberculosis, Robert Koch formalized the criteria eventually called Koch's postulates to distinguish a microbe-causing disease from one that is a happenstance passenger. According to the postulates, a link between agent and disease is valid when the organism is regularly found in the lesions of the disease; the organism can be isolated in pure culture on artificial media; inoculation of this culture produces a similar disease in experimental animals, and the organism can be recovered from the lesions in these animals. These postulates require modification for viruses, however, because they cannot be grown on artificial media (viruses require living cells for their replication), and some are pathogenic only for humans. Nevertheless, these experiments with ferrets, humans, and influenza virus filled the bill for a modified Koch's postulate. Considering the role serendipity played in the use of ferrets and the initial isolation of human influenza virus, one agrees with Pasteur: "Chance favors the prepared mind."

Macfarlane Burnet, the eminent Australian scientist, whose contributions to poliomyelitis virus research were mentioned in Chapter 7, was to play an important role in the investigation of influenza. From 1933, when the human influenza virus was isolated, until the early to mid-1950s, when tissue culture systems became available, Burnet pioneered both the technology and conceptual approaches to using embryonated eggs for the study of influenza (23–25) and other viruses. This model became the standard for investigating viral replication and genetic manipulations. Hemagglutination, that is, the clumping of red blood cells, is a simple and reliable test for establishing the presence of many viruses. The principle of hemagglutination was first uncovered when George Hirst of the New York Public Health Institute accidentally tore the blood vessel of an influenza-infected chicken (26,27). Red blood cells escaping from the wound agglutinated, or clumped, around influenza viruses in the infected fluid. From this simple event, Hirst realized that hemagglutination could signal the presence of virus.

The influenza viruses that afflict humans are divided into three types: A, B, and C. Influenza A is responsible for the epidemics of historical fame and infects not only man but also pigs, horses, seals, and a large variety of birds (3,6). Indeed, influenza A has been isolated worldwide from both domestic and wild birds, primarily waterbirds including ducks, geese, terns, and gulls and domesticated birds such as turkeys, chickens, quail, pheasants, geese, and ducks. Studies of wild ducks in Canada from 1975 to 1994 indicated that up to 20 percent of the juveniles were infected, and fecal samples from their lakeshore habitats contained the virus. These birds usually shed the virus from five to seven days (with a maximum of thirty days) after becoming infected even though they show no sign of the disease. Obviously, this virus and its hosts have adapted mutually over many centuries and created a reservoir that ensures perpetuation of the virus. Duck virus has been implicated in outbreaks of influenza in animals such as seals, whales, pigs, horses, and turkeys. Extensive analysis of the virus's genetic structure, or nucleic acid sequences, supports the hypotheses that mammalian influenza viruses, including those infecting man, likely originated in aquatic birds.

Influenza A viruses from aquatic birds grow poorly in human cells, and vice versa. However, both avian and human influenza viruses can replicate in pigs. We have known that pigs are susceptible to influenza viruses that infect man ever since the veterinarian J. S. Koen first observed pigs with influenza symptoms closely resembling those of humans. Retrospective tests of human blood indicate that the swine virus isolated by Shope in 1928 was similar to the human virus and likely played a role in the human epidemic. Swine influenza still persists year-round and is the cause of most respiratory diseases in pigs. Interestingly, in 1976, swine influenza virus isolated from military recruits at Fort Dix was indistinguishable from virus isolates obtained from a man and a pig on a farm in Wisconsin. The examiners concluded that animals, especially aquatic birds and pigs, can be reservoirs of influenza virus. When such viruses or their components mix with human influenza virus, dramatic genetic shifts can follow, creating the potential of a new epidemic for humans.

The influenza virus continually evolves by antigenic shift and drift. Early studies in this subject area by Robert Webster and Graeme Laver established the importance of monitoring influenza strains in order to predict future epidemics (28–30). Antigenic shifts are major changes in the structure of the influenza virus that determine its effect on immune responses. Of the viral proteins, the hemagglutinin, a major glycoprotein of the virus, plays a central role in infection because it is responsible for attachment to the host's cells. The breakdown of hemagglutinin into two smaller units is required for virus infectivity. Shifts in the composition of the hemagglutinin (H) or neuraminidase (N), another glycoprotein, of influenza virus were observed in the 1933, 1957, 1968, and 1977 epidemics:

1933: H1N1
1957: H2N2 (Asian flu)
1968: H3N2 (Hong Kong flu)
1977: reappearance of H1N1, called the Russian flu

The reappearance in 1977 of the Russian flu, a virus of near-complete genetic identity with the H1N1 viruses that abounded in 1933, raises the possibility that the virus had been preserved at some undefined location, probably in frozen storage.

Beginning in 1995, Jeff Taubenberger and his colleagues at the Armed Forces Institute of Pathology in Washington, DC, started analyzing lung tissues from individuals who died in the 1918 influenza pandemic. In March of 1997, part of the influenza virus nucleic acid was isolated from a formalin-fixed sample of lung tissue from a twenty-one-year-old army private who died during the 1918–19 Spanish influenza pandemic (31).

Over the next ten years, with collections of additional formalin-fixed tissues and a piece of lung tissue from a native Alaskan who died during the pandemic of 1918–19 and was buried in the permafrost (akin to tissue being stored in a freezer), the extinct 1918 influenza virus was resurrected (32), a marvel of molecular biology and serendipity.

The technology not only involved isolation of RNA from diseased tissue of a victim from the long-past pandemic and copying the DNA blueprint but also the use of reverse genetics independently, first described by Peter Palase of Mount Sinai Medical School in New York and then Yoshi Kawakara of the University of Wisconsin. The combination of this technology and creative scientists allowed the recovery of an active replicating influenza virus from the 1918 pandemic. Again, serendipity played a role. As Jeff Taubenberger told me, "having completed my medical and research training (in immunology), I took a position as head of a molecular pathology laboratory at the Armed Forces Institute of Pathology in Washington DC." When asked by his supervisor to plan, in addition to his major research interest, immunology, a project using samples at the Armed Forces Institute, Jeffrey chose to utilize tissues from a formalin-fixed collection of living tissues plentifully stored at the institute to seek out genomic sequences from the pandemic influenza virus. This was not a novel approach, since investigators from multiple laboratories had been engaged in such a fossil search. The advantage for Taubenberger was finding tissue samples from the 1918 influenza pandemic that were not compromised by secondary bacterial infections, which would have injured the viral RNA sequences.

Because the first influenza viruses were not isolated until the 1930s, characterization of the 1918–19 strain relied on molecular definition of the viral RNA. Subsequent reconstruction of the influenza virus containing all eight of its subunits and using reverse genetics to generate infectious virus has yielded new and unexpected information (32–37). First, unlike the influenza viruses of the 1957 and 1968 pandemics in which hemagglutinin and neurominodase genes were reassorted with avian (bird) genes (as listed above the two preceding paragraphs), the H and N genes of the 1918 pandemic flu virus originated from a purely avian source and crossed to humans after genetic adaptation. That is, H1N1 sequence analysis of the pandemic 1918 influenza virus compared to multiple species sequences indicated an avian ancestral origin, since the H1N1 sequence was more closely related to avian H1N1 sequences than human influenza H1N1 sequences. The latter genes differed (genetically distinct) by twenty-five changes in the protein sequence from all known avian flu genes. Perhaps the type of bird that carried these original sequences is no longer living or was an avian-pig-avian-human mix. However, no reports of the 1918–1919 period mentioned abnormal mortality or illness of waterfowl or other birds. Detective virology hunters are now evaluating bird collections at the Smithsonian Institute obtained around 1918–19 for influenza viruses.

Detailed research at the molecular level showed that the reconstructed 1918 influenza pandemic strain bound to α-2,6 sialic acid receptors (human influenza receptor), not the α-2,3 sialic acid receptor (avian influenza receptor). Moreover, one H gene isolated from the 1918 strain bound only to the α-2,6 sialic acid receptor, whereas a second H gene isolate bonded dually to α-2,6 and α-2,3 sialic acid receptors suggesting mixtures of circulating influenza viruses. Importantly, the resurrected 1918 influenza virus replicated in the absence of added protease trypsin. Most pathogenic influenza virus H molecules contain a cleavage site of basic residues and require cleavage inside host cells for replication. Thus, to grow influenza viruses in cultured cells, the virologist adds a proteolytic enzyme like trypsin. By contrast, the 1918 pandemic influenza virus H molecule has a single basic residue and can replicate in cells without the addition of trypsin.

No single gene of the 1918 influenza virus accounts for its high degree of pathogenicity. Therefore, we are forced to conclude that the lethal effect is caused by many viral genes (polygenic). The definition of this profound lethality is that the resurrected 1918 virus is 100 times more lethal than other strains for experimental animals so-infected; it replicates in some instances to produce 39,000 more virus particles than other influenza strains, and it causes severe lung injury in mice and monkeys very similar to that in lungs from humans who died from the 1918–19 influenza virus infection. Further, unlike other influenza viruses, the 1918 resurrected virus is lethal when injected into chick embryos. Although many of its genes may participate in the virulence, both the hemagglutinin and polymerase genes likely play the dominant roles.

Other clues as to the virulence of the 1918 influenza virus have come from recent studies in monkeys (38). Infection of cynomologous monkeys with a contemporary influenza strain led to mild symptoms and minimal pathology in the lung. In contrast, the revived 1918 influenza virus spread rapidly through their lungs and was lethal. Particularly important was an outcome of 1918 influenza virus infection in which the monkeys' immune systems went into overdrive causing an increased production of host proteins called cytokines. This immunopathologic effect is called a "cytokine storm." The implication is that such host-derived molecules, in addition to damage from the virus itself, are responsible for tissue injury and death. Cytokine storms have also been blamed for severe respiratory disorders in humans infected with SARS or Hanta viruses. Several of these cytokines provide signals for the migration of macrophages and polymorphonuclear cells that significantly add to the destruction of the lung by compromising air exchange and breathing.

As influenza viruses cause disease, surveillance centers established by the World Health Organization (WHO), other agencies, and individual

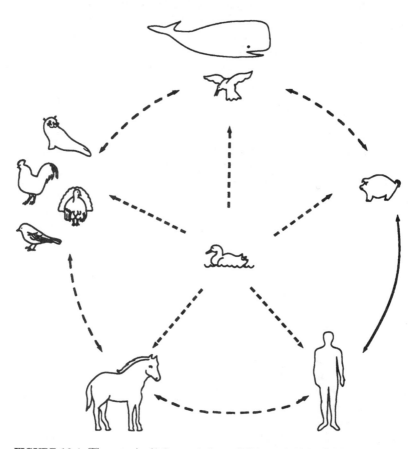

FIGURE 16.4 *The reservoir of influenza A viruses. Wild aquatic birds are believed to be the primary reservoir for avian and mammalian species. Solid lines indicate the known transmission to man from pigs; dashes show possible spread. Diagram courtesy of* Fields' Virology *(Philadelphia: Lippincott-Raven, 1996).*

countries all over the world obtain influenza viruses that are studied for alterations, primarily in the viruses' hemagglutinin. According to the evidence from these centers, species identified as dangerous in late spring are excellent indicators of potential problems in the following winter.

Both avian and human influenza viruses can replicate in pigs, and genetic reassortants or combinations between them can also be demonstrated experimentally. A likely scenario for such an antigenic shift in nature occurs when the prevailing human strain of influenza A virus and an avian influenza virus concurrently infect a pig, which serves as a mixing vessel. Reassortants containing genes derived mainly from the human virus but with a hemagglutinin and perhaps polymerase gene from the avian source are able to infect humans and initiate a new pandemic. In rural Southeast Asia, the most densely populated area of the world, hundreds of millions of people live and work in close contact with domesticated pigs and ducks. This is the likely reason for influenza pandemics in China. Epidemics other than the 1918–19 catastrophe have generally killed 50,000 or fewer individuals in that area, although within a year over one million people had been infected with these new strains.

Three major hypotheses have been formulated to explain antigenic shifts. First, as described above, a new virus can come from a reassortant in which, for example, an avian influenza virus gene substitutes for one of the human influenza virus genes. The genome of human influenza virus group A contains eight RNA segments, and the current wisdom is that the circulating influenza hemagglutinin in humans has been replaced with an avian hemagglutinin. A second explanation for antigenic shifts that yield new epidemic-quality viruses is that strains from other mammals or birds become infectious for humans. A third possibility is that newly emerging viruses have actually remained hidden and unchanged somewhere but suddenly come forth to cause an epidemic, as the Russian H1N1 virus once did. H1N1 first was isolated in 1933, then disappeared when replaced by the Asian H2N2 in 1957. However, twenty years later, the virus reappeared in a H1N1 strain isolated in northern China then spread throughout the world. This influenza virus was identical in all its genes to the one that caused epidemics among humans in the 1950s. Where the virus was for twenty years is not known. Could it have been inactivated in a frozen state, preserved in an animal reservoir, or obscured in some other way? If this is so, will the Spanish influenza virus also return, and what will be the consequences for the human population?

Currently the world has focused on a new reassortment and potential influenza pandemic from the H5N1 bird flu. Bird flu has currently infected over 370 humans with a mortality of 63 percent (Table 16.1). On May 10, 1997, a three-year-old child in Hong Kong was admitted to the hospital with influenza and died eleven days later. Isolation and characterization of the virus revealed that it was a new human pathogen, formerly known to infect only birds (39,40). By the end of December 1997, eighteen cases were confirmed with a mortality rate of 33 percent. Molecular analysis revealed that the virus's outer coat protein, the influenza hemagglutinin, was of bird origin, typed as hemagglutinin-5. The ability of this avian virus to replicate in humans was surprising and of great concern. Only because this influenza virus failed to adapt sufficiently to allow easy spread among humans was a new pandemic avoided. The H5N1 virus was traced to the poultry markets in Hong Kong, and subsequently over a million and a half domestic birds were quickly slaughtered to prevent possible adaptation of the virus for transmission among humans. By this means, the spread of the virus was limited, and its potential adaptation to humans was interrupted. H5N1 bird flu, first isolated in 1997, had by 2008 killed about 60 percent of those humans sickened with the infection but had not yet jumped repeatedly or easily from human to human. Some transmissions among humans have been reported, and these occurred in clusters. In such circumstances, the WHO and local health officials are alerted, come to the disease site, kill all the poultry, and supply aid to humans in contact with infected animals. The anti-influenza viral drug Tamiflu is often used as blanket protective therapy for individuals in and around the affected area. The strategy of sacrificing all birds that might harbor the virus decreases the virus's opportunity to replicate and spread.

To be effective against bird flu and prevent a return of the 1918-like influenza pandemic requires a sophisticated and well-organized global network. The one currently in place monitors the spread of H5N1 and the evolution of influenza viruses. Collecting that information allows public health teams to rapidly enter potentially infected areas and to initiate the production of protective vaccines. However, the preparation of a vaccine currently takes six to nine months. If we are to have any realistic hope of detecting, treating, and containing such outbreaks before they spread around the world, the absolute requirement is close cooperation among countries and universal organizations like the WHO through the United Nations, World Bank, and so forth. For an individual

TABLE 16.1 Total Number of Confirmed Bird Flu Cases in Humans and Mortality Rate

Country	Cases	Deaths
Azerbaijan	8	5
Cambodia	7	7
China	30	20
Djibouti	1	0
Egypt	47	20
Indonesia	129	105
Iraq	3	2
Lao	2	2
Myanmar	1	0
Nigeria	1	1
Pakistan	1	1
Thailand	25	7
Turkey	12	4
Vietnam	106	52
TOTAL	**373**	**236**[1]

[1] %mortality = 63%
Source: (WHO, March 2008)

country, such as the United States, federal, state, and local (city, county) governments and committees must plan and act cooperatively. Public health and medical personnel, hospitals, and security agencies need coordinated plans of action. Diagnostic tests must be widely available and anti-influenza viral drugs and vaccines stored. Currently, the United States is stockpiling anti-influenza drugs. States can purchase 31 million courses of these drugs with a 20 percent federal subsidy. Of course, states vary on how much they wish or can afford to store. Further, bureaucratic lethargy and government inertia are never-ending blockages. An estimated 75 million drug courses would treat 25 percent of the population. As for vaccine makers, if they know what influenza virus to target, working twenty-four hours per day would enable them to produce 500 million doses of vaccine per year. This amount is, of course, short for vaccinating the approximate 6.7 billion people on this planet.

Current federal guidelines have been established to deal with a theoretical pandemic influenza outbreak. Such guidelines were based on how forty-four cities fared in the 1918–1919 influenza pandemic. Guidelines include (1) closing all schools for up to three months; (2) cancelling athletic events; (3) closing churches, theaters, and areas of assembly; (4) working staggered hours to ensure less crowding in public transportation vehicles; (5) limiting contact with the sick by isolating and quarantining them in their homes or treatment centers, preventing public gatherings, encouraging use of face masks, and providing public education.

In an op-ed piece in *The New York Times* on June 6, 2005, then Senator Barack Obama (Democrat) and Senator Richard Lugar (Republican) spoke in one bipartisan voice, "Avian flu outbreak is the most important threat we are facing now." Two of the three conditions needed for a flu pandemic have been realized in that, first, a new strain of influenza virus H5N1 has emerged and, second, the strain has jumped across species. Missing is the third requirement that the virus mutates sufficiently to a form that allows easy transmission from human to human. The White House strategy for implementing a plan to control a potential influenza pandemic can be accessed at http://www.whitehouse.gov/homeland_security, and related information appears at http://www.pandemicflu.gov.

The potential seriousness of a coming H5N1 influenza pandemic has been expressed sternly by some experts in this medical field. For example, Yoshi Kawaoka at the University of Wisconsin has stated, "never has a virus so lethal for poultry become so widespread and continued for such a long time, thus increasing the risk for mutations." However, this view is not universally accepted. Another leader in the area of influenza investigation, Peter Palese, points out that blood collected in the 1990s from people in China indicates that millions of them had antibodies to H5N1. The point being that before making antibodies, one must become infected and recover without serious clinical disease.

Where did H5N1 virus originate and how and where has it spread? Available evidence indicates that this influenza virus originated in southern China where millions of people and chickens live close together. The transport and selling of infected birds spread the infection regionally. However, H5N1 virus has escaped China on the wings and in the guts of migratory birds. The Qinghai Lake Region of western China witnessed a dramatic outbreak of H5N1 virus in waterfowl with deaths of over a thousand migratory birds (41). The outbreak was first identified in bar-headed geese, which migrate over the Himalayan Mountains. These and other migratory birds have spread H5N1 throughout Southeast Asia, Africa, and into Europe where chickens, swans, and turkey have been infected (42–44). Cats and dogs have also become infected, presumably from eating dead birds. Thus, the H5N1 virus continues to sweep across the globe. H5N1 has been found in areas from Nigeria to Iraq to Russia, to Romania, France, and England. Thus, since 2005 the H5N1 avian flu has spread to Africa and Europe. While not yet in North America, its appearance is likely just a matter of time. The cause of this spread appears to be migratory birds and the poultry trade.

How the world's communities handle this spread and the dilemma it causes are mixed. In poor countries where nourishment and trade often depend on poultry and poultry products, instances of refusal to report outbreaks of ill/dying birds have multiplied. This has been partially overcome by governments and organizations that reimburse for culled birds. Other countries, like Indonesia, which is composed of thousands of islands with a limited central government, pose problems of enforcing public health measures in rural areas. Countries like China, where image is often greater than responsibility (see chapters on SARS and HIV), have governments that do not always report infections of humans and wildlife at the regional and even national levels. Some countries have refused to share H5N1 samples from their sick citizens, saying that the viruses are their own intellectual property. Still, several of these incidents were not one sided, and many have or are being resolved. The fact remains that any chain is as only strong as its weakest link—in this case the chain is a barrier to wide-sweeping infection.

Scientists, like all humans, have their own conflicts and egos. In 2006, Ilaria Capua of the Istituto Zooprofilattico Sperimentale delle Venezie in Italy led a charge to have all sequences obtained from H5N1 bird flu released into the public domain as they became available. The purpose was to bring about rapid understanding of how the virus evolves and circulates. She then followed this principle by releasing the sequences she had derived to all engaged in those studies. In contrast, the WHO has a select circle of approximately fifteen laboratories that share H5N1 sequences on a password-protected Internet site. The reason is, evidently, that sharing data compromises scientific credit and that without a form of confidentiality some would not submit samples at all. Another point of view was expressed by Jan Brown, director of the Veterinarian Laboratory Agency in the United Kingdom, which is the reference laboratory for the European Union. Brown was quoted in the journal *Science* (311:1220, 2006) as justifying the refusal to release sequencing information by citing intellectual, proprietary, and monetary expectations. He said, "The staff in this institute is working 24/7 (24 hours, 7 days a week) to provide this service. I don't think its unreasonable to expect some reward (publications) for their endeavors." The analogy made by the Russian poet Yevtushenko that racehorses are not needed but workhorses that pull together appear appropriate.

Human-to-human infection by bird flu virus has now been confirmed. An Indonesian man died after contracting the virus infection from his ten-year-old son. In the family's home clustered in a remote village on Samaha Island, six of seven members died. The first to die was a woman who sold vegetables in a market where birds were also purchased. She became ill and was coughing heavily within her family group. Five of those family members later became ill, and subsequent sequence analysis proved that all of them were infected with the identical strain of H5N1 as the woman. The seed virus mutated slightly in the sixth victim, a child, and he passed the mutated virus onto his father who helped nurse him in the hospital. Samples of viruses were obtained so that mutations could be evaluated for evidence of human-to-human transmission. Previously, when human-to-human transmission was suspected, investigators had no virus samples to test, so infection of one patient by another or between patients and poultry could not be proven. Although the H5N1 virus does not spread easily to humans or among humans, some few instances have been clearly documented. Now, of course, the worry is that the virus will mutate to acquire that property.

The H5N1 bird flu virus binds (receptor) to sialic acid linked to galactose sugar by an α-2,3 linkage (45). The sialic acid receptor to which the H5N1 bird flu virus binds is found primarily deep in the respiratory tract at a junction bronchiole between the respiratory and alveolus (45). In contrast, the H1N1 pandemic 1918 influenza (as well as H1, H2, H3 influenzas) binds to sialic acid linked to galactose by α-2,6 linkage, a receptor that is predominant in the upper respiratory tract—the nasal mucosa, paranasal sinuses, pharynx, trachea, and bronchi. The disparate location of receptors is often proposed as an explanation for H5N1 bird flu's limited ability to infect and spread among humans, although the virus efficiently replicates in the lungs and, conversely, for why H1N1 virus (as well as H2, H3 influenzas) easily replicates and spreads among humans as well as efficiently replicating in the lung.

Recently, Zhang and colleagues (46) provided a new twist to the influenza pandemic episode. They reported preservation of influenza A viral genes in ice and water from high latitude lakes that are frequently visited by migratory birds. Could influenza virus be preserved in lake ice that melts during spring warming as a source of infecting migratory birds? Certainly, more questions remain to be answered before this report has biologic meaning; nevertheless, it raises a number of interesting issues.

In addition to pandemics with antigenic shift and alterations in the 1918 influenza virus, both of which signify major changes in existing viruses, antigenic drift permits slight alterations in viral structure. Such drift follows pinpoint changes (mutations) in amino acids in various antigen domains that relate to immune pressure, leading to selection. For example, the hemagglutinin molecule gradually changes while undergoing antigenic drift. A mutation of this kind allows the virus to escape attack by host antibodies generated during a previous bout of infection. Because these antibodies would ordinarily protect the host by removing the virus, this escape permits the related infection to remain in the host and the population.

With the difficulties posed by antigenic shift and drift as well as animal reservoirs with respect to making an influenza vaccine as effective as those for smallpox, poliovirus, yellow fever, or measles, it is not surprising that problems arise. Another complication is that immunity to influenza virus is incomplete; that is, even in the presence of an immune response, influenza viruses can still infect. Even so, the challenge of developing vaccines based on surveillance studies has been met. A chemically treated, formalin-inactivated virus has been incorporated in a vaccine that is about 70 percent effective in increasing resistance to influenza virus. The vaccine decreases the frequency of influenza attacks or, at least, the severity of disease in most recipients, although protection is not absolute. In addition, the secondary bacterial infections that may accompany influenza are today treatable with potent antibacterial drugs that were previously unavailable. Nonetheless, of the plagues that visit humans, influenza is among those that require constant surveillance because we can be certain that in some form influenza will return.[1]

---

[1] In April of 2009 an outbreak of swine influenza occurred. It spread, by late April, to multiple countries, and its passage from human-to-human led the World Health Organization to issue a Phase 5 alert of a pending pandemic. As of this time since the denominator, that is the numbers of those infected is unknown, it is difficult to judge the seriousness of the outbreak. However, the fact that the viral disease is occurring in the spring, as opposed to the usual occurrence in the fall, is infecting young adults and is rapidly spreading is a matter of concern. That this virus is of type H1N1 suggests that those persons exposed to the H1N1 virus in 1977 (32 years of age and older) should have some protection against this latest outbreak.

World Health Organization

Cumulative Number of Confirmed Human Cases of Avian Influenza A/(H5N1) Reported to WHO

10 September 2008

Country	2003		2004		2005		2006		2007		2008		Total	
	cases	deaths	cases	deaths	cases	deaths	cases	deaths	cases	deaths	cases	deaths	cases	deaths
Azerbaijan	0	0	0	0	0	0	8	5	0	0	0	0	8	5
Bangladesh	0	0	0	0	0	0	0	0	0	0	1	0	1	0
Cambodia	0	0	0	0	4	4	2	2	1	1	0	0	7	7
China	1	1	0	0	8	5	13	8	5	3	3	3	30	20
Djibouti	0	0	0	0	0	0	1	0	0	0	0	0	1	0
Egypt	0	0	0	0	0	0	18	10	25	9	7	3	50	22
Indonesia	0	0	0	0	20	13	55	45	42	37	20	17	137	112
Iraq	0	0	0	0	0	0	3	2	0	0	0	0	3	2
Lao People's Democratic Republic	0	0	0	0	0	0	0	0	2	2	0	0	2	2
Myanmar	0	0	0	0	0	0	0	0	1	0	0	0	1	0
Nigeria	0	0	0	0	0	0	0	0	1	1	0	0	1	1
Pakistan	0	0	0	0	0	0	0	0	3	1	0	0	3	1
Thailand	0	0	17	12	5	2	3	3	0	0	0	0	25	17
Turkey	0	0	0	0	0	0	12	4	0	0	0	0	12	4
Viet Nam	3	3	29	20	61	19	0	0	8	5	5	5	106	52
Total	4	4	46	32	98	43	115	79	88	59	36	28	387	245

Total number of cases includes number of deaths.
WHO reports only laboratory-confirmed cases.
All dates refer to onset of illness.

http://www.who.int/csr/disease/avian_influenza/country/cases_table_2008_09_10/en/print.html [11/18/2008 1:16:13 PM]

FIGURE 16.5 *The highly pathogenic avian influenza A (H5N1—bird flu) has killed over 60 percent of those infected since its discovery in 2003 according to cumulative mortality table provided by WHO (reprinted by permission of the World Health Organization, http://www.who.int/csr/disease/avian_influenza/country/cases_table_2008_09_10/en/ index.html).*

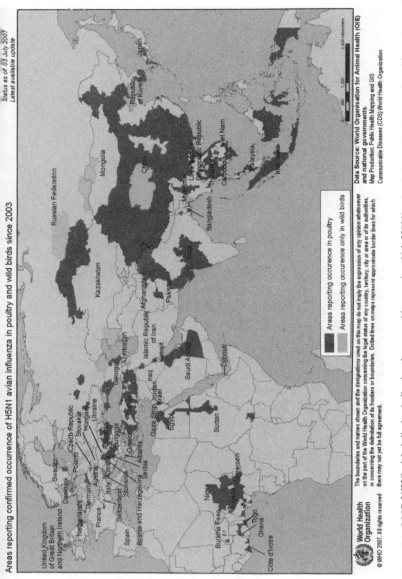

FIGURE 16.6 *2007 WHO global display indicating the geographic areas in which H5N1 avian influenza has been confirmed in poultry and wild birds since 2003 (reprinted by permission of the World Health Organization, http://gamapserver.who.int/mapLibrary/app/searchResults.aspx).*

17

Conclusions and
Future Predictions

From the mid-nineteenth to early twentieth century, the understanding that microbes, not miasmas or ill winds, caused infectious diseases of humans led to euphoric prophecies that humankind now had the power to vanquish plagues from our midst. Yet in 1926, when Paul deKruif's classical book *Microbe Hunters* (1) was published, almost every viral disease known continued unabatedly and relentlessly to claim victims. An effective vaccine against smallpox had been available since the early 1800s, yet millions of people continued to die from that infection each year, including the year deKruif's book was published. Even though attenuated vaccines could protect chickens from fowl cholera or humans from rabies, medical doctors had no vaccine to use against measles, yellow fever, or poliomyelitis, and these infections continued to kill or cripple. It was true that understanding the biological cycle of yellow fever infection led to public health measures to reduce or eliminate the mosquito vector and that, by the early twentieth century, control of this infection had increased dramatically. Yet Paul deKruif remained pessimistic, even resigning his research position at the Rockefeller Institute in the early 1920s. In his autobiography, *The Sweeping Wind* (2), published in 1962, he wrote:

> What was the use of knocking myself out at microbe hunting in these days of the beginning 1920s when the universal life-saving advances predicted

by the immortal Pasteur seem to have come to a dead end?...The blooming golden days of the old microbe hunters were done. What had become of the brave prophecy of Pasteur's—that it was now in the power of men to make microbic maladies vanish from the face of the globe?...Where were the hopes for preventive vaccines?

However, deKruif spoke too soon, because fifty to sixty years later, smallpox, yellow fever, measles, and poliomyelitis were under control, as he could never have visualized. Still, as viruses evolve and new types emerge, so our perceptions continuously change about their potential for hatching plagues. What can and should be done? We now have to face the possible return of smallpox and its use as a weapon of bioterrorism (3). We have witnessed the return of yellow fever to the United States, the first case in seventy-four years. The vector that spreads that disease, the *Aedes aegypti* mosquito, now dwells in our midst. Even as the march to contain measles and poliomyelitis viruses continues at an impressive pace, bumps and setbacks have been encountered along the way.

Measles viruses recently infected humans in the tens of thousands in Brazil and in the hundreds of thousands in Japan. New cases also surfaced in the United States, as recently as 2008 in San Diego, California. The return of epidemic-size measles infections highlights its near universal infectivity (over 99 percent) for susceptible populations, the growing pool of susceptible individuals, the difficulty in eliminating the virus, and resistance by some to immunization.

In Malaysia, a recent outbreak of disease from a "mysterious virus" killed hundreds of people. The Centers for Disease Control (CDC) identified the virus as a member of the paramyxovirus family to which measles belongs. Further defined as a Hendravirus, this agent resembles the one that attacked two humans in Queensland, Australia. The Australian Hendravirus is associated with horses and spread by bats, whereas the Malaysian Hendra-like virus is associated with pigs. These far-flung examples signify not only the geographic diversity of just one class of viruses, measles, but also their aptitude for remaking themselves so as to cross the former barriers of species susceptibility.

Since immunization, paralytic poliomyelitis has disappeared from the Americas. Yet polio vaccination was temporarily curtailed in Northern Nigeria despite new outbreaks of the disease and its spread from Africa to Asia by Muslim pilgrims returning from Mecca. Correspondingly, since 1991, the world's total number of recorded cases has diminished more than 89 percent, from over 35,000 to about 2,000 currently. More than two-thirds of children under five years of age, approximately 420 million individuals worldwide, have been vaccinated during the last two years. The hope is that continued immunizations will have blanketed the globe's population to wipe out the poliomyelitis virus. However, many argue that containment rather than eradication is the feasible goal.

Yet, even now, immunization must be required and practiced diligently not only in Third World countries but also in the United States. As an example, when Dirk Kempthorne, governor of Idaho, decided to enhance vaccination of children susceptible to polio, he appointed Jim Hawkins to oversee the program. Because Hawkins was infected with the poliomyelitis virus as a child, he knew its horrors well. Despite this, he was confronted with opposition groups from the Christian Coalition, other religious factions, and antigovernment groups who did not want any agency or organization telling them what to do with their children. As a consequence, Idaho ranked low among states for polio-vaccinated residents, with only 70 percent coverage for its children. As a consequence of such bias and neglect, the pool of unvaccinated children grows, and the risk to all citizens increases. This danger prevails despite proof that protection through immunization succeeds only when the numbers of susceptible people decrease.

The newfound viruses, so far, afflict relatively few persons in limited areas of the world, but the human immunodeficiency virus (HIV) continues its devastating march; AIDS, the disease HIV causes, has already killed 10 to 25 percent of the population in regions of Africa. Similar reports appear with increasing regularity in Asia, and a yearly incidence of around 40,000 new cases continues in the United States. In Western countries, although no individual is yet considered cured of AIDS, aggressive antiviral triple-drug therapy has dramatically reduced the expected death rate and prolonged life. Those infected will likely die of other diseases, that is, heart failure, cancer, stroke, and so forth. Even so, persisting HIV infection endures in these patients' bodies and thus remains a source of continued spread.

No one knows whether the human form of "mad cow" disease will rise in incidence. This disease presumably caused by prions, is a variant of the relatively rare CJD. Because the incubation period for prion disease is so long, about fifty years or more, it is too early to know if a widespread epidemic is likely. But since the emergence of a mad cow-like disease in humans during the early 1990s, such a plague may be a distinct possibility (4). Concern for such an eventuality in the United States is evident in the ban preventing persons who lived in England during the mad cow disease epidemic from donating to blood banks as a way of protecting the country's blood supply. This ban eliminates a pool of donors who formerly provided up to 10 percent of the U.S. blood supply. Evidence from the United Kingdom asserts that blood can retain this agent, which has been passed via transfusions to four individuals according to related reports.

Prominent in this list of potential assaults by well-known or modified viruses is fear of a new influenza plague. In late 1998, a novel influenza virus, which killed over a third of the humans it infected, was found to contain an outer glycoprotein coat—the hemagglutinin—of birds. This influenza virus protein had never before been isolated in humans (5,6). Fortunately, this time around, the virus that jumped species from birds to humans has failed to routinely spread from human to human. Further, the major source of this human disease was traced to poultry markets in Hong Kong. The rapid elimination of millions of ducks, geese, and chickens removed a large reservoir of the virus, thereby likely preventing the infection of more humans. This strategy, so far, has prevented the evolution of a viral variant that could afflict large numbers of humans, as did the massive influenza epidemic of 1918–1919. A search of the past few years has intensified efforts to find and identify the 1918–1919 flu virus and to learn what made it so deadly. Just below the Arctic Circle and in Alaska, scientists made energetic attempts to obtain permanently frozen tissues from victims of the 1918–1919 outbreak in anticipation that their corpses would contain nucleic acid fingerprints from that long-past virus (7). Others recovered viral nucleic acid sequences from formalin-fixed lungs of influenza-infected patients who died in the 1918/1919 epidemic (8). RNA was recovered, and current molecular and virologic technology allowed the recovery of the virus's amino acid sequence and its reconstruction. However, many of its lethal effects are still to be decoded.

Yellow fever first returned to the United States after an absence of seventy-two years (9). In July 1996, a forty-five-year-old Tennessean vacationed in Brazil but neglected to receive the mandatory vaccination for yellow fever. During a nine-day fishing trip on the Amazon and Rio Negro rivers, he was bitten by a mosquito carrying the yellow fever virus. Upon return to Knoxville, he developed fever and chills, as Kate Bionda did in Memphis ninety-eight years earlier, when the yellow fever virus also entered her blood, then set off an epidemic (see Chapter 5). Similarly, he deteriorated, vomited blood, and died. As with the Memphis outbreak in 1878, the *Aedes aegypti* mosquito was now loose in Knoxville. But unlike that earlier plague, no other yellow fever infections developed. However, cases of yellow fever and deaths still occur in South America, including in Brazil, where the virus is endemic, where the mosquito dwells, and where the Tennessee traveler was infected.

Edward Jenner, too, would have been discouraged had he known how long the wait would be between his great discovery of a vaccine against smallpox and eradication of the disease. In 1800, only four years after his success, he wrote:

> May I not with perfect confidence congratulate my country and society at large on the beholding—an antidote that is capable of extirpating from the earth a disease which is every hour devouring its victims; a disease that has ever been considered as the severest scourge of the human race!

Some 177 years passed before the world's last case of endemic smallpox occurred in Somalia, although in the next year a laboratory accident in Birmingham, England, led to the death of one person. Nevertheless, by 1979, a global commission formed to evaluate the control of smallpox certified that smallpox had been conquered. The Thirty-Third World Health Assembly in 1980 accepted this final report and the certification of smallpox eradication. Thus came fulfillment of the first part of Pasteur's prophecy.

With the total elimination of smallpox infection in nature, the debate shifts to a new focus. Should smallpox as a species be removed from our planet? Opinions on this matter are mixed. Several arguments against destruction of smallpox stocks remain on the table. First, although depositories in the United States and in Russia continue to sequester stocks of this virus for research, who can ensure that rogue states or societies have not secretly stockpiled the infectious agent elsewhere? Even the elimination of smallpox from these two sites may not keep the agent from reappearing. Although there are now better biological warfare agents than smallpox, it may be quixotic to think that others with secret caches will abandon their supplies. This possibility suggests the second issue, the risk of a continuously expanding human population that is susceptible to smallpox. A third argument is that the functions of most genes of the smallpox virus are not known. The majority of these genes are not concerned with the virus's basic replication strategy per se, but rather alter the infected host so as to favor the virus. The products from such interactions may prove to have therapeutic value in humans with other diseases. Last, there is the intellectual concern that all living things are part of the cosmic universe and to regard any form of life as a foe and eliminate it completely will one day be considered a philosophically poor action for all.

Smallpox's natural host is man. There are no animal intermediates, and since the virus does not linger in the form of a persistent infection, it is amenable to permanent eradication—that is to say, removal from the world. But because the virus no longer circulates in any community, the numbers of never vaccinated or previously infected/vaccinated, susceptible individuals increase. Complete or efficient immunity of those previously vaccinated is likely to wane in ten to twenty years or less. As a consequence, the pool of highly susceptible individuals would expand enormously.

In the recent past, some countries and individuals have actually chosen to develop more dangerous smallpox viruses by inserting lethal materials alongside the natural genes. For example, the Soviet Biologic Weapons Program near Novosibirsk in western Siberia continued such work using a component of Ebola virus, despite attempts from Gorbachev to curtail it. With the breakup of the Soviet Union, government-funded research decreased dramatically, and scientists working in biowarfare programs often found themselves without jobs. Some went abroad looking for employment by the highest bidder. Several emigrated to the United States or Great Britain as consultants in the defense against such biological weapons, even as the Offensive Biological Weapons Program was discontinued in the United States during the Nixon presidency. Others, perhaps mercenary biologists, have simply disappeared from Russia. One can only guess that they ended up in Iraq, Syria, Libya, Iran, or perhaps other areas with their stocks of smallpox and their technical knowledge to initiate and expand a bioweapons program. However, no one really knows where they are. But because of that threat, several specialists who earlier led the fight to remove smallpox from our planet and destroy the entire virus species as well as public health and government officials have stockpiled vaccines against smallpox and other pathogens. The Clinton administration agreed in late 1998 to request $300 million for this purpose, and the Bush administration continued the program. President Bush was himself revaccinated with the smallpox vaccine (see Chapter 4). Implicit in the goal of eradication and elimination of smallpox or other plague-inducing agents is removing all need to vaccinate the population. The billions of dollars saved by not having to make or use vaccines would then be available to control other health problems. In recent years, smallpox disease has become more of a curiosity than a medical issue and has been removed from teaching curriculums of many medical schools. Even the retraining of physicians and public health officials in diagnosis of small-pox, which was advised by some experts, has been discontinued at most medical schools.

The last natural case of smallpox occurred in 1977 in Somalia at a time when many countries had already discontinued routine vaccination. All countries ceased vaccination programs eight years later. However, in 1978, a photographer working at the University of Birmingham, England, became infected and died. Supposedly, the source of infection was a secure laboratory for smallpox research located a considerable distance from the room in which the photographer worked. This lethal episode emphasizes the danger of any viable smallpox virus during the posteradication era. As a result of that accident, all strains of small-pox stored in laboratories were supposedly destroyed or transferred to depositories at the CDC in Atlanta or the Research Institute for Viral Preparations in Moscow.

Although humans and their collective institutions have the power to accomplish dramatic good, some have the ability to do overwhelming evil. For the latter reason, smallpox, one of the most intently studied viruses in the past and the killer of millions, could reappear. Clearly, the possibility remains that smallpox in the hands of evildoers could resurface to be seen once again by practitioners of medicine.

This debate does not end with smallpox but could encompass poliomyelitis and measles viruses. Both viruses have been targeted for elimination in the twenty-first century by WHO and the scientific community. However, whether this can be achieved remains questionable.

Eradication of infections caused by poliovirus is still considered by WHO as feasible. In 1994, almost 80 percent of children under one year of age throughout the world were immunized against poliomyelitis through the Expanded Program of Immunization (EPI) (10). During 1995, half the world's children under five, roughly 300 million, were immunized as part of the plan to eradicate the disease globally. In pursuing this grand campaign, and reflecting what can be done with active collaboration and goodwill among countries, WHO, other health organizations, medical doctors, and pharmaceutical houses immunized over 160 million children in India and China during just two weeks of December 1995. A month earlier, in war-torn Sri Lanka and in Afganistan in 1996, a short truce was arranged. Called a day of tranquility, it was organized to enable children on both sides of the conflict to be immunized. The model for this and other programs is the successful campaign that eradicated smallpox in 1979. To accomplish that goal, widespread immunization programs were enforced. In addition, when a case of smallpox was uncovered, everyone around the infected individual was vaccinated. But poliovirus infection differs from smallpox in an important way. The symptoms of smallpox are easily recognized, yet fewer than one in one hundred persons infected with poliovirus shows any manifestation of the disease. For that reason, a poliovirus eradication campaign will require near-universal immunization. The total elimination of poliomyelitis virus from mankind, overcoming all objections and interference from every source, will be a great event in human history and should be honored as such.

With measles virus infection, eradication may be more difficult. Although the current vaccine is excellent, scientific advisors to WHO and those knowledgeable about measles are not confident that it will be effective enough for total elimination of the virus. I am among those who share this concern. But why this divergence of opinion? Measles remains one of the major childhood killers, accounting for more children's deaths than all other vaccine-preventable diseases combined (10). Yet of all the vaccines currently administered by EPI and WHO, measles virus when compared with the other five vaccines administered for childhood diseases provides the least degree of protection (10). Why is the measles virus vaccine so much less effective?

All agree that the current measles virus vaccine has a proven track record of success, strongly arguing in favor of its ability to eradicate measles virus infection. For example, before the EPI launched its vaccination campaign in 1974, the death rate from measles virus was 8 million individuals per year. By 1990, global immunization reached 80 percent coverage, and the associated mortality dropped nearly eightfold. Death rates for the last several years have been at a low point of slightly more than one million individuals per year. By 2007, the death rate fell to nearly 300,000. Even better, parts of the Caribbean and Central and South America have had virtually no new cases of measles. In 1996, the Pan-American Organization and CDC observed the total eradication of measles virus in Cuba following enforceable national vaccine days. Nevertheless, as long as even 200,000 or somewhat fewer susceptible persons are available in any one place—the number believed required for the continued circulation of measles virus in an area—there will always be a risk of reinfection. Vaccine coverage is still incomplete not only in Third World countries but also in some industrial countries. For example, in the 1990s and early 2000s, in some regions of Japan and France coverage of susceptible inhabitants was less than 70 and 60 percent, respectively, and in Italy there was only approximately 50 percent vaccine coverage.

Even so, what is the problem with the current attenuated vaccine? Unlike the poliomyelitis vaccine, which is effective within the first few months of life, the attenuated measles vaccine is not effective as early. Many babies carry antibodies to measles virus obtained from their mothers, and these antibodies inactivate the vaccine for a period of several postnatal months. Therefore, even though the current vaccine is effective, work to produce a better vaccine that will not be inactivated by antibodies from the mother should be continued so that an alternative is available.

When *Microbe Hunters* was published in 1926, no one knew that viruses caused influenza or that infections by the hemorrhagic viruses, SARS and HIV, lay in the future. Today, monitoring stations worldwide watch for newly emerging variants of the influenza virus and for the return of well-known types. The recent appearance of the hemorrhagic fever viruses, SARS, and West Nile virus in the Americas and HIV throughout much of the world provided challenges to a new generation of microbe hunters, as did smallpox, poliomyelitis, measles virus, and yellow fever to medical researchers in the past. Evolving viruses, whose mutations cause changes in their genomes, combined with the intrusion of human populations into lands used only for agriculture and virgin forests, routinely allow new agents to infect humans and incite disease. With the appropriate resources to do the work, talent to undertake the task, and continuing technologic advances, the viruses causing hemorrhagic fevers, West Nile virus, and SARS should be as controllable as smallpox, yellow fever, measles, and poliomyelitis viruses have been. However, HIV and other similar infections provide unique problems and stand apart from what has been observed earlier. HIV infection continues to survive in and thus defy the presence of an anti-HIV immune response. Therefore, strategies that have successfully tamed the most virulent acute infections will have to be modified and rethought to control the long-lasting persistent viral infections.

Since 1953, when James Watson and Francis Crick discovered the structure of DNA, the molecule that contains genetic directions and transmits them from one generation to the next, scientific dogma has asserted that all genetic information is encoded by nucleic acids. However, the recent revelation of prion proteins introduced a new player into microbiology: Some argue that this protein can also provide genetic directions from one generation to the next. Prions arise as a result of mutations in a normal cell gene, and many believe that the conformational change from a normal prion to an abnormal one is the cause of spongiform encephalopathies. Current interest focuses on the possibility that prion disease of cows, the bovine spongiform encephalopathy, or mad cow disease, or possibly chronic wasting disease of deer and elk can cross the species barrier and affect humans, leading to progressive dementia and death. The prion, in itself, could be the infectious agent able to transmit disease. A related suggestion is that prions are the cause of other diseases of aging. At issue is not the "scare" value of this information but the prospect of scientific inquiry that will eventually identify and overcome the disease agent.

Using a different strategy, certain viruses infect cells without killing them and, instead, cause a persistent infection. During this long-lived infection, viruses can alter the functions of cells where they hide. For example, viruses can prevent nerve cells from making molecules necessary for cognitive function and normal behavior, inhibit endocrine cells from making hormones needed to maintain metabolism and growth, and block the immune system from making cytokines, other growth factors, and antibodies required for providing protection from microbes and cancers. Research is currently focused on the molecular basis of how these afflictions occur and whether diseases affecting the brain, endocrine and immune systems, heart, and other organs of humans are caused by viruses.

In the final analysis, the history of viruses, plagues, and people is an account of our world and the events that shaped it. Central players in that history are individuals who worked toward the conquest of viruses and the diseases they cause. From the time of Pasteur's great discovery of living vaccines, a large cadre of men and women has joined in the battle against viruses. Their great legacy to our society is painstakingly dissecting diseases that once took millions of lives with ease and devising methods to control or eradicate them. In the end, the splendor of human history is not in wars won, dynasties formed, or financial empires built, but in improvement of the human condition. The obliteration of diseases that impinge on our health is a regal yardstick of civilization's success, and those who accomplish that task will be among the true navigators of a brave new world.

REFERENCES

CHAPTER 1: A GENERAL INTRODUCTION

1. D. A. Henderson. "Smallpox Eradication." In *Microbe Hunters Past and Present*, ed. H. Koprowski and M. B. A. Oldstone, pp. 39–43. Bloomington, IN, 1996.
2. D. Hopkins. *Princes and Peasants: Smallpox in History*. Chicago, 1983.
3. H. Thomas. *Conquest: Montezuma, Cortes, and the Fall of Old Mexico*. New York, 1993.
4. W. H. McNeill. *Plagues and Peoples*. New York, 1976.
5. D. Malone. *Jefferson the President: First Term 1801–1805*. Boston, 1970.
6. J. E. Gibson. *Dr. Bodo Otto and the Medical Background of the American Revolution*. Springfield, 1937.
7. J. R. Paul. *A History of Poliomyelitis*. New Haven, 1971.
8. S. Gard. Presentation speech for the Nobel Award in physiology and medicine, 1954.

CHAPTER 2: INTRODUCTION TO THE PRINCIPLES OF VIROLOGY

1. P. B. Medawar and J. S. Medawar. *Aristotle to Zoos*. Cambridge, 1983.
2. M. S. Hirsch and James Curran. "Human Immunodeficiency Virus." In *Fields' Virology*, ed. B. N. Fields et al., pp. 1953–76. New York, 1990.
3. Q. J. Sattentau et al. "Epitopes of the CD4 Antigen and HIV Infection." *Science* 234 (1986):1120.
4. D. Naniche et al. "Human Membrane Cofactor Protein (CD46) Acts as a Cellular Receptor for Measles Virus." *J. Virol.* 67 (1993):6025.
5. R. E. Dorig et al. "The Human CD46 Molecule Is a Receptor for Measles Virus (Edmonston Strain)." *Cell* 75 (1993):295.

6. M. Manchester, M. K. Liszewski, J. P. Atkinson, and M. B. A. Oldstone. "Multiple Isoforms of CD46 (Membrane Cofactor Protein) Serve as Receptors for Measles Virus." *Proc. Natl. Acad. Sci. USA* 91 (1994):2161–2165.

7. R. Johnstone, B. E. Loveland, and I. F. McKenzie. "Identification and Quantification of Complement Regulator CD46 on Normal Human Tissues." *Immunology* 79 (1993):341.

8. M. B. A. Oldstone. "Virus Neutralization and Virus-Induced Immune Complex Disease: Virus-Antibody Union Resulting in Immunoprotection or Immunologic Injury—Two Sides of the Same Coin." In *Progress in Medical Virology*, Vol. 19, ed. J. L. Melnick, pp. 84–119. Basel, 1975.

9. M. B. A. Oldstone. "Molecular Anatomy of Viral Disease." *Neurology* 37 (1987):453–460.

10. M. B. A. Oldstone. "Viruses and Diseases of the Twenty-First Century." *Amer. J. Pathol.* 143 (1993):1241–1249.

11. D. I. Ivanovski. "Ueber die Mosaikkrankheit der Tabakspflanze." *Zentbl. Bakt. ParasitKde*, Abt. II 5 (1899):250–254.

12. M. W. Beijerinck. "Bemerkung zu dem Aufsatz von Herrn Iwanowsky uber die Mosaikkrankheit der Tabakspflanze." *Zentbl. Bakt ParasitKde*, Abt. I 5 (1899):310–311.

13. F. Loeffler and P. Frosch. "Berichte der Kommission zur Erforschung der Maul und Klauenseuche bei dem Institut fur Infektionskrankheiten in Berlin." *Zentbl. Bakt. ParasitKde*, Abt. I 23 (1898):371–391.

CHAPTER 3: INTRODUCTION TO THE PRINCIPLES OF IMMUNOLOGY

1. J. L. Whitton and M. B. A. Oldstone. "Immune Response to Viruses." In *Fields' Virology*, 3rd ed., ed. D. Knipe and P. Howley, pp. 285–320. Philadelphia, 2001. T. J. Braciale, Y. S. Hahn, and D. R. Burton. "The Adoptive Immune Response to Viruses." In *Fields' Virology*, 5th ed., ed. D. Knipe and P. Howley, pp. 275–326. Philadelphia, 2007.

2. C. A. Biron and G. Sen. "Innate Responses to Viral Infections." In *Fields Virology*, 5th ed., ed. D. Knipe and P. Howley, pp. 249–278. Philadelphia, 2007.

3. U. H. Koszinowski, S. Jonjic, and M. J. Reddehase. "The Role of CD4 and CD8 T Cells in Viral Infections." *Curr. Opin. Immunol.* 4 (1991):471–475.

4. P. C. Doherty, S. Hou, and R. A. Tripp. "CD8$^+$ T-Cell Memory to Viruses." *Curr. Opin. Immunol.* 6 (1994):545–552.

5. E. J. Wherry and R. Ahmed. "Memory CD8$^+$ T Cell Differentiation During Viral Infection." *J. Virol.* 78 (2004):5535–5545.

6. R. Ahmed and D. Gray. "Immunologic Memory and Protective Immunity: Understanding Their Relationship." *Science* 272 (1996):54–60.

7. M. Matloubian, R. J. Concepcion, and R. Ahmed. "CD4+ T Cells Are Required to Sustain CD8+ Cytotoxic T-Cell Responses During Chronic Viral Infection." *J. Virol.* 68 (1994):8056–8063.

8. A. Tishon, H. Lewicki, G. Rall, M. von Herrath, and M.B.A. Oldstone. "An Essential Role for Type I Interferon-Gamma in Terminating Persistent Viral Infection." *Virology* 212 (1995):244–250.

9. G. J. V. Nossal. "Life, Death and the Immune System." *Scientific American*, September 1993, pp. 53–62.

10. M. B. A. Oldstone. "Virus Neutralization and Virus-Induced Immune Complex Disease: Virus-Antibody Union Resulting in Immunoprotection or Immunologic Injury—Two Sides of the Same Coin." In *Progress in Medical Virology*, Vol. 19, ed. J. L. Melnick, pp. 84–119. Basel, 1975.

11. R. S. Fujinami and M. B. A. Oldstone. "Antiviral antibody reacting on the plasma membrane alters measles virus expression inside the cell." *Nature* 279 (1979):529–530.

12. D. B. McGavern, U. Christen, and M. B. A. Oldstone. "Molecular anatomy of antigen-specific CD8(+) T cell engagement and synapse formation in vivo." *Nat. Immunol.* 3 (2002):918–925.

13. J. D. Miller et al. "Human Effector and Memory CD8+ T cell Responses to Smallpox and Yellow Fever Vaccines." *Immunity.* 28 (2008):710.

14. I. J. Amanna, N. E. Carlson, and M. K. Slifka. "Duration of Humoral Immunity to Common Viral and Vaccine Antigens." *N. Engl. J. Med.* 8 (2007):1903.

15. I. J. Amanna, I. Messaoudi, and M. K. Slifka. "Protective Immunity Following Vaccination: How is it Defined?" *Hum. Vaccin.* 4 (2008): 316–319.

16. D. Homann, L. Teyton, and M. B. A. Oldstone. "Differential regulation of antiviral T-cell immunity results in stable CD8$^+$ but declining CD4$^+$ T-cell memory." *Nat. Med.* 7 (2001):913.

17. D. Naniche et al. "Decrease in measles virus-specific CD4 T cell memory in vaccinated subjects." *J. Infect. Dis.* 190 (2004):1387–1395.

CHAPTER 4: SMALLPOX

1. F. Fenner and D. A. Henderson. *Smallpox and Its Eradication.* Geneva, 1988.

2. D. A. Henderson. "Smallpox Eradication." In *Microbe Hunters Past and Present*, ed. H. Koprowski and M. B. A. Oldstone, pp. 39–44. Bloomington, IN, 1996.

3. F. Fenner. "Poxviruses." In *Fields' Virology*, ed. B. N. Fields et al., pp. 2673–2702. New York, 1996.

4. W. H. McNeill. *Plagues and Peoples.* New York, 1976.

5. D. Hopkins. *Princes and Peasants: Smallpox in History.* Chicago, 1983.

6. A. M. Behbehani. "Life and Death of an Old Disease." *Microb. Rev.* 4 (1983):455.

7. F. Fenner. "History of Smallpox." In *Microbe Hunters then and now,* ed. Koprowski and Oldstone, pp. 25–38. Bloomington, 1996.

8. J. A. Poupard and L. A. Miller. "History of Biological Warfare: Catapults to Capsomeres." *Ann. N.Y. Acad. Sci.* 666 (1992):9.

9. K. C. Wong and L. T. Wu. *History of Chinese Medicine,* 2nd ed. Shanghai, 1936.

10. Rhazes (Al-Razi, Abu Bakr Muhammad). *De Variolis et Morbillis Commentarius.* Londini, G. Bowyer, 1766. English translation in *Med. Class.* 4 (1939):22.

11. H. Thomas. *Conquest: Montezuma, Cortes, and the Fall of Old Mexico.* New York, 1993.

12. J. Duffy. "Smallpox and the Indians in the American Colonies." *Bull. Hist. Med.* 25 (1951):324.

13. L. James. *The Rise and Fall of the British Empire.* St. Martin's Press, New York, 1994.

14. H. Bouquet. Letter, June 23, 1763. MSS 21634:295. British Library, London.

15. H. Bouquet. Letter, July 13, 1763. MSS 21634:321. British Library, London.

16. C. Ward. *The War of the Revolution.* New York, 1952.

17. H. Thursfield. "Smallpox in the American War of Independence." *Ann. Med. Hist.* 2 (1940):312; J. E. Gibson. *Dr. Bodo Otto and the Medical Background of the American Revolution.* Springfield, IL, 1937.

18. D. Jackson and D. Twohig, eds. *The Diaries of George Washington.* University of Virginia Press, Charlottesville, VA, 1976.

19. C. F. Adams, ed. *Familiar Letters of John Adams and His Wife Abigail Adams, During the Revolution.* Hure and Houghton, New York, 1876.

20. D. McCullough. *John Adams.* Simon and Schuster, New York, 2001.

21. J. Adams. *Diary and Autobiography of John Adams,* ed. L. Butterfield. Harvard University Press, Boston, 1961.

22. E. Jenkins. *A History of the French Navy.* McDonald and James, London, 1973.

23. D. Hopkins. *Princes and Peasants.* University of Chicago Press, Chicago, 1983.

24. Editorial. "The True Issue." *Richmond Enquirer,* March 23, 1861.

25. Editorial. "The Terrors of Submission." *Charleston Mercury,* October 11, 1860.

26. J. R. Lowell. The Question of the Hour. *Atlantic Monthly.* 7 (1861):120.

27. D. Donall. *Lincoln.* Simon and Schuster, New York, 1995.

28. D. Hopkins. *Princes and Peasants.* University of Chicago Press, Chicago, 1983.

29. C. Smart. *The Medical and Surgical History of the War of the Rebellion.* U.S. Government Medical Office, 1888.
30. C. M. Green. *Washington: Village and Capital, 1800–1878.* Princeton University Press, Princeton, NJ, 1962.
31. M. Shutes. *Lincoln and the Doctors.* Pioneer Press, New York, 1933.
32. M. Leech. *Revelle in Washington, 1860–1865.* Harper Brothers, New York, 1941.
33. E. B. Long. *Civil War Day by Day.* Doubleday, New York, 1971.
34. C. Sandberg. *Abraham Lincoln: The War Years.* Harcourt Brace and Co., New York, 1939.
35. F. Fenner, ed., *The Biology of Animal Viruses.* New York, 1974.
36. W. Osler. *Practice of Medicine.* D. Appleton and Company, New York and London, 1904, p. 56.
37. J. Thresh. The Hospital Ships of the Metropolitan Asylums Board and the Dissemination of Smallpox. *Lancet.* 495, 1902.
38. E. Timoni. "An Account or History of the Procuring of the Smallpox by Incision or Inoculation: As Has for Some Time Been Practiced at Constantinople." Phil. Trans. Royal Society, 1714.
39. E. Jenner. *An Inquiry into the Causes and Effects of Variolae Vaccine, a Disease Discovered in Some of the Western Counties of England, Particularly Gloucestershire, and Known by the Name of the Cowpox.* London, 1798.
40. J. B. Blake. *Benjamin Waterhouse and the Introduction of Vaccination.* Philadelphia, 1957.
41. B. Waterhouse. *A Prospect of Exterminating the Smallpox.* Boston, 1800.
42. R. H. Halsey. *How the President, Thomas Jefferson and Dr. Benjamin Waterhouse Established Vaccination as a Public Health Procedure.* History of Medicine Series 5. New York, 1936.
43. D. Malone. *Jefferson the President: First Term 1801–1805.* Boston, 1970.
44. S. E. Ambrose. *Undaunted Courage.* New York, 1996, p. 115.
45. World Health Organization. Official Records, no. 151. Geneva, Switzerland.
46. Ibid., no. 152.
47. D. A. Henderson. Personal communication, 1995.
47a. M. Bliss. *Plague. A Story of Smallpox in Montreal.* Harper-Collins, Toronto, 1991.
47b. J. Haegerty. *Four Centuries of Medical History in Canada.* John Wright and Son, Bristol, United Kingdom, 1928.
48. P. Wehrle et al. "An airborne outbreak of smallpox in a German hospital and its significance with respect to other outbreaks in Europe." *Bull. Org. WHO* 43 (1970):669.
49. F. Fenner et al. *Smallpox and Its Eradication.* World Health Organization, Geneva, 1988.

50. The National Academy of Sciences Report. *Old guard against an old nemesis: IOM advises immunization effort against smallpox.* 2003.
51. C. Stalberg and L. Altman. "U.S. public health officials instruct states to be prepared to vaccinate up to 1 million people in 10 days in the event of a smallpox attack." *New York Times*, September 24, 2002.
52. K. Alibek. *Biohazard.* Random House, New York, 1999.
53. D. A. Henderson. "The looming threat of bioterrorism." *Science* 283 (1999):1279.
54. D. A. Henderson. Smallpox eradication. A sage of triumph and betrayal. The Pfizer/IDSP Discovery Series, Article 23, 1999.
55. M. B. A. Oldstone. *Viruses, Plagues, and History.* Oxford University Press, New York, 1998.
56. The National Academy of Sciences Report. *Old guard against an old nemesis: IOM advises immunization effort against smallpox.* 2003.
57. Morbidity and Mortality Weekly Report. *Vaccinia vaccination.* Volume 50, June 22, 2001.

CHAPTER 5: YELLOW FEVER

1. J. M. McFarland et al. "Imported Yellow Fever in a United States Citizen." *Clin. Infect. Dis.* 25 (1997):1143–1147.
2. World Health Organization. "Yellow Fever Vaccine." WHO position paper. *Weekly Epidemiol. Rev.* 78 (2003):349–359.
3. Centers for Disease Control and Prevention (CDC). "Fatal Yellow Fever in a Traveler Returning from Venezuela, 1999." *MMWR Morb. Mortal. Wkly. Rep.* 49 (2000):303–305.
4. Centers for Disease Control and Prevention (CDC). "Fatal Yellow Fever in a Traveler Returning from Amazonas, Brazil, 2002." *MMWR Morb. Mortal. Wkly. Rep.* 51 (2002):324–325.
5. J. Bryant, E. Holmes, and A. Barrett. "Out of Africa: A Molecular Perspective on the Introduction of Yellow Fever Virus into the Americas." *PLoS Pathogens* 3 (2007):668–673.
6. J. D. Goodyear. "The Sugar Connection: A New Perspective on the History of Yellow Fever." *Bull. Hist. Med.* 52 (1978).
7. H. Thomas. *Conquest: Montezuma, Cortes and the Fall of Old Mexico.* New York, 1993.
8. G. K. Strode et al. *Yellow Fever.* New York, 1951.
9. D. S. Freestone. *Yellow Fever Vaccine.* In: Vaccines, 2nd edn (Eds Plotkin, S. A. and Mortimer, E. A.). WB Saunders Company, London, 1994, pp. 741–779.
10. W. H. McNeill. *Plagues and Peoples.* New York, 1976.

11. H. R. Carter. *Yellow Fever: An Epidemiological and Historical Study of Its Place of Origin.* Baltimore, 1931.
12. H. Bloch. "Yellow Fever Epidemic in Philadelphia 1793." *N.Y. State J. Med.* 73 (1973): 2606–2609.
13. W. Currie. A Description of the Malignant, Infectious Fever Prevailing at Present in Philadelphia; with an Account of the Means to Prevent Infection, and the Remedies and Method of Treatment, Which Have Been Found Most Successful. Philadelphia, 1793.
14. D. Geggus. "Yellow Fever in the 1790's: The British Army in Occupied Santo Domingo." *Med. Hist.* 23 (1979):38–58.
15. J. H. Powell. *Bring Out Your Dead. The Great Plague of Yellow Fever in Philadelphia in 1793.* New York, 1970.
16. A. W. Woodruff. *Benjamin Rush, His Work on Yellow Fever and His British Connections: Am. J. Trop. Med. Hyg.* 26 (1977):1055–1059.
17. D. Malone. *Jefferson the President, 1st Term 1801–1805.* Boston, 1970.
18. S. R. Bruesch. "Yellow Fever in Tennessee in 1878." *J. Tenn. Med. Assoc.* 71 (1978): Part 1 887–896; 72 (1979): Part 2 91–104.
19. T. H. Baker. "Yellow Jack: The Yellow Fever Epidemic of 1878 in Memphis, Tennessee." *Bull. Hist. Med.* 42 (1968):241–264.
20. J. M. Keating. *A History of the Yellow Fever. The Yellow Fever Epidemic of 1878 in Memphis, Tennessee.* The Howard Association, 1879. Keating was the editor of the newspaper *The Daily Appeal*, as well as an active member in the Howard Association and Citizen's Committee.
21. G. Rosen. *A History of Public Health.* New York, 1958.
22. *The Daily Appeal*, August 13, 1878.
23. *The Sisters of St. Mary at Memphis: With the Acts and Suffering of the Priests and Others Who Were There with Them During the Yellow Fever Season of 1878.* New York, 1879.
24. M. Wingfield. *The Life and Letters of Dr. William J. Armstrong.* West Tennessee Historical Society Papers, Vol. IV, 1956.
25. *The Centennial History of the Tennessee State Medical Association 1830–1930.* Tennessee State Medical Association, 1930.
26. W. Reed and J. Carroll. "The Etiology of Yellow Fever." *Amer. Med.* 3 (1902):301–305.
27. A. Agramonte. "The Inside History of a Great Medical Discovery." *Sci. Monthly* 1 (1915):209–237.
28. J. Carroll. "Yellow Fever—A Popular Lecture." *Amer. Med.* 9 (1905):907–915.
29. J. Carroll. "A Brief Review of the Aetiology of Yellow Fever." *N.Y. Med. J.* 79 (1904):241–245, 307–310.
30. A. Agramonte. "The Transmission of Yellow Fever." *J. Am. Med. Assoc.* 40 (1903):1660.

31. C. Finlay. "El mosquito hipoteticamenti considerado como agente de transmision de la fiebre amarella." *Anales de la Real Academia Ciencias Medicas, Fisicas y Naturales de la Habana* 18 (1881):147–169.
32. C. Finlay. *Carlos Finlay and Yellow Fever*. New York, 1940.
33. F. Delaporte. *The History of Yellow Fever*. Cambridge, MA, 1991.
34. F. de Lesseps. *Recollections of Forty Years*. New York, 1888.
35. J. C. Rodrigues. *The Panama Canal. Its History, Its Political Aspects and Financial Difficulties*. New York, 1885.
36. I. E. Bennett. *History of the Panama Canal. Its Construction and Builders*. Washington, 1915.
37. D. McCullough. *The Path Between the Seas*. New York, 1977.
38. T. Roosevelt. *An Autobiography*. New York, 1920.
39. A. Stokes, J. Bauer, and N. Hudson. "Experimental Transmission of Yellow Fever to Laboratory Animals." *Am. J. Trop. Med.* 8 (1928):103–164.
40. W. Lloyd, M. Theiler, and N. Ricci. "Modification of the Virulence of Yellow Fever Virus by Cultivation in Tissues In Vitro." *Trans. R. Soc. Trop. Med. Hyg.* 29 (1936):481–529.
41. W. Sawyer, S. Kitchen, and W. Lloyd. "Vaccination Against Yellow Fever with Immune Serum and Virus Fixed for Mice." *J. Exp. Med.* 55 (1932):945–969.
42. M. Theiler and H. Smith. "The Effect of Prolonged Cultivation In Vitro upon the Pathogenicity of Yellow Fever Virus." *J. Exp. Med.* 65 (1937):767–786.
43. M. Theiler and H. Smith. "The Use of Yellow Fever Virus Modified by In Vitro Cultivation for Human Immunization." *J. Exp. Med.* 65 (1937):787–800.
44. M. Theiler. Nobel Prize in Physiology of Medicine Lecture, 1951.

CHAPTER 6: MEASLES VIRUS

1. E. Norrby and M. N. Oxman. "Measles Virus." In *Fields' Virology*, ed. D. Knipe et al., pp. 1013–1044. Lippincott, Williams and Wilkins, Philadelphia, 1990; Diane E. Griffin. "Measles Virus." In *Fields' Virology*, ed. D. Knipe et al., pp. 1551–1585. Lippincott, Williams and Wilkins, Philadelphia, 2007.
2. Current Topics in Microbiology and Immunology, "Measles Virus." Ed. M. B. A. Oldstone and D. Griffin. Volume 329, Springer-Verlag, Berlin, 2008.
3. Jennifer Steinhane quoting Cybil Carlson in the *New York Times*, March 21, 2008.
4. D. Naniche et al. "Decrease in measles virus-specific CD4 T cell memory in vaccinated subjects." *J. Infect. Dis.* 190 (2004):1387.

5. A. A. Parker et al. "Implications of a 2005 measles outbreak in Indiana for sustained elimination of measles in the United States." *N. Engl. J. Med.* 355 (2006):447.

6. L. E. Markowitz and Samuel L. Katz. "Measles Vaccine." In *Vaccines,* ed. S. A. Plotkin and E. A. Mortimer, Jr., pp. 229–276. Philadelphia, 1988.

7. W. Squire. "On Measles in Fiji." *Trans. Epidem. Soc. (London)* 4 (1877):72.

8. P. Christensen et al. "An Epidemic of Measles in Southern Greenland, 1951. Measles in Virgin Soil." *Acta. Med. Scand.* 144 (1952):430.

9. Michael McChesney and Michael B. A. Oldstone. "Virus Induced Immuno-suppression: Infections with Measles Virus and Human Immunodeficiency Virus." *Adv. Immunol.* 45 (1989):335.

10. W. Osler. *The Principles and Practice of Medicine.* New York, 1904.

11. C. von Pirquet. "Das Verhalten del kutanen Tuberkulin-Reaktion Wahrend der Masern." *Dtsch. Med. Wochenschr.* 34 (1908):1297.

12. R. Wagner. *Clements von Pirquet: His Life and Work.* Baltimore, 1968.

13. R. W. Blumberg and H. A. Cassady. "Effect of Measles on Nephrotic Syndrome." *Am. J. Dis. Child.* 63 (1947):151.

14. W. H. McNeill. *Plagues and Peoples.* New York, 1976.

15. H. Thomas. *Conquest: Montezuma, Cortes and the Fall of Old Mexico.* New York, 1993.

16. L. Spier. *Yuman Tribes of the Gila River.* Chicago, 1933.

17. G. Rosen. *A History of Public Health.* New York, 1958.

18. S. Krugman et al. Studies with the Live Attenuated Measles-Virus Vaccine. *Am. J. Child.* 103 (1962):353.

19. P. L. Panum. *Observations Made During the Epidemic of Measles on the Faeroes Islands in the Year 1846.* New York, 1940.

20. P. E. Steiner. *Disease in the Civil War.* Springfield, IL, 1968.

21. H. H. Cuningham. *Doctors in Gray.* Baton Rouge, LA, 1958.

22. The United States Surgeon-General's Office. *The Medical and Surgical History of the War of the Rebellion 1861–1865.* Washington, DC, 1870–88.

23. R. E. Lee. *The War of the Rebellion: A Compilation of the Official Records of the Union and Confederate Armies.* Washington, DC, 1880–1902, p. 657.

24. R. E. Lee. Ibid., 817.

25. F. L. Black. "Measles Endemicity in Insular Populations: Critical Community Size and Its Evolutionary Implications." *J. Theoret. Biol.* 11 (1966):207.

26. M. S. Bartlett. "Measles Periodicity and Community Size." *J. R. Stat. Soc. Ser.* A120 (1957):40.

27. Rhazes (Al-Razi, Abu Bakr Muhammad). *Med. Class.* 4 (1939):22.

28. T. Syndenham. "The Works of Thomas Syndenham." *Syndenman Soc. (London)* 4 (1922):250.

29. J. F. Anderson and J. Goldberger. "Experimental Measles in the Monkey: A Preliminary Note." *Pub. Health Rep. (Wash.)* 26 (1911):847.

30. S. Gard. Presentation Speech for the Nobel Award in Physiology and Medicine, 1954.

31. A. Carrel. "Some Conditions of the Reproduction In Vitro of the Rous Virus." *J. Exp. Med.* 43 (1926):647.

32. H. B. Maitland and M. C. Maitland. "Cultivation of Vaccinia Virus." *Lancet* 2 (1928):596.

33. T. Weller. "History of Varicella Virus." In *Microbe Hunters Then and Now*, ed. H. Koprowski and M. B. A. Oldstone, pp. 165–172. Bloomington, IL, 1996.

34. R. Chanock and S. Katz. Personal communication, 1997. Dr. Chanock, a former student of Albert Sabin's, is former Director of the Laboratory of Infectious Diseases at the National Institutes of Health, Allergy and Infectious Disease Institute, Bethesda, Maryland. Dr. Katz was a student of John Enders' and is currently Professor of Pediatrics at Duke University School of Medicine, Durham, North Carolina.

35. E. Jenner. *A Continuation of Facts and Observations Relative to the Variolae Vaccine, or Cow Pox*. London, 1800.

36. D. Hopkins. *Princes and Peasants*. Chicago, 1983.

37. F. Home. *Medical Facts and Experiments*. London, 1759.

38. F. Loeffler and P. Frosch. "Berichte der Kommission zur Erforschung der Maul und Klauenseuche bei dem Institut fur Infektionskrankheiten in Berlin." *Zentbl. Bakt. ParasitKde, Abt. I* 23 (1898):371–391.

39. J. F. Enders and T. C. Peebles. "Propagation in Tissue Culture of Cytopathic Agents from Patients with Measles." *Proc. Soc. Exp. Biol. Med.* 86 (1954):277.

40. Editorial, *New York Times*, September 17, 1961.

41. J. F. Enders. Letter to the *New York Times*, October 1, 1961.

42. C. Dagger. "Mothers of Nepal." *New York Times*, April 30, 2006.

43. M. Fitzpatrick. *MMR and Autism: What Parents Need to Know*. Routledge, London, 2004.

44. R. Horton. *MMR Science and Fiction: Exploring a Vaccine Crisis*. Granta, London, 2004.

45. K. Gardner. "Autism's cause may reside in abnormalities at the synapse." *Science* 317 (2007):190.

CHAPTER 7: POLIOMYELITIS

1. F. C. Robbins. "Polio—Historical." In *Vaccines*, ed. S. Plotkin and E. Mortimer, Jr., pp. 137–154. Philadelphia, 1994.

2. J. R. Paul. *A History of Poliomyelitis*. New Haven, CT, 1971.

3. S. Gard. Presentation Speech for the Nobel Award in Physiology and Medicine, 1954.
4. J. Salk, J. A. Drucker, and D. Malvy. "Non-infectious Poliovirus Vaccine." In *Vaccines*, ed. S. A. Plotkin and E. A. Mortimer, pp. 205–228. Philadelphia, 1994.
5. G. Courtois et al. "Preliminary Report on Mass Vaccination of Man with Live Attenuated Poliomyelitis Virus in the Belgian Congo and Ruanda-Urundi." *Br. Med. J.* 26 (July 1958):187.
6. H. Koprowski. "A Visit to Ancient History." In *Microbe Hunters Past and Present*, ed. H. Koprowski and M. B. A. Oldstone, pp. 141–152. Bloomington, IL, 1996.
7. A. B. Sabin. "Oral Poliovirus Vaccine: History of Its Development and Use and Current Challenge to Eliminate Poliomyelitis from the World." *J. Infect. Dis.* 151 (1985):420.
8. T. Syndenham. "The Works of Thomas Syndenham." *Syndenham Soc. (London)* 2 (1922):250.
9. M. Underwood. *A Treatise on the Diseases of Children with General Directions for the Management of Infants from the Birth.* London, 1789.
10. J. Heine. *Beobach tungen uber Lachmungs zustande der unteren Extremitatien und diren Behandlung.* Stuttgart, 1840.
11. J. M. Charcot. *Lectures on the Diseases of the Nervous System.* London, 1881. Rpt. New York, 1962.
12. C. Bell. *The Nervous System of the Human Body as Explained in a Series of Papers Read Before the Royal Society of London.* London, 1844.
13. F. Loeffler and P. Frosch. "Berichte der Kommission zur Erforschung der Maul und Klauenseuche bei dem Institut fur Infektionskrankheiten in Berlin." *Zentbl. Bakt. ParasitKde, Abt. I* 23 (1898):371–391.
14. K. Landsteiner and E. Popper. "Mikroscopische Praparate von einem menschlichen und zwei Affenruckenmarken." *Wein. Klin. Wschr.* 21 (1908):1830.
15. K. Landsteiner and E. Popper. "I. Ubertragung der Poliomyelitis Acuta auf Affen." *Z. Immun. Frosch. Exp. Ther.* 2 (1909):377.
16. K. Landsteiner and C. Levaditi. "Surlaparalysie infantile experimente." *C.R. Seanc. Soc. Biol.* 67 (1909):787.
17. K. Landsteiner and C. Levaditi. "La transmission de la paralysie infantile auxsinges." *C.R. Seanc. Soc. Biol.* 67 (1909):592.
18. S. Flexner and P. A. Lewis. "The Nature of the Virus of Epidemic Poliomyelitis." *J. Am. Med. Assoc.* 53 (1909):2095.
19. *New York Times*, March 9, 1911.
20. M. Burnet and J. Macnamara. "Immunologic Differences Between Strains of Poliomyelitic Virus." *Br. J. Exp. Path.* 12 (1931):57.
21. T. Gould. *A Summer Plague: Polio and Its Survivors.* London, 1995.

22. A. V. Burns. "The Scourge of 1916—America's First and Worst Polio Epidemic." *The American Legion Magazine*, September 1966: 12–16 and 45–47.
23. *New York Times*, July 7, 1916.
24. *New York Times*, July 14, 1916.
25. R. T. McIntire. *Twelve Years with Roosevelt*. London, 1948.
26. G. Ward. *A First Class Temperament: The Emergence of Franklin D. Roosevelt*. New York, 1989.
27. S. Neal, *Happy Days Are Here Again*. Harper-Collins, New York, 2004.
28. K. Kling, A. Petterson, and W. Wernstedt. *Experimental and Pathological Investigation (Investigations on Epidemic Infantile Paralysis)*. State Medical Institute of Sweden, 1912.
29. J. L. Melnick. "Enteroviruses: Polioviruses, Coxsackieviruses, Echo- viruses, and Newer Enteroviruses." In *Fields' Virology*, ed. B. N. Fields et al., pp. 655–712. New York, 1996.
30. *British Medical Journal*, November 18, 1911.
31. J. F. Enders, F. C. Robbins, and T. H. Weller. "The Cultivation of the Poliomyelitis Viruses in Tissue Culture. Nobel Lecture 1954." *Rev. Infect. Dis.* 2 (1980):493.
32. J. L. Melnick. "Live Attenuated Poliovirus Vaccines." In *Vaccines*, 2nd ed. S. A. Plotkin and E. A. Mortimer, pp. 155–204. Philadelphia: WB Saunders, 1994.
33. R. Carter. *Breakthrough*. New York, 1966.
34. F. Horaud. "Albert B. Sabin and the Development of Oral Polio Vaccine." *Biologicals* 21 (1993):311.
35. S. Rosenstein and L. Garrett. "Polio's Return: A Who Done It"? *The American Interest* (2006):19.

CHAPTER 8: AN OVERVIEW OF NEWLY EMERGING VIRAL PLAGUES: THE HEMORRHAGIC FEVERS

1. B. LeGuenno. "Emerging Viruses." *Scientific American*, October 1995.
2. W. H. McNeill. *Plagues and Peoples*. New York, 1976.
3. Y. Riviere and M. B. A. Oldstone. "Genetic Reassortants of Lymphocytic Choriomeningitis Virus: Unexpected Disease and Mechanism of Pathogenesis. *J. Virol.* 59 (1986):363–368.
4. C. Scholtissek et al. "Correlation of Pathogenicity and Gene Constellation of Influenza A Virus. II. Highly Neurovirulent Recombinants Derived from Non-Virulent or Weakly Neurovirulent Parent Virus Strains." *Virology* 95 (1979):492–498.
5. D. H. Rubin and B. N. Fields. "Molecular Basis of Reovirus Virulence. Role of the M2 gene." *J. Exp. Med.* 152 (1980):853–857.
6. B. N. Fields et al., ed. *Fields' Virology*. New York, 1990.

7. E. M. Leroy, et al. "Fruit bats as reservoirs of Ebola virus." *Nature* 438 (2005):575–576.
8. J. S. Towner, et al. "Marburg virus infection detected in a common African bat." *PloS ONE* 2 (2007):e764.

CHAPTER 9: LASSA FEVER

1. J. B. McCormick. "Arenaviruses." In *Fields' Virology*, ed. B. N. Fields et al., p. 1215. Now York, 1990
2. J. D. Frame et al. "Lassa Fever, a New Virus Disease ot Man from West Africa." *Am. J. Trop. Med. Hyg.* 19 (1970):670.
3. J. D. Frame. "The Story of Lassa Fever. Part I: Discovering the Disease." *N.Y. State J. Med.* 92 (1992):199.
4. J. D. Frame. "The Story of Lassa Fever. Part II: Learning More About the Disease." *N.Y. State J. Med.* 92 (1992):264.
5. W. Cao et al. "Identification of alpha-dystroglycan as a receptor for lymphocytic choriomeningitis virus and Lassa fever virus." *Science* 282 (1998):2079.
6. N. Sevilla et al. "Immunosuppression and resultant viral persistence by specific viral targeting of dendritic cells." *J. Exp. Med.* 192 (2000):1249.
7. S. Kunz et al. "Molecular analysis of the interaction of LCMV with its cellular receptor (alpha)-dystroglycan." *J. Cell. Biol.* 155 (2001):301.
8. E. I. Zuniga et al. "Persistent virus infection inhibits type 1 interferon production by plasmacytoid dendritic cells thereby facilitating opportunistic infections." *Cell Host & Microbe* 4 (2008): 374–386.
9. S. Kunz et al. "Posttranslational modification of alpha-dystroglycan, the cellular receptor for arenaviruses, by the glycosyltransferase LARGE is critical for virus binding." *J. Virol.* 79 (2005):14282.
10. S. Kunz et al. "Characterization of the interaction of lassa fever virus with its cellular receptor alpha-dystroglycan." *J. Virol.* 79 (2005):5979.
11. P. C. Sabeti et al. "Genome-wide detection and characterization of positive selection in human populations." *Nature* 449 (2007):913.
12. S. Kunz and M. B. A. Oldstone. Unpublished studies, 2008.
13. G. P. Holmes et al. "Lassa Fever in the United States, Investigation of a Case and New Guidelines for Management." *N. Engl. J. Med.* 323 (1990):1120.

CHAPTER 10: EBOLA

1. J. S. Towner et al. "Marburg virus infection detected in a common African bat." *PloS ONE*, 2 (2007):e764.
2. A. Sanchez, T. Gersbert, and H. Feldman. "Filoviridae: Marburg and Ebola Viruses." In *Fields' Virology*, 5th ed., ed. D. Knipe et al., pp. 1409–1448. Philadelphia, 2007.

3. C. A. Zanpieri, N. J. Sullivan, and G. J. Nobel. "Ebola perspective." *Nature Immunol.* 8 (2007):1159.
4. B. LeGuenno. "Emerging Viruses." *Scientific American*, October 1995.
5. *Newsweek*, May 22, 1995.
6. T. W. Geisbert et al. "Association of Ebola-Related Reston Virus Particles and Antigen with Tissue Lesions of Monkeys Imported to the United States." *J. Comp. Pathol.* 106 (1992):137.
7. E. M. Leroy, et al. "Fruit bats as reservoirs of Ebola virus." *Nature* 438 (2005): 575–576.

CHAPTER 11: HANTAVIRUS

1. B. W. J. Mahy and C. J. Peters. "Current Problems with Viral Hemorrhagic Fevers." In *Microbe Hunters Past and Present*, ed. H. Koprowski and M. B. A. Oldstone, pp. 257–266. Bloomington, IL, 1996.
2. J. M. Hughes et al. "Hantavirus Pulmonary Syndrome: An Emerging Infectious Disease." *Science* 262 (1993):850.
3. L. H. Elliott et al. "Isolation of the Causative Agent of Hantavirus Pulmonary Syndrome." *Am. J. Trop. Med. Hyg.* 51 (1994):102.
4. F. Gonzalez-Scarano and N. Nathanson. "Bunyaviruses." In *Fields' Virology*, ed. B. N. Fields and D. M. Knipe, et al., pp. 1473–1504. New York, 1996.
5. B. LeGuenno. "Emerging Viruses." *Scientific American*, October 1995: 56–64.

CHAPTER 12: SEVERE ACUTE RESPIRATORY SYNDROME (SARS): THE FIRST PANDEMIC OF THE TWENTY-FIRST CENTURY

1. Y. Guan et al. "Isolation and Characterization of Viruses Related to the SARS Coronavirus From Animals in Southern China." *Science* 302 (2003):276.
2. T. Svoboda et al. "Public Health Measures to Control the Spread of the Severe Acute Respiratory Syndrome during the Outbreak in Toronto." *N. Engl. J. Med.* 350 (2004):2352.
3. C. M. Booth et al. "Clinical Features and Short-Term Outcomes of 144 Patients with SARS in the Greater Toronto Area." *JAMA.* 289 (2003):2801.
4. S. M. Poutanen et al. "Identification of Severe Acute Respiratory Syndrome in Canada." *N. Engl. J. Med.* 348 (2003):1995.
5. "The Impact of SARS on Toronto's Business Community: A Survey of Toronto Employers." Toronto: Toronto Board of Trade, May 2003.
6. KPMG. "Toronto Tourism Revenue Loss Exceeds Quarter of a Billion." Press release of KPMG Canada, Toronto, July 2, 2003.
7. M. M. C. Lai, S. Perlman, L. J. Anderson. "Coronaviridae." In *Fields' Virology*, 5th ed., ed. D. Knipe et al., p. 1305, Philadelphia, 2007.

8. F. R. Beaudette and C. B. Hudson. "Cultivation of the Virus of Infectious Bronchitis." *J. Am. Vet. Med. Assoc.* 90 (1937):51.

9. F. S. Cheever et al. "A Murine Virus (JHM) Causing Disseminated Encephalomyelitis with Extensive Destruction of Myelin." *J. Exp. Med.* 90 (1949):181.

10. L. P. Doyle and L. M. Hutchings. "A Transmissible Gastroenteritis in Pigs." *J. Am. Vet. Assoc.* 108 (1946):257.

11. C. Drosten et al. "Identification of a Novel Coronavirus in Patients with Severe Acute Respiratory Syndrome." *N. Engl. J. Med.* 348 (2003):1967.

12. T. G. Ksiazek et al. "A Novel Coronavirus Associated with Severe Acute Respiratory Syndrome." *N. Engl. J. Med.* 348 (2003):1953.

13. J. S. Peiris et al. "Coronavirus as a Possible Cause of Severe Acute Respiratory Syndrome." *Lancet* 361 (2003):1319.

14. P. A. Rota et al. "Characterization of a Novel Coronavirus Associated with Severe Acute Respiratory Syndrome." *Science* 300 (2003):1394.

15. L-F. Wang et al. "Review of Bats and SARS." *Emerg Infect Dis.* 2006 Dec. Available from http://www.cdc.gov/ncidod/EID/vol12no12/06-0401.htm.

16. R. H. Xu et al. "Epidemiologic Clues to SARS Origin in China." *Emerg Infect Dis.* 10 (2004):1030.

17. Centers for Disease Control and Prevention. "Prevalence of IgG Antibody to SARS-Associated Coronavirus in Animal Traders—Guangdone Province, China, 2003." *MMWR Morb. Mortal Wkly Rep.* 52 (2003):986.

18. M. Wang et al. "SARS-CoV Infection in a Restaurant from Palm Civet." *Emerg. Infect. Dis.* 11 (2005):1860.

19. L. F. Wang and B. T. Eaton. "Bats, Civets and the Emergence of SARS." *Curr. Top. Microbiol. Immunol.* 315 (2007):324.

20. D. Normile. "Researchers Tie Deadly SARS Virus to Bats." *Science* 309 (2005):2154.

21. W. Li et al. "Bats Are Natural Reservoirs of SARS-Like Coronaviruses." *Science* 310 (2005):676.

22. A. P. Dobson. "What Links Bats to Emerging Infectious Diseases?" *Science* 310 (2005):628.

23. J. Kahn. "China Bars U.S. Trip for Doctor Who Exposes SARS Cover-Up." *New York Times*, July 13, 2007.

24. C. Mason. "Poor Hospital Practices Blamed for 2003 SARS Epidemic in Toronto." *New York Times*, January 10, 2007.

CHAPTER 13: WEST NILE VIRUS: DEATHS OF CROWS AND HUMANS

1. B. Lindebach, H. Thiel, and C. Rice. "Flaviviridae: The Viruses and Their Replication." In *Fields' Virology*, 5th ed., ed. D. Knipe et al., p. 1191. Philadelphia, 2007.

2. J. Strauss and E. Strauss. *Viruses and Human Disease.* Academic Press, San Diego, 2002, p. 93.
3. Available at http://www.cdc.gov/ncidod/dvbd/westnile/control.htm.
4. GAO Report to Congress, *West Nile Virus Outbreak: Lessons for Public Preparedness: GAO/HEHS-00-180.* September 2000.
5. Centers for Disease Control and Prevention. *Expecting the Unexpected: Lessons from the 1999 West Nile Encephalitis Outbreak.* Atlanta, July 2000.
6. D. Asnis et al. "The West Nile Virus Outbreak of 1999 in New York: The Flushing Hospital Experience." *Clin. Infect. Dis.* 2000 (2000):413.
7. Editorial, "Exotic Diseases Close to Home." *The Lancet* 354 (1999):1221.
8. X. Y. Jia et al. "Genetic Analysis of West Nile New York 1999 Encephalitis Virus." *The Lancet* 354 (1999):1971.
9. R. S. Lanciotti et al. "Origin of the West Nile Virus Responsible for an Outbreak of Encephalitis in the Northeastern United States." *Science* 286 (1999):2333.
10. M. Enserink. "Groups Race to Sequence and Identify New York Virus." *Science* 286 (1999):206.
11. ——. "New York's Lethal Virus Comes from Middle East, DNA Suggests." *Science* 286 (1999):1450.
12. W. J. Shieh et al. "The Role of Pathology in an Investigation of an Outbreak of West Nile Encephalitis in New York, 1999." *Emerging Infect. Dis.* 6 (2000):370.
13. T. Briese et al. "Identification of a Kunjin/West Nile-like Flavivirus in Brains of Patients with New York Encephalitis." *The Lancet* 354 (1999):1261.
14. J. F. Anderson et al. "Isolation of West Nile Virus from Mosquitoes, Crows, and a Cooper's Hawk in Connecticut." *Science* 286 (1999):2331.
15. K. E. Steele et al. "Pathology of Fatal West Nile Virus Infections in Native and Exotic Birds During the 1999 Outbreak in New York City, New York." *Vet. Pathol.* 37 (2000):208.
16. N. Komar et al. "Serologic Evidence for West Nile Virus Infection in Birds in the New York City Vicinity During an Outbreak in 1999." *Emerg. Infect. Dis.* 7 (2001):621.
17. M. Eidson et al. "Dead Bird Surveillance as an Early Warning System for West Nile Virus." *Emerg. Infect. Dis.* 7 (2001):631.
18. K. C. Smithburn et al. "A Neurotropic Virus Isolated from the Blood of a Native of Uganda." *Amer. J. Trop. Med. Hygiene* 20 (1940):471.
19. E. B. Hayes and D. J. Gubler. "West Nile Virus: Epidemiology and Clinical Features of an Emerging Epidemic in the United States." *Ann. Rev. Med.* 57 (2006):181.
20. C. G. Hayes. "West Nile Fever." In *The Arboviruses: Epidemiology and Ecology,* Vol. 5, ed. T. P. Monath, pp. 59–88. Boca Raton, FL, 1988.
21. C. G. Pollock. "West Nile Virus in the Americas." *J. Avian Med. Surg.* 22 (2008):151–157.

22. N. Komar. "West Nile Virus: Epidemiology and Ecology in North America." *Adv. Virus Res.* 61 (2003):185.

23. M. S. Godsey et al. "West Nile Virus Epizootiology in the Southeastern United States, 2001." *Vector-Borne Zoon Dis.* 5 (2005):82.

24. O. Komar et al. "West Nile Virus Transmission in Resident Birds, Dominican Republic. *Emerg. Infect. Dis.* 9 (2003B):1299.

25. C. Rahbek. "The Silence of the Robins." *Nature* 447 (2007):652.

26. M. Iwamoto et al. "Transmission of West Nile Virus from an Organ Donor to Four Transplant Recipients." *N. Engl. J. Med.* 348 (2003):2196.

27. L. N. Pealer et al. "Transmission of West Nile Virus through Blood Transfusion in the United States in 2002." *N. Engl. J. Med.* 349 (2003):1236.

28. T. Wang et al. "Toll-like Receptor 3 Mediates West Nile Virus Entry into the Brain Causing Lethal Encephalitis." *Nat. Med.* 10 (2004):1366.

29. A. C. Brault et al. "A Single Positively Selected West Nile Viral Mutation Confers Increased Virogenesis in American Crows." *Nat. Genetics* 39 (2007):1162.

30. S. L. LaDeau, A. M. Kilpatrick, and P. P. Marra. "West Nile Virus Emergence and Large Scale Declines of North American Bird Populations." *Nature* 447 (2007):710.

31. N. Komar, N. A. Panella, and E. Boyce. "Exposure of Domestic Mammals to West Nile Virus During an Outbreak of Human Encephalitis, New York City, 1999." *Emerg. Infect. Dis.* 7 (2001):736.

32. M. Schoch-Spana. "A West Nile Virus Post-Mortem." *Biodefense Quarterly* 1 (1999). Available at www.hopkins-biodefense.org/pages/news/quarter1_3.html

33. L. K. Altman. "Virus in Encephalitis Outbreak Resembles Israeli Strain." *The New York Times*, December 5, 1999.

34. "West Nile Virus Similar to Israel '98 Virus." *Family Practice News* 30 (2000):12.

35. Y. Yevtushenko. In *20th Century Russian Poetry*, ed. A. Todd and M. Haywood. New York, 1993.

CHAPTER 14: HUMAN IMMUNODEFICIENCY VIRUS (HIV): AIDS, THE CURRENT PLAGUE

1. M. S. Gottlieb et al. "*Pneumocystis carinii* Pneumonia and Mucosal Candidiasis in Previously Healthy Homosexual Men." *New. Engl. J. Med.* 305 (1981):1425.

2. R. C. Gallo et al. "Isolation of Human T-Cell Leukemia Virus in Acquired Immune Deficiency Syndrome (AIDS)." *Science* 220 (1983):865.

3. F. Barré-Sinoussi et al. "Isolation of a T-Lymphotropic Retrovirus from a Patient at Risk for Acquired Immune Deficiency Syndrome (AIDS)." *Science* 220 (1983):868.

4. M. Essex et al. "Antibodies to Cell Membrane Antigens Associated with Human T-Cell Leukemia Virus in Patients with AIDS." *Science* 220 (1983):859.

5. M. S. Gottlieb et al. "The Acquired Immunodeficiency Syndrome." *Annals. Int. Med.* 99 (1983):208.

6. Martin S. Hirsch and James Curran. "Human Immunodeficiency Viruses." In *Fields' Virology*, ed. B. N. Fields et al., pp. 1953–76. New York, 1996.

7. J. C. Gluckmann. "AIDS Virus History." *Science* 259 (1993):1809.

8. Robert Gallo. *Virus Hunting: AIDS, Cancer and the Human Retrovirus.* New York, 1991.

9. J. Cohen. "Increase in Those Living with HIV Due to Antiviral Therapy." *Science* 318(2007):1360.

10. B. R. Schackman et al. "The Lifetime Cost of Current HIV Care in the United States." *Med. Care.* 44 (2006):990.

11. L. Altman. "Rethinking Is Urged on a Vaccine for AIDS." *The New York Times*, March 26, 2008.

12. J. Cohen. "Did Merk's Failed HIV Vaccine Cause Harm?" *Science* 318 (2007):1048.

13. J. Cohen and B. Lester. "Trials of NIH's AIDS Vaccine Get a Yellow Light." *Science* 318 (2007):1852.

14. "Cold Shower for AIDS Vaccine." Editorial. *Nat. Med.* 13 (2007):1389.

15. D. L. Barber et al. "Restoring Function in Exhausted CD8 T Cells During Chronic Viral Infection." *Nature* 439 (2006):682.

16. D. G. Brooks et al. "Interleukin-10 Determines Viral Clearance or Persistence In Vivo." *Nat. Med.* 12 (2006):1301.

17. M. Ejrnaes et al. "Resolution of a Chronic Viral Infection After Interleukin-10 Receptor Blockade." *J. Exp. Med.* 203 (2006):2461.

18. D. G. Brooks et al. "IL-10 Blockade Facilitates DNA Vaccine-Induced T Cell Responses and Enhances Clearance of Persistent Virus Infection." *J. Exp. Med.* 205 (2008):533.

19. S. J. Ha et al. "Enhancing Therapeutic Vaccination by Blocking PD-1-Mediated Inhibitory Signals During Chronic Infection." *J. Exp. Med.* 205 (2008):543.

20. C. L. Day et al. "PD-1 Expression on HIV-Specific T Cells is Associated with T-Cell Exhaustion and Disease Progression." *Nature* 443 (2006):350.

21. G. J. Freeman et al. "Reinvigorating Exhausted HIV-Specific T Cells Via PD-1-PD-1 Ligand Blockade." *J. Exp. Med.* 203 (2006):2223.

22. D. E. Kaufmann et al. "Upregulation of CTLA-4 by HIV-Specific CD4$^+$ T Cells Correlates with Disease Progression and Defines a Reversible Immune Dysfunction." *Nat. Immunol.* 8 (2007):1246.

23. "Role of IL-10 in HIV Patients." B Walker Laboratory and A. McMichael Laboratory, unpublished results, personal communications 2007, 2008; M. A. Brockman et al. "IL-10 is upregulated in multiple cell types during

viremic HIV infection and reversibly inhibits virus-specific T cells." *Blood* in press (2009).

24. P. Borrow et al. "Virus-Specific CD8+ Cytotoxic T-Lymphocyte Activity Associated with Control of Viremia in Primary Human Immunodeficiency Virus Type 1 Infection." *J. Virol.* 68 (1994):6103.

25. B. D. Walker et al. "HIV Specific Cytotoxic T Lymphocytes in Seropositive Individuals." *Nature* 328 (1987):345.

26. X. Wei et al. "Viral Dynamics in Human Immunodeficiency Virus Type 1 Infection." *Science* 373 (1995):117.

27. A. Fauci. "AIDS: Newer Concepts in the Immunopathogenic Mechanism of Human Immunodeficiency Virus Disease." *Proc. Assoc. Am. Phys.* 107 (1995):1.

28. T. W. Chun et al. "Relationship Between the Size of the Human Immunodeficiency Virus Type 1 (HIV-1) Reservoir in Peripheral Blood CD4+ T Cells and CD4+:CD8+ T Cell Rations in Aviremic HIV-1-Infected Individuals Receiving Long-Term Highly Active Antiretroviral Therapy." *J. Infect. Dis.* 185 (2002):1672.

29. T. W. Chun et al. "Persistence of HIV in Gut-Associated Lymphoid Tissue Despite Long-Term Antiretroviral Therapy." *J. Infect. Dis.* 197 (2008):714.

30. M. Guadalupe et al. "Severe CD4+ T-Cell Depletion in Gut Lymphoid Tissue During Primary Human Immunodeficiency Virus Type 1 Infection and Substantial Delay in Restoration Following Highly Active Antiretroviral Therapy." *J. Virol.* 77 (2003):11708.

31. C. Wiley et al. "Cellular Localization of Human Immunodeficiency Virus Infection Within the Brains of Acquired Immunodeficiency Syndrome Patients." *Proc. Natl. Acad. Sci. USA* 83 (1986):7083.

32. A. V. Moses and J. A. Nelson. "HIV Infection of Human Brain Capillary Endothelial Cells—Implications for AIDS Dementia." *Adv. Neuroimmunol.* 4 (1994):239.

33. T. Pierson, J. McArthur, and R. F. Siliciano. "Reservoirs for HIV-1: Mechanisms for Viral Persistence in the Presence of Antiviral Immune Responses and Antiretroviral Therapy." *Annu. Rev. Immunol.* 18 (2000):665.

34. S. Le Gall et al. "Nef Interacts with the Mu Subunit of Clathrin Adaptor Complexes and Reveals a Cryptic Sorting Signal in MHC 1 Molecules." *Immunity* 8 (1998):483.

35. P. Stumptner-Cuvelette et al. "HIV-1 Nef Impairs MHC Class II Antigen Presentation and Surface Expression." *Proc. Natl. Acad. Sci. USA* 98 (2001):12144.

36. O. O. Yang et al. "Nef-Mediated Resistance of Human Immunodeficiency Virus Type 1 to Antiviral Cytotoxic T Lymphocytes." *J. Virol.* 76 (2002):1626.

37. R. Wyatt et al. "The Antigenic Structure of the HIV gp120 Envelope Glycoprotein." *Nature* 393 (1998):705.

38. P. D. Kwong et al. "Structures of HIV-1 gp120 Envelope Glycoproteins From Laboratory-Adapted and Primary Isolates." *Structure* 8 (2000):1329.

39. T. W. Chun and A. S. Fauci. "Latent Reservoirs of HIV: Obstacles to the Eradication of Virus." *Proc. Natl. Acad. Sci. USA* 96 (1999):10958.

40. J. McFadyean and F. Hobday. "Notes on the Experimental Transmission of Warts in the Dog." *J. Comp. Path. Ther.* 11 (1898):341.

41. H. Zur Hausen. "Human Papillomaviruses and their Possible Role in Squamous Cell Carcinomas." *Curr. Top. Microbiol. Immunol.* 78 (1997):1.

42. D. R. Lowy and J. T. Schiller. "Prophylactic Human Papillomavirus Vaccines." *J. Clin. Invest.* 116 (2006):1167.

43. I. H. Frazer. "Prevention of Cervical Cancer Through Papillomavirus Vaccination." *Nat. Rev. Immunol.* 4 (2004):46.

44. F. Loeffler and P. Frosch. "Berichte der Kommission zur Erforschung der Maul und Klauenseuche bei dem Institut Fur Infektionskrankheiten in Berlin." *Zentbl. Bakt. ParasitKde., Abt I.* 23 (1898):371.

45. V. Ellermann and O. Bang. "Experimentelle Leukamie bei Huhnern." *Zentbl. Bakt. I. Orig.* 46 (1908):595.

46. P. Rous. "A Sarcoma of Fowl Transmissible by an Agent Separate from the Tumor Cells." *J. Exp. Med.* 13 (1911):397.

47. J. B. Moloney. Personal communication.

48. B. J. Poiesz et al. "Detection and Isolation of Type C Retrovirus Particles from Fresh and Cultured Lymphocytes of a Patient with Cutaneous T-Cell Lymphoma." *Proc. Natl. Acad. Sci. USA* 77 (1980):6815.

49. B. J. Poiesz et al. "Isolation of a New Type C Particle Retrovirus in Primary Uncultured Cells of a Patient with Sezary T-Cell Leukemia." *Nature* 294 (1981):268.

50. R. C. Gallow and L. Montagnier. "The Discovery of HIV as the Cause of AIDS." *New. Engl. J. Med.* 349 (2003):2283.

51. D. A. Morgan, F. W. Ruscetti, and R. C. Gallo. "Selective In Vitro Growth of T-Lymphocytes from Normal Human Bone Marrow." *Science* 193 (1976):1007.

52. Y. Hinuma et al. "Adult T-Cell Leukemia: Antigen in a CTL Cell Line and Detection of Antibodies to the Antigen in Human Sera." *Proc. Natl. Acad. Sci. USA* 78 (1981):6476.

53. B. F. Keele et al. "Chimpanzee Reservoirs of Pandemic and Nonpandemic HIV-1." *Science* 313 (2006):523.

54. F. Van Heuverswyn et al. "Human Immunodeficiency Viruses: SIV Infection in Wild Gorillas." *Nature* 444 (2006):164.

55. F. Gao et al. "Origin of HIV-1 in the Chimpanzee Pan Troglodytes Troglodytes." *Nature* 397 (1999):436.

56. M. L. Santiago et al. "Simian Immunodeficiency Virus Infection in Free-Ranging Sooty Mangabeys (Cercocebus Atys Atys) from the Taï Forest, Côte

d'Ivoire: Implications for the Origin of Epidemic Human Immunodeficiency Virus Type 2." *J. Virol.* 79 (2005):12515.

57. F. Van Heuverswyn et al. "Genetic Diversity and Phylogeographic Clustering of SIVcpzPtt in Wild Chimpanzees in Cameroon." *Virology* 368 (2007):155.

58. M. Worobey et al. "Origin of AIDS: Contaminated Polio Vaccine Theory Refuted." *Nature* 428 (2004):820.

59. R. Shilts. *And the Band Played On: Politics, People, and the AIDS Epidemic.* New York, 1987.

60. D. Douek. "HIV Disease Progression: Immune Activation, Microbes, and a Leaky Gut." *Top HIV Med.* 15 (2007):111.

61. L. J. Picker. "Immunopathogenesis of Acute AIDS Virus Infection." Curr. Opin. *Immunol.* 18 (2006):399.

62. S. Mehandru et al. "The Gastrointestinal Tract is Critical to the Pathogenesis of Acute HIV-1 Infection." *J. Allergy Clin. Immunol.* 116 (2005):419.

63. S. Mehandru et al. "Lack of Mucosal Immune Reconstitution During Prolonged Treatment of Acute and Early HIV-1 Infection." *PLoS Med.* 3 (2006):e484.

64. J. M. Brenchley et al. "Microbial Translocation is a Cause of Systemic Immune Activation in Chronic HIV Infection." *Nat. Med.* 12 (2006):1365.

65. J. Brown. "Money/Profit and Politics in the USA." *New York Times*, September 22, 2007.

66. J. Kramer. "Bad Blood." *The New Yorker*, October 11, 1993.

67. E. Rosenthal. "African Children Often Lack Available AIDS Treatment." *New York Times*, November 15, 2006.

68. N. Kristof. "The Deep Roots of AIDS." *New York Times*, September 19, 2006.

69. G. Abbadessa et al. (107 Accential around the world), Unsung Hero Robert C. Gallo. *Science* 323: 206, 2009.

70. R. S. Werss. "On Viruses Discovery and Recognition." *Cell* 135: 983, 2008.

CHAPTER 15: MAD COW DISEASE AND ENGLISHMEN: SPONGIFORM ENCEPHALOPATHIES—PRION DISEASE

1. C. Besnoit. "La tremblante ou nevrite peripherique enzootique du mouton." *Rev. Vet. Toulouse.* 24 (1899):265.

2. J. Cuillé and P. L. Chelle. "Pathologie animal-la maladie dite tremblante du mouton est-elle inoculable." *C. R. Acad. Sci. (Paris)* 203 (1936):1552.

3. J. Cuillé and P. L. Chelle. "Investigations of Scrapie in Sheep." *Vet. Med.* 34 (1939):417.

4. D. C. Gajdusek and V. Zigas. "Degenerative Disease of the Central Nervous System in New Guinea. The Endemic Occurrence of 'Kuru' in the Native Population." *N. Engl. J. Med.* 257 (1957):974.

5. D. C. Gajdusek. "Kuru." *Trans. R. Soc. Trop. Med. Hyg.* 57 (1963):151.

6. D. C. Gajdusek. "Kuru in New Guinea." In *Slow, Latent, and Temperate Virus Infections,* NINDB Monograph No. 2, pp. 3–12. Bethesda, MD, 1965.

7. W. J. Hadlow. "Scrapie and Kuru." *Lancet* 2 (1959):289.

8. B. Chesebro and B. N. Fields. "Prion Protein and Transmissible Spongiform Encephalopathy Disease." *Neuron* 24 (1999):503.

9. D. C. Gajdusek. "Infectious Amyloids: Subacute Spongiform Encephalopathies as Transmissible Cerebral Amyloidosis." In *Fields' Virology,* ed. B. N. Fields et al., pp. 2851–2900. Philadelphia, 1996.

10. S. B. Prusiner. "Prions." In *Fields Virology,* 5th ed., ed. D. Knipe et al., pp. 3059–3091, Philadelphia, 2007.

11. S. B. Prusiner. *Prion Biology and Diseases.* Cold Spring Harbor Laboratory Press, Cold Spring Harbor, NY, 1999.

12. C. A. Donnelly et al. "Implications of BSE Infection Screening Data for the Scale of the British BSE Epidemic and Current European Infection Levels." *Proc Biol Sci.* 269 (2002):1279.

13. R. M. Anderson et al. "Transmission Dynamics and Epidemiology of BSE in British Cattle." *Nature* 382 (1996):779.

14. D. Butler. "BSE Researchers Bemoan Ministry Secrecy." *Nature* 383 (1996):467–468.

15. D. Butler. "CJD Variant Stirs Debate on Release of Data." *Nature* 384 (1996):658.

16. S. J. Sawyer et al. "Creutzfeldt-Jakob Disease in an Individual Occupationally Exposed to BSE." *Lancet* 341 (1993):642.

17. P. T. G. Davies et al. "Creutzfeldt-Jakob Disease in Individuals Occupationally Exposed to BSE." *Lancet* 342 (1993):680.

18. P. E. M. Smith et al. "Creutzfeldt-Jakob Disease in a Dairy Farmer." *Lancet* 346 (1995):898.

19. T. C. Britton et al. "Sporadic Creutzfeldt-Jakob Disease in a 16-Year-Old in the UK." *Lancet* 346 (1995):1155.

20. D. Bateman et al. "Sporadic Creutzfeldt-Jakob Disease in a 18-Year-Old in the UK." *Lancet* 346 (1995):1155.

21. R. G. Will et al. "A New Variant of Creutzfeldt-Jakob Disease in the UK." *Lancet* 347 (1996):921.

22. E. Masood. "Mad Cow Scare Threatens Political Link between Food and Agriculture." *Nature* 380 (1996):273.

23. "Lessons from BSE for Public Confidence." *Nature* 380 (1996):271.

24. D. Butler. "Slow Release of Data Adds to BSE Confusion." *Nature* 380 (1996):370.

25. C. O'Brien. "Scant Data Cause Widespread Concern." *Science* 271 (1996):1798.

26. J. Collinge et al. "Kuru in the 21st Century—An Acquired Human Prion Disease with Very Long Incubation Periods." *Lancet* 346 (2006):2068.

27. M. S. Palmer et al. "Homozygous Prion Protein Genotype Predisposes to Sporadic Creutzfeldt-Jackob Disease." *Nature* 352 (1991):340.

28. S. Mead et al. "Balancing Selection at the Prion Protein Gene Consistent with Prehistoric Kurulike Epidemics." *Science* 300 (2003):640.

29. P. A. Lewis et al "Codon 129 Polymorphism of the Human Prion Protein Influences the Kinetics of Amyloid Formation." *Gen. Virol.* 87 (2006):2443.

30. A. Tahiri-Alaoui et al. "Methionine 129 Variant of Human Prion Protein Oligomerizes More Rapidly than the Valine 129 Variant: Implications for Disease Susceptibility to Creutzfeldt-Jacob Disease." *J Biol Chem.* 279 (2004):31390.

31. I. Baskakov et al. "The Presence of Valine at Residue 129 in Human Prion Protein Accelerates Amyloid Formation." *FEBS Lett.* 579 (2005):2589.

32. C. A. Llewelyn et al. "Possible Transmission of Variant Creutzfeldt-Jakob Disease by Blood Transfusion." *Lancet* 363 (2004):417.

33. A. H. Peden et al. "Preclinical vCJD After Blood Transfusion in a PRNP Codon 129 Heterozygous Patient." *Lancet* 364 (2004):527.

34. C. Lasmezasi et al. "BSE Transmission to Macaques." *Nature* 381 (1996):743.

35. A. Aguzzi and C. Weissmann. "A Suspicious Signature." *Nature* 383 (1996):666.

36. C. O'Brien. "Protein Test Favors BSE-CJD Link." *Science* 274 (1996):721.

37. J. Collinge et al. "Molecular Analysis of Prion Strain Variation and the Aetiology of 'New Variant' CJD." *Nature* 383 (1996):685.

38. S. Stocklow. "US Falls Behind in Tracking Cattle to Control Disease." *Wall Street Journal,* June 21, 2006.

39. Advancing Prion Science. Institute of Medicine, National Academy of Sciences, 2003.

40. M. E. Bruce et al. "Transmissions to Mice Indicate that 'New Variant' CJD Is Caused by the BSE Agent." *Nature* 389 (1997):498.

41. J. Collinge et al. "Molecular Analysis of Prion Strain Variation and the Aetiology of 'New Variant' CJD." *Nature* 383 (1996):685.

42. P. Brown et al. "Bovine Spongiform Encephalopathy and Variant Creutzfeldt-Jackob Disease: Background, Evolution and Current Concerns." *Emerging Infect. Dis.* 7 (2001):6.

43. L. B. Schonberger. "New Variant Creutzfeldt-Jackob Disease and Bovine Spongiform Encephalopathy." *Infect. Dis. Clinics of N. America.* 12 (1998):111.

44. A. F. Hill et al. "The Same Prion Protein Causes vCJD and BSE." *Nature* 389 (1997):448.

45. M. R. Scott et al. "Compelling Transgenic Evidence for Transmission of Bovine Spongiform Encephalopathy Prions to Humans." *PNAS* 96 (1999):15137.

46. P. E. Hewitt et al. "Creutzfeldt-Jakob Disease and Blood Transfusion: Results of the UK Transfusion Medicine Epidemiological Review Study." *Vox Sang.* 91 (2006):221.

47. E. S. Williams and S. Young. "Chronic Wasting Disease of Captive Mule Deer: A Spongiform Encephalopathy." *J. Wildlife Dis.* 16 (1980):89.

48. E. S. Williams and S. Young. "Spongiform Encephalopathy of Rocky Mountain Elk." *J. Wildlife Dis.* 18 (1982):465.

49. E. S. Williams and M. W. Miller. "Chronic Wasting Disease in Deer and Elk in North America." *Rev. Sci. et Tech.* 21 (2002):305.

50. B. Caughey et al. "Scrapie infectivity Correlates with Converting Activity, Protease Resistance and Aggregation of Scrapie-Associated Prion Protein in Guanidine Denaturation Studies." *J. Virol.* 71 (1997):4107.

51. B. Caughey and B. Chesebro. "Transmissible Spongiform Encephalopathies and Prion Protein Interconversions." *Adv. Virus Res.* 56 (2001):277.

52. S. Prusiner. "Novel Proteinaceous Infectious Particles Cause Scrapie." *Science* 216 (1982):136.

CHAPTER 16: INFLUENZA VIRUS, THE PLAGUE THAT MAY RETURN

1. L. Hart. *A Complete History of the World War.* New York, 1936.

2. A. Livesey. *Great Battles of World War I.* New York, 1989.

3. B. Murphy and R. G. Webster. "Orthomyxoviruses." In *Fields' Virology,* ed. B. N. Fields et al., pp. 1397–1446. Philadelphia, 1996.

4. W. Beveridge. *Influenza: The Last Great Plague.* New York, 1978.

5. L. A. Crosby. *Epidemic and Peace, 1918.* Westport, CT.

6. C. H. Stuart-Harris and G. C. Schild. *Influenza: The Virus and the Disease.* Littleton, MA, 1976.

7. N. P. Johnson and J. Mueller. "Updating the Secounts: Global Mortality of the 1918–1920 Spanish Influenza Pandemic." *Bull. Hist. Med.* 76 (2002):105.

8. J. E. Osborn, ed. *Influenza in America 1918–1976.* New York.

9. B. Easterday. "Animal Influenza." In *The Influenza Viruses and Influenza,* ed. E. D. Kilbourne, pp. 449–82. New York, 1975.

10. E. D. Kilbourne. "The Influenza Viruses and Influenza." In *The Influenza Viruses and Influenza,* ed. E. D. Kilbourne. New York, 1975.

11. N. D. Camugliano, *The Chronicles of a Florentine Family, J. Cape, London, 1200–1470.* 1933.

12. D. O. White and F. J. Fenner. *Medical Virology.* San Diego, California, 1994.
13. T. Willis. "Epidemics in 1658." In *Annals of Influenza,* ed. T. Thompson, p. 11. London, 1885.
14. T. Thompson. *Annals of Influenza or Epidemic Catarrhal Fever in Great Britain from 1510–1837.* London, 1852.
15. C. Creighton. *A History of Epidemics in Britain.* Cambridge, England, 1894.
16. D. Finkler. "Influenza." In *Twentieth-Century Practice: An International Encyclopedia of Modern Medical Science by Leading Authorities of Europe and America,* ed. T. L. Stedman, pp. 3–249. New York, 1898.
17. E. S. Thompson. *Influenza.* London, England, 1890.
18. J. Skchel. "The Discovery of Human Influenza Virus and Subsequent Influenza Research at the National Institute for Medical Research." In *Microbe Hunters: Then and Now,* ed. H. Koprowski and M. B. A. Oldstone, pp. 205–210. Bloomington, IL, 1996.
19. J. S. Koen. "A Practical Method for Field Diagnosis of Swine Disease." *Am. J. Vet. Med.* 14 (1919):468.
20. R. E. Shope. "Swine Influenza. I. Experimental Transmission and Pathology." *J. Exp. Med.* 54 (1931):349.
21. R. E. Shope. "Swine Influenza. III. Filtration Experiments and Etiology." *J. Exp. Med.* 54 (1931):373.
22. W. Smith, C. H. Andrews, and P. P. Laidlow. "A Virus Obtained from Influenza Patients." *Lancet* 1 (1933):66.
23. F. M. Burnet. "Influenza Virus on the Developing Egg. I. Changes Associated with the Development of Egg Passaged Strain of Virus." *Br. J. Med. Path.* 17 (1936):282.
24. F. M. Burnet and P. E. Lind. "Studies on Recombination with Influenza Viruses in the Chick Embryo. III. Reciprocal Genetic Interaction Between Two Influenza Virus Strains." *Aust. J. Exp. Med. Sci.* 30 (1952):469.
25. F. M. Burnet. "Influenza Virus Infections of the Chick Embryo by the Amniotic Route." *Aust. J. Exp. Med. Sci.* 18 (1940):353.
26. G. K. Hirst. "The Agglutination of Red Blood Cells by Allantoic Fluid of Chick Embryos Infected with Influenza Virus." *Science* 94 (1941):22.
27. G. K. Hirst. "Adsorption of Influenza Haemagglutinins and Virus by Red Blood Cells." *J. Exp. Med.* 76 (1942):195.
28. R. G. Webster et al. "Molecular Mechanisms of Variations in Influenza Viruses." *Nature* 296 (1982):115.
29. W. G. Laver and R. G. Webster. "Selection of Antigenic Mutants of Influenza Viruses. Isolation and Peptide Mapping of Their Hemagglutinating Proteins." *Virology* 34 (1968):193.
30. R. G. Webster, C. Campbell, and A. Granoff. "The 'In Vivo' Production of 'New' Influenza A Viruses. I. Genetic Recombination Between Avian and Mammalian Influenza Viruses." *Virology* 44 (971):317.

31. J. K. Taubenberger et al. "Initial Genetic Characterization of the 1918 'Spanish Influenza Virus.'" *Science* 275 (1997):1793–1796.

32. T. M. Tumpey et al. "Characterization of the Reconstructed 1918 Spanish Influenza Pandemic Virus." *Science* 310 (2005):77.

33. J. C. Kash et al. "Genomic analysis of Increased Host Immune and Cell Death Responses Induced by 1918 Influenza Virus." *Nature* 443 (2006):578.

34. D. Kobasa et al. "Enhanced Virulence of Influenza A Viruses with the Haemagglutinin of the 1918 pandemic virus." *Nature* 431 (2004):703.

35. J. K. Taubenberger et al. "Initial Genetic Characterization of the 1918 'Spanish' Influenza Virus." *Science* 275 (1997):1793.

36. A. H. Reid et al. "Origin and Evolution of the 1918 'Spanish' Influenza Virus Hemagglutinin Gene." *Proc. Natl. Acad. Sci. USA* 96 (1999):1651.

37. A. H. Reid et al. "1918 Influenza pandemic Caused by Highly Conserved Viruses with Two Receptor-binding Variants." *Emerg. Infect. Dis.* 9 (2993):1249.

38. D. Kobasa et al. "Aberrant Innate Immune Response in Lethal Infection of Macaques with the 1918 Influenza Virus." *Nature* 445 (2007):319.

39. K. Subbarao et al. "Characterization of an Avian Influenza A (H5N1) Virus Isolated from a Child with Fatal Respiratory Illness." *Science* 279 (1998):393.

40. N. Zhou et al. "Rapid Evolution of H5N1 Influenza Virus in Chickens in Hong Kong." *J. Virol.* 73 (1999):3366.

41. H. Chen et al. "Avian Flu: H5N1 Virus Outbreak in Migratory Waterfowl." *Nature* 436 (2005):191.

42. H. Chen et al. "Properties and Dissemination of H5N1 Viruses Isolated During an Influenza Outbreak in Migratory Waterfowl in Western China." *J. Virol.* 80 (2006):5976.

43. D. Butler. "Bird Flu: Crossing Borders." *Nature* 436 (2005):310.

44. B. Olsen et al. "Global Patterns of Influenza A Virus in Wild Birds." *Science* 312 (2006):384.

45. K. Shinya, M. Ebina, S. Yamada, M. Ono, N. Kasai, and Y. Kawaoka. "Influenza Virus Receptors in the Human Airway." *Nature* 440 (2006): 435.

46. G. Zhang, D. Shoham, D. Gilichinsky, S. Davydov, J. D. Castello, and S. O. Rogers. "Evidence of Influenza A Virus RNA in Siberian Lake Ice." *J. Virol.* 80 (2006):12229.

CHAPTER 17: CONCLUSIONS AND FUTURE PREDICTIONS

1. P. de Kruif. *Microbe Hunters*. New York, 1926.

2. P. de Kruif. *The Sweeping Wind*. New York, 1962.

3. *New York Times*, 7 March 1999, p. 19.

4. R. G. Will et al. "Deaths from Variant Creutzfeldt-Jakob disease." *Lancet* 353 (1999):979; Editorial, "Tragedy of Variant Creutzfeldt-Jakob disease." *Lancet* 353 (1999):939.
5. K. Subbarao et al. "Characterization of an Avian Influenza A (H5N1) Virus Isolated from a Child with Fatal Respiratory Illness." *Science* 279 (1998):393–396.
6. N. Zhou et al. "Rapid Evolution of H5N1 Influenza Virus in Chickens in Hong Kong." *J. Virol.* 73 (1999):3366–374.
7. R. Webster, "1918 Spanish Influenza: The Secrets Remain Elusive." *Proc. Natl. Acad. Sci. USA* 96 (1999):1164–1166
8. A. Reid et al. "Origin and Evolution of the 1918 'Spanish' Influenza Virus Hemagglutinin Gene." *Proc. Natl. Acad. Sci. USA* 96 (1999):1651–1656.
9. J. McFarland et al. "Imported Yellow Fever in a United States Citizen." *Clin. Infect. Dis.* 25 (1997):1143–1147.
10. World Health Organization. *State of the World's Vaccines and Immunizations.* Geneva, 1996, 2007.

INDEX